7/00

STATES OF MIND

JOHN F. BLAIR, PUBLISHER
WINSTON-SALEM, NORTH CAROLINA

STATES
OF
MIND

A SEARCH FOR

Faith, Hope, Inspiration, Harmony,

Unity, Friendship, Love, Pride, Wisdom,

Honor, Comfort, Joy, Bliss, Freedom,

Justice, Glory, Triumph,

and Truth or Consequences

IN AMERICA

BY BRAD HERZOG

Third Printing, 2000

Grateful acknowledgment is made to the following for permission to reprint previously published material: Excerpt from "My Back Pages" by Bob Dylan. Copyright © 1964 by Warner Bros. Music. Copyright renewed 1992 by Special Rider Music. • Excerpt from "Don't Think Twice It's All Right" by Bob Dylan. Copyright © 1963, by Warner Bros. Music. Copyright renewed 1991 by Special Rider Music. All rights reserved. International copyright secured. Reprinted by permission. • Excerpt from "Over the Hills and Far Away" by Jimmy Page and Robert Plant. Copyright © 1973 Superhype Publishing. All Rights Administered by WB Music Corp. All rights reserved. Used by permission. *Warner Bros. Publications U.S. Inc.*, Miami, FL, 33014. • Excerpt from "Shine On You Crazy Diamond (Part 7)," Lyrics by Roger Waters. Copyright Pink Floyd Music Publisher Limited • Excerpt from "That was No Lady" from *Betsy and Camille, Sisters of Destruction*. Reprinted by permission from Janice P. Buras.

PHOTOGRAPHY BY AMY HERZOG

DESIGN BY DEBRA LONG HAMPTON

The paper in this book meets the guidelines for permanence and durability of the Committee on Production Guidelines for book Longevity of the Council on Library Resources.

Library of Congress Cataloging-in-Publication Data

Herzog, Brad.
     States of mind : a search for Faith, Hope, Inspiration, Harmony, Unity, Friendship, Love, Pride, Wisdom, Honor, Comfort, Joy, Bliss, Freedom, Justice, Glory, Triumph, and Truth or Consequences in America / by Brad Herzog.
        p.   cm.
     Includes bibliographical references (p.   ) and index.
     ISBN 0-89587-187-4 (alk. paper)
     1. United States—Description and travel. 2. United States—History, Local.
     3. Herzog, Brad—Journeys—United States.
   I. Title.
E169.04.H465 1999
973—dc21   99–24574

To Amy,

for seizing

the day with me

CONTENTS

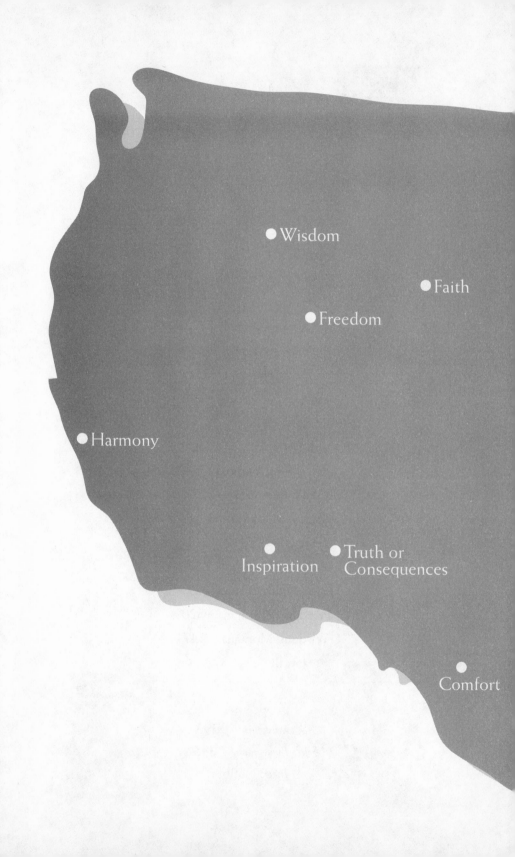

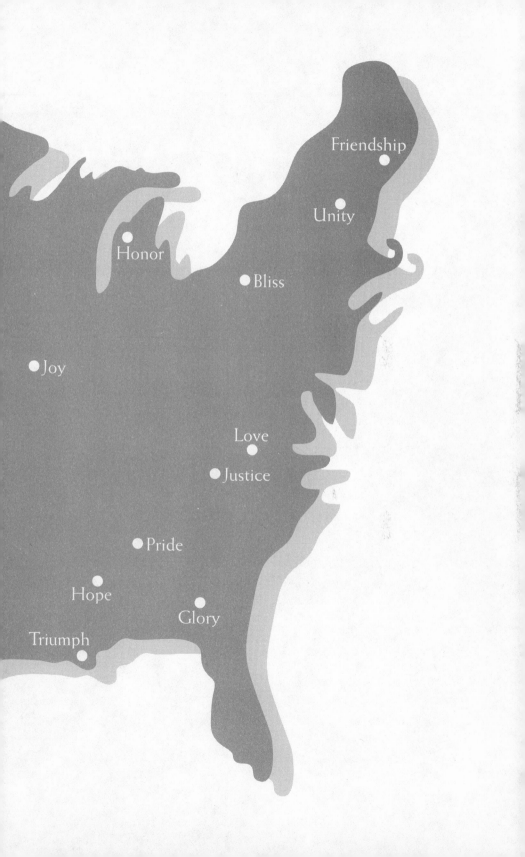

*Our destination is never a place but rather a
new way of looking at things.*

Henry Miller

*Mellow is the man
Who knows what he's been missing
Many many men
Can't see the open road.*

Led Zeppelin

PROLOGUE/EPILOGUE

I t's an imperfect day in Big Sur. Rain has been falling in fits and starts, washing the air clean along California's central coast. After sleeping late, only now is the sun beginning to yawn an appearance, its midafternoon rays, backlit against wizard-gray clouds, forming shapely shadows on the water. This stretch of the Pacific always seems utterly empty, which is why I'm drawn to it. But it's mid-January, which means that beneath the surface, the gray whales are migrating southward from Alaska to Baja. Look carefully and you can see them break the silence periodically, announcing themselves with a spectacular sigh.

I am sitting eight hundred feet above the waves with my back to the ocean and my face to the fire, a blazing hearth in the center of a magnificent redwood-and-adobe structure decorated with wicker chandeliers and driftwood candleholders. There's gentle music coming from somewhere, the kind that makes itself known only when it stops and you feel a void. Built on land Orson Welles once bought for Rita Hayworth, this place has evolved into a manifestation of California dreams—a restaurant serving poached shrimp, pale ale, and serenity on the edge of the earth. In the months since I arrived here, permanence on my mind, it has become my place of refuge. Here is the journey's end. *Nepenthe*, the owners call it. Greek for "no sorrow."

My journey began two years ago, also in the dead of winter, only it was the numbing dead of a Chicago winter, when the wind stiffened the soul. There was a fire there, too, a log burning in an old potbelly fireplace in a Lincoln Park apartment. We were staring at the flames, my wife and I, two newlyweds taking stock of our lives. Marriage should have seemed the culmination of a journey all its own. It had started with dinner, a movie, and a kiss good night when I was seventeen and Amy was sixteen and the world was at our feet. But a decade later, when the final thank-you note was mailed and the last vase returned, there was something missing—not between us, but within ourselves and beyond ourselves. There must be more out there, we felt, despite the rumors.

I'm a cynic by nature. More accurately, I'm a cynic by nurture. We are all born with a capacity for wonder, a propensity toward optimism, but it is whittled away by the years. I was born in August 1968, eight months after the Tet offensive, four months after Martin Luther King collapsed on the balcony in Memphis, two months after Robert Kennedy lay vacant-eyed in a kitchen hallway at the Ambassador Hotel. At the very moment I took my first breath, Chicago cops were beating the hell out of America's youth twenty miles away. It makes for an ironic arrival into the world.

A generation later, people my age were called names. We were Slackers, Baby Busters, Boomerangs, the MTV Generation, the Yo Generation, the Why Me Generation, the Whiny Generation, Grunge Kids, the Atari Wave, Generation X. The media, dominated by baby boomers, characterized us at one time or another as aimless, apathetic, unmotivated, disappointing, overly sensitive, low-energy, lazy, overqualified, underachieving, illiterate, irreverent, aloof, jealous, nihilistic, and morally obtuse.

If you believe what you read, then I should be a flannel-wearing, goatee-bearing, body-piercing, politically correct yet apolitical, half-employed slacker sitting around a gourmet coffeehouse complaining about the godforsaken mess I've inherited. But generalizations are generally bad form. As the early nineties became the late nineties, the stereotype dissolved into a thousand unique forms. For every twenty-six-year-old snowboarding weed hound, there was a twenty-six-year-old bank vice president. Sometimes, they were the very same person. The X in Generation X was revealed to be just what it is—a variable of infinite possibilities.

But one characteristic that seems pervasive is a sense of surrender. Somewhere along the line, "Have a nice day!" turned into the contemptuous shrug that defines Generation X: "Whatever." Succinct cynicism. But I am a cynic because, in my heart, I am an idealist. Skepticism and scorn are simply a reaction to unfulfilled expectations. I expect so much, thus I am impressed by so little. If that seems like a contradiction, so be it.

Walt Whitman knew there was more out there. "Other states indicate themselves in their deputies," he wrote, "but the genius of the United States is not best or most in its executives or legislatures, nor in its ambassadors or authors or colleges or churches or parlors, nor even in its newspapers or inventors . . . but always most in the common people." So he made himself the poet of the open road.

Some people have always known there was more. It's just way out there, past the shock headlines and the schlock newsmakers, hidden in the nooks and crannies of America. John Steinbeck claimed, "The honest bookkeeper, the faithful wife, the earnest scholar get little of our attention compared to the embezzler, the tramp, the cheat." So he and his dog, Charley, set off to remedy that. Charles Kuralt stated, "The front pages were full of selfishness, arrogance and hostility toward others. The back roads were another country." So he brought the back roads into our living rooms.

Sitting by the fire on that bitterly cold evening in Chicago, Amy and I suddenly saw our future laid before us, and it didn't satisfy. Like the empty Pacific, all appeared calm and orderly on the surface. Amy had embarked on a fine career, rising through the ranks with a public-relations firm in the Loop. I appeared to be doing the same, having just completed my first book. But she felt like one of the herd, the colorless stampede of professionals who have traded a life for a living. And I found myself sitting in front of a computer terminal ten hours a day, a chronicler of the world whose own world was limited to a back room with a view of an icy parking lot. We had both lost a sense of Out There. We needed a permanent shift of perspective. We needed to get out of town.

The need to cleanse one's soul and restore one's confidence through travel goes by many names. Steinbeck's "virus of restlessness" was Whitman's "resistless call of myself" and Thomas Wolfe's "hunger for voyages." It can take many forms—a meandering journey without itinerary, a Kerouacian dive into the fringes of society, a rush to the farthest point from departure. We decided ours would be a mission in the form of destinations, an experiment to find out if cynicism was justifiable—if our generation reflected the state of the union or merely misjudged it.

We would search for the things that seem elusive in modern America by seeking out Pride (Alabama), Faith (South Dakota), Wisdom (Montana), and Inspiration (Arizona). Some may call them virtues; I call them states of mind. After all, one man's pride is another's arrogance; one man's faith is another's folly. Knowing nothing about these places except what emanated from the fine print of the atlas, we would embark on a literal and figurative search for states of mind often overwhelmed by many Americans' states of panic.

We headed for the middle of nowhere. More people squeeze into a stadium for a typical pro basketball game than can be found in all eighteen towns, villages, and hamlets we visited combined. But as the Zen believers say, one can learn much about the tree by studying the simple shrub. Large insight is the amalgam of small discoveries.

The clouds have opened, and the sun is blinding. I find my way to a porch on the western edge of Nepenthe, where the rays reflect off rain-soaked tables, leaving a smoky cedar scent. The porch overlooks the ocean, which the sun has softened so that it could almost be the tops of clouds. To my left and far below is a promontory, green and smooth and perfect, jutting into the Pacific as if it were a golf hole carved into paradise. A lone baby cypress tree rises from its center, bent away from the ocean, its leaves blown eastward like trailing hair. I feel as if I'm standing removed, looking at myself looking at the view. I look content.

One month before we left on our journey, we almost lost it all in the blink of an eye. I had been assigned to write a magazine article about a fellow in Louisville, Kentucky. For some reason, I decided to drive there from Chicago, and Amy decided to join me. We were returning home through the lonely blackness of U.S. 65, the only sign of life the occasional brake light in the distance, when it happened. It was November—hunting season—and the hunted were being forced from the woods that lined the highway. For a split second as we zoomed through the darkness at sixty-five miles per hour, I saw the deer in my headlights, standing frozen in our lane. I didn't even have time to hit the brakes. There was a sickening crunch and then chaos. The hood of the car crumpled like a tin can. A streak of blood stretched along the passenger side. The air bags deployed and deflated, releasing a stream of smoke and a pungent odor. I thought the smoke was coming from the car, and I had visions of a fiery explosion as we rumbled to the side of the road.

Amy's first words were strangely calm: "I think I might have to go to the hospital." She'd been leaning slightly forward when the impact came, and the air bag had struck her in the face. She blacked out for a few seconds and then woke to blood flowing from her right eye. She couldn't see. I remember handing her a T-shirt to stem the flow and helping her out of the car, my frantic mind still fearing an explosion, then leaning back in to dial 911 on the car phone we'd installed for just this kind of emergency that would never happen. I remember my voice shaking as I explained the situation to a dispatcher and she asked me where we were.

I had no idea. As happens so often, we had been rushing from one place to another without attending to life in between. We were some-where in a rural stretch of Indiana. That's all I could offer. Amy was left to shiver by the car, holding a bloody rag to her face while I ran up the highway to a lighted road sign in the distance. It was not a moment I'd like to relive.

In the end, the accident was far worse than the aftermath. Amy re-covered quickly. Contrary to Jasper County Hospital's sky-is-falling di-agnosis, she'd suffered only minor injuries. The cuts and burns to the right side of her face proved superficial. The detached iris was perma-nent but not debilitating, requiring just a few trips to the ophthalmolo-gist. The car, less than a year old, was irrecoverable but well insured. The deer was dead. A sense of reaffirmation was the most significant residue of the incident. When time is suddenly revealed as something of inesti-mable value, you want to spend it wisely.

A few days later, Amy quit her job, and we scraped up a down payment for a 1996 Winnebago Adventurer. Tradition calls for liter-ary travelers to take along only the bare necessities, and for the end of the journey to coincide with the near-demise of the travelers' car or van or bus. We decided to take the opposite route. If we were really going to do this, we were going to do it in comfort. The Winnebago was thirty-four feet long, complete with television, microwave, stove, oven, bedroom, bathroom, shower, the works. Our first home. The following day, we bought a used car to tow behind the RV, our means of accessing those hard-to-reach places. Five days into our adventure, we forked over two bucks for a Route 66 antenna ball, which waved at us through the rear window for the next ten months. A young couple driving a Winnebago, trailing a Saturn, and extolling the memory of the Mother Road, we oozed Americana.

Having substantial time—and a mission—on our hands, we felt a need to name our means of travel. Steinbeck had Rocinante; Hunter S. Thompson drove the Great Red Shark to death; the Merry Pranksters piloted Furthur. Toward that end, we examined why we felt such a need to take to the road, and we realized it was an attempt to stave off the mundane, to drink in life, to celebrate the profundity of experience. What was it Bob Dylan said? "I was so much older then; I'm younger than that now." That's what we wanted out of it. Ours was a mission to enjoy youth—to avoid gathering moss, as it were. So, with a nod to Dylan, we named our thirty-four-foot monster the Rolling Stone. Naturally, it followed that, with a wink to John Lennon, the Saturn became the Day Tripper. But mostly, we called them the RV and the car.

An older couple walks into Nepenthe, one of only a handful of patrons to brave what had threatened to be an uninviting day. They sit two tables away, and I gather snippets of their conversation. He's beefy and bearded, with a professorial air. She's slim and demure. There's a certain distance to their body language, a formality to their dialogue, but it may just be the years. They were married in 1946, he tells the waiter, and then he shows his love by explaining to his wife how to load film into their camera.

It was Amy's job to snap film on our journey—sixty rolls in all. It was my job to drive—21,300 miles over 314 days. The Rolling Stone was slightly worse for wear when we finished—a bent bumper here, a scraped awning there, a windshield cracked by a flying pebble in the last days of the trip. The Day Tripper, another 14,000 miles on the odometer, was still waving at us, though the antenna ball was covered with the dust and debris of forty-eight states.

Along the way, we sampled a full helping of the American experience, visiting Disneyland and Graceland, Gettysburg and Williamsburg, Montgomery's Civil Rights Memorial and Washington's Vietnam Memorial, the Texas School Book Depository in Dallas and the Lorraine Motel in Memphis, the Alamo and Appomattox, Monticello and Hearst Castle, the Rose Bowl and Camden Yards, Dupont Circle and Times Square.

We tasted dim sum in San Francisco, green chili in Albuquerque, fresh guacamole in San Antonio, barbecued ribs in Kansas City, grits in Tuscumbia, crawfish étouffée in New Orleans, shrimp gumbo in Savannah, crab cakes in Baltimore, lobster in Maine, beef pasties in Michigan, and the Circus Circus breakfast buffet in Las Vegas. We listened to "Georgia on My Mind" while driving through Atlanta, "Sweet Home Alabama" in Muscle Shoals, "Rocky Mountain Way" while cruising through Colorado, and, of course, the Eagles' "Take It Easy" while passing a corner in Winslow, Arizona.

We visited Plains, Georgia, and Hope, Arkansas; Woodstock, Vermont, and Mystic, Connecticut. We watched the sun rise in Maine and set in Malibu. We traversed Seventeen-Mile Drive, Bourbon Street, Fifth Avenue, Elvis Presley Boulevard, the Apache Trail, the Blue Ridge Parkway, the Pacific Coast Highway, and the Golden Gate Bridge. We marveled at the White Sands of New Mexico, the Black Hills of South Dakota, the Green Mountains of Vermont, gray whales, redwoods, Yellowstone, and the House of Blues.

But sitting here at journey's end, my most vivid memories of ten months on the road are the faces and stories of the residents of eighteen small towns whose names were cause for investigation, men and women who opened heart and home to us and turned a yearlong adventure into a lifelong lesson.

The old professor attracts the waiter's attention again, rests his elbows on the table, and uses his hands for emphasis. "I've got a question for you," he says, leaning forward. "Where exactly is Big Sur?" The waiter smiles at the opportunity to pass on his wisdom. "You're in it."

"It's not a place?"

"It is a place, and you're in it," replies the waiter. "But it's . . . more of an area."

It is, I want to tell him, a state of mind. Arrival depends upon the perspective of those who come here by whatever means, for whatever reason. It is a coastal rhythm, a forested shroud, a smoky campsite, a steep climb, a Sunday drive, an earthy reality, an airy overlook, a hermit hole, a hippie trip, a Hollywood jaunt, a continent's end, a new beginning.

HARMONY,
CALIFORNIA

> *Everything falls into place, irrelevancies relate,*
> *dissonance becomes harmony, and nonsense wears*
> *a crown of meaning.*
>
> John Steinbeck

The search began in Malibu, of all places, on a mist-shrouded Tuesday morning in January. It was the kind of coastal phenomenon in which the sky becomes darker and the sea lighter until they blend into a gray void where the horizon is supposed to be. The horizon is perspective, and already it was gone.

We had started in late December, heading from Chicago to Los Angeles along the bastard sons of Route 66—I-55, I-44, I-40, I-15, and I-10, a new generation of interstates with almost no romantic folklore. Steinbeck described the Mother Road as "the path of a people in flight." Nowadays, you see more of America by actually flying.

We planned to make it past St. Louis on the first day of our journey,

but our plans were derailed by the infamous Auspicious Beginning. We had a decent excuse. An apparently mild morning turned into an abnormally gusty afternoon—and this in the Windy City. Suddenly, there were forty-five-mile-per-hour winds and a trailer advisory. I had test-driven the RV exactly once and had never otherwise steered anything larger than a sedan. The Rolling Stone was as aerodynamic as it was compact, so I did what any sane adventurer would do. I panicked. We spent the rest of the day and the night in Joliet, one hour south, a city of gamblers and maximum-security prisoners. Camp was a corner of a Kmart parking lot. Frost gathered on the inside of our bedroom window, and a parade of windblown shopping carts slammed us to sleep.

We contemplated our next move for fear of regretting our prior one.

Over the next few weeks, we made our way through Missouri, Oklahoma, the Texas panhandle, New Mexico, and Arizona, finally arriving in Malibu on New Year's Eve. And why not Malibu? If you're going to embark on a journey to find the real America, why not choose as a jumping-off point a place where reality is obscured by silicone and sunblock? Driving through Los Angeles in a thirty-four-foot motor home was a bit like shuffling along a fashion runway in overalls. It felt good.

On a January morning, we headed north on Highway One, dwarfed on our right by the Santa Monica Mountains and on our left by the Pacific. Far in the distance, a vessel drifted through the grayness at a ghostly pace. It appeared to be a ship riding high in the ocean but turned out to be a blimp riding low in the clouds. The heavy air hugged the coastline, which revealed itself only gradually with each curve of the highway.

We took the Pacific Coast Highway to U.S. 101, which we then followed back to the Pacific Coast Highway. There was an international flavor to the journey. Our route took us past Goleta Beach, where the Japanese attacked in 1942—the only attack on the continental United States since the War of 1812. We drove through Santa Barbara, rebuilt in Spanish Colonial style following a devastating 1925 earthquake, and past the mock-Danish town of Solvang. We rolled by Santa Maria and Nipomo and San Luis Obispo.

But the road doesn't just take you through places, it takes you past thoughts and themes. On this day, this particular highway took us past surfers shooting the waves, a film crew shooting a movie, and soldiers shooting rifles at a practice range; past orchards, vineyards, graveyards, and a banana garden touting fifty exotic varieties; past windblown telephone poles bending toward the sea; past a sign for Santa Claus Lane in a town called Summerland and another shouting *Buellton: Home of Split Pea Soup,* where the landscape suddenly changed to rolling countryside; past a white stallion prancing proudly in a mud-brown stable, ignoring his ignoble surroundings, a unicorn amid trolls; past plowed fields resembling corrugated paper and sharp peaks surrounded by harmless foothills; past three huge smokestacks hovering over a rumbling bay like a polluted candelabra. One can think about such nonsense forever, until it is not nonsense at all, but a kind of language of observation. This became my language.

All the while, the ocean dodged in and out of view according to the whim of the road and the lay of the land. And all the while, there was a nagging fear that, this being our first destination, we might never find what we were looking for—until we did. I stopped the Rolling Stone, having arrived at a coincidence of time and place, and we ran to the shore just as the dying sun tossed its parting rays against feathered clouds and exploded in a pink frenzy. We were in the vicinity of Harmony, at a place called Morro Bay, which would be our base camp.

Harmony and California don't normally go hand in hand. Yes, three Olympic Games have been held here. Yes, the United Nations Charter was drawn up in San Francisco in 1945. Yes, it became the thirty-first state as part of something called the Compromise of 1850. But this was also a place claimed by Spain, England, Russia, and Mexico before a war with the latter officially brought it into American hands. California was where the gold rush began at Sutter's sawmill in 1848 and ended with

Sutter's bankruptcy four years later, where Japanese Americans were imprisoned by their countrymen in World War II internment camps, where the no-fault divorce originated, where Sirhan Sirhan altered history. It is a state where lumber companies and naturalists scuffle over redwoods and spotted owls, where immigration battles and labor conflicts and race riots are as common as earthquakes and wildfires and mud slides.

But the following morning, we saw a promising sign. If we couldn't find what we were looking for here, we might as well turn around, pack up, head home. *Town of Harmony, turn right 1 mile*, the billboard alongside the highway explained. *Working artists, restaurants, arts, crafts, wine tasting, wedding chapel*, it announced. *Population 18*, it nearly shouted.

I imagined a throwback commune, a patchwork family, a son named Earth, a daughter named Rainbow, two dogs named Steve. I expected art for the sake of creativity, or maybe creativity for the sake of art. What is harmony? Something more than accord, perhaps a melodious understanding. Is it the same as peace? Absolutely not. Peace can be passive. It seems to imply something thrust upon us rather than achieved, with tension and force as prerequisites. In a continuum with harmony on one end and disharmony on the other, peace is in the middle. Harmony is actively bettering the world; peace is just not making it worse. Harmony is the opposite of war; peace is merely the absence of it. Certainly, harmony is easiest to find in manageable quantities of humanity. Harmony among the masses is unimaginable. Harmony among eighteen is not.

We turned right on Harmony Valley Road and then left toward a half-dozen buildings of various sizes at the end of a dead-end street— the town of Harmony. Our first sight at our first stop was a gold banner on a rust-colored fence adjacent to a sky-blue house: *TOWN FOR SALE*, it said in big red letters. I checked my wallet. Twenty-four bucks. Three hundred years ago, that was enough to get Manhattan. I had learned my first lesson: You can buy Harmony. By the end of the day, I also learned that you can't.

Because the town, ten miles south of Hearst Castle in San Simeon, is just off the Pacific Coast Highway, I had expected it to cozy up to the ocean. The map suggested it. For some reason, so did the name. Instead, I found myself surrounded by waves of pastureland, the vague smell of the sea the only reminder that it was close.

We escaped the Day Tripper and encountered more signs. The wine shop was this way, the glassblower that way, the restaurant here, the post office there. Arrows pointed the way. No one place of interest was more than a hundred feet in any direction. On the side of the post office was a painted scroll five feet wide and eight feet high, flowing with calligraphy like a medieval proclamation. It was an explanation of Harmony's origin.

The name sprang from discord. The area was settled in 1869 as a collection of dairy farms but something less than a community. Rivalry spawned feuds, and on one occasion, a feud led to a fatal shooting. But a

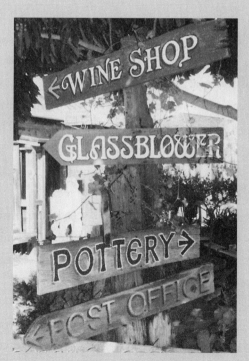

Signs of Harmony

truce was called, and shortly thereafter, the hamlet was named Harmony. The cynic in me whispered that it was a tourism trick as old as Eric the Red's giving ice-layered Greenland its name, shortly after being banished from Norway for manslaughter. I read on.

At the turn of the century, twenty local farmers incorporated the Harmony Valley Creamery Association, which was soon producing some of California's finest butters and cheeses. The town grew around the company. At its peak, Harmony boasted a large residence for management, a bunkhouse for employees, a schoolhouse, a livery stable, a blacksmith, a general store, and a post office. The highway ran directly through town, and William Randolph Hearst himself was said to have stopped here often on the way to his ranch, which was far larger than Harmony. Prosperity in Harmony lasted nearly half a century, until the dairy business moved thirty miles south to San Luis Obispo in the 1950s. The creamery closed its doors, and except for the post office, Harmony was abandoned.

In 1970, however, the ghost town amid ranch land was purchased, appropriately, by people named Casper and Fields. Ralph and Janet Casper and Paul and Doris Fields bought the two-and-a-half-acre plot on which the creamery stood and began the restoration of Harmony, drawing artists and shopkeepers to the forgotten village. There were now several shops in the old creamery building, a brick walkway leading to a potter's studio and shop, and a gallery and a glassblowing studio in an old rust-roofed barn across the street. Harmony had been reborn and recast.

Were the town's saviors still around? We went searching. Steinbeck believed that the best places to eavesdrop on a local population were bars and churches. The Harmony Chapel consisted of four pews and two stained-glass windows in an area the size of a large walk-in closet. It was empty except for windblown leaves. We tried the saloon.

The Harmony Saloon was a bar, literally—five stools and a wooden counter. I sat on a low-backed stool loose on its hinges. Amy sat next to me, and we ordered sandwiches and drinks from the bartender. A woman, fortyish with a sun-creased face, sat at the other end of the bar conquering the local newspaper. "Hmm. There's an article in here about caffeine," she said to no one in particular. "I can't drink coffee or Pepsi anymore. I get so I can't concentrate on anything." She walked out of the saloon for a few seconds, came back, and read some more. "Hmm. Can't even eat anything anymore—chocolate, pain relievers. Do you believe they put caffeine in pain relievers? Says it right here."

Amy responded by saying she found it hard to believe and by posing a question: "Do you live in Harmony?"

Were we anywhere else, it would have been a rather loaded inquiry. The jittery woman shook her head and said she lived in Cambria, a whaling center turned artist colony four miles up the highway. "We don't know who lives here. There's eighteen people. We don't know who they are." She paused and then added, "It's for sale, you know. The owners live in that blue house across the street."

I asked the obvious: "How does one get to own a town?"

She answered the obvious: "Just buy it, I guess. They're just common folk, but they bought it." She shouted into the kitchen, "Bill, how did they get to own the town? That's my husband, Bill. He's the bartender."

Bill the Bartender appeared with our turkey sandwiches. "Just bought it. It's not incorporated or anything—it's a township, I guess." And he left it at that.

The voice of Eric Clapton rose from the radio, spicing up a Dylan tune. "I ain't saying you treated me unkind. / You could've done better, but I don't mind. / You just kind of wasted my precious time. / But don't think twice, it's alright."

Our eyes drifted as our stomachs filled. Mine wandered to old steel barstools in one corner, the kind that were intended to be shaped for rear ends but resembled some sort of torture machine. Amy's roamed to the photographs on the wall. There were more than a dozen portraits, most of them awkward class photos from the 1960s, complete with beehives, flips, and other prehistoric designs. The Bartender's Wife explained that some of them were waitresses in the adjacent restaurant and some were customers.

"That one on the left, near the bottom, is a singer here in town." She meant Cambria. "That one on the right, her teeth are usually blackened because her ex-boyfriend always comes in and draws funny glasses and stuff on her. I can see he hasn't been here in a while."

I turned to Bill the Bartender and asked how he came to be behind Harmony's bar. "Well, I was on the other side of the bar for a long, long time. I just got drafted, I guess."

And again, he left Eric Clapton to do the talking. "I wish there was something you would do or say / to make me change my mind and stay. / But we never did too much talking anyway. / Don't think twice, it's alright."

Another customer strolled in, a likable-looking fellow with a ruddy complexion. Conversation soon revealed him to be the owner of the winery up the road, Harmony Cellars. We were five now—Amy and I, Chuck the Winemaker, Bill the Bartender, and the Bartender's Wife. Amy inquired about another photograph, that of a large brown animal with a thatch of white on its neck. That's when we learned about Freddy the Cat.

Six months earlier, Freddy had been Harmony's most renowned citizen. He was a Maine Coon cat, and the best anybody could tell, he was in his twenty-second year when he finally expired. According to Harmony lore—and there were photographs to back it up—he was big enough to catch squirrels and send St. Bernards whimpering in retreat. He was beloved enough to have the run of the town, with food and bed in every shop and the occasional cat cocktail—milk with an umbrella in it—in the saloon. He was famous enough to have shirts bearing his likeness sold in a local shop. And he was revered enough, according to Bill the Bartender, to be Harmony's honorary mayor.

"When it was time for the election, he just ran unopposed," he said, refilling my water glass. "He was deaf the last couple years, so people would write him notes to communicate with him. But I don't know if he read them himself or if someone read them to him and he read lips."

We laughed. The Bartender's Wife shook her head. "It was devastating when he died." She pointed her thumb to the rear of the old creamery. "He's buried out back."

I peered at a sign posted above the bar—*Friendly Henry*, it said—and the talk turned to Hank, the owner of the Harmony Saloon and the Old Harmony Pasta Factory next door. Hank, the bartender explained, had been neighboring Cambria's honorary mayor. He thought for a second. "In fact, it was about the same time Freddy ruled Harmony. I never thought there might have been a conspiracy between the two." He cocked a mischievous eyebrow. "But it's possible."

Chuck the Winemaker joined in. "If you dig deep enough, you could come up with some dirt, I'm sure."

"I can show you where to start," laughed the bartender, nodding toward Freddy's grave. "You'd definitely come up with something."

Outside the saloon, a golden retriever wagged his way past us, followed by a large cat, perhaps the new mayor. A wedding party had arrived at the chapel: a striking, pregnant blond woman on the arm of a handsome black man with a ponytail running down his spine. Dogs and cats living together. Black and white in matrimony. It was too much—too surface.

We wandered to the front of the old creamery building, a six-thousand-square-foot concrete structure the color of its product. In fact, it still said *Harmony Valley Creamery Assn.* in bold letters on the side. A few feet lower was another sign over a doorway. *Hart and Co.*, it read, *in the heart of beautiful downtown Harmony, CA*. It was a boutique smaller than the saloon.

"Hello," said a voice belonging to a longhaired brunette who wore what seemed to be a constant smile. Her name was Linda. She owned the store with her sister and a friend. The friend was named Hart, and the

Harmony Valley Creamery Association

sisters were the Company. Linda had been raised in Vermont. She moved to California in 1978.

"I was involved in the new-homes industry, which for a while I enjoyed," she explained. "But then I could see that it was just destroying the environment. There was too much building going on. It's one thing to supply the housing to people, because everybody has a right to have it. But it's another thing to overtax the land, so I had to get out of it."

Her sister had settled in Harmony in 1987 and started the store. Two years later, Linda joined the business, selling hand-painted boots, hand-painted vests, hand-painted sweatshirts, hand-painted jackets. There were also Harmony postcards, Harmony shirts, Harmony magnets, Harmony history scrolls. Harmony was indeed for sale.

"We used to have a store in Cambria as well, and we used to be in wholesale manufacturing. We had a line of women's sportswear, but we lost our butts in that business. It was just too tough. We made a lot of . . . Hey there!"

She smiled at the doorway, where stood a man with his right arm in a sling and his considerable pants held up by suspenders designed to look like tape measures. Dominick was his name, and he looked like a cross between a wise guy and a muppet. He was selling produce door to door. Linda bought a dozen oranges for four dollars. Dominick asked if I wanted any. I stammered a non-reply. When he went to his truck, Amy told me we already had plenty of oranges in the RV. It's amazing how a man can spend half his life peering into a refrigerator and still not see a thing. Dominick brought back a bag and set it triumphantly on the floor. I apologized and told him we didn't actually need any. He shrugged and walked away, apparently a pushover. I should have known better. Later, after he'd made his rounds of Harmony, he caught me again, this time giving me the hard sell. I bought a pound of pistachios.

I asked Linda if she lived in Harmony. She lived in Cambria, too. Did anybody live in Harmony?

"When we first came up here, there were a few rogue artists who sort of camped out on the premises, but the real residents of the town are farmers and ranchers around here whose names go back to before the turn of the century. This area is an old Swiss-Italian settlement, so you have names like Tartallia, Bordoglio, Souza, Molinari. A lot of them will come here and pick up their mail."

I peered at a petition on the counter. The addresses next to the signatures ranged from Tennessee to Washington State. It was a petition to save the post office. "It's a small office. Whenever the postmaster retires from a little office, they try to close it," Linda explained. "They're going to have to have some kind of resolution soon, so what I'm doing is showing that this is also a tourist attraction. It's a part of U.S. postal history. They say, 'Oh, nothing historic has happened here.' And I say, 'That's not the point. It's part of your history. You want to preserve something like this.'"

Somehow, she managed to smile all the way through this. I added my signature to the petition.

"Sometimes, I think we're a tiny little microcosm of the universe," she said, still smiling, when I asked her about the name of the town. "There's sometimes disharmony in Harmony, but usually we get along pretty well."

"Disharmony? Over what?"

"You know, little things that come up. Sometimes, there are little feuds between the shopkeepers, or you might hear some gossip about some of the neighbors. . . ."

I must have seemed interested, because she looked around as if watching out for Big Brother. Then she sighed and continued, as if confessing, "I'm going to be very honest with you. It needs to be said. This town's history, there was violence here, and that's why they came up with the name Harmony. But I think this place still has to be exorcised, because it seems like there's still some feuds between the families and there's still some feuding here in the town. I guess in every town there's some difficulties, but this place is so little that it seems to show up more. For a few months at a time, everything will be golden, and then all of a sudden, that negative spirit will be back again. I'm thinking now, though, that the most positive people are staying and some negative people have left."

She tried to smile again. It wasn't working this time.

Try the artists, I figured. John the Potter owned Harmony Pottery. He was a gnomelike man, small in stature, bald of head, with a cherubic face and a dusty orange goatee flowing from his chin. Amid the ashtrays and the urns and the ornaments and the comings and goings of customers, he was a rather unexcitable lump of clay. In a shy, sleepy voice, he offered memories grudgingly.

He had been here since 1973, since just after Harmony's reemergence. He lived up the road, the only Harmony artist with a Harmony address. He had survived three different landlords and had seen dozens of businesses come and go. It was quiet at the beginning, he nearly whispered. Business had been better over the past five or six years, but he wasn't sure why. Generally, most people got along, he said, but not always and not everybody. And that was about all I got out of John the Potter.

Maybe one of the newer tenants would point me in the right direction. In front of the barn turned gallery, I stopped a gentleman who looked like he knew his way around—that is, if he could see from above an untamed beard and below a wide, floppy hat. His name was Larry, he was an artist, and he worked with glass. "I contacted some dentists that I know, got little tiny diamond burrs, and started scratching them on glass," he explained. "I found some glass called flash glass from Italy and France. It's not laminated, but the way they make it, there's different colors in it. So you hit a certain depth, and you reach a different color."

Larry was engaged to Kat, the owner of the gallery, who had been here barely eighteen months. Already, they didn't get along with John the Potter. "He started handling glass back there. We had agreed not to handle pottery if he didn't handle glass. . . . I don't know. We don't really get into each other's business here. We say hi, they say hi. It's not as close as you would think a town like Harmony would be."

I was beginning to think this entire journey was a bad idea. If it was supposed to restore my belief in the inherent goodness of humanity, it wasn't working. Like Larry, I was just scratching the surface, poking here, rubbing there, and I wasn't enjoying the colors I was finding. This wasn't my utopian vision of harmony.

During the Civil War, at about the time Harmony was founded, the rank and file of both the Union and Confederate armies tended to refer to one another by slang nicknames derived from their home states. Those from Michigan were Wolverines, those from Maine were Foxes, those from Maryland were Claw Thumpers, those from Mississippi were Tad Poles. And Illinois? People from Illinois were Suckers. And maybe we were. Perhaps harmony is indeed the smile of the fool.

I knocked on the door of the owners' blue house, hoping to find a silver lining. It was opened by a woman in her sixties wearing a hand-painted sweatshirt from Hart and Co. She gave a hello that indicated she thought she knew us from somewhere. Once she realized she didn't, she invited us in anyway. As she went off to fetch her husband, I noticed a trio of oversized books on a shelf in their living room: *The Norman Rockwell Collection*, the *Great Book of Wine*, and *Cosmos* by Carl Sagan. Nostalgia, nurturing, and a recent understanding of space and time—the story of Jim and Kay Lawrence.

Jim Lawrence limped into the room. He had sprained his ankle days earlier. It appeared to be the least of his health concerns. He was moving slowly and coughing slightly. I'd let him tell me about it.

"So what can we do for you?" he offered, settling on the couch as I was swallowed by an easy chair.

"Well, I was wondering what leads a person to say, 'I think I'll buy a town.'"

Kay, sitting across from me, let out a laugh. I don't think I'd known what a guffaw was until then. "Ego trip." She winked. "It was pretty quiet when we bought the town, and for some reason or another, we thought we could turn it around. We felt it was something special and it needed some life turned into it. We thought we could do it. I don't know why." She laughed again.

"Are you from this area originally?"

Jim shook his head. "Originally, we were raised in southern California. Kay was from Whittier. I was from Pomona. We left there in '72, went to the San Joaquin Valley for about ten years, and then came over here."

Jim and Kay Lawrence

"Jim was a C.P.A., and I was a dental hygienist," Kay explained. "And then Jim got into farming in the valley—almonds, table grapes, wine grapes. And then he sold some of it and bought Harmony." Another laugh. "I guess that's the short of it."

I asked for the long version, and I liked it better. She was born in Utah, he in Oklahoma, both in the midst of the Depression. In 1941, both of their families moved to the Los Angeles area, hers to join up with relatives, his to escape the Dust Bowl. They met in 1952. He joined the army; she went off to college. Six years later, they reunited and were married.

It was a piano that brought them to Harmony. In 1979, while running their ranch in the valley town of Delano, the Lawrences purchased a second home, a beach house about two hours west in Cambria. They were unimpressed by the high school in Delano, so they sent their daughter to school in Cambria. Kay and she moved there, while Jim spent half his time on the coast and half in the valley.

"The actual story of how we came here," said Jim, "was Kay wanted me to bring the piano over from Delano for our daughter to play here, and I thought it was too much to move. I told her to see if she could buy a used one, and we found one being advertised. We called, the price was right, and it happened that they were living in this house right here. It was the mother of the fella that owned the town, and it was for sale."

After getting Harmony on its feet again, the Caspers and Fieldses had sold the town to a Beverly Hills developer in 1977. He had planned on moving his family north, but his wife took ill and refused to leave southern California. In 1981, he sold the town to Jim and Kay for $650,000.

"When we were on the ranch, we had a house that sat on two and a half acres, same size as this town. And there were several thousand acres that Jim was managing," Kay explained. "So when we came over here, it didn't really dawn on me that it was that big a deal. It was like a weekend project. It would give him something to do. He never could quite make it over to the coast. He always had something tying him up in Delano. Well, if he had something to keep him occupied on the weekends here . . ."

They never actually meant to live in Harmony, but it soon became apparent that somebody had to be here to oversee the property. They sold the ranch. They sold the beach house. They became the only permanent residents of downtown Harmony. The town's other residents—the owners of the sprawling green countryside surrounding Harmony's half-a-block business district—might as well have been a thousand miles away. "We see each other, speak to each other," said Jim. "But you just don't get real close to the people. They're busy running their ranch."

Jim and Kay concentrated on their new purchase instead of their new neighbors. The previous owner had tried to make some changes, but he had pushed too hard. By the time the Lawrences arrived, there were only two artists remaining in town. But within a few years, all of the available space in Harmony was being leased. It stayed that way for nearly eight years.

And then Freddy the Cat died. It may have been a coincidence, but all hell broke loose in Harmony.

"We had one person that some people were unhappy with, so we settled with getting her out of her lease and letting her go," Jim began. "Someone rented the shop right away, coming out of Los Angeles, on a two-year lease. He was going to move the family here, then his wife basically told him she found someone else. He was going to take custody of the children, and that meant going back to southern California. There was no need trying to hold him to the lease. Then we had another that had been rented out to the same people seven or eight years. They had a split in the partnership. They were brothers. I guess they hadn't personally gotten along for years. And then we leased it right off the bat to someone else. They were opened and everything, and then two weeks later, they left. We found out there had been some problem with bankruptcy."

Kay continued the litany of incompatibility. "And this glassblower and his wife moved in here. I think it was less than a year, and they split up. She started a shop here in Harmony just this last year, until she decided it just wouldn't work being right next to him. She sold it to Kat, who owns the gallery now. Kat's ex-husband actually signed the lease, and the next thing I know, they're separating."

She shrugged. "For years, things were going well, and I basically told anybody who got married in the chapel that they were being married in Harmony, so they had to stay in harmony, but lately I don't know."

Harmony was for sale for $1.68 million. The Lawrences had originally asked more, but that was when they weren't necessarily eager to sell. That had all changed recently, and the fact that there were now three vacant spaces in the old creamery had little to do with it. It took a shock of a different kind.

"I had smoked for forty years and had quit just before," Jim explained. "I had a cough, and it wouldn't go away. They said I had chronic bronchitis, but I couldn't get rid of it, and I said, 'Hey, that's not bronchitis. That's something else.' I wanted x-rays and a complete physical. Everything. That's when I found out I had a little spot on my lungs."

He said it as if describing a fishing trip, but I knew a fishing trip could be a spiritual experience. "They got all of it with surgery," he continued confidently. "The chemotherapy and radiation are just insurance, to make sure. You know, cells can get loose. But from the time they found the spot until I found out it was operable, it was about a week or ten days, and it made me do a lot of thinking—about a lot of things I haven't done that I'd like to do."

"Like what?"

"Well, being a C.P.A., that was a lot of work. I was basically going all the time. And then we had four or five hundred employees on the ranch. They kept me going. Sometimes, you'd be up at five o'clock and you're home at five. And then we built this up here, and there's different things to worry about. Right now, a couple of years without doing too much sounds good."

For some, it is a lifelong goal; for others like Jim Lawrence, it is a grudging surrender to exhaustion. He had come to the point in his life where he was tired of adding and growing and nurturing and striving and formulating and generating. He simply wanted to savor. But he couldn't quite get himself to say the word.

Amy, who had been sitting quietly, said it for him: "You basically want to retire."

Kay nodded her head. Jim looked as if he were considering it. "Well, I guess that's it. What we really want to do is travel," he said, and his eyes lit up as he leaned forward. "I've taken trips, but I haven't really gotten out of the cities much. I've been to Washington, D.C., to Chicago. But outside of Chicago? I've never seen that area. Once, we went to Kenosha, I think. I've never been to Lake Louise in Banff. And down south? We've never really been down south besides one trip to New Orleans. And Kay would like to see the fall colors in Vermont and New Hampshire and that area. There are just a lot of places we would like to see that we haven't really taken the time to see."

In one breath, he had taken himself thousands of miles. He then put the reverie in his pocket and leaned back again. "It's just if some emergency happens, somebody's gotta be here. It's tough to take off more than a couple of weeks. So we'd just like to be rid of any responsibility, and if we decide we wanted to go tomorrow, we could."

"We've had this town for fifteen years," Kay pointed out. "It's time for someone else to go on with it."

They'd still keep a house in the area, Jim explained. Just not the same house and not the same town. It would be too tough, like watching another parent raise your child. "The two people who started this town, Casper and Fields. Casper's been here once or twice. But Paul Fields . . . His wife's been here, but Paul won't come. It's too emotional. It's not that they don't come because they don't like Harmony. They don't come because they love it."

Amy and I left Harmony in a buoyant mood, more confident than ever in our decision to fend off the inevitable regret of later times by spending a year on the road in the prime of our lives. Confidence is like that. Sometimes, you need to hear other people's desires to lay claim to your own. The Lawrences had finally discovered priority, consonance, peace of mind. They had achieved a sort of inner harmony, and the prospect of their future gave us a warm memory to hang on to—until we opened the *New York Times* a year later to find a brief feature on the California hamlet of Harmony. Kay Lawrence, it noted, was still trying to sell the town, having dropped the price significantly. Jim Lawrence had died four months after our visit.

INSPIRATION,
ARIZONA

Inspiration at its best means breath, but only too frequently means wind.

Lord Chesterton

Having made our way down the coast to San Diego and begun our trek east along Interstate 8, we were accompanied by a hefty breeze traveling in the same direction. The highway here hugs the Mexican border, bouncing close to it repeatedly like an insect at a wall and passing hybrid towns like Calexico and Mexicali, which reflect the ambiguity of the American fringe.

We were leaving the coast, heading toward the desert, and it came upon us suddenly. Trees shrank, mountains grew, and the land became harsh, the naked earth exposing itself. Blemishes of outcroppings, pock-marked hillsides, bald peaks, wrinkled valleys, a rash of red here, a gash of rock there, as if the forest had been sheared away by a razor. Vegetation receded into rock, leaving mountains littered only with the debris of themselves.

The desert, perhaps more than any other landscape, topples expectations. It is not a place of colorless monotony. Color is visible when light falls upon it, and this is a sun-punished setting. The colors emerge in contrasts—burgundy and slate gray, peach and mint green, red-orange and gold.

We inched through Mountain Spring Pass, taking heed of the warnings constantly thrown at desert travelers. *Runaway Truck Ramp 5 Miles. 6% Grade Next 9 Miles. Loose Gravel 500 Feet. Strong Winds Possible Next 12 Miles.* Mountain ranges were stacked one behind the other, like heads peeking over shoulders at an accident scene.

Crossing the state border into Yuma, Arizona, we discovered a city with barely fifty thousand full-time residents in the summer, but with nearly that many recreational vehicles squeezed into its dozens of RV parks in the winter. They call themselves Snowbirds. Nomadic elders. This was Retirement City, located on the banks of the Colorado River, which springs from the grand Rockies, summers in the Grand Canyon, and winds its way to winter with grandparents.

The sun began to sink, and we decided to pull off and rest, unwilling to brave the desert night. Arizona is a state of violent contrasts. From day to night, mountain to desert, summer to winter, the temperature can change dramatically. At its hottest, Arizona sizzled at 127 degrees in the town of Parker on the western border in 1905. At its coldest, sixty-six years later, Arizona froze at 40 degrees below zero at Hawley Lake, only 250 miles east. Indeed, it is not uncommon for two different Arizona communities to record the nation's highest and lowest temperatures in the same day.

Steinbeck viewed the desert as a classroom of sorts. He called it an arena in which to observe "the infinite variety of techniques of survival under pitiless opposition." There are dozens of endangered species in Arizona. In fact, of the three dozen species of fish native to the state, more than two-thirds are threatened, primarily because dams and other building projects have altered the course of streams. Still, there are animals that have conquered the desert with Darwinian aplomb. For instance, the kangaroo rat, which obtains moisture while digesting food and can live its entire life without a sip of water, and the pronghorn goat, whose four-part stomach serves as a built-in fermentation vat.

Generation upon generation of desert life has bred survivalists, but we came from the Midwest, we were thirsty, and our one-part stomachs were empty. We stopped for the night in the dusty, gray community of Wellton. Judging by the tumbleweeds, it appeared to be struggling to survive itself.

The Rolling Stone came equipped with a nineteen-inch color television placed dramatically above the expansive windshield. It won't work while the vehicle is in motion, the salesman told us—though the simple fact that it was necessary to design such a turn-off system was indictment enough of modern American culture. Like self-flushing toilets. The view out the window was more interesting and certainly more educational, but the local news became a staple of our experience, if only because there may be no better way to gauge the interests, scope, and sensibilities of a region. Whether it was a young anchor in Joplin, Missouri, stumbling over her words on her way to a job in a larger market, or a well-groomed sportscaster in Amarillo, Texas, doing his best to maintain his enthusiasm as he moved from Dallas Cowboys football to high-school girls basketball, or a glitzy Los Angeles news team surrounding stories about drive-bys with a smug weather report by a talking head named Dallas Rains, the look and the feel of a region were usually encapsulated by the look and the feel of the evening news.

The evening news that night in Wellton, however, took us toward a surreal nightmare. It is a common science fiction theme. Confident city slickers enter sleepy small town and soon find out that they have actually entered a different dimension. When we turned on the local newscast and heard, "Sixty humans attended a fiddling contest today" and "Dozens of humans were on hand to watch a flag football game between the police and fire departments" and "Humans are in for nice weather this week," we half-expected Rod Serling to appear. Until we realized they were saying *Yumans*, I wondered if it weren't only true that Mars was a desert but also that the desert was Mars.

The following morning, we watched Wellton disappear into our rearview mirror as we continued along Interstate 8, the Castle Dome Mountains to the north and the Mohawk Mountains to the south. A hundred-car freight train slept silently alongside the highway, and as we passed it moving east, another train just as long passed it moving west. It was the arrival of the railroad that had marked the end of the rugged western frontier, but not before boom towns sprouted up with names to match the environment—Whiskey Bar, Lousy Gulch, Show Low, Gouge Eye, Total Wreck, Rough and Ready, and, of course, Tombstone.

The wind blew us forward until we came upon Gila Bend and Route 85 heading north-south. Going south, the road made straight for Why, Arizona, reportedly named when travelers kept asking, "Why would you want to live here?" This valid question was answered by an enormous saguaro cactus on the side of the road, its arms raised in a shrug. Another, a dozen feet away, seemed to point its arms to one side, as if ushering us south. But Inspiration was our goal, and that meant turning north. As I did so, I peeked behind us, and I could have sworn I saw a third saguaro, two arms on each side giving it the appearance of a five-fingered hand, the middle finger upraised.

Now, the Gila Bend Mountains were to our left and the Maricopa Mountains to our right, cloud and sun combining to turn them into monuments of shadow and light, the swirls changing as the sky moved. Within minutes, we met up with another east-west artery, Interstate 10. We drove past a smiling sign welcoming us to the friendly town of Goodyear (followed quickly by a sign of caution: *State Prison—Do Not Stop for Hitchhikers*) and zoomed through Phoenix and its parasitic suburb

*S*uperstition Mountain

cities of Mesa and Scottsdale before finally arriving at our planned base in Apache Junction. We stopped in the shadow of the Superstition Mountains, a great, broad-shouldered stretch of rock that didn't rise up from the region as much as it looked down upon it, like a stern overseer. Here, we discovered the spell of the Lost Dutchman Mine.

Jacob Waltz was a native of Germany but a son of the American frontier. For some reason, he was known as "the Dutchman." A loner and an alcoholic, he had a mysterious heart and a vein of gold. According to legend, there was treasure in the Superstitions. It was originally found by Mexicans, who loaded their mules with as much gold as they could carry and then ran into Apaches on the way home. The Apaches believed the gods were angered by the treasure's removal and killed all but two of the Mexican caravan. Years later, one or the other told Waltz the location of the gold mine. Waltz told nobody.

He is said to have dipped periodically into the treasure trove, taking gold when he needed it. Many tried to follow him through the maze of canyons and ridges to the secret mine. If he couldn't elude them, he killed them. It was only on his deathbed that he left a vague clue, whispering,

"Where Weaver's Needle casts its long shadow at four in the afternoon, there you will find a vein of rose quartz laced with gold wire, and you will be rich beyond your wildest dreams."

Many have since searched for the Lost Dutchman Mine in the Superstitions. No one has found it. Some say that each of the ghostly white rocks in the nearby foothills represents a prospector who never returned. Local Pima and Maricopa Indians believed those who entered the mountains fell victim to diabolic possession. One man's dream is another man's demon.

The legend is pure Arizona. The state's motto—*Ditat Deus*, or "God enriches"—seems to conjure the search for the mother lode. The Spaniards, the first Europeans to arrive, came in search of the legendary Seven Cities of Cibola. Francisco Vasquez de Coronado set off with hundreds of soldiers and Indians in 1540 and spent two years scouring the region for cities of gold and silver, only to find pueblos of mud and stone. Three centuries later, the prospector replaced the soldier-explorer. The gold rush brought treasure seekers through the desert with a pick in one hand and a gun in the other. By 1863, enough mineral riches had been discovered to lead Abraham Lincoln to create the Arizona Territory.

Mark Twain claimed that wherever there was a rumor and a hole in the ground, someone built a town around it. Arizona offered a mineral belt of rumor 450 miles long and 70 miles wide, stretching northwest to southeast across the state. Strikes were made, and tent cities sprang up. The demand for beef brought ranchers, the demand for protection from the "Indian menace" brought soldiers, and the money trail brought merchants. A man named Studebaker built and sold wheelbarrows to prospectors. Another named Levi Strauss created trousers out of canvas intended for tents. Others mined the miners, running gambling halls and whorehouses.

The life span of a boom town was often fleeting. Once the treasure was gone, the makeshift community created around it soon faded. Some mining towns became cities, but most became memories. Gila City, one of the first boom towns in Arizona, sprang up around a gold strike in 1858. Six years later, all that remained, it was said, were three chimneys and a coyote. The map was littered with towns that used to be. We decided to take Robert Frost's advice: "Don't loaf and invite inspiration. Light out after it with a club."

Ten centuries ago, the Salado Indians used a foot trail along the canyons of the Salt River and its tributaries. Ten decades ago, it was used by Native American traders and white settlers. It was by then known as the Tonto Trail. From 1905 through 1911, Roosevelt Dam was constructed to store and regulate the river's water, and a supply road was created along much of the old trail leading to the dam site. Teddy Roosevelt himself dedicated the dam and declared the trail, chosen as the state's first Historic Road, "one of the most spectacular best-worth-seeing sights of the world." According to our map, this road, forty-four miles of remarkable scenery now known as the Apache Trail, led toward Inspiration.

Five miles along, as we rounded the northwest base of the Superstition Mountains, we came upon the town of Goldfield, where gold was discovered a century earlier. *Welcome to Goldfield ghost town*, said the sign, which is a bit like saying, "You are now entering Atlantis, the Lost City." It wasn't much of a ghost town. It was in fact a replica built in 1988, boasting the Superstition Mountains Museum, a steakhouse and saloon, a leather shop, an ice cream shop, live music nightly, mine tours, a livery, and a gift shop selling everything from onyx ashtrays to prickly pear jelly. There were cars pulling in and out of Goldfield every thirty seconds. There was even handicapped parking. The only piece of reality I could find was an old man wearing a cowboy hat and bolo tie, smoking a pipe and giving directions to tourists through missing teeth. I asked him about Inspiration.

"Inspiration?" he sort of whistled. "That's a ghost town, isn't it?"

I was afraid he meant a real ghost town. We moved on, past Lost Dutchman State Park and Weaver's Needle Vista, as the black road twisted its way through a forest of saguaros. Standing an arm's length apart, the cacti mimicked nearby telephone poles, raising their arms and cheering us on—or begging us to stop. We paused at a cliff overlooking Canyon Lake and watched two silent motorboats race opposite ways through the green stillness. Two miles later, the road brought us to Tortilla Flat, population six. There were five times that many cars parked alongside the road. It was another lost town that had found tourism.

There were two patchwork wooden buildings in the town, one boasting the Superstition Saloon, the other a gift store. On the door to the saloon, a sign: *Shirts and shoes required, bra and panties optional.* Next to the door, a hanging wooden toilet seat with enough room to poke a picture-perfect smile through it. In front of the store, a wash basin and the words, *Wyatt Earp was washed heah.* Next to that, a wooden box bearing a warning: *Beware of baby rattlers.* Inside it were actual plastic baby rattles. Kitsch, it seems, survives in the desert, too.

We stepped inside the gift store and found every available inch of wall space taken up by signed dollar bills from around the globe, apparently a common practice in towns conceived around separating tourists from their money. When visitors didn't have dollar bills, they taped coins to the wall. When they didn't have either, they actually wrote out checks for one dollar. The majority of bills had business cards stapled to them, from carpenters and country-western singers, bank managers and photographers, mechanics and paper-doll makers. Of course, most of the patrons' dollar bills went toward postcards, pocketknives, pot holders, mugs, magnets, thermometers, "Old West" incense cones, and assorted other Tortilla Flat souvenirs.

I asked the man behind the counter—adorned in a desert grunge uniform of goatee, boots, and backward baseball cap—whether he had heard of Inspiration. He shook his head.

"Hey, Angie, ever heard of a town called Inspiration?"

Angie poked her head out from a back room. "Inspiration? What's that?"

In the saloon, there were more dollars bills. The barstools were actual leather saddles, and the patrons drank out of jelly jars. I approached a man behind the counter. He was wearing a sheriff's badge and selling envelopes filled with rattlesnake eggs.

"Inspiration? Isn't it down in the Globe area? I'm just not familiar enough with that area to give you any information."

He turned his attention to a customer who was opening an envelope to inspect the eggs. When the contents—a bent paper clip wound by a rubber band—made a startling rattling noise, the customer jumped. The sheriff laughed, probably for the thousandth time.

I walked out of the saloon and directly into the belt buckle of a giant cowboy complete with chaps and six-shooters, his wild hair and eyes giving him the look of a cartoon character. He was exceptionally tall and exploited it to its maximum potential, allowing husbands to take photographs of their wives pointing a gun at his back as he held their purses and adopted an over-the-top look of terror. "Don't tell anyone you saw me here," he told a giggling wife. "Tell them you saw me in New Mexico on a slow horse going south." Of course, he always tagged on an addendum: "Did I mention I gladly accept tips?"

When they gave him a dollar, he gave them a business card: *Big Dave Murra, Terror of the Rockies. Wanted: Alive or Otherwise. Description: 300 lbs., 7 ft. 2 in., Eyes of Blue, 16 in the Shoe. From the Black Hills of Dakota Territory. Gunfighter, claim jumper, dry gulcher, all-around nasty guy.*

Thirty-five-year-old Big Dave Murra claimed to be a resident of Deadwood, South Dakota. "I do live theater," he told me. "Western gunfights, comedy shows. I die three times a day onstage. It's set in the days of 1876 or so. It's about a guy who finds a gold mine, gets fleeced out of the gold mine, and then gets shot in the end."

I assumed he didn't mean he got shot in the rear. "So you're a good guy?"

"Sort of."

In the winter months, the Terror of the Rockies flew south, where he posed for photos and appeared in the Renaissance Festival, his specialty being tests of strength. "I've done shows as small as a hundred people and as large as seventeen thousand in the St. Paul Civic Center," he explained. "I've been in *People* magazine, *Good Morning America*, and *Easy Rider* magazine. I did carnivals before this, doing everything from eating fire to working on the rides. We went to Key West, Saskatchewan, Arizona, California, Wyoming, Montana, North Dakota, South Dakota, Nebraska. I've been around the block."

"Ever been to Inspiration, just a little ways east of here?"

From my vantage point below, he seemed to be scratching his head. "Inspiration? No. I've been to Kearney, Hayden, Winkelman. But Inspiration? Never heard of it."

The blacktop turned to gray two miles past Tortilla Flat, and the saguaros turned to prickly pears. There were more desert warnings: *Mountain Grades Next 37 Miles. Watch for Animals. Flash Flood Area Next Mile. Road Narrows. No Pavement Next 22 Miles.* After this last sign, the pavement faded into a dirt trail, and Fish Creek Hill plunged into Fish Creek Canyon. We had the good fortune of heading downhill along the two-mile grade, and so we hugged the sheer wall on our right side instead of the cliff's edge on our left. It used to be that stagecoaches stopped at the top of the hill, where a mule was hitched to the rear and walked backward to brake the coach on the steep descent. I fought the urge to call this a backward-ass place.

At the bottom of the canyon, we crossed a one-lane bridge over the trickle of water constituting Fish Creek. Next came our first view of Apache Lake, a long, narrow body of water as green as the cacti and shrubs that surrounded it. We stopped for lunch at the Apache Lake Marina and Resort, where the waiter-proprietor said this of Inspiration: "A ghost town, right? Or is that the open-pit copper mine? There are mines all over the place here."

We were getting closer to Inspiration, and the clues were adding up to confusion. After lunch, we plodded through more twists and turns—and ten more miles of Apache Lake masquerading as a still river—until we finally arrived at Roosevelt Dam, the world's largest masonry dam, and the end of the Apache Trail. From there, it was south on Highway 88 to the strange, twisted oasis of Claypool, a collection of mobile homes, tilted windmills, and forsaken ranches. We pulled up alongside a man walking toward nowhere, the only sign of life in town.

"Excuse me, is there a place called Inspiration nearby?"

"Inspiration? Go up five or six miles to the lights and make a right."

"So it exists?"

"Yeah, it's in Miami."

"Does anyone live there?"

"No, not really. It's up on the hill."

We followed his directions until Highway 88 met U.S. 60 where three towns—Globe, Central Heights, and Miami—rested side by side. Here, tucked between the Pinal and Apache Mountains, was the heart of copper country. Surrounded by black slag piles and bleached-out copper tailings were lawless desert boom towns that had lasted.

Miami emerged, according to legend, when a gentleman called Black Jack Newman (he had a long Polish name, so the locals just referred to him as the "new man") discovered a rich mineral prospect and proposed to name it after his girlfriend, Mimi Tune. At the same time, a group from Miami, Ohio, staked a claim nearby. The two sides compromised by spelling their fledgling community *Miami* but pronouncing it *Mimi*.

Globe derived from the Globe Mine, the product of an 1873 strike. According to one story, prospectors considered the source of ore "as big as the globe." Another claims that prospectors came upon a globe-shaped boulder of pure silver. According to the latter theory, a man named Munson, unable to move the silver, scrawled "This is Munson's chunk" on the back of an envelope, placed it under a nearby rock, and hurried back to town for help. He was able to break the treasure into movable pieces and sell them for a total of twenty thousand dollars. Of course, this being the Wild West, the story ended with Munson spending his money on whiskey, getting hit in the head during a bar brawl, being tossed out, and dying of exposure.

Indeed, Globe was the kind of place where, when it was discovered that a new school was unlawfully located within four hundred feet of a house of ill repute, and a group of concerned citizens asked that the house be closed, an equally large group suggested moving the school. When precise measurements found that the four-hundred-foot limit extended four feet into the brothel's parlor, the sheriff simply told the madam to confine her business to the back rooms.

Globe, we discovered, was actually rather quaint, its rough edges smoothed over by time. Miami was sandy tailings and empty storefronts. Central Heights was a town slowly wasting away. Cluttered yards. A house gutted by fire. Trailers and boats fallen into disuse and serving as lawn ornaments. Stray dogs. White picket fences left gray and toothless.

Finally, we spotted a hill that seemed to fit the clues we'd been given. It was an industrial mound of sorts, all bins and boilers and shafts and smelters. Smoke wafted from two small smokestacks and one large one, the three rising like a thick black cigar and two cigarettes. At the entrance were a red-and-white-striped gate, a guardhouse, and a guard.

"Hi. Can I help you?" There was suspicion in her eyes. Or maybe dust.

"We're looking for a town called Inspiration."

"The town of Inspiration no longer exists." She pointed to the hill. "It used to be up there."

"Right there?"

"When Inspiration shut down, they shut down Inspiration, too."

I asked her to run that by me again.

"When the mine shut down. It's now owned by Cyprus, but they don't have housing up there anymore at all. You'll have to turn around."

For thirty centuries, beginning around 2500 B.C., the eastern Mediterranean island of Cyprus was the most abundant source of the "Cyprian metal," or *kypros*, which we now refer to as copper. The Cyprians bent the red metal into knives and axes, distinguishing themselves from their Stone Age enemies. It was an immeasurably valuable commodity. When the Cyprians could no longer find red boulders of pure copper, they took to burning brilliant green rocks of copper carbonate and finding lumps of pure copper in the ashes. For dozens of generations, the Ionians, the Phoenicians, the Greeks, and finally the Romans worked the Cyprus copper mines, until the industry came to a sudden and inexplicable end. The mines were forgotten until the early twentieth century, when a young engineer named D. A. Gunther explored the island's hidden treasures and spawned Cyprus Minerals Company, which began to acquire mines all over the world.

Meanwhile, back in Arizona, copper was king. Often referred to as an "ugly duckling" in comparison to the more glamorous gold and silver, it had become Arizona's most vital resource as the age of electricity introduced a need for copper wire. In fact, since 1888, Arizona has been the nation's leading copper producer.

The turn of the century brought the opening of the Inspiration Mine,

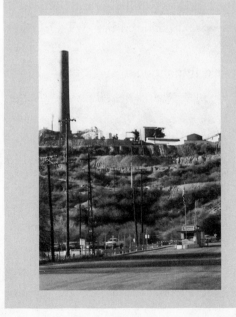

*C*yprus Miami Mining
Corporation
(formerly Inspiration)

located adjacent to the claims of the Miami Copper Company. In 1909, several claims were consolidated to form the Inspiration Copper Company. Here again, the derivation of the name has faded into legend. One version has the original claimants experiencing a dream or vision of the mine. Another says that they were "inspired" to borrow from a bank to jump-start their operation. A third version—the most appealing—points to a fortuneteller who shared office space with the prospectors. Her name was Madame Inspiration.

By 1910, just before Inspiration merged with another operation to become the Inspiration Consolidated Copper Company, the *Arizona Silver Belt* reported that "in naming this marvelous mining property, the original owners manifested a degree of foresight. In looking back over the past history of the mine, it seems that nothing less than an inspiration on the part of its owners could have brought it to its present stage of development and proven wealth in so short a time."

By 1931, Inspiration ranked second in the nation in underground copper, having produced nearly 660,000 tons. After production was suspended for forty-two months during the Depression, financial and geological considerations led engineers to switch to open-pit mining in 1948. Inspiration increased its mining capacity from 5,000 tons of ore a day to 60,000.

The mine on the hill thrived, and a company town complete with a post office, school, and general store thrived around it. But by the late 1970s, the winds of change led to the demise of Inspiration. The school closed its doors; the post office shut down; company housing was slowly phased out. The last residents moved off the hill in the early 1980s. In 1988, Cyprus Minerals Company purchased the operation and gave it a less inspired name: Cyprus Miami Mining Corporation. Inspiration had lost its town and now its name.

If there's one principal thing Generation X is perceived as lacking by those who call us nihilistic and unmotivated, it is inspiration. Yet here I was, a self-appointed representative of the so-called slacker demographic, actively searching for Inspiration, and the gate was down, the *No Trespass-ing* sign up, the former life gone.

But maybe the problem was this: You don't search for inspiration. It comes to you. It smacks of spontaneity, imagination, a flash of creation. From the Latin *inspirare*, it is literally the act of "breathing in"—inhala-tion—and thus involuntary. We can no more find inspiration than we can discover oxygen. We can look for it, but if it's there, it's there, and if it's not, it's not. And it wasn't.

Undeterred, Amy and I set out to examine the Inspiration that used to be. The Human Resources Department at Cyprus pointed us to a man just a few miles away in Central Heights who had spent thirty years mining Inspiration. We wondered if he found anything.

The Johnsons lived on Chaparral Hill, a collection of a dozen or so modest but comfortable homes overlooking Central Heights. Area resi-dents referred to it as "Snob Hill," a lesson in relativity. We pulled up to a red-brick ranch house with barrel cacti lining both sides of the drive-way, rang the doorbell, and heard the sound of anxious dogs pawing at the door. Then a deep, reverberating voice: "Kill! Kill!" The dogs, obvi-ously used to their master's sense of humor, ignored him. Dave Johnson showed us in.

"You need a drink?" He poured himself a full glass of scotch. I had the feeling it wasn't his first. "I had a tough day."

Dave Johnson had the big-boned look of a former athlete. He had a ravaged face, wore glasses over a bulbous nose, and swept his hair across his scalp like a throw rug. His wife, Ilene, her hair in a bun, sat on the floor cooing at their grandchild as the rest of us took up residence on the living-room couch. Three dogs and a cat pranced in and out as the Johnson saga unfolded.

"I'm the fella who recognizes the ore and tells 'em where to look," he explained.

"A prospector," I offered.

Dave Johnson

"That's it, I'm a prospector. But I'm a modern-day prospector with a college education."

"I've read that a prospector is an artist who knows where to dig."

"He's also a man with a hole in the ground who's a liar."

He poured himself a refill and embarked on a boy-meets-girl story. Dave Johnson, I learned, was a storyteller.

He was born in Hammond, Indiana, grew up in Gary working at a dairy, and graduated from the Michigan College of Mines as a geological engineer in 1956. Within weeks, he was hired by the Inspiration Consolidated Copper Company. Ilene was born nearby in Miami, attended Arizona State University, became a teacher, and moved back to the area in 1957.

"The fella where I got my gas told me there was a teacher coming to town who wanted to be introduced to some engineers at the mines, so that she'd have someone to date," Dave began. "He told me that she drove a blue Ford, so every time I drove by his place and the blue Ford was there, I kept going. August went by. September went by. Then I went down there one day in October. I was going quail hunting, and I just told him to put a little gas in. He reached in, took the keys to the car, and said, 'The girl we've been trying to introduce you to is here.' I looked around and said, 'But her car's not here!' He said, 'She walked.' And then I thought, 'God, I'm trapped.' "

Instead of going quail hunting, Dave took Ilene out to dinner. That was on a Friday night. He saw her again on Monday and Tuesday. On Wednesday, they attended a dinner party. On Thursday, they were engaged. A week or so later, they were married. A justice of the peace performed the ceremony in Phoenix. That night, they ate Sunday dinner at Ilene's parents' house. Ilene wandered into the kitchen to talk to her parents, who had been told nothing. She promptly came out and quietly informed Dave that they were no longer married. At least, not yet. They spent the rest of the night discussing their upcoming wedding at a Presbyterian church in Globe.

"So we've celebrated two wedding anniversaries ever since," said the prospector. "The first was October 26; the second was November 8. The parents never knew about the first one."

"So the first one was inspiration," I determined, "and the second one was obligation."

He almost spilled his drink laughing. "It pacified the parents."

They moved to Inspiration, a community divided into three neighborhoods—Upper Circle, Lower Circle, and Moonshine Hill—all of them connected by Main Street. Moonshine Hill was where the foremen lived. Lower Circle housed the supervisor's staff. Upper Circle was where the general manager's staff lived. It was subsidized housing for the mine's key employees. At Inspiration's peak, some 120 families lived on the hill.

"We moved up there in 1957 into a one-bedroom house," Dave explained. "Paid five dollars per major room. We had a kitchen, a living room, and a bedroom, so it cost fifteen dollars a month. Water and gas were furnished, and electric cost ten dollars a month. You had to live on the hill, and as houses became vacant or you got a promotion, there was a pecking order. So then in November 1960, we moved into a two-bedroom with a basement and paid twenty dollars. But I got a garage in the bigger house, so we paid twenty-one dollars."

The more the Johnsons revealed about Inspiration, the less inspiration the Johnsons revealed. You cannot create inspiration, but you can facilitate it. You can provide an environment amenable to flashes of insight and energy. Paper the walls with diversity, unpredictability, flexibility. Set the stage for chance encounters.

Inspiration didn't. From the sound of it, this was a village of uniformity and rigidity. Inexpensive and comfortable, yes, but systematized to an Orwellian extent, virtually militaristic. It should have been named Order. Or maybe Conformity.

"We not only lived in a company town, we had a company post office, a company gas station, and a nonprofit company store," Dave explained. "If our children ever wanted anything, they just walked to the store only fifteen or twenty houses away, picked out what they wanted, signed a little piece of paper, and it would come out of my paycheck."

This was a town where your neighbors were your coworkers, where all the houses had stucco exteriors and hardwood floors, and where there were strict rules and schedules and obligations. When your house needed repairs, someone from the company had to do it. If you were on the general manager's staff, you were expected to host two cocktail parties a year. If you paid your five-dollar dues to join the company's country club, you were expected to take a turn hosting the monthly bridge tournament, and you were expected to host it wearing hat and gloves. The Benjamin Franklin School was surrounded by housing for the teachers and had a motto inscribed at its entrance: *God is industry*.

"It was very regimented," Ilene admitted, "but at the same time, we felt very protected."

"We never locked the door," Dave added. "As a matter of fact, we never even had keys for the house on Main Street. There were locks, but no one knew where the keys were."

I was struck by the contrast between the anarchy of traditional mineral-strike frontier communities and the regulation and segregated elitism of the modern version. Corporate organization had sterilized mining, taking it from the dreamers and gamblers and putting it in the hands of scientists and managers. Give me the days of claim conflicts and whorehouses and saloon brawls. I sensed that Dave Johnson felt the same way.

"Back in my days, we used to go to the Miami Copper Club, and everybody brought their own bottle. You danced the night away, and nobody went home until all the bottles were empty. And if you went home early, then who were you? So the best mining engineers and the best geological engineers and the best foremen at the mine were always gauged by who could drink who under the table. We'd start off the evening, and you'd drink scotch and then bourbon and then gin and then vodka, then beer, then wine. And if you were still on your feet, you'd finish up any bottles that were left around. Those were the people that everybody remembered."

Dave looked at his empty glass and then helped himself to another scotch. His voice rose in volume. "There's still a prospecting mentality around here. There are still people who have a dream of finding the taproot of the Andes, made out of solid gold. Prospectors knock on the door and say, 'I think I found it—the mother lode of mother lodes.' And you have to remember that a prospector's a man with a hole in the ground, and you'll never change his opinion of his hole in the ground. But he'll damn sure change his opinion of you."

Inspiration, the mine and the town, had left nothing to chance. And yet its hallmark had been practicality without permanence. Such is the nature of a community built around depleting nature's resources while admitting that someday the well will run dry.

"I always felt there was sort of a mining-camp mentality here, the thinking that when the ore is gone, we will go," claimed Ilene. "So people don't really put down deep roots. In the early days, the miners spent more on gambling and drinking than they did on their homes and churches, and there's still some of that here. People don't spend much on their property—even the people at Inspiration were like that. They were practically given their housing. If they were fired or the mine gave out, it wouldn't take much for them to pack up and go."

The Johnsons packed up and moved from Inspiration in 1971, fifteen years before Dave retired as the company's senior exploration geologist. They built their own house, using their own plans and their own preferences. The old house—the twenty-one-dollar cookie-cutter perk— had provided no closet space for their four children, had allowed unwanted sunlight after late-night shifts, had been built with stucco walls facing west that grew hot to the touch. The new house boasted a walk-in closet for each child, a master bedroom without windows, a western wall of cool brick.

Later, I began to recognize in the story of the Johnsons some surprising similarities to my own background and my reasons for packing up and moving away. The company town's lack of inspiration was the product of a rather sheltered, trouble-free existence. In many ways, it mirrored my own childhood. I have often considered how I am among the luckiest one-tenth of one percent of the people in the world. The difficulties faced by my generation and my countrymen—the national debt, the murder rate, the dumbing-down of America, whatever—are distant problems, not intimate struggles. The facts are these. I was born in the most powerful and prosperous country in world history. I was raised in a stable, upper-middle-class household and never wanted for food, clothes, love, or support. I was educated by educated people. Unlike many members of my generation, I never had to suffer through the pain of divorce. I didn't attend a funeral until I was twenty-five. I never considered a stint in the army, forced or otherwise. I didn't even have any college loans to pay off, for God's sake. It was a wonderful way to grow up, and I remain grateful for my good fortune.

But it was a lousy way to be inspired. I remember seeing an interview with Paul McCartney in which he was asked why it was that John Lennon was considered the deep, arty, soulful Beatle, while he was perceived as a happy-go-lucky mop-top. He said that in order to draw on the same angst and anger Lennon had, he would need to trade childhoods with him, and he wouldn't want to do that.

Ditto for me. As a writer, I have an embarrassing lack of troubled times to draw on. Inspiration is a product of notable experience. Much like the Lawrences in Harmony reaffirmed the timing of my journey, the Johnsons in Inspiration reminded me of the principal reason for it: I have had too few experiences, too much sheltered sameness in my life. And I was hoping to remedy that situation.

Though the Johnsons moved away from Inspiration, they still had a view of the industrial skyline to the west, the smokestacks silhouetted by the setting sun. But the view was from a distance, from up high, where the breathing was easier.

TRUTH OR CONSEQUENCES,
NEW MEXICO

> *Whatever satisfies the soul is truth.*
>
> Walt Whitman

B y mid-February, we found ourselves heading south from Albuquerque along the oldest road in the United States. El Camino Real, the Spaniards called it when it was established in the late 1500s—"the King's Highway." Now, it was Interstate 25, a modern incarnation of the trail connecting Chihuahua, Mexico, with Santa Fe. As we drove the highway, baked into a vivid maroon by the sun and the dust, the landscape began to seem less mountainous but more rough-hewn than Arizona. A peach color crept into the ridges and mesas. Mauve and magenta and muted green, too. If Arizona is a brilliant desert painting, New Mexico is a palette, its colors adjacent but not necessarily intermingled. Indeed, its cultural heritage is the same—a meeting of Indian, Spanish, and English that is unique among the fifty states.

The Rio Grande, trailing Interstate 25 for three hundred miles, runs like a backbone down the length of New Mexico. It is a magnet drawing all the state's entities together—cliff dwellers and Ph.D.'s, artists and soldiers, ranchers and retirees. The Land of Enchantment is a place of side-by-side contrasts as incongruous as adobes and observatories. New Mexico's hallmarks are its extremes—ancient and futuristic, historic and cutting-edge.

The aged New Mexico can be found in the Spanish missions, the Indian drums, the crumbling ruins. It's in the nine-hundred-year-old mountain village of Acoma, the oldest continuously inhabited site in the United States. It's in Santa Fe, colonized by the Spaniards a decade before the Pilgrims reached Plymouth Rock. It's in the Old West icons.

Doc Holliday operated a dental office in Las Vegas, New Mexico. Wyatt Earp ran a gambling hall in Albuquerque. Jesse James worked on the New Mexico railroads while hiding out from the law. In the 1880s, gunfights were so common in the territory that newspapers stopped covering them and instead printed monthly summaries of all the killings. Horse thieves, bandits, and assorted outlaws proliferated, men with nicknames like the Human Exterminator, One-Eared Dodge, and Icicles. And the most notorious of all—Henry McCarty, a.k.a. William Antrim, a.k.a. William Bonney. "Billy the Kid." After leading a band of outlaws in various cattle wars and killing as many as twenty-seven people, he was finally shot to death in 1881. The Kid was all of twenty-one, so young and so old, just like the modern version of his adopted home.

In his essay "New Mexico," D. H. Lawrence wrote, "In the magnificent fierce morning of New Mexico one sprang awake, a new part of the soul woke up suddenly, and the old world gave way to the new." This land of ancient cultures is also a leading center of space and nuclear research. It is home to the Rio Grande Research Corridor, a 340-mile stretch of universities, national laboratories, and high-tech companies. Sandia Laboratories in Albuquerque, which conducts research on the uses of nuclear energy, is the largest private employer in the state—a state that ranks first in the nation in supercomputers per capita. New Mexico is the frontier, both historically and scientifically.

Halfway between Albuquerque and our destination, we stopped for gas in the city of Socorro, where the Old San Miguel Mission was constructed in 1626. Three and a half centuries later and fifty miles west, another construction site typified New Mexico's bewildering juxtapositions. It was a group of gigantic, dish-shaped antennas, each eighty-two feet in diameter and weighing 230 tons, arranged in a Y shape along the Plains of St. Augustin like enormous sci-fi ray guns aimed at unseen enemies. It was called what it is—the Very Large Array, part of the National Radio Astronomy Observatory. The geographic isolation prevented radio interference. The seven-thousand-foot altitude and clear, dry air put the stars at astronomers' fingertips. The twenty-seven antennas formed the equivalent of a single radio telescope twenty-one miles in diameter.

That was New Mexico, too. The black holes and spinning pulsars were for the lucky few, but this desert region was all about space—ample, endless, uncluttered space. Montana may be Big Sky Country, but it has nothing on New Mexico. The air is clean, the views clear, the landscape devoid of any visual deceit. You can behold freight trains in their entirety. You can discern where towns begin and end—in one glimpse. Rural establishments here have names like the Middle of Nowhere Café not because it's cute but because it's true. Our Rolling Stone, normally as conspicuous as a refrigerator on a skateboard, was little more than a pebble on an endless stretch of pavement.

When you can see forever, your thoughts either expand to fill the surroundings or shrink into themselves. As we rolled down the King's Highway, I came to recognize in the passing scenery a proper setting for our state of mind. New Mexico was simple and huge and undisguised. It was plateaus eroded into mesas and mesas eroded into buttes. No veneers or facades. Just vast, abraded landscape leaving the truth exposed.

Just south of Socorro was a godforsaken place called Jornada del

Muerto. It was here in mid-July 1945 that a group of soldiers and scientists waited in carefully placed bunkers to observe one of the most significant moments in human history. Unlike us, they had already found truth—a scientific discovery that would usher in the modern era. Over the previous two years, a city of six thousand inhabitants had been constructed from the ground up in Los Alamos, just northwest of Santa Fe. There, under the direction of Dr. J. Robert Oppenheimer, a theoretical physicist from the University of California, the nation's most fertile minds had been working feverishly to complete the most secret of top-secret missions. The goal of the Manhattan Project, the largest scientific project in history, was to use atomic energy for military purposes. Now, it was time to unveil the creation.

The site for the detonation of Fat Man—the nickname given to an implosion bomb constructed in the Los Alamos labs—was carefully chosen. The scientists considered locations ranging from the sand dunes of Colorado to sand barriers in the Gulf of Texas, but they settled on this thinly populated stretch of New Mexico desert. Jornada del Muerto means "journey of death." Oppenheimer christened the specific site—a piece of land eighteen miles wide and twenty-four miles long at one corner of the air force's Alamagordo Bombing Range—the Trinity Site.

Even as the bomb was being raised to the top of its 110-foot-high structure, the outcome was in doubt. Weather watchers worried about storms moving in, meaning that winds might spread the fallout to surrounding towns. Meanwhile, senior scientists obsessed over dire predictions, some fearing that the bomb would ignite the atmosphere. If it didn't destroy all human life, they warned, it certainly might destroy all life in New Mexico. As the bomb neared the top, a skate holding a cable slipped and rattled down the side of the tower. The bomb swayed precariously but didn't fall. At precisely 5:29:30 A.M. on July 16, 1945, an explosion rocked southern New Mexico, a blast so powerful that it was seen 160 miles away, shattered windows 120 miles away, and left a crater 8 feet deep and 1,200 feet across. One observer described it as a desert sun appearing in the middle of the night. "A few people laughed, a few people cried," said Oppenheimer. "Most people were silent."

Three weeks afterward, on the morning of August 6, the specially adapted B-29 bomber *Enola Gay* dropped a uranium-fueled bomb nicknamed Little Boy on the city of Hiroshima, Japan. It leveled the center of the city, destroyed more than sixty thousand buildings, kindled a fire that swept across the landscape, and killed between eighty thousand and two hundred thousand people. On August 9, Fat Man, a duplicate of the implosion bomb tested at Trinity, was dropped on the city of Nagasaki. Had it not been for low clouds and fog over Kokura, the first-choice target, Nagasaki would have survived. Instead, nearly a hundred thousand people there were killed or maimed. Five days later, the war was officially over, and President Harry Truman told the world, "We have spent $2 billion on the greatest scientific gamble in history—and won."

But it didn't feel like victory for the so-called father of the A-bomb. Only nine weeks after the bombings, when Oppenheimer received a Certificate of Appreciation from the army on behalf of the Los Alamos lab, he told the gathering, "If atomic bombs are to be added to the arsenals of a warring world, or to the arsenals of nations preparing for war, then the time will come when mankind will curse the name of Los Alamos and Hiroshima."

By 1946, he was desperately trying to introduce a system of international control for nuclear weapons. Oppenheimer would later fall prey to his own politics and his own remorse, losing his security clearance and finding himself accused of being a Soviet agent. He came to represent a dilemma that has grown more common as the world has become more technologically advanced: moral problems rising out of scientific discoveries. Advancement weighed against effect. Discovery versus danger. Truth and consequences.

While the Manhattan Project was under way, Oppenheimer focused on completing the mission, not examining its moral implications. In a statement he would later come to regret, he told reporters, "A scientist cannot hold back progress because of fears of what the world will do with his discoveries." It is an ongoing debate.

Indeed, as we rumbled past the Trinity Site in the desert Southwest, a couple of Scottish scientists were engrossed in another act of discovery with profound ethical repercussions. Soon, they would announce that they had succeeded in using DNA from a six-year-old sheep to create a genetically identical lamb. It was the first cloning of an adult mammal. The stuff of science fiction had become reality. Dolly the lamb was her mother's identical twin.

Soon after, word came that researchers in Oregon had cloned two rhesus monkeys, the first primates cloned. We were getting perilously close to human cloning, a step so unfathomable that it had been thought impossible only a few years earlier. The implications scared leaders into action. Declaring that "we have a responsibility to move with caution and care," President Clinton called for a moratorium on the use of federal funds for human-cloning research. But as with splitting the atom, Pandora's box had already been opened. Just like rogue nations' development of the bomb, cloning can be regulated, but it can't be prevented.

At the heart of the matter is the same debate that swirled around the Manhattan Project's scientists—whether it is appropriate to stifle intellectual progress in any form. Thomas Jefferson, for one, stated, "There is no truth existing which I fear, or would wish unknown to the whole world." But his French contemporary Voltaire believed, "There are truths which are not for all men, not for all time." Such is the dilemma.

Technological advancement is often a double-edged sword. When we explored the atom's nucleus, we discovered a new source of energy but also a new means of warfare. We have invented chemicals that solve problems and cause pollution. Computers have wired the world into a global village, but they've also meant terrible security risks. The invention of the automobile meant intercity travel would take hours instead of days, but it also meant the loss of a hundred thousand lives a year. For every truth discovered, there is a consequence uncovered.

Certainly, cloning might provide us tremendous benefits. We might clone animals for biomedical research, discover further secrets about DNA, perhaps even gain some insight into the origin of cancer and certain hereditary diseases. We might clone commercial farm animals for better meat and greater yields of milk. But there is also an ethical gray area. There are more questions than answers.

Is it a theological issue? What's the price if we start playing God, messing with Mother Nature, toying with millions of years of evolution? Has Adam's rib become Dolly's chops? Was Martin Luther King, Jr., right when he suggested our scientific power has outrun our spiritual power? "We have guided missiles," he said, "and misguided men."

Is it a philosophical issue? Is this our moment of decision—whether to take control of technology's bounty and guide its use or let it roll over us with the inevitable consequences? Walter Cronkite once said of George Orwell's *1984* that it "fails as a prophecy because it succeeded as a warning." Perhaps forethought is the only antidote to scientific truth run amuck.

Is it a political or social issue? If ethical misgivings cannot stop scientific discovery, should we worry more about practical applications? Armies of cloned egomaniacal millionaires. Human hybrids. Slave hatcheries. Movie studios concocting starlets out of petri dishes. Childless couples ordering designer offspring. If cloning is a step toward achieving genetic perfection, who is to decide what is perfect? Doesn't that change with each passing century?

We may be achieving what scientists once thought impossible, but as it turns out, that's the easy part.

My head spinning beneath the massive New Mexico sky, we pulled into an oasis with a name longer than its voting roll. The sign said, *Truth or Consequences—pop. 5,219, elevation 4,576.* Twenty feet away, another sign put the elevation at 4,260. Truth lay somewhere in between.

Sierra County, larger than Rhode Island and Delaware combined, covers 4,231 square miles. In its eastern section lie huge cattle ranches

and the White Sands Missile Range. In its west are the forested Black Range and the Continental Divide. Truth or Consequences lay smack-dab in the center, surrounded by southwestern space. It was a town almost completely lacking obstructions. Just a crisscross of treeless streets and squat buildings plopped down in the middle of the arid wilderness. And no pretensions either. City hall was on City Hall Road. The library was on Library Road. The two main thoroughfares were Main Street and Broadway. It was as simple as sagebrush.

Time crept here. The business district only gradually seemed to be shedding its Eisenhower-era decor. It was drab brown and lusterless save for a couple of enormous water tanks painted with murals depicting the area's history, its changing landscape, and its people—mineral springs, Native Americans, gold prospectors, charging buffalo, longhorn cattle. It was as if the murals and the years had drained the color from the community itself.

Confident that the chances of finding a scientist or philosopher in town were about equal to the odds of locating a sushi bar, I switched gears in my metaphysical journey and tracked down a trio who provided insight into the notion of truth as it applies to human endeavor.

Bob Tooley was first. Nothing happens in Truth or Consequences unless Bob Tooley says it does. He *is* the news, has been for nearly half a century. His family owns the *Herald*, the local newspaper that shouts from its front page, "There is NOTHING more powerful than the TRUTH." His brother composes the pages. His son runs the computers. His wife and daughter-in-law oversee the advertising and keep the books. Bob him-

*Truth or Consequences
water tank*

self has been in town and in the newspaper business since he started cleaning presses at age nine. He began running those presses at age twelve. He has agate in his blood.

So the stale air of the *Herald*'s newsroom fairly crackled with anticipation when Bob Tooley pulled up a chair, scratched his chin, and revealed the most significant news ever to grace the pages of the family Bible. "The biggest thing that ever happened here happened back in 1950," he announced, conviction in his voice and newsprint on his hands. "That's when Ralph Edwards came to town."

Upon hearing it, I thought of swinging saloon doors, bourbon straight up, whispers about the mysterious stranger who'd arrived out of the cold. Truth or Consequences, New Mexico. The name conjured up Old West, high-noon, quick-draw images. But that would be fiction, and truth is stranger than fiction. Ralph Edwards essentially named the town, but he was no gunfighter or lawman or frontier explorer. He was a game-show host.

"See," said Bob Tooley, "this all started as a publicity stunt. It wasn't going to go on forever." But it has, an April Fools' joke carried into perpetuity.

Edwards was no ordinary game-show host. He was the fastest game-show host in the West. Now well into his eighties, he has long since

Bob Tooley

evolved into an iconic producer. The brains behind *This Is Your Life* and *The People's Court*, he has never been off the air since 1940. It was in his Hollywood boardroom that the fate of this desert town was sewn.

In January 1950, Edwards was meeting with the staff of his wildly popular radio game show, *Truth or Consequences*, planning their tenth-anniversary celebration. The show was built on a simple premise. Contestants were asked to answer an unanswerable question—for example, What color is a hiccup? A wrong answer meant they had to face the consequences, usually a bizarre physical assignment. There was the time, for instance, when two contestants were each given half of a thousand-dollar bill. Starting from opposite ends of the country, they were instructed to find each other by yelling "Heathcliff!" in Chinese restaurants across America. It wasn't *Jeopardy*. It wasn't even *Wheel of Fortune*. But in the days before humor acquired a cynical edge, it was an unqualified hit. *Truth or Consequences* would last fourteen years on radio and another twenty-eight on television.

For the tenth anniversary of the show, Edwards wanted to do something special, something eye-catching. A member of his staff offered a suggestion. Perhaps, just maybe, some American town would be willing to change its name to match that of the show. That would really get people talking. The program would then broadcast its tenth-anniversary show from the newly renamed community. Edwards was sold immediately. He announced the offer during a broadcast and received bids from several towns, including a tiny sawmill outpost in Montana and a suburb of Denver. But the one that appealed to him most came from the town of Hot Springs, New Mexico, known at the time for its bubbly, medicinal mineral baths and the recreational opportunities at nearby Elephant Butte Lake.

There were dozens of towns named Hot Springs around the county. In that era before zip codes, mail to this New Mexico hamlet was sometimes delivered to Hot Springs, Arkansas, or Hot Springs, California. There was little to differentiate this resort town from other resort towns, little to separate this Hot Springs from all the others. So a local cattleman and state senator named Burton Roach grew enamored with the possibility of advertising the town free of charge. He broached the idea with the city council, which voted unanimously to discuss the proposition with a representative of the program. The wheels were turning. All the townspeople had to do was change the name—sell out, in a manner of speaking. But for a good price. Soon, the talk turned from a temporary change to a permanent one.

"WHOLE TOWN 'JUMPING UP AND DOWN' OVER PROPOSAL" announced the *Hot Springs Herald*, which was then run by Bob Tooley's parents.

The prospective name change sparked vigorous debate.

On one side were those who figured it was a resort town, so why not resort to this? They were intrigued by the possibilities, excited by the publicity, and perhaps a bit awed by celebrity. Hollywood would be coming to their corner of the desert. It was heady stuff. "Personally, I am for it. It is too good an advertising deal to pass up," wrote Paul O. Tooley, Bob's father, in his newspaper. "When people in other towns oppose changing the name of Hot Springs it can be for two reasons only: they are lacking information on what actually lies behind the move or fear that Hot Springs will grow to the point of menacing the business of other towns. I really believe this is true in Albuquerque."

On the other side were dissenters who felt that Hot Springs was a far more durable name. They believed the character of the town—a place with frontier origins, a noble past, and leading citizens with names like Catfish Williams and Skinny Davis and Doc Huckabee—was not in keeping with a Hollywood whim. They suspected Edwards was using the town strictly for his own publicity. Indeed, they felt the whole idea was rather silly.

They lost. On March 31, the town voted in a special city election, and the result was 1,294 in favor of changing the name, 295 against. "I honestly feel the voters of Truth or Consequences, NM have made a great move that will prove beneficial to suffering humanity over the nation," gushed Paul O. Tooley. "It's a silly name for a town, but then my own name is a bit on the odd side."

On April Fools' Day 1950, Ralph Edwards received a hero's welcome. Riding a white palomino, he led a parade along a two-mile route lined with ten thousand spectators, some from as far as Arizona and Texas. Eighty members of the Sierra County Sheriff's Posse mounted their horses and rode behind him. At Main Street, they put on a show, forcing Edwards to strip to his long johns at gunpoint, then dressing him in a sheriff's uniform and badge. You're one of us now, they seemed to suggest, though few believed it at the time.

That night came the live broadcast—"coast to coast," as they liked to say in those days—from the adopted home of the nation's favorite game show. Though the local radio station, KCHS, was not an NBC affiliate, the network gave it special permission to broadcast the program. No one seemed fazed by the fact that the station's call letters stood for Keep Coming to Hot Springs.

"Hello there!" Edwards shouted at precisely 6:30 P.M. Fifteen hundred spectators applauded in the packed Hot Springs High School auditorium. Some 19 million listeners tuned in. "Here we are," Edwards continued, "the whole lock, stock, and barrel of us in Truth or Consequences, New Mexico. What a name! What a city!"

Edwards inaugurated the festivities by breaking a fake bottle of champagne over Burton Roach's head. When he told another local resident to bring an elephant back from Elephant Butte Lake, the audience laughed. When the fellow came back with a live pachyderm that the producers had snuck into town, the audience howled. It was only a half-hour show, but those thirty minutes transformed a town.

For years after, a small but persistent faction continued to deplore the name change, not least because it was so long-winded. One of them was newspaperman Will Harrison. Most locals refer to the town as "T or C," which probably saves them a good ten minutes a year when all is said and done, but occasionally Harrison found it necessary to write out the full name in his stories. Each time, he inserted the expression "Ugh!" after it. In response, those who approved the name would retaliate in kind. "Hey, there goes Will Harrison Ugh!" It wasn't quite black hats and white hats at high noon.

The dissenters remained steadfast. Three more times over the next seventeen years, they filed protests. Three more times, the town returned to the polls. Three more times, Truth or Consequences won.

It's been three decades since the last vote. The name change is no longer a tender subject in town. But I, a visitor to the area, felt some of the unease the early dissenters must have experienced. What's in a name? Some history, to be sure. Some identity. Had the town lost a portion of both?

"You can't change history. The history of the town remains constant," Bob Tooley insisted. "As a matter of fact, one hundred years down the road, why, there'll be a lot of history about Truth or Consequences."

Playing devil's advocate, I threw out a hypothetical that was more a snide analogy than a legitimate query. "What if Alex Trebek came along and suggested you change the town's name to Jeopardy?"

"No, I don't think they'd go for that now. People's attitudes change. We were actually looking for something to boost the town in those days, and we were thinking that might help."

"But *Jeopardy* is hot now."

"It probably is, but I don't think that would appeal to them." Bob moved forward on his chair. "Now, if he came in and said, 'Hey, we'll dump a quarter of a billion dollars in this area if you change the name to Jeopardy,' we might think about that pretty hard."

All too true, I'm sure. But as it turned out, it wasn't a pile of money that proved to be the most significant residue of that fateful day in 1950. It was a remarkable relationship—between a town and a man. The early dissenters may have been right about Ralph Edwards's plan. Two generations removed from the show's heyday, the name has about as much cachet as a $64,000 grand prize. But they were wrong about Ralph Edwards.

Without fail, Edwards returns every May to emcee the Ralph Edwards Fiesta, a weekend of rodeos, beauty contests, golf tournaments, and a once-a-year episode of the old game show. Until 1975, when a local Fiesta Committee was formed, Edwards funded the entire event himself, paying for hotel rooms, food, parties, and appearances by his stable of B-list celebrities—Wayne Newton in 1964, Ann B. Davis (Alice from *The Brady Bunch*) in 1969, Judge Joseph Wapner in 1987, Jamie Farr in 1992. Most estimates put Edwards's annual bill for the affair at about twelve thousand dollars, but in return, the man whose house is a Beverly Hills mansion found a home in southern New Mexico.

Edwards has delivered a sermon at a local church. He is the subject of an entire room—the Ralph Edwards Wing—in the local museum. There is a Ralph Edwards Drive in town. There is a Ralph Edwards Park. Perhaps it's true that he used the town for his own publicity in 1950, back when his arrival was a thrill for the town. But a half-century later, in the twilight of his life, it may be that the town is a thrill for Ralph Edwards.

"Hello there, we've been waiting for you." That was Edwards's signature opening to *Truth or Consequences*. Now, the tables are turned. Now, the town says it to him.

I asked Bob Tooley about truth as it applies to journalism, and he handed me a copy of his newspaper, making no apologies for the fact that his family's production is decidedly old-fashioned in appearance and outlook. There are no splashes of color, no tabloid headlines, nothing of the fast-food frenzy that elsewhere grips American journalism. He makes no claims to being the conscience of the community or the watchdog of the world. He just prints the news.

"Our primary obligation is to make a profit," he explained. "Because if we don't, we don't stay in business. It's just like any other business. Second, our obligation is to give the public the information that they need as to how the town is being run, what's happening in the town, and what's coming up in the future. We're not a crusading newspaper. We don't think we're knights in shining armor riding big white horses. We're just here doing the job."

There is a Turkish proverb that says, "Whoever tells the truth is chased out of nine villages," which is similar to a Yugoslav proverb: "Tell the truth and run." The essence is that truth hurts, but that's the case only if it serves as an unwelcome agent of change, rather than as a reflection of the status quo. Who's to say which is better? In an era when mass access has diminished reliance on corroborating sources, when the barrier between news and entertainment has been smashed into a thousand pieces, and when no private matter is too intimate or insignificant for public consumption, are media outlets really seeking the truth? Or is it the scoop and the ratings they're after? Who's more truthful, the journalists who aim for fame and fortune under the guise of aiming for the real story, or the ones without pretentious claims?

"You know," he said, a smile creeping onto his face, "there's an old story that's been around forever about people who live in a small town. They already know what's going on. They just read the paper to find out who got caught."

He is still the truth teller of Truth or Consequences, but the truth need not be shrouded in secrecy or salaciousness. In a town where an investigative report amounts to asking the locals what's new, where survival depends on promoting the community, Bob Tooley is acutely aware of the role his newspaper serves. So, yes, it says "There is NOTHING more powerful than the TRUTH" on the *Herald's* masthead. But slightly higher on the page, in a slightly larger font, it says this: "ADOPTED CITY OF RALPH EDWARDS."

Museum curator Ann Wellborn sat among the artifacts of a town's history and pondered how that history was altered by a game show. "You know, the people who were all for the name change probably were looking for the goose that laid the golden egg. They figured Ralph Edwards would come in here, and he would bring lots of money and lots of advertising," she explained. "As a result, over the years, it backfired."

Ann has lived in Truth or Consequences for all of her fifty-seven years, save for a four-year stint seventy miles south at New Mexico State University. After a quarter-century as a schoolteacher, she retired and wanted nothing further to do. She climbed the hills outside town, hunted rocks, walked her dogs. It was while doing a little bit of each one day that she came across what looked like a fossil. It turned out to be a mastodon skull, and it led her to the museum that surrounded us.

"I didn't want it to be stuck somewhere in a basement, and no one would ever be able to see it," she said, punctuating her thoughts with occasional giggles that didn't seem to match her stern countenance. "So I

Ann Wellborn

got involved with the museum, just to keep it here. And things evolved. First thing I knew, I was on the board. Next thing I knew, they needed someone to run the place. I was going to do it temporarily." She shrugged. "I've been here five years so far."

You could say that Ann stumbled on a piece of history and it changed her direction. You also could say that the exact opposite happened when Hot Springs became Truth or Consequences—a town stumbled on a new direction and changed its history. Or at least its memory. Ann thought it was a change for the worse. "It didn't give the people the initiative to go ahead and do things for themselves. They kept waiting for that golden egg, for all the advertising and stuff to pay off," she said. "You know, it used to be called the 'City of Help,' and people came here by the thousands, literally, to take hot baths. Then it became Truth or Consequences, and they let that slide. They didn't promote the bathhouses like they should have. I think they just stepped back and kept waiting. It's just in the last ten or fifteen years that people have begun to realize if we're gonna make this town happen, we're gonna have to do it ourselves."

Long before there was any town in need of promotion, the bubbling mineral baths of Sierra County drew travelers. The first local homestead, established by a fellow named Fount Sullivan in 1905, included a bathhouse where guests could soothe themselves free of charge. Eleven years later, the village that sprouted around it was chartered as Palomas Hot Springs, *Palomas* being Spanish for "doves." Soon, the village dropped the Spanish altogether, ditching the symbol of peace for the prospect of tourism-driven prosperity in Hot Springs.

But the hot springs were a desert oasis long before they were marketed as such. The area was a stop along El Camino Real for Spanish conquistadors transporting copper ingots, a place where they could find shelter and protection when they were unable to ford the Rio Grande. Aware of the healing power of the hot mineral waters, they called the area Los Remedios. To the Native Americans, the mineral baths were sacred. They came from all over the continent to soothe their aching muscles, to heal battle wounds, to celebrate the magical powers of gurgling mud and wisps of steam that seemed to come from the center of the earth.

It was said that each spring had specific medicinal qualities. Bathing in one gave relief from swollen joints. Drinking from another alleviated digestive problems. If a woman used the white mud from a third as a face pack, legend declared she would become beautiful. Indian warriors laid down their weapons at the hot springs, setting aside animosities in a pilgrimage for spiritual and physical healing. One of these warriors, again according to legend, was Go Khla Yeh. The Spaniards called him Geronimo.

Born in 1829 and raised among the Bedonkohe band of Apaches, who believed four to be a magic number, Geronimo was the fourth child among four boys and four girls. He had four full-blooded Bedonkohe wives and four more of mixed heritage. Four of his children were killed by Mexicans, as were his first wife and mother. Four more of his children were captured by the United States government. Geronimo's life was magical and terrible. It was one of consequences, of revenge—against Mexicans, white settlers, United States soldiers. He was never an official Apache chief, but his people were willing to let him lead them in a fight for cultural survival, resisting the government's attempt to force them to reservations. Geronimo was fearless, it was said, because he once had a vision in which he saw himself growing old and escaping a battlefield death. That vision came true, but it had a price. Pursued for years by some fifty-five hundred American soldiers, he was finally captured in 1886 and exiled to Florida, then to Alabama, then to Fort Sill in Oklahoma. He tried his hand at farming, even joined a church, but the soil was no match for battle, and the church expelled him for gambling. In the end, he became a tourist attraction at fairs and exhibitions. He lived to be eighty, but he probably lived too long.

The building we sat in was the Geronimo Springs Museum, named after the hot mineral spring located under a roofed brick grotto next door. The museum was a hodgepodge of history. One room was devoted to Ralph Edwards, another to local artists, a third to local veterans of foreign wars. There was a replica log cabin complete with a wax miner sitting at a table with a corncob pipe in his mouth. You could view Native American pottery from 200 A.D. and *Truth or Consequences* episodes from the twentieth century. There were antique eyeglasses, sewing machines, snowshoes. In one room was a photograph of Geronimo, in the next a publicity shot of Richard Dawson. It was a medley of local interests combined under one roof like an anthropological garage sale.

The gift shop in the museum had bookshelves separated into Good Guys (Bat Masterson, Wyatt Earp, Tom Horn) and Bad Guys (Billy the Kid, Butch Cassidy, Josey Wales). But historical truth is rarely so black and white. As history becomes longer, memories become shorter. We latch onto stories, elevate them to myths, repeat them as facts. Eventually, we all have our own interpretation of what happened. Take Hot Springs, for instance. Ann remembered it as the "City of Help," but Bob Tooley pointed out that the mineral baths provided an excuse for gamblers to come to town and cavort with prostitutes and other unsavory types. "A lot of people will say that when they changed the name, they ruined the bathhouses," he said. "Well, what ruined the bathhouses was when the governor issued an order that gambling would no longer be tolerated. That was in 1950, too."

Maybe Hot Springs had been no more true to itself than Truth or Consequences. What bothered me was not any distaste over a community chasing publicity. That's what chambers of commerce are for. But I suspected that the most lasting towns were the ones that changed naturally. Sitting in a museum, surrounded by the natural history of the region, I got the impression that the change that took place in 1950 was too formulated, too contrived.

When you throw unnatural evolution into your historical mix, you come out with a muddled self-perception. Forty-six years after the fact, Truth or Consequences still revealed itself as a community searching for an identity. There were ghost towns on its outskirts, whispers of Billy the Kid, monuments to a Native American past. Was it a frontier outpost? The population swelled each winter with snowbirds who valued the climate and cost of living. Was it a retirement mecca? More than a million watersports enthusiasts visited Elephant Butte Lake each year. Was the town right in billing itself as the "Recreation Paradise of the Southwest"? Was it still a hot-springs haven? Or had Truth or Consequences sacrificed its history and origins for novelty—a novelty that was now a half-forgotten remnant of radio days?

Even adopting an icon like Geronimo solely because he passed through the area a handful of times smacked of grasping at historical legitimacy. Even history is at the mercy of interpretation. Facts are finessed by biases and lost paper trails. Museums don't hold absolute truths any more than journalists are absolute truth tellers. Geronimo was a warrior, perhaps the ultimate warrior. Yet Truth or Consequences celebrated an annual Geronimo Days Peace Gathering, which was a bit like starting a George S. Patton Pacifists Club.

"He was a renegade Indian who hated Mexicans and spent his whole life getting even. There are people who would argue with me on that. But when I did that room," said Ann Wellborn, pointing to a section devoted to the Apache warrior, "I did a lot of reading on Geronimo. I read his autobiography that he dictated to one of the army officers at Fort Sill, and that's all he talked about. That's all he could remember. He couldn't remember his wives' names after the first one or two, but he could remember that in this year, we went to the Sierra Madres and we killed this and we killed that. A lot of people would argue with you that he was a great leader, and he really wasn't."

That was one attempt at the truth via one interpretation of historical events. It was a matter of separating fact from fiction, Ann explained, all the while understanding that they became less distinguishable as the years passed.

"You just have to wade through it and get one hundred different stories, and in those one hundred stories, there will be some things that are repeated over and over and over, so you can pretty much take that as the truth. And the rest of it . . . It's just like we have the Apache Kid, who was killed in the mountains just a few miles from here. He was another renegade Native American. There are fifty dozen different stories as to how he was killed, and that's because the men who killed him wouldn't talk. They never told their story, so everybody else is having to guess at what really happened. So 90 percent of what you hear is not the truth. It's just guesswork."

A hundred years from now, the evolution of Truth or Consequences may seem perfectly natural, fiction remembered into fact. Maybe the dissenters' votes will disappear from the histories. Maybe their descendants will make that so. It happens all the time. John F. Kennedy was elected president in 1960 with 49.7 percent of the vote. After his death three years later, a nationwide poll revealed that 65 percent of Americans recalled casting their vote for him. We recall selectively, until that recall becomes fact. As George Santayana philosophized—and Ralph Edwards revealed—we sometimes have to change the truth in order to remember it.

Jay Rubin knew little of the evolution of T or C. The name change occurred nine years before he was born, and two thousand miles away. Jay grew up in the suburbs of Philadelphia, the son of a pharmacist. He attended the Wharton School of Business at the University of Pennsylvania, thinking he might follow in his dad's footsteps—until his dad died when Jay was nineteen and Jay began to look at things differently. He turned to law school and to North Carolina, enrolling at Wake Forest University. During his final year there, his Wake Forest club team won a water polo championship. Jay was the starting goalie. With a law degree in one hand and a trophy in the other, Jay Rubin then did exactly what you wouldn't expect a nice Jewish water polo player from the Philadelphia suburbs to do. He headed for the desert.

"I had clerked in Philadelphia for a couple of years when I was in law school, and I didn't really have any great desire to practice in a town that had twenty thousand lawyers in it. And I guess I'd had one too many northeastern winters, too. So I thought, 'If I'm gonna go somewhere else, why not just do something really interesting with my life and go somewhere I've never been before?' So I tried the Southwest. I kind of narrowed it down to New Mexico and Arizona, and I kind of thought the trend was that everyone was moving to Arizona, so I would do something different. I would go to New Mexico. There's only one law school in the state, so I figured there may not be so many lawyers here. So I graduated from law school and just basically got in my car and got the heck out here."

"Strange place for a kid from Philadelphia to end up," I told him, as I stared at a football on his shelf autographed by Randall Cunningham, another Philly refugee.

"Well, it wasn't like I was laying in bed one night and said, 'I'm gonna live in Truth or Consequences.' I mean, I narrowed it down to New Mexico and then went to Albuquerque, and I was going to practice there. I took the bar exam, and afterward I decided I was going to drive around a bit and see a little of New Mexico. I just love the water, so that's what attracted me to Elephant Butte Lake. So I thought I'd come

*J*ay Rubin

down here, and while I was here, I'd interview a couple of local attorneys. Well, that's what I did, and one fellow made me an offer to be his associate, and I took it. A year later, we became partners. Then I eventually bought him out. Now, I'm alone."

As he spoke these last words, he let out a big burst of laughter. His voice was deep and resonating, but the laugh was high and unfettered. At the moment, in his short-sleeved shirt, his tie loose around his neck and his hair unkempt, he seemed remarkably boyish. His surroundings were those of a small-town lawyer, but the face didn't fit. He was Jerry Lewis playing Atticus Finch. I couldn't picture him in a high-powered big-city firm.

"When I was clerking in a Philadelphia law office, I would walk into the office in the morning, and you could just feel the tension in the air, you know? There were a few lawyers there, and you could see they were all uptight. The secretaries were uptight. The clients who were walking in were all uptight. I just felt uncomfortable. I just didn't like it. It's a different way of life out here."

But an Ivy Leaguer in the land of Geronimo and Billy the Kid? "Still," I guessed, "at first, you had to feel like a fish out of water."

He laughed again. "I remember when I passed the bar exam. I took it in July, and then I came here to work. I even remember the dates. My first day on the job here was September 12, 1983, and we didn't expect to get the exam results until October. One of my friends who I studied with in Albuquerque called me on September 13 and told me the results were out and that I could call up to get them. I figured this is one of those existential moments when I find out in the next five minutes whether I passed it or not. It was the happiest day of my life when I found that I'd passed it, and I decided I was going to go out and celebrate. That's when the culture shock set in. There was nowhere to go to celebrate. I remember driving around town, and there was nowhere to go. There were just a couple of country-and-western bars open, and I hate country-and-western. It was like nothing I had experienced before. I think I went home at about nine in the evening and lit up a cigar. That was my cele-bration. That's when it struck me that I was really in a different place."

Amy told him that our driving a Winnebago around the country was in part an attempt to do something different, to take the road less trav-eled. She sensed the same thing in him, and that the three of us had found our way to T or C for the same reasons.

"Oh yeah," said Jay, nodding his head vigorously. "I just had no in-terest in putting myself in some stuffy firm in Philadelphia or New York or Washington. I mean, I just couldn't see doing something like that. I saw everyone else doing that, and I just thought it seemed awful. So getting out here was perfect."

"And what do your old friends from Philly think?" I wondered.

"They all ask, 'What are you doing in New Mexico?' Nobody un-derstands it," he said, smiling an epiphany-spawned smile. "To me, it just seemed like a natural thing. To me, it just made sense to do something like this. But I guess a lot of people don't look at it that way. They think you've grown up in Philadelphia, and this is your home. They can't un-derstand why someone would want to live somewhere else."

Amy and I would explore that notion further as our journey contin-ued. Stay or go. The ultimate dilemma. Jay had gone, and then he'd stayed, even if it wasn't the original plan. He figured it would be temporary, but by the time we arrived in Truth or Consequences, Jay was firmly en-sconced. Not only did he have a private practice as one of only a handful of attorneys in town, but he was also the city attorney, the man who gave legal advice to the city commission, handled zoning questions, prosecuted cases under the jurisdiction of the municipal court. He was a criminal defense lawyer one day, a city prosecutor the next. Different hats, though by no means black hats and white hats. More like shades of gray.

Because it was the law—and a certain restlessness—that had brought Jay to Truth or Consequences, I asked the question that had led me to him: "Is your role to seek out the truth?"

He paused for a moment, and his face transformed from boy to barrister. His expression suggested he relished the question. "Well, you know, yes and no. Of course, as a matter of ethics, you always have to be truthful. I mean, I'm not going to go to court and lie for someone, and I'm not going to expect someone to lie to me either. What you're doing here is you're trying to present the best argument on behalf of your client. The purpose of the adversarial position is to have two competing sides here, and between the positions being advanced, the truth will come out."

"That's the theory, at least," I said, unconvinced.

"Yeah. Yeah. Well, I take my role as a small-town lawyer seriously. I think I have a reputation here of being very honest. That's very important to me, and I think people know that."

"How do you balance the search for truth with the search for an advantage?"

"Well, it depends what you're talking about. For example, if I'm involved in a criminal case, representing a criminal defendant, it isn't my job to prove my client innocent. It's the prosecution's job to prove my client guilty. Even if I have knowledge that my client may have committed a particular crime, it's up to them to prove it. I don't necessarily have to say something that's dishonest. You can win a case by doing nothing."

I shifted in my seat and pressed the issue. "Some people," I said, clearly meaning me, "have a problem with that notion of law—that it's not truth, really. It's proof."

"Well, that's true, and you have to evaluate cases based upon what you think you can prove. And when we settle cases, it's based on what I think I can prove and what the other side can prove. I mean, look, everybody is entitled to a defense, including mass murderers. They're entitled to be defended vigorously. You have to remember that when you have a case that's tried in front of a jury or a judge, the issue isn't necessarily the question, Did the guy or didn't the guy do it? The question is, Did the prosecution prove its case beyond a reasonable doubt? And you have to recognize the distinction there."

"So let's be honest then," I said. "Law really isn't about truth."

He shook his head. "I don't agree with that. I think it is a search for truth. We have good judges in this area, and regardless of how I argue my position or the other attorney argues their position, the judges are going to try to get to the bottom of the matter. The other thing you have to recognize is it isn't just a search for the truth. You can have two lawyers who have an honest difference as to what the law is in a particular case. You know, a lot of times we go to court not necessarily because we don't agree on the facts. But I may think the law is one thing, and my adversary may think it's another, and we have to have the judge tell us."

Philosophers have written of the difference between truth and the spirit of truth. Perhaps jurisprudence is more concerned with the latter, a sort of consensual understanding that if rules have been met and rights have been protected, chances are good that the truth will prevail. Truth in law, like truth in science and news and history, is a matter of interpretation and balance and spin.

But Jay believed that truth was accessible in Truth or Consequences. "I have to deal with the same lawyers day after day after day. If I were to say something that weren't true, or they were to catch me doing something less than honest, they'd never trust me again. And vice versa. That really opens up a lot of advantages, because we even cut down on the amount of work that has to be done to get ready for the hearings. They give me their stuff. I give them my stuff. You get to the truth a lot quicker that way. In a big city, even in Albuquerque, you may go up against a lawyer that you'll never see again, and I guess the tendency up there is to think, 'Well, why do I have to worry about what this person thinks of me? I'll probably never work with him again anyway.' Here, you don't have that."

The faster the pace, the easier the deception, the more elusive the truth. Jay had migrated to the desert to do something different. Maybe that meant being a lawyer for all the right reasons. Maybe he found, like we did, that a small town in a big desert can illuminate, and that even if you don't find absolute truth, there's something in the search after all.

COMFORT,
TEXAS

> *The wanderer's danger is to find comfort.*
> William Least Heat Moon

O ne expects the states to have more than just a psychological border, but they don't. In most cases, states blend into each other seamlessly. A traveler can experience far greater change by moving from one end of Colorado to the other, for instance, than by moving from, say, Kansas to Nebraska. A state line is a state of mind.

Eastern New Mexico and west Texas were no exception. The only means of knowing that we had crossed from the former to the latter was the sign that said, *Welcome to Texas*. Otherwise, it was more of the same as we screamed along Interstate 10—a rust-colored highway surrounded by sprawling nothingness, the blue-and-white sky crashing hard against a green-and-gray prairie, an occasional oil rig dipping into the sun-baked soil, the mountain peaks too distant and diminished to be anything more than a faint backdrop. West Texas is a treadmill of a region.

The monotony of the landscape was broken by the diversity of the land cruisers. America has as many ways of moving as it has places to go. A community on wheels filed past us, going who knows where but always going: spit-polished motorcycles, Jeeps and pickup trucks, campers, mini motor homes, fellow fully equipped RVs, conventional trailers, a fifth-wheel trailer hitched to a hardworking Ford, countless tractor-trailers, and a mobile-home wide load. There was a pale green school bus, a lemon-yellow Volkswagen van, and a stark white Corvette convertible. A Greyhound bus headed west, filled with tourists, and a huge diesel bus with *Klink's Kaboose* stenciled on the back headed east, filled (we assumed) with Mr. and Mrs. Klink. There were garbage trucks, cement trucks, cattle trucks, trucks with double and triple trailers. There was an empty flatbed truck, a flatbed carrying enormous spools of cable, a flatbed carrying a bulldozer, even a flatbed truck carrying a flatbed carrying another flatbed.

The United States has the world's largest trucking industry, with more than 36 million vehicles in service. On our trip, we came to know the trucking companies like familiar faces in a high-school hallway: Covenant Transport, Consolidated Freightways, Jim Palmer Trucking, Marten, J. B. Hunt. The same was true of motor homes and trailers: Pace Arrow, Fleetwood Bounder, Itasca Suncruiser, Dutchman, Dolphin, King of the Road, some 9 million in all. Hunter S. Thompson revealed a sobering truth when he wrote, "Old elephants limp off to the hills to die; old Americans go out to the highway and drive themselves to death with huge cars."

Rivers used to be the great arteries of American transportation and expansion, spawning ports. Then it was the railroads, whose stations sprouted into communities. For the past half-century, it has been miles and miles of pavement. Places with nothing more to offer than an exit ramp and a truck stop now call themselves towns. Businesses line the interstates and are entirely dependent on them: Budget Inn, Comfort Inn,

Quality Inn, Holiday Inn, Best Western, Super 8, Shell, Exxon, Chevron, Texaco, Shoney's, Hardee's, Jack-in-the-Box, Dairy Queen. Uniqueness has been rendered secondary to catering to the sheer volume of traffic, so that a Burger King and a Wendy's can be found next to each other, and a McDonald's can appear every ten miles. Fast food, quick fuel, brief shelter. It is the American way.

The movement is not just a matter of travel and transport; it is reinvention and relocation. Each year, about 10 percent of the American work force changes occupations. Corporate relocation is a $15 billion industry in the United States. According to the 1990 census, only 8 percent of residents in metropolitan areas had lived in the same house for thirty years. Each year, more than 15 million American households relocate. Not surprisingly, this is primarily a phenomenon of the young. Annually, nearly one-third of Americans in their twenties relocate.

But is this movement anything new? Steinbeck, for one, suggested it might in fact be inevitable. He pointed out that our nomadic ancestors followed the weather and the food supply, agriculture and land ownership being relatively recent developments in human history. The American heritage is one of colonists, pioneers, frontiersmen, and immigrants. We came here aboard the *Mayflower*, via Ellis Island, along the Oregon Trail, across the Rio Grande, over the Bering Strait. The only people who didn't arrive as restless wanderers were brought here in chains. We are all in some sense hyphenated Americans; we are a nation of shallow roots. "Perhaps we have overrated roots as a psychic need," wrote Steinbeck. "Maybe the greater urge, the deeper and more ancient, is the need, the will, the hunger to be somewhere else."

What is it all these people are searching for, from the Indians following the buffalo herds to the wagon trains probing the frontier, from Irishmen in Boston to Cubans in Miami, from corporate consultants accepting a promotion and relocation to newlyweds moving from the city to the suburbs? What do they want?

I asked myself because I was part of the phenomenon.

Amy and I had entered the nomadic RV culture, but it was more than that. We were also on the move in a more profound sense. Over hours of discussion and reflection, we had decided that once our trip across America was over, we were going to relocate. We both grew up in the same town and returned to the area after college. Our parents lived just a few miles apart. Indeed, dozens of friends and family were entrenched in and around Chicago. But we were restless, and we needed a new perspective. Was that American? It meant shedding something that could only be described as roots. It meant more than a little guilt. It was something we would struggle with throughout our journey.

So I asked myself, "What am I searching for? What are we all searching for?" And I came up with an answer: comfort. It can be physical, financial, emotional, but for us, I think, this was a pursuit of spiritual comfort and the knowledge that we had sampled life's options before settling on a home.

This dominated my thoughts as we rolled through the arid flatlands of west-central Texas, past lonely Lone Star towns, and finally into the green woodlands of the Texas Hill Country, where we were met by a welcoming committee of cypress trees and a sign touting, *Historic Comfort—A Haven in the Hills.*

The following morning, February 19, the thermometer approached a hundred degrees as we explored the "Haven in the Hills." Nestled near the junction of Cypress Creek and the Guadalupe River, this community of fourteen hundred residents in rural Kendall County consisted of about three dozen square blocks. First Street through Eighth Street ran northwest and southeast and intersected Front Street, High Street, Main Street, Broadway, and Water Street. Standing guard over all of it was a faded blue water tower, *Comfort* written on it in big, black letters. A joke around town went like this: "Right now I live in Comfort, but tomorrow I could be in Welfare," Welfare being a town a few miles down the road.

The residential area of town had the haphazard appearance of many rural communities—solid nineteenth-century buildings with carefully cropped lawns alongside flimsy mobile homes. Each home had its own lawn ornament—a basketball goal here, a Ford Tempo without tires there, a trampoline, a clothesline, a doghouse. Comfort High School stood in the northeastern part of town, Altgelt Stadium toward the southwest. The latter was a football field dying of thirst, like the rest of the region that February, scattered blades of grass sticking up from one hundred yards of dirt.

Located throughout the town were dozens of buildings that predated the twentieth century, many of them in the business district on High Street between Seventh and Eighth, bookended by the Comfort Public Library and the Comfort Museum. The row of buildings included a couple of cafes, a soda shop, a general store, a bed-and-breakfast, and an art gallery or two. But mostly, there were shops selling antiques, collectibles, crafts, and old potpourri cleverly packaged. One could find wagon wheels, butcher blocks, oilcans, minnow buckets, clothes ringers, stained glass, an old Boy Scout handbook, a 1950 world atlas, a special bicentennial Hunt's Catsup "Spirit of '76" decanter, and a mug in the shape of Roy Rogers's head.

The town itself was an antique. It was the kind of place where people arrived at Sunday brunch still dressed for church, where half the store windows bore a message that the circus was coming to town, where roosters crowed in the distance, and where the soda shop had old 45s nailed to the walls. Here, friends played checkers in front of the barbershop, boys rode their bikes down Main Street whistling, men sat on rocking chairs on front porches whiling the day away, and passersby responded to a "How ya doin'?" with a "Fine, just fine. If I was any better, it'd be scary."

The heat made us hungry, so our first stop was for brunch at Arlene's Country Cafe on Seventh Street. A homey little eatery in a turn-of-the-century yellow Victorian, it was a local hangout, but the guest book at the entrance included visitors from Chagrin Falls, Ohio; Dodge City, Kansas; Sandy Hook, Connecticut; and even South Africa. We sat at a small table in the back. The meal was small-town delicious. Amy ordered vegetable lasagna, salad, and iced tea. I had a south-of-the-border quiche, soup, and a biscuit smothered in honey butter. For dessert, we shared a piece of sawdust pie, a concoction of pecans topped with coconut, fresh bananas, and whipped cream in a graham cracker crust.

Halfway through our soup and salad, the owner, Arlene Lightsey, stopped by to chat. A San Antonio native, she still wrote occasional food features for the *San Antonio Express-News* while running the cafe and a gift shop next door. She had lived in Comfort for the past twelve years, which, compared to the others we would come to know, made her a relative newcomer in town. She sat down at our table like we were old buddies.

"A lot of our friends thought we had absolutely lost our minds when we told them we were moving to Comfort," she explained. She had a soft southern drawl that came out quicker than I thought it was supposed to. "They said, 'My God, everybody's gonna know everything. They're gonna know how much you do or don't have in the bank, they're gonna know how frequently you drink a glass of water, you name it.' And you know, I have nothin' to hide, and I kind of like that."

She offered a story that captured the pros and cons of Comfort. When she and her husband moved to town, their paperboy was an old man pushing eighty—meaning his age *and* his average speed. The older he got, the faster he drove. Arlene's husband, Doug, was still employed by the San Antonio Fire Department at that time. He worked twenty-four- and forty-eight-hour shifts, so he was gone quite a bit. In Comfort, people knew when he was home and when he wasn't. One day when the old man came by just before dawn, Doug was standing on the front porch waiting for the paper. As he watched the paperboy roar up the street and crank his arm back, he ducked behind the bushes to avoid catching it in the face.

"Well, the old fellow saw somebody behind the bushes and assumed I was home alone and that somebody was about to get me." Arlene chuckled. "Here I was, still sleeping in the front bedroom, and I'm not kidding, in maybe five minutes, there was all these pickups, the sheriff, floodlights in front of the house."

She shook her head, smiling, and rose to greet some familiar faces. "In San Antonio, someone could have murdered me. I could have been dead for a month before they ever discovered my body." She offered us a parting wink. "So people knowing what's goin' on doesn't bother me at all."

The key to Comfort was not in the antiques and the old buildings that were the remnants of history, but in the history itself. It began with the German revolution of 1848 and the subsequent suffering of a people faced with deteriorating economic conditions and a loss of political and religious freedom. Searching for their own brand of comfort—the comfort of being left alone—thousands of Germans pulled up their roots and set out for America. They sailed into New Orleans and Galveston and soon migrated inland to central Texas, pioneering numerous settlements in the region north of San Antonio.

In 1854, a twenty-two-year-old German immigrant named Ernst Altgelt, an employee of a New Orleans cotton merchant, led a survey party of seven people to the banks of Cypress Creek and laid out a town in three hundred lots. The settlers wanted to call their community Gemutlichkeit, a German word with tones of tranquility and fellowship. Perhaps out of consideration for mapmakers or future generations of residents, they decided to shorten and Anglicize the name to Camp Comfort. It was one of the few concessions the Germans made.

Unlike most German settlements in the region, Comfort wasn't settled by an organized group but by individuals. Better educated than most immigrants, the majority of these people were fiercely independent intellectuals known as "freethinkers." They were leery of organized religion and intrusive government, both having been forced on them in the old country. "Live and let live" and "We'll take care of our own" were their mottos. It would be nearly forty years before the town had its first church, more than fifty years before it organized its first bank.

By 1856, there were more than 130 families or individual men in the Comfort area. Freethinkers stocked their cabins with books, paintings, and musical instruments and often spoke Latin to one another, so that neighbors began to refer to the area as the "Latin Colonies." Though the immigrants pledged their allegiance to the nation that had accepted them, Comfort was still a slice of the old country amid the American frontier. Some years later, when children established play areas under the trees outside Comfort's school, they called one section "Comfort," another "San Antonio," and another "Deutschland." Such was the delineation of their universe.

One of the earliest settlers of Comfort was Peter Joseph Ingenhuett. He built a store in 1867, moved it to a more permanent location down the street thirteen years later, and became one of the town's leading citizens. Peter's son, Paul, operated the store starting in 1891 and diversified the merchandise to include groceries, dry goods, leather goods, hardware, farm machinery, saddles, and clothing. In 1921, Paul's son, Peter C. Ingenhuett, took over. He ran the business for thirty-four years before leaving it to his daughter, Gladys Ingenhuett Krauter, and her husband, Jimmy, in 1955. Gladys, an adventurer, was the first native Hill Country female to earn her pilot's license. She died in 1995.

We went searching for Gladys's son, the great-great-grandson of Peter Joseph Ingenhuett. All we had to do was stroll to the west end of High Street and stop at the 116-year-old building that bore the sign, *Peter Ingenhuett, Fancy Groceries, Hardware and Implements*. Gregory Krauter was a gaunt man forty-five years old, with a thin sheath of sandy brown hair, a slight beard, and tinted glasses. He had the kind of unprepossessing face you could place in nineteenth-century Germany. Surrounding him in a store that hadn't been remodeled in nearly half a century was a selection of merchandise so varied it would make Sam Walton blush. There were horse saddles and earthenware crocks, chicken feeders and horseshoe nails, cowbells and meat grinders, pickles and pecans. Adding it all up was a cash register too rudimentary to figure tax.

What Krauter sold as practical goods, others touted as antiques. There is a difference between living history and nostalgia. It struck me that Gregory Krauter's life breathed the themes of continuity and the maintenance of roots.

"I guess, being that we are the oldest continuously operated general store in Texas, and possibly the southern U.S., that makes it more important to try and keep it going. My family ancestors, they believed very much in a person living on through their children, so it's important to me," he explained, a space between his teeth flashing when he talked.

"I still consider myself a freethinker. You know, an emphasis on reason, rationale, logic, and also I guess my feelings against big government and too much control. It's pretty rare, I guess. Most of the remaining few that I'd consider still subscribing to that way of thought around here are pretty old people, and they're quickly dying out. There aren't too many more my age who would probably admit it."

The difference, I think, is that today they call themselves libertarians. Regardless, Comfort still retained much of its independent character. The town had never been incorporated, and just as the earliest settlers shied away from any form of local government, there remained not a single elected official in Comfort. One resident described the situation as "benevolent anarchy."

The Krauters

"There's a small group recently that started talking about incorporation, but I don't think it's going to fly, because I think there's still enough people who have that independent sense around here and that distrust of government," said Gregory.

He went on to explain the reason for the incorporation issue. "In the past ten or fifteen years, we've had a tremendous influx of Hispanics, a large number of them illegal aliens, and it's really impacted the area in a negative way, unfortunately. Up until even the 1940s, there were prominent families all over the Hill Country that sent their kids to live with cousins here in Comfort just to go to school here. That's how good a school we had. And even when I was in school, it was well above average, but not anymore. A large part of it is because education is suffering all over the United States. But here in Comfort, a large part of it is due to the tremendous percentage of illiterate Hispanics that have come to the area."

It was ironic, of course, this "Hispanic problem," in light of the state's history. After Mexico gained its independence from Spain in 1821 and Texas became a Mexican state, new settlers from the United States were welcomed. The large influx of Americans led to skirmishes with Mexican troops and then to outright revolt in 1835. In early March 1836, about the time Texas declared its independence from Mexico, Colonel William Barret Travis turned to his 183 companions, who were surrounded by 4,000 Mexican troops at the Alamo, just forty-seven miles from what later became Comfort. He drew a line in the sand and asked all who would fight to the death to cross over to him. "Do as you think best," he said, "but no man can die with me without affording me comfort in the hour of death." That's what he was hoping for in his hour of death—comfort.

All but one man—Lewis Rose, who would escape around midnight and survive—crossed the line and sealed their fate. Santa Anna's troops attacked the following morning and slaughtered the inhabitants of the rebuilt mission. But Texas won the war and raised the Lone Star flag over its own republic. Nine years later, it accepted annexation as the twenty-eighth state in the union. The flag of the republic of Texas was officially lowered on February 19, 1846. Our visit to Comfort marked the exact sesquicentennial anniversary of that event.

The state of Texas rose because Mexicans allowed Americans to settle there. The community of Comfort emerged because Americans allowed German settlement. A century and a half later, these descendants of rootless people were rooted and protective of their own, and they weren't about to return the favor.

One block west and one block south of Gregory Krauter's store, on the corner of Main and Seventh, a man in a camel-colored cap and silver horn-rimmed glasses sat atop a block of limestone. His thin, drawn face was a collection of deep lines. These, combined with his gentle voice and reserved demeanor, made him appear older than his sixty-one years.

He was Gregory's distant cousin. His great-grandfather was Gregory's great-great-grandfather August Faltin II, a Comfort patriarch who learned the mercantile business from his father in Danzig, Prussia, which is today Gdansk, Poland. When he emigrated to Comfort as a twenty-six-year-old in 1856, he purchased a general store and called it Faltin & Company.

August Faltin IV

Like Peter Joseph Ingenhuett, Faltin became a leading businessman in the Hill Country, the money he brought with him financing everything from land development to lumbermills. The Faltin General Store was

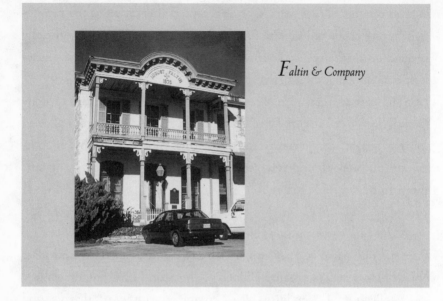

Faltin & Company

built in 1879, the first two-story stone building in the area. Faltin's son Richard succeeded his father as store owner in 1889, and Richard's younger brother, August III, soon joined him. They ran the store for nearly two decades before selling it to their brother-in-law, Dan Holekamp, and his sons in 1907. Holekamp & Sons survived until 1962. After that, the only people with the run of the property were occasional teenage vandals.

Meanwhile, Richard Faltin's son, Albert, worked as a bank teller in Comfort for fifty years, becoming such an institution that the town named Faltin Street and Faltin Baseball Field after him. In 1968, Albert repurchased the original store property for his family. Upon his death four years later, when the Faltin estate was distributed, Albert's son said he would revive the business. He was the man sitting before us, a descendant of a "Haven in the Hills" original, the closest thing to Comfort royalty. His name was August Faltin IV.

After walking over from Gregory Krauter's store, we had approached August inside Faltin & Company, housed in the same Victorian-Italian edifice built by his ancestor 117 years earlier. The proprietor had been very reluctant to speak to us at first. "I don't think I have much to say," he claimed, more apology than disdain in his voice. With a little urging, he grabbed an antique wall mirror and some polish and told us to follow him outside to a couple of limestone blocks in front of the building. He planned to get some polishing in while we talked. As it turned out, he never touched the mirror.

I began by asking about an ancient-looking log cabin being restored right next to the store. A chamber-of-commerce brochure touted it as "Comfort's oldest building still in its original location," and it showed every bit of its 132 years.

"That," said August, "is our family's first American home."

"What do you hope to do with it?"

The suggestion of a smile raised the corners of his mouth. "Live in it."

I began to suspect that he was testing me, waiting to see if I was a conversationalist worth his time, an intellect up to his standards. I had the feeling he said little but had lots to say. He carried himself like a scholarly man. Indeed, he had taught biology for fourteen years before scratching his ancestral mercantile itch. Only this time, the store would sell not general merchandise but antiques, which was entirely appropriate. History was August's passion.

As we spoke of Comfort's German settlers and the obstacles they faced, both physical and psychological, his reticence faded into reverence. "It was difficult for them to pull up their roots and leave their family and come over here to this unknown area," he pointed out.

"This was the frontier," I agreed, "even for Americans. This area must have been some sort of oasis of enlightenment in the middle of nowhere."

He nodded. "They brought their books, their music, and they weren't farmers. It's remarkable that they even survived." And then his eyes flickered. "Of course, when the Civil War came, that just dissolved. I mean, that whole concept was lost."

"You mean the monument?"

He nodded again. We had seen the monument, a slab of stone amid cypress trees, when we first strolled into town. It was on High Street between Third and Fourth, across the street from Comfort High School. In front of the school was a marquee that read, *Doubts today can hinder tomorrow.* In light of what we would learn about the Treue der Union monument, I wondered if the school officials appreciated the irony.

From the beginning, the immigrants who settled the Hill Country felt they owed their loyalty to the nation that had provided them with a new way of life. When Texas seceded in 1861, the Germans were only a few years removed from their pledge to the Union. Most believed not only that an oath of allegiance to the new Confederacy was disloyal, but also dishonorable.

"They came over here, and their allegiance was to the Union—to the country that granted them citizenship," August explained. "That's where the roots were. They didn't have slaves, and they weren't into this Deep South stuff. So they were just at odds from the very beginning. They really didn't want anything to do with it, but they weren't permitted to stay neutral."

Local citizens formed the Union Loyal League, ostensibly to protect the area from Indians and prevent discord between Union and Confederate partisans. But Confederate officials viewed it, not unwisely, as a militant organization, and martial law was declared in the Hill Country. August Faltin II saved himself by acting quickly. He found it necessary to return to the country he had fled in order to show support for the country that had taken him in. He had to leave the United States to show allegiance to it.

"My great-grandfather didn't want any part of the Confederacy, so he finally left," said August, who now seemed more willing, even eager, to talk. "He went into Mexico and then to Germany and came back after the war. He was nearly hanged out here by some of his competitors, who came down on horseback, in disguise, with the handkerchiefs and all that business. They tried to eliminate him. He knew they'd be back, so he said, 'I'm getting out of here while I'm still alive.' I don't know who ran the business. His wife stayed back, but I've gone and researched the deed records, and you can see where he saw trouble coming. He deeded all of his property to his wife."

On May 30, 1862, Confederate captain James Duff, who had previously been court-martialed and dishonorably discharged from the United States Army, was sent from San Antonio to the Hill Country to order all males over age sixteen to take the oath of allegiance to the Confederacy or be treated as traitors. He began to burn crops and homes and arrest prominent citizens. As many as 150 men, young and old, may have been lynched during what amounted to a reign of terror.

August leaned forward. The sound of violins drifted through the open door of his store, providing an eerie score to the story. "There was a lot of dirty stuff going on here, just bad, bad stuff. They were pressured to either take the oath or leave and face the consequences. And that's basically what happened."

In an act of desperation, nearly a hundred Union loyalists from the Hill Country, all of them men under the age of thirty-five, decided that they would leave for Mexico; some planned to eventually find their way up north and enlist in the Union army. At the last minute, about a third of the men turned back. On August 1, 1862, the remainder set out for the border, expecting to cross the Rio Grande in about ten days. They weren't aware that an informant had revealed their plans to Confederate officials, and that a large detachment of Texas Rangers was after them.

The attack came early in the morning on August 10, as the group approached the Nueces River, about fifty miles from the Mexican border. In what became known as the Battle of the Nueces—or, more accurately, the Nueces River Massacre—the Texas Rangers killed nineteen men and wounded nine more, whom they later executed. Two months later, eight more Hill Country refugees were gunned down as they tried to cross into Mexico. In all, thirty-six men lost their lives in a run for freedom.

The massacre decimated the population of young males in Comfort and several surrounding communities. It wasn't until August 1865, after the war had ended, that friends and family dared to retrieve the victims' remains and return them to Comfort. A year later, on August 10, 1866, a simple, white obelisk was erected over a mass grave in the part of Comfort that came to be known as Monument Hill. They called it the Treue der Union—"True to the Union"—monument. In 1991, at the 125th anniversary of the dedication, Congress designated the memorial as only the sixth mass-burial site in the nation permitted to fly the American flag at half-staff in perpetuity. It is believed to be the only monument to the Union on Confederate soil.

"When you look at it now, it took a lot of courage and guts to do what they did," August declared. "They could have gone the easy route and said, 'Yeah, we'll sign your stupid allegiance to the Confederacy.' But they didn't. They had principles. They knew it wasn't the easy course, but they went ahead and did it. It took a lot of courage—a lot of courage— to do what they did. It was just pure blood murder, savagery at its highest, and this community never forgot that."

Treue der Union monument

Yet the monument was crumbling. Its spire was missing, its pedestal eroded, the chain barrier around it worn and rusting. It was in the process of being restored by the Comfort Heritage Foundation, and an official rededication was planned for later in the year. But at the moment, the Treue der Union monument was little more than a memory.

"Did it just fall apart?" I asked.

"Well, it deteriorated," August explained. "It was limestone, and it just deteriorates with time."

"When people walk in here and ask, 'Are you a native?' I say, 'Yes, fourth generation.' They look at you and just can't believe, just cannot fathom, that you can have four generations on any property," August marveled. "It's not that unusual in the Hill Country, but in a lot of other places, people are moving every three years to someplace else."

"But even your family started from someplace else," I replied defensively, realizing he could have been describing me.

"But they stuck it out. They said, 'We're going there, and we're going to make the most of it.' Today, it's so easy to move. I mean, look at your transportation. I know an airline pilot who lives two doors down. He's gone three days, he comes back, and where he's been in three days is just mind-boggling. I mean, it's incredible! It's so easy to move today. You can get in your car, and in one day, you can drive one thousand miles."

"Is that bad?"

August shook his head. "Look at your problems today. I mean, that's what it starts with. They have no roots. They have nothing to tie into. This mobility is good, but it's bad, too. If you know where you're coming from, it just stabilizes everything."

But that's just it, I felt. I happened to be going someplace else, but that didn't preclude an understanding of where I came from. Was it the monuments we should value, or the memories?

A couple of hours earlier, Gregory Krauter had reflected that people like August and himself were becoming oddities, because staying was no longer a viable option. "When I was young, up until the late sixties, you could still make a living of ranching and farming if you worked hard at it and had enough land," he claimed. "But it's almost an impossibility now, between the low prices you get for your produce, be it livestock or feed or whatever, and the high taxes, the cost of maintenance and materials and things. In other words, kids are less apt to be able to stay here and make a good living."

As August bemoaned the dissolution of America, I began to consider the reasons for it, and I decided Gregory's evaluation of Comfort could be extended into a broader analogy. One reason many Generation Xers struggle with the notion of staying somewhere is that the American Dream, as we interpret it, seems to be leveling off. Generations before us treasured the potential to build upon the success of their ancestors, considering it a privilege. For us, it seems more of a right or an expectation. As products of American success stories, perhaps we expect too much comfort—and we do so at a bend in history when we can no longer plan to out-achieve our parents. We're at the top of the American Dream curve and heading down.

Call it the Maria Taft Syndrome. When Maria was a schoolgirl, her teacher asked her to write a brief family history. "My great-grandfather was President of the United States," she wrote. "My grandfather was Senator from Ohio. My father is Ambassador to Ireland. . . . I'm a Brownie." It's an extreme example, of course, but many young Americans in the 1990s are faced with a choice: lower their expectations or look elsewhere to construct them.

Struggling with my own guilt about my plans to start a new life distant from my old one, I began to use bits and pieces of my Comfort experience as fodder for rationalization. For instance, I discovered that neither of the men we had talked to was married or had children. Lesson: Reverence for the past is important, but so is regard for the future. I also realized that many Hill Country settlers had left Germany, but Germany had never left them. Lesson: We take the best of our memories with us. Finally, many of those German settlers had escaped their new country for their old during the Civil War, only to return to their families afterward. Lessons: No decision is final, distance doesn't diminish relationships, and you *can* always go home again.

It was possible, in fact, that my ancestors were part of that same nineteenth-century migration that had brought the Faltins and the Ingenhuetts to the frontier. My paternal great-grandmother was born in El Paso, her parents having emigrated from Hungary. And there is a Herzog Street in Kerrville, Texas, right in the heart of the Hill Country.

I thought back to August Faltin II and found myself identifying with that immigrant freethinker who had first set foot in his new world in his late twenties. He had planted seeds deep in American earth in the hope that new roots would take hold. He and others had done so with a kind of determination my generation will likely never know. Lo and behold, in a place called Comfort, those new roots had grown into old ones.

PRIDE,
ALABAMA

> *The tyrant is a child of pride.*
>
> Sophocles

I t was early April by the time we reached Memphis and embarked on our four-week tour of the South. We hopped on U.S. 72 heading southeast, and the first half-hour along the highway provided us with a quick lesson in community demographics. The road began as Poplar Avenue, rolling east from Riverside Drive through the heart of Memphis, past corporate suites and street-corner saxophonists. On the outskirts of the city, the highway snaked through affluent Germantown, with its upscale malls and downy landscapes. Minutes later, we were in a land of white-steepled Baptist churches, rolling hills, and mud the color of a robin's breast. And kudzu, lots of kudzu, an eerie and omnipresent vine creeping alongside the highway like some sort of scientific experiment gone haywire. We had gone from skyscrapers to soccer moms to septic tanks in less time than it takes to cross the Verrazano Bridge.

The Mississippi state line came upon us quickly. U.S. 72 took us through the extreme northeast corner of the state, a ninety-mile journey over wooded hills and through towns with names like Slayden, Walnut, Corinth, and Glen. Five miles past the town of Iuka was the Alabama state line. Six miles more and we reached our destination. It has been said that most towns in America are named after either the first white person to arrive or the last Indian to leave. We set up camp ten miles east of Pride in the town of Cherokee.

There is a rich Native American tradition in Alabama. The first armed conflict between Europeans and Indians took place here when the Spaniards under Hernando De Soto killed thousands of Chief Tuscaloosa's warriors at the Battle of Mauvilla in 1540. The name *Alabama* came from Indian words meaning "to clear vegetation." Before the nineteenth century, this land was home to nearly two dozen Indian tribes, including the Koasati, Tuskegee, Natchez, Okmulgee, Apalachicola, Mobile, Chatot, Yamasee, Napochi, Sawokli, Tohome, Taensa, Pawokti, Shawnee, Chickasaw, Choctaw, Creek, and Cherokee peoples.

But today, Native Americans make up less than half of one percent of the state's population. There are no Cherokees in Cherokee, Alabama. The story of their struggle is a lesson in pride.

At its peak, the Cherokee Nation encompassed 124,000 square miles of land, including parts of what would become eight southeastern states. The Cherokees considered themselves the "principal people," the "People of Fire." Their land was the center of the earth. Starting in 1721, however, they began to cede land to white settlers. After the American Revolution, these so-called voluntary cessions evolved into forced ones, and by 1783, the Cherokee Nation was down to 70,000 square miles. Two years later, the Cherokees signed a treaty with the United States government protecting the tribe's territory against further intrusions.

George Washington's Indian policy was one of acculturation. Civilize the savages through education, agriculture, industry, religion, the arts. Little thought seems to have been given the difficulty of the task, the prospect of transforming a wandering, hunting, spirit-worshiping, communal people into a sedentary, agricultural, landowning, monotheistic culture. And there seems to have been little worry, too, that the strategy might backfire, that an attempt to assimilate might result in entrenched resistance.

But the Cherokees were realistic. They understood the odds. And so, more than any other native people, they attempted to adopt Anglo-American culture. They intermarried with whites to a significant extent, and the mixed-blood offspring rose to dominate tribal government. The women took to spinning and weaving. The men planted crops and raised livestock; some even built large plantations and owned dozens of slaves, black, white, and red. A man named Sequoyah created a Cherokee syllabary, which evolved into the first Native American written language. The tribe welcomed white missionaries and eventually translated the New Testament into Cherokee. It established schools and introduced written laws. It even organized a republic—modeled after the United States government—that included a supreme court, a constitution, and a capital, called New Echota.

Yet at the same time, Cherokee lands became increasingly attractive to white settlers, particularly after the invention of the cotton gin. In 1803, after the Louisiana Purchase doubled the size of the country, there emerged an alternative to assimilation: removal. Compared to the genocide advocated by some frontiersman, relocation was perceived by many as a compassionate compromise. Letting the Cherokees be was not a consideration.

Voluntary migration became the government's goal. In 1817, a treaty was signed that included a provision for removal. Nearly 3 million acres of Cherokee lands were to be exchanged for territory in northwestern Arkansas. As many as fifteen hundred Cherokees voluntarily moved. But Americans continued to push west, and the Cherokees' holdings continued to dwindle. By 1819, they could claim only 17,000 square miles of the original 124,000. In less than a century, they had lost more than 85 percent of their land.

The conflict entered a new era in 1828 with the election of Andrew Jackson as president. Jackson had become a national figure in the War of 1812, aided in large part by the Cherokees, who had fought alongside him against the Creeks in the Battle of Horseshoe Bend, the victory that made him famous. But Jackson was a devout expansionist. He would go on to push the Indian Removal Act through Congress, and by the end of his two terms, he would negotiate seventy removal treaties affecting nearly forty-six thousand Native Americans.

Soon after the 1828 election, he sent this message regarding the "Indian problem" to a Georgia congressman: "Build a fire under them. When it gets hot enough, they'll move."

It got hottest in Georgia. In 1802, the federal government had promised the state that, in return for relinquishing its claim to the western lands that later became Alabama and Mississippi, it would erase all Indian titles to Georgia land. Georgians grew impatient waiting for the federal government to keep its promise. The state legislature passed laws abolishing Cherokee government and prepared to distribute Cherokee land by lottery to Georgia citizens. When gold was discovered on the land, treasure seekers arrived without regard for ancient land claims, and the situation intensified.

Meanwhile, the Cherokee council vowed not to cede another acre of land. Elias Boudinot, a formally educated Cherokee and the editor of the *Cherokee Phoenix*, the first newspaper printed by and for Native Americans, gave an impassioned plea to the Georgia legislature: "We have seen everywhere the poor aborigines melt away before the white population. . . . We have seen, I say, one family after another, one tribe after another, nation after nation pass away; until only a few solitary creatures are left to tell the sad story of extinction. . . . They hang upon your mercy as a garment. Will you push them from you, or will you save them? Let humanity answer."

On April 7, 1835, an answer appeared in the form of a letter sent to newspapers. It was addressed "to the Cherokee Tribe of Indians East of the Mississippi River." "How under these circumstances, can you live in the country you now occupy?" it asked. "Your condition must become worse and worse, and you will ultimately disappear, as so many tribes have done before you. . . . You cannot remain where you are now. Circumstances that cannot be controlled, and which are beyond the reach of human laws, render it impossible that you can flourish in the midst of a civilized community. You have but one remedy within your reach and that is to remove to the West."

It was signed, "Your friend, Andrew Jackson."

By 1835, a minority faction of the Indians, including Boudinot, believed that removal was inevitable and that they may as well negotiate the best possible deal and save the Cherokee Nation. Though the vast majority of Cherokees vehemently disavowed that stance, the group signed what became known as the Treaty of New Echota. The Cherokee Nation, with the exception of a separate faction in the Smoky Mountains, would move west. In spite of a petition from over fifteen thousand Cherokees protesting the treaty, the United States Senate ratified it by a margin of one vote. On May 23, 1836, Jackson signed it into law. The Cherokees had two years to emigrate peacefully; after that, they would be moved by force.

By 1838, only four thousand of the twenty thousand Cherokees had capitulated. The rest still didn't believe they would be forced to leave. Call it naivete or reluctance. Call it pride. Regardless, it proved costly. In May, seven thousand United States soldiers began rounding up Cherokees at bayonet point. They rushed them from their homes and herded them into stockades, from which they were to depart in shifts along a water route. The Cherokees would follow the Tennessee River to its confluence with the Mississippi, float down that river to the Arkansas, and then travel upstream to their destination in the West. To the superstitious among them, rivers were the ways to the underworld; west was the direction taken by the spirits of the dead. When low water forced them to take an alternate route overland under the scorching summer sun, hundreds died.

The Cherokees soon petitioned to conduct the removal themselves. They would go by land, they decided, through central Tennessee, western Kentucky, southern Illinois, Missouri, and Arkansas. They would wait until September to begin and would separate into thirteen staggered detachments of nearly a thousand people each.

The average journey took 153 days, lasting through the bitter cold of winter. The average detachment lost nearly a fifth of its members along the way. Old campsites became new cemeteries. Due to thin blankets, spoiled rations, scarce wagons, paltry shelter, and inadequate medicine, as many as four thousand Cherokees died. They died from the heat of day and the cold of night, from accidents and starvation. They died from influenza, pleurisy, smallpox, dysentery, malaria, cholera, gonorrhea, tuberculosis, pneumonia, and whooping cough. They died at the hands of rifle-toting soldiers flush with power and vengeance. One Georgia volunteer who became a Confederate colonel later admitted, "I fought through the Civil War and have seen men shot to pieces and slaughtered by thousands, but the Cherokee removal was the cruelest work I ever knew."

The Cherokees named the journey *Nunna daul Isunyi*—literally, "the Trail Where We Cried." But the tragedy didn't end with the journey. The new Indian territory was rife with conflict between the settlers who had moved before the treaty and the deportees, who were themselves divided between treaty supporters and detractors. The treaty signers escaped most of the hardships of the dispossession until a day in June 1839, when they were all assassinated.

For more than a decade, civil war threatened to destroy the Cherokees. They then became further divided by the American Civil War, during which most sided with the South. After the Union victory, the government forced the Indians to surrender more land and to allow railroads to be built through their territory. Once again, settlers came by the score, and promises were broken. Sacred ground gave way to land runs; the Cherokee Nation was trampled by Manifest Destiny; the Indian territory became Oklahoma. Said Will Rogers, "We spoiled the best territory in the world to make a state." By 1930, almost all the land originally allotted to the Cherokees was gone.

Today, the tribe is enjoying a revitalization of sorts. In 1970, the Cherokees regained sovereignty over the choice of their leadership. In 1976, they adopted a new constitution. In 1987, Wilma Mankiller was elected principal chief, the first Cherokee woman to serve as such. Today, the Cherokee Nation is the largest American Indian tribe, boasting more than three hundred thousand members, about a fourth of whom are active in tribal life. The flame still burns in the People of Fire. It was dimmed for a while but not extinguished by the Trail of Tears.

Pride, Alabama, less than a dozen miles from Cherokee, is located in the foothills of the Appalachians hard against the Tennessee River, right along the Trail of Tears. The region was settled by white men after Andrew Jackson passed through it en route to the Battle of New Orleans in 1814. Some of his men were so taken by the area's beauty that they returned after being released from service. One of them, Major William Russell, built a trading post that went by the name of Russellville and became the seat of Franklin County, which was established in 1818.

Eventually, there arose a distinction between the prosperous Tennessee Valley region in the north of Franklin County and the hill country in the south. During the Civil War, the northern part of the county was generally loyal to the Confederacy, and the southern part was not. In 1867, the northern portion became a separate county and was named in honor of Chickasaw Indian chiefs Levi and George Colbert, who had been removed west three decades earlier. Colbert County's seat, Tuscumbia, later became famous as Helen Keller's birthplace.

Pride, in the dead center of the county, is a blink-and-it's-gone hamlet, an unincorporated and undistinguished community of a couple of churches and cemeteries, a few clusters of houses, a mobile-home park, and perhaps two hundred residents when every hill and dale is accounted for. One of those residents is the indomitable William "Chicken" Owen Foster, an immensely proud man, for better or for worse.

We were led to him by his nephew, George, who runs Foster's Service Center, the only commercial establishment in Pride. "He's my uncle, my daddy's brother," said George. "He can probably tell you anything and everything about Pride. He has nothing but time on his hands." George began to chuckle when he said this. He stopped long enough to call his uncle, who lived a few hundred yards away, and set up an appointment for us to meet him at the garage at eight o'clock the following morning. He then began to chuckle again and looked at us with something resembling compassion in his eyes. "One more thing," he said as we were walking out the door. "Don't be intimidated by him." As we closed the door, I was sure I heard him giggling.

We were a bit late the next morning. We arrived to find a truly awesome spectacle. He was six-foot-eight, some 340 pounds, and six weeks

William "Chicken" Owen Foster

shy of his seventy-sixth birthday. He chewed on a mangled, hand-rolled cigar like it was a Tootsie Roll. His pale face was a blotch of jowls and liver spots and ears the size of portobello mushrooms, all capped off by a stubble-topped point of a head. Put some baggy overalls on the Chrysler Building and you have Chicken Owen.

He rose to his full height, looked down at me, and boomed, "According to this ol' one-dollar watch, it's eight-twenty-two. Where ya been, boy?"

I didn't know whether to laugh or run. He made the decision for me, enveloping me in a huge bear hug and nearly breaking a few ribs in the process. The other men in the garage chortled, as if to say, "Oh, that Chicken Owen. He just scared the crap out of another one." They were right. We sat down, and he took charge.

"What's your name, boy?"

"I'm Brad."

"Tell me all of it, baby."

"Brad Herzog."

He turned to my wife. "And yo' Mrs. Brad."

"Or Amy."

"All right, I'll jus' call her Missus Herzog. Or Missus Brad. I got one I've had fifty-four years over at the house."

"You've been married fifty-four years?" I asked.

"She says I have. She keeps up with ever'thin'."

I decided to begin by asking him for a little background about himself. As I did so, the man next to him—another nephew, I think—rolled his eyes. It was the kind of expression Don Meredith must have used when Frank Gifford would turn to Howard Cosell and ask, "Howard, what do you think?"

Chicken Owen began his autobiographical account with these words: "Well, I sucked mah mammy over 'bout three miles from here."

"You what?"

"I sucked mah mammy three miles from here," he repeated. "I was raised on a farm. I sawmilled. I drove lots of mules. I broke some o' the meanest horses ever breathed. And I like a tough man."

That will be his epitaph, I imagine. I asked if he was born in Pride.

"I said I sucked mah mammy right over there three miles!"

"But is that in Pride?"

He grew suddenly impatient. "You ride with me. Get in, and I'll show ya. And then I'm gonna tell ya all of it. C'mon. Get up, youngun."

I looked at Amy. She looked at me. What the hell . . .

They say a dog begins to resemble its owner. The same may be true of a pickup truck. Chicken Owen's had been white once, but it was now covered with Alabama dust. A faded sticker—*Old Glory, New Pride*—adorned the bumper. The windshield was cracked; the seats were torn, stuffing and springs popping out at random; the floorboards and door hinges were rusting away; frayed wires bloomed from the console where a radio should have been. Six chewed cigars, a fly swatter, and a rusted chain sat atop the dashboard. We climbed into the front seat, Chicken Owen driving, Amy huddled by the passenger window, me in the middle. I turned to our driver. "How old is this truck?"

"I dunno. I'll run it till it falls down, then I'll get out of it and get another. It gets me around jus' as much as I wanna go."

A mangy dog with one brown eye and one blue eye stood in the bed of the pickup scratching at the rear window. "What's the name of your dog?" Amy asked.

"Dog," was his reply. "He'll set right up there in yo' lap if ya want, but Dog rides behind when I tell 'im to. Dog does what Daddy tells 'im to do."

So Chicken Owen and Dog and Amy and Brad were set to embark on a tour of Pride. Before the motor even coughed to a start, our guide began to recite his version of the town's history. Our research the previous day had revealed that Pride wasn't a state of mind at all. It was a last name.

"At one time, this property here was all Thompson Pride's. They owned sev'al thousan' acres. They had three girls and a boy, Thompson did. He was the son o' the man who owned these Pride slaves here. And he lived up there." He pointed across the highway.

Thompson Pride was the regional patriarch when Chicken Owen was a child, but he wasn't the original Pride in Pride. That honor belonged to his great-grandfather, Edward Mitchell Pride, who is believed to have been a descendant of an original settler in America's original settlement, at Jamestown, Virginia. Born in North Carolina in 1755, Edward Mitchell Pride was a Methodist minister who served as a chaplain and major in the Revolutionary War. In 1817, the "Fighting Parson" and his wife moved their three daughters and six sons to Tuscumbia, where Edward owned and operated a tavern. A couple of years later, he acquired some land a dozen miles west and built a log cabin overlooking the Tennessee River. That place came to be known as Pride's Landing. When the Memphis and Charleston Railroad arrived, so did Pride's Station. In time, the name was shortened to Pride.

Major Pride's oldest son, Jack, lived to see the first twenty-three United States presidents, finally keeling over in 1891 just sixty-nine days short of his hundredth birthday. He had one daughter and five sons. The two youngest sons died fighting for the Confederacy. The daughter, Jacqueline, married Colonel Sam Thompson, who became a landowner in Pride. Another son, Joe, was the father of Laurence Thompson Pride, which brings us back to the front seat of the pickup.

"And then ol' man Thompson Pride married a Mhoon woman," Chicken Owen explained. That was Mary Mhoon, Thompson Pride's first cousin. "They was landowners down there. Now, she had a . . . Girl, help me watch! I don't want to kill you."

We were turning onto the highway. "Okay," said Amy, "all clear."

"Clear?"

"Yep."

"Talk up to me, woman. Don't play wit' me. I'm ol' and hardheaded."

He pulled out of the parking lot and headed west on U.S. 72. Traffic zoomed past us at seventy miles per hour; we maintained a steady speed of twenty. Whether it was the truck's choice or the driver's, I'm not sure. Between the cigar in his mouth and the syrup in his drawl and the cough of the motor and the cars whizzing by, it was even more difficult for us to understand Chicken Owen than for Chicken Owen to hear us.

He pointed to a house just south of the highway. "I live right yonder. That ol' woman that lives with me lives right there. I stay aroun' close." We crossed Cane Creek, which led north to the Tennessee River. Railroad tracks paralleled the highway between us and the river. "Now, that railroad track, it would run befo' the slaves were free. Ol' man Tom Pride's daddy had slaves that knocked them rocks out up through yonder. The slaves, they built this railroad here prob'ly two hundred years ago. I'm not hardly ol' enough to know that fo' a fact. But I did know some of the ol' kin o' the slaves, chillun of some of them ol' slave folks. They dead now. There's one of 'em ninety-nine years old, she's buried right up there. And her brother's buried up there. He's ninety-five. The

*P*ride *Estate*

other brother lived right yonder. And they all come out of a Pride slave line, ya know."

"Those are the children of the slaves?"

"Yeah. The mammy of 'em and the daddy of 'em were slaves. I knew Willis. I knew Bette. I knew Abe. I knew Tom Christmas. And all of them was born out of slave folk. Ol' Abe died right here, at a lil' ol' place over there, when he got heart trouble. There's his ol' house there. Ol' Abe was a hundred and twenty-two, accordin' to the recollections. His name was Abe Pride. And that was fifty or sixty years ago, so ol' Abe himself was a slave. A young slave."

We turned off the highway and headed south along a lonely stretch of road. "Now, this is what we call the Red Rock community. Mah grandpa come in here 'bout a hundred years ago and brought mah daddy in here. That ol' house right there is one hundred and twenty years old. That's where one of mah sisters lives. Right there."

"I saw in the phone book that a lot of people in this area are named Pride."

"No whites. Don't know any white folks left by the name of Pride. Ol' man Tom Pride's boy—the only one he had left—he died a long time ago. Some o' the blacks are still named Pride. They were the descendants of the ol' slaves. . . . This is Red Rock Road, boy. Most 80 percent o' these folks are cousins over here."

"Cousins of yours?"

"Yeah, cousins of me. They can't help it." He rumbled a laugh. "Some of 'em won't claim it, some of 'em will. But I ain't met one of 'em that could hold me yet. Heh-heh."

The tour continued. "How many people live in Pride?" I asked.

"Damn few. A lot more work there than live there. . . . Now, this is where I sucked mah mammy right up here on that hill. The ol' house burned up 'bout a year ago. It'd only been there 'bout seventy years. See the chimney? Now, if ya look over there, you'll see Red Rock."

George Foster had told us about Red Rock. "There's a myth that there were so many Indian battles there that you can see the blood?" Amy asked. "Is that it?"

"Yeah. This is Indian country. Right in here, this piece o' ground was the last they took from the Indians. They claim they'd been in here ten thousand years, them Indians. They dug up ol' things on land I own. I just got tired of them diggin' up ol' bones, so I told 'em don't ever dig no more."

One man's sacred ground is another man's property. I noticed we were turning on to a dirt road. "So where are we going now?"

"I ain't gonna kill ya, boy. You gettin' scared? Heh-heh."

"Just curious," I lied.

"Well, am I telling you enough or am I not? This was Colonel Joe Thompson's ol' land here. See, he and Tom Pride was cousins. They owned everything everywhere we went except one lil' street so far. They used to gamble right over yonder, had a gamblin' house where they went and played cards on the weekend."

"Tell me a little bit more about yourself. You've been married for fifty-four years, you said?"

"That's what that woman says. Worst woman I ever married, boy. Never had any before I met her, but she's bound to be the worst. Heh-heh. How many you had?"

"Just this one," I said, trying not to look at Amy for fear of laughing.

"Well, that's the worst one you ever had, too. . . . I slept on them rocks over yonder, boy, in mah day."

"Why'd you do that?"

" 'Cause I wanted to. I'm a man. I been a man a long time. I was a man when I was fourteen years ol'. I laced up with the roughest and the best. Never saw a mean man. I been all over the country, but I never saw a mean man."

"Have you visited a lot of places?"

"I go when I want to and come back when I want to. I don't know whether I been a lot of places. Ain't many states I haven't been in the United States."

"Any special reason why you travel?"

" 'Cause I want to."

"What was your profession, mainly?"

"Farmin' and sawmillin', trainin' mules, enjoyin' life. If I made money, I spent money. If I didn't make it, I didn't spend it."

"Were you ever in the military?" Amy shouted from her end of the seat.

"No, I was too big. They couldn't draft me, baby, 'cause I was 'bout that much too high. You don't mind if I call ya baby, do ya?"

Amy doesn't let anyone but me call her baby. That much I know. She looked at Chicken Owen and forced a smile. "Go right ahead."

"I had enough education out of Auburn that they offered me West Point, baby, but I didn't take it. I just married that woman, and I thought I was a sport, see? That's where ya make a mistake. The woman gets ya down. She was pregnant and right ready to have chillun, and I didn't wanna leave her. And so I didn't volunteer."

"You went to Auburn?" I admit I didn't expect it.

"Yeah, you know I did, boy."

"Did you play football?"

"At one time, I did. I'm too old now."

"Did you graduate?"

"No. I come back here about three months before I graduated and didn't go back. I married that gal. I thought she was the only thing on earth. Heh-heh-heh. You know how it is. Heh-heh."

"How many children do you have?"

"That woman over at the house got fo'."

I took the bait. "And how many do *you* have?"

"Heh-heh. A man can't swear to the younguns. All he can do is take the woman's word. She says they's mine. But I told you the truth. I said that woman in the house got fo'. I know because I seen them all born.

Them folks say they resemble me, but I can't swear to it, because I didn't have 'em. Heh-heh. I got one, though, he got a mark on his hand. You see this lil' ol' blue mark there? Same place! I believe he's mine. And the others act more like me than I do myself. . . . Now, right over there was where they had a doctor's office, right over there on the Whiteside place. But it was the Pride place then."

"Where's the nearest doctor now?"

"Oh, Tri-Cities got more doctors than they got Jews."

Okay, he might have said "than they got to use." I'm not sure. Forgive my Woody Allen persecution complex, but tolerance wasn't one of Chicken Owen's strong suits. By Tri-Cities, he meant nearby Florence, Tuscumbia, and Muscle Shoals. Beyond that, I'm not sure what he meant.

"See, mah mammy come from the other side of Mus' Shoals. Mah grandpa first give the thirty-five acres to Mus' Shoals fo' the airport to be started. They's supposed to name it after him, and they didn't do nothing."

I steered the conversation in a different direction. "Did you ever stop and think about the word *pride?*"

"Huh?"

"Did you ever stop and think about the word *pride* and what it means?"

"No. No more than I just use it. They owned these slaves. . . . I just thought, 'Pride is Pride, and that's all it is.' "

"But . . ."

"Let me show you what them slaves dug up here."

We had made our way back to the highway. This time, we crossed it toward the river. I phrased my next question carefully. "Do people get along around here, black and white?"

"Yeah. I called a black man a black buck a few days ago. But I'm inclined to if one of 'em gets smart. Only thing I hate about the blacks, they try to go with these lil' ol' white girls, boy. And that's against Daddy's rules, now. Mah rule is, I don't touch a black woman, and I don't want no black man touchin' no white woman. That's mah rule! They tryin' to put the white folks down. Normally, they are stronger than lots of weak folks, but not me."

I suppose I wasn't surprised. This was Alabama, after all. The birthplace of Booker T. Washington, Rosa Parks, Joe Louis, Jesse Owens, Willie Mays, Henry Aaron, and Nat King Cole was also the stomping ground of George Wallace and Bull Connor and the setting for the bus boycott in Montgomery, the Freedom March from Selma, the church bombing in Birmingham. This was the Birthplace of the Confederacy. The Land of Cotton. The Heart of Dixie.

For many, intolerance is not an aversion to people but rather an aversion to change. Status means less to the Chicken Owens of the world than does the status quo. But consider Alabama's history. First explored by the Spaniards, it was settled by the French, who ceded it to the British, who relinquished it to the United States. It was part of Florida, then Georgia, then the Mississippi Territory before entering the nation in 1819 as the twenty-second state. It was worshiped by Native Americans, cultivated by African Americans, and dominated by European Americans. Change, in many respects, is Alabama's historical constant, yet obduracy may be its hallmark.

"We used to ship our timber out here on the railroads," Chicken Owen continued. "In nineteen-and-thirty-five, we drove a truck to Memphis with a kerosene lantern hung up fo' a taillight, boy. Heh-heh. I drove the truck. I was fifteen."

"So you've been all over the country?"

"I've been enough places."

"Is there anyplace you like as much as this?"

"I dunno. I had a woman here, and I liked the way she smelled, I reckon. Heh-heh. Don't you? Tell it like it is, boy. Heh-heh. I told 'em that over in Tuscumbia when they put one of them things in mah heart. They operated on me—seven bypasses. Then they put another little deal in over here on this side, 'bout that big around."

"A pacemaker?"

"Yeah. They were over there examinin' it, and I told 'em in the hospital, 'Get me back down there where that woman is. I like the smell o' her.' But just 'cause I like the smell o' her ain't sayin' somebody else would. Heh-heh-heh."

"How many heart operations have you had?"

"Well, they cut me one time and put in seven bypasses, and then put in that thing, and they've cut my guts out twice, all of 'em. And I been knocked in the head, right up here, boy. Put yo' hand here! Put yo' hand up there!"

"No, I'll take your word for it."

"No, by God, I want you to feel what they done to my head."

It felt like an overripe pumpkin. "How'd that happen?"

"I just wanted to be a man. He caught me setting down half-asleep, knocked me in the head there. I got up and broke both his legs. He's on crutches now. So he didn't win after all."

There was a pause in the conversation. Then Chicken Owen returned to an earlier topic that must have been rattling around in his head. "Do ya think it's right fo' a black man to raise a family by a white woman? Say yes or no to me, boy. Don't play with me!"

Now, remember, this man was four inches short of seven feet and weighed about a sixth of a ton. We were in his pickup driving through an isolated thicket of trees in the middle of nowhere. And we later discovered there was a pistol stuffed below the seat. His inquiry created an inner battle between self-respect and self-preservation.

"Well, now, do ya think it's right, boy?"

"Yes, actually, I do." Self-respect had won.

"You do? Well, I don't believe it is. That's where me and you differ. I ain't gonna fool with no black woman, and I don't want no black man foolin' with white women. Now, I'm not against 'em. I was raised with 'em, boy. And I'll do as much for a black man as I will a white man. I raised a lot of black chillun. They were on my land. I like 'em, do anything for 'em. I just don't believe in them breedin' a white woman. A white woman is a weakness. Ain't many white men who would breed a black woman in this country. But these white women are weak. I think it's wrong. I think it's takin' advantage of the race. Because the birds don't do it. I don't see the crow breedin' the buzzard. I don't see a hawk breedin' a crow. I don't see a jaybird breedin' a dove. I don't see nothin' like that. Everything goes with their own species. And I believe that's the way it oughta be. Those are mah rules, boy."

We passed what appeared to be a dead black Labrador sprawled on the side of the road. Dog, still standing in the back, looked back at it for a moment and then turned his attention forward again without a change of expression. Chicken Owen steered the pickup down a narrow road into a cemetery.

"Now, this is a lil' ol' graveyard where they bury most of us. Eighty percent of these folks I knew. Ya see that over there? They had a Civil War battle right over yonder. The North and the South. Now, I don't believe in slavery, ya know what I mean? Only thing I don't believe in is breedin' a black to a white. We need to keep a pure white race and a pure black race, so we know where we at. If you goin' to get a mixed race, you goin' to get a race that has really no chance. Now, a pure Indian is a pure Indian. I like them."

"But don't you think the races are mixed already?"

"Yeah, lots are mixed. Seventy percent o' folks around here . . ." He lost his train of thought amid the tombstones. "That's ol' Pieface right out there. See . . . Copeland. He played football with me. I called him Pieface. He's dead right there."

"Were you a star player in high school?"

"I ain't never been a star in nothing, boy. I do what I want to. I don't count no stars. O. J. Simpson was a star, but I believe he killed that white woman and that white boy. They proved he didn't, and I accept it, but that don't change my mind at all, you hear me? A Nigro"—that's how he pronounced it—"is jealous of a white woman when he goes with her."

He returned his attention to the tombstones. "Here's where mah folks are buried right there, both sides of the road. This is mah mammy, mah daddy, and mah two oldest sisters. Right there. This is mah grandpa and mah great-grandpa. Right here."

"So your family's been here a long time."

"Well, I'm showin' you the graves, ain't I?"

"Do you know where your ancestors came from?"

"On mah mammy's side of the house, they were from that Rhine River in Germany. And mah grandma on mah mammy's side of the house was a Dutch woman, come out of Holland, so they tell me. She had thirteen chillun by that ol' German . . . uh . . . count. And on mah daddy's side of the house, the Fosters was Englishmens. And I don't know what breed mah grandma was."

More tombstones. "This is mah wife's folks, the Cookes and the Chambers and the Braggs. And these McWilliamses was all mah uncles. These are mah daddy's cousins right here, and mah great-uncle Dick. He was a long, tall kind of a man. Now, these bunch of Thompsons weren't kin to Colonel Joe Thompson, but they was kin to mah brother's wife. That's her folks in there."

"So you're related to just about everyone here."

"One way or the other."

Chicken Owen was telling us about some of the finer things in life. "One of the bes' rattlesnakes I ever saw was six feet long or longer," he explained. "Good eatin', boy. If ya cut it off below the rectum, skin it back, that's the prettiest white meat ya ever saw. Then if ya take that tenderloin on both sides of his backbone, it's all right. But if ya just cut his guts out and try to cook that, it's not as good."

I had no response. Still can't think of one. But it did raise a related question: "How'd you get the name Chicken Owen, anyway?"

"Fought chickens all my life. And I guess I was scared o' them, too."

I laughed. Amy laughed. Chicken Owen didn't. "You take it like you want to. But I'm gonna tell you before you start foolin' with me, there's three men got plastic jaws on account of they thought I wasn't game. I just broke their lil' ol' jawbones. . . . I'm goin' to the rooster fights 'bout a week from now. Down in Louisiana."

"Your roosters?"

"No, I quit foolin' with 'em. See where that one got me?" He pointed to a scar with pride. "Some Japanese are comin' over and Filipinos and whatnot. They all gonna fight down there. There's gonna be over a three-thousand-dollar purse down there."

"Isn't that illegal?"

"I dunno whether it is or not. Ain't nothin' illegal unless you make it. I never saw nobody that was legal in everything. . . . Hey, Homer!" He waved to a man standing in his driveway. "Known him seventy years. Heh-heh. That's the tightest man I ever saw."

We turned onto a dusty road heading into a grove of trees. By now, he had chewed his cigar into submission.

"Looks like you like cigars."

"Huh?"

"You like smoking cigars?"

"You ain't seen me burn a hole in one of 'em yet."

"You like the taste of it?"

"I reckon I do. You like the taste o' tobacco?"

"Not really."

"Do ya take a drink o' liquor?"

"I've been known to."

"You see, I ain't never done that. I never did take a drink o' liquor. I'm a man. I don't have to put it in me. But I'm not religious. I jus' saw so many fools . . ."

"So you've never tried alcohol?"

"Didn't I jus' say that, boy?"

"Never?"

"You heard me, didn't you? Never did drink no whiskey, no beer. And I ain't scared of nobody who does it. Them boys of mine take a drink, get drunk. That's their business. My business was I didn't want to. Ain't that peculiar? I done jus' exactly like I wanted to, boy. I drive this ol' truck here 'cause it's cheap. If I get out and leave it here, I ain't lost nothin'. . . . See now, there used to be a slave house right up there. They would unload the boat down here and put black folks in it. I don't believe in that, now, ya understand me? I do not believe in making a slave. I never knew any of mah ancestors on mah mammy's side owning a slave. They come out of Germany 'bout the time of the Civil War. But the Fosters . . . There's a lot of black folks in the country named Foster. But I still don't believe in a man bound to another man. I don't even believe in a woman bound to a man. I think a woman got as much right as any man. But I don't think a man oughta be bound to a woman neither."

He pointed a crooked finger ahead of us. "Now, over there's the Barton land. Ol' man Barton used two black women to breed his chillun. And Mrs. Franklin D. Roosevelt was one-eighth black, and she had a Barton descendant up above her. Ya hear me?"

"Eleanor Roosevelt?"

"Mrs. Franklin D. Roosevelt was one-eighth black. And her ancestor was born right over yonder where the cemetery is."

"You're saying Eleanor Roosevelt—"

"Didn't I jus' say that, boy?" He pointed to the side of the road. "I saw two dead folks here one time. A drunk killed 'em."

The pickup continued at a snail's pace past the green and red of an Alabama spring. We passed a teenage boy with medium-length hair walking along the road. "Hey, Rooster!" Chicken Owen shouted. "I call them kind o' folks Rooster, 'cause they got long hair. Heh-heh."

"What do you call people with no hair?" I asked, instinctively patting my pate.

"I like 'em. You don't look like no woman. See, one thing I hate is a lizbin. I had a lizbin workin' for me one time. I thought she was a boy when she was first hired to me. I looked at her the next day or two, and I saw she looked like a woman. I said to her, 'Are you a woman?' She said yeah. I said, 'I don't want your trash. I don't run no show like that. You work or you'll be gone.' I kept her five years. She worked. No reason arguing 'bout it as long as she produced. I didn't care what breed she was, but I didn't want her to be out there clownin' around, ya know what I mean? I done made it plain. But she was 'bout as good a truckdriver as I ever had. She could run any piece of equipment."

If there's one thing Alabamans can do, it's talk. Take the long route to a short answer. It's been that way from the beginning. Alabama's state constitution is 174,000 words in length—twice as long as any other state's, and twenty-five times the size of Vermont's. In fact, combine the number of words in the state constitutions of Vermont, New Hampshire, Indiana, Minnesota, Connecticut, North Carolina, Utah, Rhode Island, Kansas, Montana, Iowa, Alaska, Illinois, Maine, and Wisconsin, and you'd still have fewer words than Alabama used.

We held our breath as Chicken Owen inched back on to the highway, and I switched gears in the conversation. I was wondering about the people he admired as a child. Who were his heroes? Ask a stupid question . . .

"I ain't never looked up to nobody. Do it for yourself, I say. Ya be your own hero." I was confident he had taken his own advice. He turned to me. "Do you look up to folks?"

"Sure."

"Such as who? Clinton?"

"I like him."

"I don't like him. He ain't right. He ain't much of a man. Didn't he run off when they tried to send him to the army? Huh? Tell Daddy."

"I don't know. He may have had good reason."

"Sure, tryin' to save his ass is all. He ain't got no guts. Really, we ain't got no one runnin' for president of the United States that I like. I don't like Dole, and I don't like him. I voted for Clinton over Bush, though. Yeah, I voted for him. But I hated ever' minute of it. Ya see, his wife is over him, the way I figure it. She's really the one that's been bossin'."

"What about Pat Buchanan?"

"I like him. He got some guts, ain't he? Tell it like it is. Heh-heh."

"What about Ross Perot?"

"He got some guts, too."

"A little loony, though."

"I don't give a damn about that. He got more guts than they have. Heh-heh. He tickles me. He got a lot of good points."

"Were you a fan of Kennedy?" Amy asked.

"Who?"

"John F. Kennedy."

"He was all right. But I don't like this one up there now, because he drowned that woman. Ya don't drown no woman. If you a man, ya don't hurt no woman."

"What about LBJ?" I wondered.

"Johnson? I think he caused Kennedy's death. That's my opinion. No proof."

"So you don't like him?"

"Johnson?"

"Yeah."

"He's dead. Ain't no use talkin' 'bout him now."

"How about Richard Nixon?"

"Nixon? I think I voted for him, and he got impeached. Heh-heh. He died tryin' to protect the rest of 'em, didn't he? You ever get in trouble like that?"

"Nope."

"Well, then you ain't never done much," he said as we rolled back into the parking lot of Foster's Service Center. "I've had one hell of a life, boy. I made money and enjoyed life. The more you learn, the more it makes you wanna go. I could drive a mule. I could drive a truck. I could run a sawmill. I could cut timber. And I could sleep in when I want to. And damn few folks can do that."

Pride is a dichotomous concept. Theologians tell us it is the deadliest of the seven deadly sins. In the story of the Cherokees, it can be seen in the white man's arrogant sense of entitlement. Yet pride is a virtue when it inspires dignity and self-confidence—as in the Cherokees' noble endurance. As likable as he was, Chicken Owen represented the slippery slope whereon self-confidence leads to conceit and dignity breeds condescension. It appears that pride is a virtue in moderation, a sin in excess.

"Naw," concluded our tour guide, "you ain't never done much if you ain't got in trouble. If you don't make folks mad at you sometimes, you ain't no-'count nohow."

HOPE,
MISSISSIPPI

> *Nothing to look backward to with pride,*
> *and nothing to look forward to with hope.*
>
> Robert Frost

It was June 21, 1964, the longest day of the year, and three young civil-rights workers were combing through ashes and rubble in the heart of rural east-central Mississippi. Just forty-eight hours after Congress had passed the first comprehensive civil-rights act since Reconstruction, that was all that was left of Mount Zion Methodist Church in Neshoba County's all-black community of Longdale. Ashes and rubble. Five days earlier, a gang of armed men, members of the Mississippi White Knights of the Ku Klux Klan, had attacked the church's leaders and then the church itself, setting fire to the sixty-five-year-old building. It was the first of more than twenty black churches fire-bombed in the state that summer.

The arsonists had come looking for one of the civil-rights workers in particular, a twenty-five-year-old Manhattan refugee named Mickey Schwerner. At a time and place where, in the words of many Mississippians, the only thing worse than a nigger was a nigger lover, Schwerner was public enemy number one. "Goatee," the Klansmen called him, for the beard he grew to make himself look older. The outside agitator. The New York Jew. Schwerner represented everything the entrenched South deplored about the civil-rights movement.

After graduating from Cornell with a sociology degree and a young president's words—"Ask not what your country can do for you . . ."—ringing in his ears, he had become a social worker in a public housing project on Manhattan's Lower East Side and had joined the Congress of Racial Equality (CORE). When four girls were killed in a church bombing in Birmingham in September 1963, Schwerner decided to apply for a southern post as a CORE field worker. "I am now so thoroughly identified with the civil rights struggle," he wrote on his application, "that I have an emotional need to offer my services in the South." In late November, just days after the young president was murdered in Dallas, Schwerner learned he would be going to the Deep South, to Mississippi.

In January 1964, he and his wife, Rita, drove from Manhattan to the city of Meridian in Lauderdale County, on the southern border of Neshoba County. They ran a community center for the area's black residents, the first of its kind in Meridian. Their success earned them the enmity of area Klansmen, whose numbers had skyrocketed as the civil-rights struggle intensified. The Schwerners received dozens of menacing phone calls and religious and racial slurs. They were tailed by cars and repeatedly picked up for questioning by police. Their gas, water, and electricity were shut off. When that didn't faze them, they were evicted from their house.

Then the church burned. Schwerner had spoken at Mount Zion Methodist three weeks earlier, urging the congregation to register to vote. "You have been slaves too long," he said. "We can help you help yourselves." With him had been a twenty-one-year-old black, James Chaney, his closest colleague at the community center, a man who had spent his life in Mississippi gritting his teeth at his second-class status. Together, they had hoped to empower the citizens of Longdale. Instead, there was a smoking ruin.

Shaken, they climbed into their blue Ford station wagon and headed back toward Meridian. Chaney, who knew the roads well, was driving. Schwerner was in the passenger seat. In the back was a twenty-year-old college student from New York City. It was Andy Goodman's second day in Mississippi.

Goodman was among the first arrivals for what was expected to be an enlightened invasion—the Mississippi Summer Project, an effort by the Council of Federated Organizations to flood the state with hundreds of northern college students. The *New York Times* called it "one of the most ambitious civil rights projects yet conceived." The volunteers would form "freedom schools" to teach disfranchised blacks about their constitutional rights and conduct a massive voter-registration drive. Secretly, some organizers suspected that the inevitable violence against these Yankee do-gooders would direct the nation's attention to the intolerable conditions in Mississippi. It was a recipe for martyrdom.

As spring turned to summer in 1964, Andy Goodman had informed his parents about his decision to be part of the Mississippi Summer Project. Being under twenty-one, he needed them to sign the permission form required of all underage volunteers. Bob and Carolyn Goodman had been progressive activists a generation earlier. Their apartment on West Eighty-sixth Street had been a gathering place for the likes of Alger Hiss, Dr. Edward Barsky, and Zero Mostel. Their middle son, Andy, was a reflection of themselves. But Mississippi?

The state's history is stained with violence and failed efforts. Hernando De Soto led the first group of white men into the region in the early 1500s. He died along with more than a hundred of his men in a futile search for the fabled City of Gold and the Fountain of Youth. Robert Cavalier, the Sieur de La Salle, claimed the lower Mississippi River Valley for France 140 years later. He then got lost and was subsequently murdered by his own companions. And the Natchez Indians of what would become southern Mississippi were exterminated in the early 1700s, after leaving two survivors in a surprise raid of a French fort, survivors who called in reinforcements.

It was a Mississippi senator, Jefferson Davis, who served as president of the Confederate States, eventually finding himself questioned by southerners and jailed by northerners. And it was a Mississippi city, Vicksburg, the "Gibraltar of the Confederacy," that fell to General Ulysses S. Grant on July 4, 1863, marking the beginning of the end for the South. Barely a third of the 78,000 Mississippians to enter the Civil War survived; in 1866, the state spent a fifth of its entire revenue on artificial limbs. Emancipation meant the end of the state's most valuable resource, a loss of 436,000 slaves worth over $218 million. The nation's fifth-wealthiest state, with more millionaires per capita than any other, suddenly became its poorest.

A century later, this was a state still reeling from defeat and clinging to antebellum attitudes. In 1964, Mississippi was twenty-two years away from electing its first post-Reconstruction black congressman, twenty-three years away from removing a ban on interracial marriage from its constitution, and thirty-one years away from actually ratifying the federal constitutional amendment outlawing slavery. It was a state with a chief executive, Governor Ross Barnett, who physically blocked the integration of Ole Miss after claiming, "The Negro is different because God made him different to punish him." Yet Barnett was only following in the footsteps of former governor Theodore Bilbo, who once called on "every red-blooded white man to use any means to keep the nigger away from the polls," and whose nickname, "the Man," came to mean an oppressive Establishment figure—and still does today.

Racial oppression was so ingrained in Mississippi that it had become a vicious circle spiraling into defeatism. The state with the highest percentage of blacks in the country had the lowest percentage of registered black voters. Only 5 percent of Mississippi's half-million African Americans were registered to vote in 1960. In eight of the state's thirteen mostly black counties, not a single black citizen had ever voted.

In their struggle for a political voice, black Mississippians were faced with literacy tests, poll taxes, and violence. Mississippi was the site of more lynchings than any other state in the nation—nearly six hundred between 1890 and 1960. In 1937, two black prisoners accused of murder were seized by a mob and roasted to death with blowtorches. In 1944, a black man was killed in southwestern Mississippi just for hiring a lawyer to firm up the title to his land. Five years later, another was murdered for "hogging the road."

The years following the *Brown v. Board of Education* decision in 1954 were particularly violent. The names of the victims still reverberate in Mississippi. There was Emmitt Till, a Chicago teen visiting family in the delta, who whistled at a young white woman in Money, Mississippi. His body was found three days later in the Tallahatchie River, a cotton-gin fan tied to his neck. There was Mack Parker, a rape suspect who was taken from his jail cell in Poplarville, Mississippi, wrapped in chains, and dumped in the Pearl River, with local law enforcement apparently aware of every move. There were Herbert Lee, who worked to register black voters and was murdered in Liberty, Mississippi, by a white state legislator, and Louis Allen, killed for witnessing the crime.

And there was Medgar Evers, the patron saint of the Mississippi civil-rights movement. After seeing a close friend lynched as a teen, he joined the army and participated in the D-Day landing at Omaha Beach. He then returned to his native state to fight the good war at home. As Mississippi NAACP field secretary, he introduced civil-rights fervor to the delta. In 1963, after his home was bombed, he told a crowd at a fund-raiser, "I love my children, and I love my wife with all my heart. And I would die, and die gladly, if that would make a better life for them." Five days later, he was assassinated in his driveway, collapsing in a pile of sweatshirts he had been carrying. The sweatshirts read, *JIM CROW MUST GO.*

Till's accused killers were acquitted by an all-white jury. Parker's death went unpunished. Lee's murderer was never arrested. In the case of Evers, an outspoken member of the White Citizens Council named Byron de la Beckwith was arrested for the assassination. The weapon used in the attack was registered to him and held his fingerprints, and several witnessed testified that he had asked directions to Evers's home. However, he went to trial twice, and the all-white juries were unable to return a unanimous verdict. It wasn't until 1993 that, with eight blacks on the jury, a new trial resulted in a murder conviction.

These were the forces at work against the Mississippi Summer Project volunteers. This is where Andy Goodman asked his parents to let him go. They felt they had little choice. "When Bobby and I talked it over," Carolyn Goodman later explained, "we realized there was no way in the world we could say no to Andy. Our lives, our values would have had a hollow ring."

Of the forty martyrs for the cause whose names are inscribed on the Civil Rights Memorial in Montgomery, Alabama, nineteen were killed in Mississippi. Three were named Schwerner, Goodman, and Chaney.

After the three drove away from Mount Zion Methodist Church, they had a choice when they reached Highway 16. They could go straight to Meridian, a distance of about twenty-five miles, or they could take a longer route through the nearby hamlet of Philadelphia. Perhaps believing it was safer, they chose the latter. As they drove Highway 16 toward Philadelphia, Neshoba County deputy sheriff Cecil Ray Price passed them going the other way. He recognized the blue Ford station wagon from the widely circulated description, made a U-turn, and took off after them. Price, it happened, was also a Klansman and was eager to impress his friends by catching Schwerner. A few miles later, just inside the Philadelphia city limits, he arrested Chaney for speeding and told the other two they would be held as suspects in the church arson.

The Mississippi volunteers had been trained to be cautious. They were given tips. Don't give a sniper a target by standing in an open window. Beware of cars without license plates and cops without badges. Know the roads in and out of the town you're assigned. Although they weren't allowed a phone call, Schwerner had previously instructed a community-center coworker to call every jail and sheriff's office along their planned route to and from Longdale if they hadn't arrived by four o'clock that afternoon. The Neshoba County Jail received a call at five-thirty. The caller was told that the men hadn't been seen all day. It was a lie. Here it was, the first day of Freedom Summer, and three volunteers were already missing in Mississippi.

It was more than six hours later, when the long day finally turned to night, that the three were released from their jail cells, Chaney having paid a twenty-dollar fine. Among the most important tips Mississippi volunteers had received before heading south was this: Don't go anywhere at night. But they left anyway, without making a phone call, a sure signal that something was wrong. Chaney drove south on Highway 19 toward Meridian. It was then that a plan hatched by Price and the rest of the local Klan was put into action. Two cars filled with Klansmen took off after the blue Ford station wagon. One car broke down; the other kept going, joined by Price in his police cruiser.

The three activists were about ten miles from the Lauderdale County line when Chaney decided to gun it, turning right on Highway 492, heading southwest. The ploy backfired. Price caught up and turned on his lights, and Chaney made the fateful decision to pull over. The Klan car arrived, and the three young men were placed in the backseat of Price's cruiser. Price and the other Klansmen, one of them driving the trio's station wagon, turned around and headed back toward Philadelphia. Before reaching the city, they turned left at an unlit, unmarked dirt road and stopped. "So you wanted to come to Mississippi," one of the

Klansmen reportedly said. "Well, now we're gonna let you stay here."

Schwerner was killed first, shot in the heart. Goodman was second, taking a bullet in the right side of the chest. Chaney was last, shot in the abdomen and the head. The three bodies were buried under ten tons of dirt in an earthen dam being constructed to create a cattle pond a few miles southwest of town. The bodies remained there for forty-four days.

At 6:55 the following morning, a phone caller learned from someone at the Neshoba County Jail that the three men had been arrested the previous afternoon for speeding. The FBI, having already begun a church arson investigation, eventually devoted 153 men to the case. Bob and Carolyn Goodman and Nathan Schwerner, Mickey's father, flew to Washington, D.C., where President Lyndon Johnson informed them that a badly burned, empty blue Ford station wagon had been found in a swamp thirteen miles northeast of Philadelphia. When the Goodmans returned home, they found a postcard their son had sent upon arriving in Mississippi. "Dear Mom and Dad," it began. "I have arrived safely in Meridian, Mississippi. This is a wonderful town and the weather is fine. I wish you were here. The people in this city are wonderful and our reception was very good. All my love, Andy."

On June 24 and 25, the story made front-page headlines throughout the country, as the press and the FBI began to suspect the involvement of law-enforcement officers. Still, Neshoba County's swaggering sheriff, Lawrence Rainey, continued to suggest the whole event was a hoax, a sentiment echoed by Mississippi's top public officials. It wasn't until late July that an unidentified Neshoba County citizen revealed where the bodies were buried. In return, he received thirty thousand dollars in reward money. On August 4, the half-decomposed bodies were uncovered in the earthen dam. Schwerner was first. Then Goodman, whose left hand was clutching soil that could have come only from the dam site, meaning he may have been alive when buried. Then Chaney, who had been beaten so horribly that a pathologist compared his injuries to the kind suffered in a high-speed auto accident or an airplane crash.

Four months later, after a couple of Klansmen became FBI informants, nineteen men were arrested for their involvement in the deaths of the three activists. The group was a motley crew of backwoods vigilantes that included Sheriff Rainey, Deputy Sheriff Price, a seventy-one-year-old Philadelphia cop, a Baptist preacher, and a seventeen-year-old high-school dropout. None was tried for murder. The Justice Department's reasons were reasonable. Because murder was not a federal offense unless it was committed on federal property, the alternative was state prosecution. But neither the state nor the county had conducted a serious investigation into the crime, and the judge who would have presided was a strict white supremacist and a distant cousin to some of the defendants. So the Justice Department reached back to a Reconstruction-era statute—a law passed to control Klan terrorism nearly a century earlier—and accused the defendants of depriving the victims of their civil rights. This meant a maximum prison sentence of ten years.

In 1965, Judge William Harold Cox of the southern district of Mississippi threw the case out of court, only to be overruled by the United States Supreme Court a year later. Finally, in 1967, thirty-eight months after the bodies were found, *United States v. Price et al* went to trial, by which time many of the defendants had become local folk heroes. Price—who said the day after he was arrested, "It took an hour to get to work this morning, I had to spend so much time shaking hands"—was even running for sheriff, and the mayor of Philadelphia was among the twelve-man defense team.

When the verdicts were returned in late October, only seven of the nineteen—including Price but not Rainey—were found guilty. Though it was the first jury conviction of white officials and Klansmen for crimes against black people or civil-rights workers in the history of the state, only two of the defendants received the maximum sentence. All were paroled early. "They killed one nigger, one Jew, and one white man," claimed the judge, inaccurately. "I gave them all what I thought they deserved."

In 1931, H. L. Mencken took it upon himself to rank the forty-eight states from best to worst. Mississippi came in dead last. Six and a half decades later, it remains in that position, at least by most statistical accounts. Pick a category, almost any category, and there's a fair chance Mississippi ranks fiftieth out of fifty in the nineties.

Education? Mississippi is last in standardized test scores, high-school graduation rate, and library funding. Standard of living? Mississippi has more births to single teenagers and more families below the poverty level than any other state. Health? Mississippi ranks fiftieth in fitness centers per capita. Culture? The state ranks last in theatrical productions, museums, and art galleries per capita. The state also ranks near the bottom in toxic emissions, drinking-water safety, education spending, college graduation rate, high-school sports participation, unemployment rate, retail sales, public safety spending, motor vehicle deaths per capita, minority-owned businesses, income disparity between the races, infant mortality rate, and life expectancy.

To be fair, Mississippi does churn out one remarkable product—artistic talent. Literary figures like William Faulkner, Tennessee Williams, Eudora Welty, Richard Wright, Shelby Foote, Walker Percy, Hodding Carter, even John Grisham. And musical legends like Jimmie Rodgers, the originator of country music; Robert Johnson, the father of the blues; and a combination of both named Elvis Presley. The blues—as typified by native sons like John Lee Hooker, Muddy Waters, and B. B. King—is a product of Mississippi misery. It is, according to Ralph Ellison, "an autobiographical chronicle of personal catastrophe expressed lyrically." It is Mississippi put to music.

It was thus with prejudices of our own and low expectations that we set out to find Hope, just outside Philadelphia. In Cherokee, Alabama, we turned from U.S. 72 onto the Natchez Trace Parkway. The trace began as a series of hunters' paths stretching from the banks of the lower Mississippi River to the Tennessee River Valley. By the nineteenth century, the crude Indian trails had evolved into a clearly marked path utilized by American farmers and traders. They would float their crops and products down the river to Natchez or New Orleans, sell their flatboats as lumber, and then make the return trip on foot or horseback along the trace. It was no easy proposition. The trail was infamous for its assassins, its land pirates, its malevolent innkeepers. In a grisly tradition of the time, the severed heads of the trace's most despised outlaws were often mounted in trees along the trail. The trail soon earned a nickname: "the Devil's Backbone."

Despite the dangers, the trace was the most heavily traveled route in the old Southwest by 1810. However, the arrival of the steamship as a safer and speedier means of transportation greatly diminished the importance of the overland route, returning a relative serenity to the path. Today, it is a 438-mile, two-lane highway meticulously maintained by the United States Park Service. It is both a scenic drive through history (Indian mounds, Civil War battlefields, Meriwether Lewis's grave) and a historic trip through scenery (dense pine forests, murky bayous, golden pastures).

We covered 160 miles on the parkway before turning from Mississippi's surreal beauty to its surreptitious back roads. As we headed east on Highway 19, the lush green roadside was replaced by harsh red clay; the thick forest gave way to a superficial row of trees with decimated acres exposed behind it. Mississippi is one of several places— Appalachia and the Canyonlands region of southeastern Utah are others—where some of the nation's most spectacular settings are juxtaposed with its most desperate circumstances. Here, we could see the deforestation through the trees. It felt like a drive through a metaphor.

Twenty miles later, we were in Neshoba County. In the late nineteenth century, the area was peopled mostly by white farmers and freed slaves and covered largely by corn and cotton. Because the hill country was not suited to the enormous plantations so often associated with southern agriculture, there were never many African Americans in the area, perhaps 15 percent of the population. The traditional attitude of Neshoba whites toward blacks was summed up by Clayton Rand, one-time editor of the *Neshoba Democrat*. "The Negro, innately happy, has written off his future as a total loss," he wrote in his memoir, "and he accepts the assets of the day as something to be untinctured with worry."

Though the railroad arrived in 1905, dirt roads crisscrossed the landscape until well into the 1940s. Neshoba County has always been a bit off the beaten path, physically isolated, emotionally entrenched. This region of the country has never tolerated "outside agitators," whether they were Yankee soldiers, carpetbaggers, federal officials exposing moonshiners, civil-rights activists, or, I suspected, a couple of visitors from the land of Grant and Lincoln come to poke around. Fifteen miles more and we came upon a sign: *Welcome to Philadelphia—Our Fair City*. I half-expected it to be followed by, *Abandon hope, all ye who enter here*.

In the eyes of many observers, Philadelphia came to symbolize the root of America's racial divide. Martin Luther King, Jr., visited the city in 1966 to lead a memorial service for the slain civil-rights workers. After he and his colleagues were attacked by a mob armed with broomsticks and ax handles, he characterized the day as one of the most frightening of his life. "This is a terrible town," he told a reporter, "the worst I've seen. There is a complete reign of terror here." *Life* magazine called it "a strange, tight little town" whose "fear and hatred of things and ideas that come from the outside is nearly pathological," and where hostile eyes

track strangers "as a swivel gun tracks a target." Even Philadelphians admitted that when the bodies of Schwerner, Goodman, and Chaney were recovered, instead of asking, "Who would have done such a thing?" the community wondered, "Who told?"

Thirty-two years later, I felt a knot in my stomach. This was a place I had long considered a bastion of wickedness far from my life, the deepest recess of the Deep South, somewhere I'd simply never be. Now, the grainy photographs in the history books suddenly came to life with startling clarity. What had been a distant knowledge leading to disgust was now a physical encounter, and it inspired an emotion closer to fear. It's one thing to read about Schwerner, Goodman, and Chaney being taken into custody at a particular street corner in Philadelphia. It's quite another to stand on that corner. When we set up camp in the darkness of a nearly abandoned state park on the outskirts of town—our only company a pair of ominous-looking trailers on the edge of the forest and the still waters of the Pearl River, the same river where Mack Parker drowned—it only heightened my anxiety.

If Philadelphia's past teaches us anything, it is to refrain from biases. But I was overcome by mine. I walked the streets wondering about the people I saw. Was that man unloading his pickup involved in the murders? Or that man laughing it up with his cronies at the diner? Or maybe him, staring silently into his cup of coffee? Philadelphians would like nothing more than to escape the shadow of 1964. I wasn't going to help them.

And yet the Philadelphia I discovered was an odd mixture of grudging evolution and sleepy stagnation. They still stared at outsiders, but it was a stare laced more with curiosity than contempt. There was still a monument to the Confederacy in front of the Neshoba County Courthouse, but the courthouse square was no longer the commercial and social center of town, having been replaced by a Wal-Mart a few miles west and a Choctaw Indian casino down the road. There were still a mostly white part of town and a black part of town literally on the other side of the tracks, but daily encounters between the races suggested a far more integrated landscape than in the South of a generation ago, or even in today's urban North. The sheriff's deputies in Neshoba County no longer swaggered about in six-shooters and Stetsons; the department even boasted interracial partnerships. Just west of town, Mount Zion Methodist Church had been rebuilt, this time in brick. And just south, there was a massive monument to James Chaney at his grave site.

If you dig a little deeper, however, you can validate your fears. You can learn that Chaney's tombstone is massive because the first two were small enough to be stolen, and that it is a lone tombstone because, though the Schwerners hoped to bury their son next to his comrade, they were told even death was segregated in Mississippi. You can hear stories about how the Ku Klux Klan is still a vibrant organization in the area, about how local law enforcement held a gun to a black man's head because he was spotted riding with a white woman, about how another young black local hanged himself in jail under "mysterious circumstances." And you can meet a fifty-two-year-old woman, a former sharecropper, who has yet to cast a vote and who still feels compelled to move off the sidewalk when a white person comes the other way. What William Faulkner said years ago still applies in Mississippi: "The past isn't dead yet; it isn't even past yet."

Hope, three miles west of Philadelphia, was dominated by the smell of Mississippi mud. The community essentially consisted of a few dozen houses clustered around Hope Baptist Church, Hope Methodist Church, a volunteer fire department, and the Hope Country Store. The store doubled as a gas station and tanning salon—or, as the sign said, *Tanin Bed*. Jerome Manning, who grew up in Hope, ran the store, which, for a community in a backwoods section of a rural region, was positively bustling. In other words, there was often more than one car at a time.

One of those cars was the talk of the store. The previous day, a family from Illinois had stopped to pick up some provisions. Mom and

Dad stepped into the store, leaving Grandma and Grandson in the car and leaving the car running. The boy reached over and put the car in drive. His grandmother tried to step on the brake but hit the gas instead. The car took out a concrete wall adjacent to the store before slamming into a tree. Grandma hit the windshield and was taken to the hospital. "They took out my air conditioner!" said Jerome, who wore a mechanic's jumpsuit. "You know how hot it was yesterday—ruined all my candy bars," he continued, still giddy twenty-four hours later. "I wish I got pictures. I was trying not to be mad. You can't get mad at people when they hurt."

Although the Hope Country Store was a multicultural crossroads, with equal numbers of white, black, and Native American customers, Hope itself was a white community. In fact, it was largely a White community. Jerome pointed to a man sitting at a bench in the store. "That's Hays White. He got about four brothers that live on his land round here—the Whites. They own all the land round here except my little six acres I got at my house. They all good people."

Hays White, seventy-four, wore a plaid shirt, a white baseball cap, and a bored expression. He had been a cotton and corn farmer, then a cattle rancher. He wasn't much of a talker. Though he had lived in Hope all but ten years of his life, he didn't know how the town got its name. In fact, nobody did.

"What's the biggest thing that ever happened in Hope?" I asked.

"Not too much," he replied, then added, "A boy and his mama run a car down behind the store yesterday."

We strolled outside and were soon accosted by three giggly teenage girls, who breathlessly asked if it were true we were writing a book. Two of them were Hays White's granddaughters, Chastity and Casey White, ages fourteen and twelve. With them was their best friend, Lindsey Harrington, age eleven and the most talkative of the trio. Not that it mattered who spoke. They were like one of those *Star Trek* creatures whose one voice speaks for three unified brains, and they proceeded to give us a

Lindsey, Chastity, and Casey

profile of every person who pulled into the parking lot.

"That's Percy. He's cool. I hope he stops. He hates the name Percy. . . . That's Pete. He's obsessed with Michael Jordan. . . . And that's my dad. Hey, Dad! This guy's writing a book! He's writing a book!"

Amy was enjoying it. "So you know just about everybody here, huh?"

"We know everybody. I'm kin to everybody in the Hope community except the preacher and Jerome and her," said Casey, pointing to Lindsey. "All my kinfolk live here, except my mama's family." She continued to point the way: "My daddy's parents live here, my daddy's stepsister lives here, and my cousins live here, and a cousin lives over there, and my other cousins live right down that road right there."

I asked if they planned on living in Hope when they got older and didn't receive the we-gotta-get-out-of-this-place response expected of fast-paced youth in an unhurried community. "Oh, I am," said Casey. "I already got my house all picked out."

"We're living here for the rest of our lives!" Lindsey nearly shouted. "We like this community. The people are nice, and there's not a lot of people. They're not mean. And they're not, like, odd."

"There ain't nobody in this community that's bad," added Chastity, a stunning girl who had already won a few local beauty pageants, was a state Bible Drill finalist, and will probably be Miss Mississippi someday.

I mean, with a name like Chastity White . . .

Then again, I wondered if she would ever be discovered. Youth and hope, of course, are supposed to be one and the same. The two places where they are most often separated, I would guess, are the urban jungle and the rural outback, both for the same reason. If you can't see beyond the neighborhood, you can't dream beyond it. At least that was my theory—until I asked the Hope trio about their favorite television shows.

"*Days of Our Lives*," said Lindsey. "It's all right, but when Marlena got possessed, it was kinda—"

"*Malibu Shores*," Casey interrupted. "That's the best show. Every Saturday night."

"My daddy's crazy about *Frasier*," said Chastity.

And so I hatched a new theory: TV has had a greater effect on the South than the TVA. It's possible that nothing has brought about the demise of regional culture as much as sitcoms and soap operas. Tupelo used to be as far from Times Square, psychologically, as Tibet. But bring Hollywood innuendo to the Mississippi farm girl, send the *Fresh Prince of Bel Air* to the back roads of the Deep South, showcase an evil twin or a love triangle or two, and it'll be a small world after all. I wondered if the images on the television seemed foreign to the girls, a portal to a different world.

"Yeah," said Lindsey. "It seems so upper-class. And we're, like, down here in Hope."

The words lingered with me as the three girls climbed into a sport utility vehicle and rumbled off down a dirt road, fourteen-year-old Chastity behind the wheel.

We headed back toward Philadelphia, disappointed that we hadn't encountered a black resident of Hope, as if the skin color and the concept were mutually exclusive here. A couple of miles down the road, I glanced to my right and caught a glimpse of a ramshackle wood-frame house. On the porch sat a black man, his face rigid under a baseball cap slightly askew. We were on the outskirts of Hope.

I turned into the driveway, and as Amy and I approached the man, a look of uncertainty crept into his eyes. "Don't talk to him!" said a voice from the driver's seat of a pickup truck set back in the driveway. We hadn't noticed the second man there at all. "Don't bother with him," he said. "His mind's like a baby's. He was born that way." The man was en route to his job driving a logging truck, but after we told him of our mission, he said, "You can talk to my wife. She's inside. . . . Ollie Mae!"

A small, frail-looking woman opened the door with that same uneasy look in her eyes. She let us in, she later admitted, only because her husband had told her to. Ollie Mae Welch had led a life of hardship and humility, yet she didn't look her fifty-two years. With her pronounced cheekbones, frizzy black hair, and bright brown eyes, she could have passed for ten years younger. When she smiled, which she did with greater frequency as the afternoon wore on, it absolutely lit up the room.

The room was well worn. We sat on three small couches with sheets and blankets draped over them. Ollie Mae's brother, Lavell, sat in a chair nearby, alternately napping, watching television, and smiling to himself beneath his baseball cap while we talked. There were dozens of pictures on the walls—children and nieces and nephews. Two Bibles and a dictionary rested on the coffee table.

What followed in the next couple of hours was a transformation. In the beginning, Ollie Mae appeared timid. She spoke haltingly, a verbal tiptoe. A still tongue, Frederick Douglass once explained, made a wise head. That was during slavery, when any critical words from the oppressed would find their way to the oppressor, and slaves would find themselves sold away from friends and family. "This is the penalty of telling the truth," Douglass wrote, "of telling the simple truth, in answer to a series of plain questions."

I sensed something similar in Ollie Mae 150 years later. I was a white stranger asking strange questions. Why was I here? What was I after? But as the minutes went by, as she realized we weren't there to trick

her or mock her, she began to open up. And what she lacked in elo-
quence she made up for in profound spirit.

"Well, anyway," she began her story, "there's been some sad days and
some happy days here. . . ."

Ollie Mae grew up in a sharecropper's shack, twelve people in two
bedrooms, no indoor plumbing. "I don't hardly discuss this with anybody too much," she said, "but it was bad back then. We was stayin' on
the place with this man, or as we called him, our bossman. And he always tried to, you know, mess around with me. And I would go and tell
my parents about it, but it wasn't nothin' they could do. When I see him
comin', I'd have to go the other way. And he would catch me by my hand
and pull on me and all that junk, and I would fight him off. Then I go
home and tell my parents, and still we worked for him. My daddy knew
he couldn't say nothin', and neither could my mama." She said this with a
weariness in her voice, as if reliving the frustration. "Eventually, he just
stopped," she explained, "and I know it wasn't nothin' but God doin' it."

On the heels of our discussion with the girls of Hope, Ollie Mae's
voice was a sobering slap of reality. Theirs was an exuberant childhood, a
future assured. Hers had been one of subjugation and sexual assault, a
past endured. We tend to think
of sharecropping as the residue
of slavery. And it was. But too
often, we ponder past tragedies
without giving thought to current scars. Here was the residue of sharecropping.

Ollie Mae Welch

When it was time to pick
cotton, Ollie Mae picked cotton.
When it was time to go to
school, Ollie Mae picked cotton. By the time she returned

to classes, she was so far behind that she eventually gave up on education. "They passed me just to get rid of me, I guess, because I don't know too much," she said. "They just moved us on. Do you know what I'm sayin'? Just moved us on."

She attended an all-black high school during the years immediately following the mandate to integrate, when Mississippi's response was contempt and defiance. In 1958, when Ollie Mae was fourteen, Alcorn College professor Clennon King, a black, applied for admission to the summer program at all-white Ole Miss. Authorities had him committed to an insane asylum. When Ollie Mae was sixteen, in 1960, another black man, Clyde Kennard, sought enrollment at Mississippi Southern College. He was sentenced to seven years of hard labor in the state penitentiary for the alleged theft of five sacks of chicken feed, a crime he didn't commit. In 1962, when Ollie Mae was eighteen, James Meredith attempted to enroll at Ole Miss. It took the Justice Department, the Mississippi NAACP, three thousand army troops, and five hundred United States marshals to get him in. Two people were killed and hundreds wounded in the subsequent rioting, and one state legislator even proposed that Mississippi secede from the Union again. Ollie Mae was twenty.

We often think of desegregation as an end to a moral struggle, when it was, to many closest to it, the beginning of a practical one. Jerome at the Hope Country Store told me he had quit school for a while when the races were mixed, not out of moral indignation but because of the volatile atmosphere it created. For two years, he lied to his father, bringing home unopened books and fake report cards while the dust settled. From an entirely different station in life, Ollie Mae had developed much the same perspective. "I remember that this mother let her daughter go to school, and she got beat up and stuff. That's when they was tryin' to mix 'em together then," she explained. "I said if I ever have any kids, if my kids had trouble, I would just take 'em out. I wouldn't let them go through that, 'cause I didn't have to."

The lessons: In close quarters, protection overwhelms principle; in hard times, high concepts don't get you through the day. Indeed, Martin Luther King and John F. Kennedy were only vague images in Ollie Mae's world. Distant people trying to help. That's all. As for Medgar Evers, who died when she was nineteen in an effort to get black Mississippians to vote, Ollie Mae had never heard of him.

"I ain't never voted in my life," she admitted. "To me, I don't know, what I see, they ain't doin' what they supposed to be doin'. Before peoples votes you in, you will do great things, you know? You say what you gonna do. If the road's all ragged and all, you'll fix it. Then you get in there and you forget the road."

I said that was because people like her weren't voting, and as I did so, I felt shame. Another Cornell graduate in his mid-twenties had come bearing the same message in 1964, only Mickey Schwerner had died for it. Here I was, thirty-two years later, giving lip service to the cause but knowing I wasn't prepared to give my life for it. I sounded more patronizing than passionate.

Ollie Mae laughed, a bit uncomfortably. "That's what a lot tells me. They say instead of sittin' back there sayin' they aren't doin', then why don't you vote?" She shrugged and looked away. "But I ain't never voted."

Ollie Mae had six children—three boys from a previous marriage to a man who "just liked to chase women" and two boys and a girl with her current husband. The three oldest boys, all in their early twenties, lived and worked in the Philadelphia area. The three youngest lived with her. "I always teach them that they can be whatever they want, if they work and strive for it. I'm hopin' the best in the future for them. That's as far as I can say." She sighed. "Now, my oldest teenage boy, he says as soon as he get out of school, he goin' to college, 'cause he say this place is so boring. You know how teenage kids are. Course, we said that ourselves—well, I did—but it was a waste of time, 'cause I didn't go nowhere."

Escape is part of Mississippi's legacy. From the end of slavery to the invention of the mechanical cotton picker in the 1940s (which produced scores of unwanted sharecroppers), the Illinois Central Railroad from Memphis to Chicago was a pipeline of hope for black Mississippians. Most of them subsequently echoed the reflection of one black man who said, "I call it *'sippi* because I don't miss it."

Ollie Mae stayed in Mississippi, but perhaps more important, the old ways of Mississippi remained in Ollie Mae. She told of how she still found herself stepping aside for white folks on the sidewalk. She admitted it sheepishly, as if marveling at her own behavior: "Yeah, I do it, because I was taught that way. The whites, okay, they got it all, and I was brought up respectin' them, and I always thought that it was wrong. It's like my daddy. He was older than the man whose place we stayed at, but he would, like, 'Mister' him and 'Yessir.' But the man wouldn't 'Mister' him and 'Yessir' him, and I was wonderin' why. But yeah, it's still there. I don't know. It's the way I was brought up, and it's still in me. And I try my best to teach my kids. I don't want my kids to come up scared like I did, and I teaches them not to be. I say, 'You as good as the white. You ain't no better than them, and they ain't no better than you.'"

Ollie Mae worked occasionally as a housekeeper for the wife of a doctor in town. She was paid twenty dollars a day. "My mama used to work for her, and you know, in a way . . . I don't know, I'm thinkin' it seem like I was supposed to do this—bein' a maid and all," she reflected. "Sometimes, I think about it. I say, 'I believe there's somethin' better for me.' Course, I got older now. Might not be too much out there now."

The doctor's wife is not a native of Mississippi. She nearly sent Ollie Mae into shock the first time she drank out of the same glass as her black maid, the time she told her grandkids to sit in the backseat of the car while Ollie Mae sat up front, and the time she told Ollie Mae to stop calling her "Miss Cannon" and use her first name instead. You can find hope in the strangest places, and Ollie Mae found it in moments like those. She found it in the fact that her oldest sons had decent jobs, that her young daughter slept over at white friends' houses, that all her children attended school instead of picking cotton. To her, there was hope in Hope, because she found hope in simple human decency.

"Well, to me, it has changed pretty much, you know, 'cause we used to be in the back or last," she explained. "Peoples, they treat you better. They speak to you. And you used to wouldn't get that, you know? And the jobs. Okay, they not only for whites anymore, you know? And they are good-paying jobs, in a lot of cases. And if we come into a store, like if we would be waited on and a white person come in, they would leave us or whatever and go to them. Well, it's a different story now. We can go in, they can wait on us, you know, and the white will have to wait until they finish with us."

My fear is that hope, as it applies to racism in America, is some sort of conceptual high jump in which we're setting the bar too low. The farther we lower our expectations, the more we perceive signs of progress. The more progress we perceive, the less we feel a need for action. That, in a nutshell, might describe a generation's apathy. We've been conditioned to believe that the hardest part is over, that the generation before us wiped out the foundations of racism, leaving only the daily manifestations. On one side are those who believe the playing field has been leveled and argue that there is no need for continued action. On the other are those who have given up the cause, who claim that separate and unequal is the best we can do. They declare black English a second language and apply for federal funding to teach it.

Hope can be a half-empty, half-full proposition. Should we feel despair that three dozen black churches were torched throughout the South in 1996? Or hope in the knowledge that this time, the president visited the rubble, Congress passed tougher church arson laws, and federal officials undertook the biggest arson investigation in United States history? Should we feel hope that in the so-called trial of the century, unfolding at the same time, a black man won a legal battle over white cops? Or despair that the most important issue of the trial was not the mountain of evidence against him, not the fact that he could afford the best lawyers money could buy, not the realization that there were significant shortcomings in the nation's criminal justice system—but ultimately that he, O. J. Simpson, was black? As we enter the twenty-first century, America's racial divide has actually widened in many ways. Signs of change are not necessarily symbols of hope.

Does it matter that there are black and white partners in Neshoba County law enforcement if there are still cops who harass black men for riding with white women? That young black Philadelphian who found a gun pointed at his temple was Ollie Mae's oldest son. "The chief of police told him to come up there and report it and tell him who it was, but he won't go," said Ollie Mae. "He told me, 'Mama, if I was up north, I would, but these people don't do nothin' down here.'"

Three decades ago, the African American citizens of Neshoba County were terrified of Sheriff Lawrence Rainey. "Ooh, I was so afraid of him, 'cause peoples talked about him, saying he's so mean, and he don't like black people," Ollie Mae recalled. "Once, I went up to the courthouse to ask for something, I don't know what it was. I went up in that place, and my heart was just beating so. Me, black, standin' up there, and there he was sittin' over there. But I asked him something, and he told me, and I felt relief, you know? There was no harsh words or anything." In 1964, Ollie Mae found solace in a modicum of civility. In 1996, she found hope in a lack of disrespect.

Ollie Mae claimed she didn't remember much about the murders in which Rainey was accused of playing a part, the tragedy that put Philadelphia on America's front pages and still seemed to echo in the hills and pines of Neshoba County. "Not too much. Only hearsay, only hearsay," she said. "Now, this lady next door, she told me . . . Uh, I don't know if I should say this or not. . . ." She paused and then continued. "The lady said we rentin' from the man that she said had a part in it. It scared me! So I don't know what to believe."

Amy and I looked at each other, eyebrows raised. "What's his name?" Amy asked.

She whispered it to us, and the name sounded familiar. We couldn't quite place it. Then we remembered. Her landlord was one of the nineteen men arrested for the murders of Schwerner, Goodman, and Chaney, the man on whose property the bodies were buried for forty-four days. He was acquitted.

Shaking a little, enlightened a lot, we said our good-byes and drove into the Mississippi darkness, never having figured out why they called it Hope.

TRIUMPH,
LOUISIANA

> *We'll bask in the shadow of yesterday's triumph,*
> *Sail on the steel breeze.*
>
> Pink Floyd

The Father of Waters begins as a gentle stream in the heart of northern Minnesota, a dozen feet wide and a dozen inches deep, trickling from the edge of a modest lake toward its destination 2,552 miles away. The lake, charted by Henry Rowe Schoolcraft in 1832 as the source of the Mississippi River, was named Itasca, a combination of the Latin words *veritas caput*, or "true head." But the true source of the great river is the rain and snow that falls on thirty-one states and two Canadian provinces from Pennsylvania to Idaho—the fourth-largest drainage basin in the world. The mighty Mississippi is an enormous rope binding a nation together. It is a storybook with chapters at every port of call.

After leaving Lake Itasca, the river wanders northward and eastward for more than eighty miles. It curls around in a lazy fishhook and connects a series of lakes before finally finding its bearings and heading south toward its first river port turned metropolis. After slicing through the heart of Minneapolis and St. Paul, it forms the Wisconsin border. By the time the river leaves Minnesota, it has traveled nearly seven hundred miles and dropped more than seven hundred feet in elevation. After heading southeast past Dubuque, where Wisconsin, Iowa, and Illinois confer, it amasses its greatest width—nearly three and a half miles—at the Iowa community of Clinton. There, it changes its mind and starts in a southwesterly direction, rolling past Nauvoo, Illinois, where Mormon Church founder Joseph Smith died, and Hannibal, Missouri, where Mark Twain was born.

Downriver from Hannibal, the Mississippi is joined by the Illinois River, one of the 250 tributaries and branches that give Old Man River a combined length of more than twelve thousand navigable miles. Barely a dozen miles later, just north of St. Louis, is its confluence with the Missouri River. The two mighty waterways flow nearly side by side for several miles, like fighters sizing each other up, before the Missouri adds its mud-red torrent and the Mississippi becomes what T. S. Eliot called the "strong brown god."

Farther downstream, at Cairo, Illinois, the Ohio River brings water from the Alleghenies, doubling the volume, and the river begins to form broad, indecisive loops. Near New Madrid, Missouri, which during the winter of 1811–12 was the center of the most violent series of earthquakes in United States history, the river nearly surrounds a slice of Kentucky, removing it completely from the rest of the state. As it winds along the Tennessee-Arkansas border toward Memphis, it changes course often, creating oxbow lakes and several of the river's 750 islands large enough to be named or numbered.

The Big Muddy rolls on southward through the Mississippi ports of Greenville, Vicksburg, and Natchez into Louisiana, where it eases eastward and thunders past Baton Rouge. So much freight passes through New Orleans eighty miles later that the port surpasses even New York.

Not only are 400 million short tons of freight transported annually on God's superhighway, but the river also dumps 500 million tons of topsoil into the Gulf of Mexico each year, enough to create a mound a mile square and 240 feet high. Over the years, the mud has gradually extended the delta. Thus, the land surrounding the Mississippi River in much of Louisiana was in fact created by it.

The last hundred miles of the mighty Mississippi, from New Orleans to the marshy delta and the four passes that fan out at the river's mouth, cut through a thin peninsula straddling the river. Louisiana is unlike every other state in that it is divided into parishes rather than counties, a remnant of French, Spanish, and Roman Catholic control. Plaquemines Parish, the land bordering both sides of the river from New Orleans to the sea, is one of the state's oldest. It was organized in 1807.

This is where Louisiana began, where La Salle stood when he claimed the entire Mississippi Valley for Louis XIV and named it for him in 1682. And it is the end of the ride. Should a raindrop fall into Lake Itasca and move with the current, it would reach this point in ninety days. Here, just thirty-two nautical miles from the gulf, is one of the last inhabitable communities along the Father of Waters. Here, on the edge of America, amid a culture all but inseparable from the river itself, along a precarious strip of land defiantly open to the fury of the sea, lies the town of Triumph.

We left the jazzy ethnicity and bourbon-stained morality of New Orleans behind as we climbed aboard Highway 23 just south of the city and headed into the delta. A southeastern route to the gulf otherwise known as the Belle Chase Parkway, Highway 23 was named after the most populous community in Plaquemines, which wasn't saying much. Though it is one of Louisiana's largest parishes, Plaquemines is also one of its most sparsely populated, with fewer than thirty thousand residents along its hundred-mile length.

Just past Belle Chase lay Idlewild, once the home of Leander Perez,

the Richard M. Daley of the delta. Judge Perez, as he was known throughout Louisiana, was the political boss of Plaquemines Parish, ruling with
an iron hand but remarkable efficiency for nearly half a century until his
death in 1969. Nationally, Perez is remembered as a leader of the mid-
century segregation movement; locally, he is something near a deity.

As I steered the Day Tripper along the west bank of the Mississippi,
I sensed in Perez's beloved Plaquemines a succession of odd juxtapositions. It was as if the end of the great river consisted of layers of culture
and industry like years of deposited topsoil. Rice and sugar plantations
dotted the early miles along the highway, followed by massive petrochemical
plants, followed by citrus groves. Each has been vital to the parish's economic survival at one time, each the dominant resource in its own era.
Side by side, however, they gave the impression that the parish had not
evolved over the years as much as it had repeatedly started over.

Plaquemines was a jumble of unrelated names—Happy Jack, Pointe
à la Hache, Port Sulphur, Myrtle Grove, Venice. It was a hodgepodge of
agriculture and industry, old and new, an indecisive dependence on the
sea, the soil, and the minerals underneath. It was an oil refinery next to a
store selling "world-famous Creole tomatoes," the salty smell of the ocean
mingled with the pungent odor of burning fuel. It was old slave quarters
and sulphur plants, oilmen and alligator hunters, tangerine trees and fishing
trawlers, kumquats and oyster bars.

At Port Sulphur, we took a left turn from the four-lane parkway to
an old two-laner that paralleled it. As we moved down the road, the
residences alongside it began to appear less permanent. Houses of stone
or brick gave way to homes of wood or tin. It was like reading "The
Three Little Pigs" backwards. The farther we went down the peninsula,
the more we encountered mobile homes and houses on stilts. I began to
sense a method to the architectural madness when we passed a church
with a marquee of black letters on a stark white background: *Sometimes
God breaks us so he can remake us.* The river was just out of sight but never
out of mind.

At the town of Empire, we waited as a boat went through the raised Doullut Canal Bridge. Just over the bridge, we stopped for lunch at a seafood restaurant. Tom's Place, it was called. All that was left above the doorway were the *T* and the *PL*. No matter. Those who needed to know knew. For the next hour, we enjoyed the best meal of our entire journey—oysters on the half shell as big as beanbags, plucked from the water three miles away and smothered in horseradish, cocktail sauce, and hot sauce. They were twice as big and tasty and a fourth as expensive as the oysters we were used to. Though we would soon discover the power of the sea to taketh away, here was the giveth part of the proverb.

We continued our southeasterly course through the town of Buras, once the heart of the region's citrus industry. Triumph was next on the map. There was no way to determine where the community began, but we did discover where it ended—at a storied fortress guarding a bend of the Mississippi.

Fort Jackson was named for Andrew Jackson, who recommended its construction. It was completed in 1832 across the river from a lesser stronghold, Fort St. Philip. By the mid-nineteenth century, only a few soldiers were garrisoned here, but at the start of the Civil War, the forts were seized by Louisiana. The prevailing military theory of the time was that it was impossible for wooden ships to outduel shore defenses of any strength, and the two forts were considered a sufficient defense for New Orleans and the Confederacy's river supply line.

In April 1862, Admiral David Farragut, a southerner who had remained loyal to the Union, decided to test that theory. He and his fleet of forty-three vessels arrived at the bend of the river intent on passing the forts and taking New Orleans. The result was one of the most important confrontations of the Civil War. Farragut's fleet bombarded Forts Jackson and St. Philip for four days and nights. Union general Benjamin Butler later described the battle this way: "Twenty mortars, 142 guns in fleet, 120 in the forts, the crash of splinters, the explosion of boilers and magazines, the shouts and cries, the shrieks of scalded and drowning men; add to this the belching flashes of guns, blazing rafts of burning steamboats, the river full of fire, and you have a picture of the battle that was all confined to Plaquemines Bend."

In all, an estimated 16,800 cannonballs were fired at the forts. On the fifth day, seventeen of Farragut's ships succeeded in passing them. The Union fleet went on to take New Orleans, and the forts eventually surrendered, thanks in no small part to a mutiny at Fort Jackson. There is no telling what might have happened had the Confederacy been able to maintain its hold on the mouth of the Mississippi. Perhaps the war might have taken a different turn altogether. As for Triumph, here in the deepest of the Deep South, it was the victorious Union soldiers who gave the town its name.

After the war, Fort Jackson was used as a prison and then as a training base. By 1927, it was declared surplus property and sold to private owners, who donated the land to Plaquemines Parish. The fort was made a National Historic Monument in 1960, and restoration began, an imposing task considering it had become a mud-filled, snake-infested, eighty-one-acre mess.

It was April 18, 1996—exactly 134 years to the day after Farragut's fleet attacked—when we arrived at Fort Jackson. Nestled against the river was a spacious, pentagonal compound surrounded by old brick ramparts and a moat the color and consistency of split-pea soup. Empty bottles and cans rested atop the murky waters. We crossed a bridge and walked through a tunnel to the center of the compound. A forlorn cannon rested in the middle of the grounds. A decidedly unhistoric vending machine leaned against a wall. Fort Jackson had the look of an aging widow still dyeing her hair to keep up appearances.

We walked into the Fort Jackson Museum, which housed a collection of old maps, cannonballs, guns, harmonicas, belt buckles, and buttons. A sixtyish woman behind a desk, assistant curator Peggy Shackelford, welcomed us. As we settled into conversation, I asked her not about the history of Fort Jackson but about Triumph. Her answers brought everything into focus. Suddenly, all of it made sense—the stilts, the mobile homes, the church sign, the agricultural struggle, the sparse population, the impermanence, the starting over.

"Everything we do and say," she explained, "begins and ends with the hurricanes."

Ever since Columbus lost a couple of ships five hundred years ago, hurricanes have been a significant part of American history. In the twentieth century alone, more than twelve thousand Americans have been killed by them. Since 1891, more than two dozen such storms have made landfall on the Louisiana coast, which is to hurricanes what California is to earthquakes and Kansas is to tornados. There are also, on average, twenty tornados a year in Louisiana, which have caused nearly 250 deaths since 1934. Often, these accompany hurricanes like hyenas follow a lion attack.

Plaquemines Parish is a hurricane magnet. The Mississippi River, creator of the fertile delta, has also been its destroyer. Hurricanes enter the delta against the current. The river's water combines with the storm surge to form a massive tide of calamity. Such was the case with Betsy and Camille.

At eight o'clock on the morning of Thursday, September 9, 1965, the weather bureau began notifying the residents of Plaquemines Parish of a threatening storm. Given the name Betsy, the tropical storm traveled rapidly and in an erratic path, which prevented emergency agencies from issuing evacuation commands until the last moment. Though residents were told to evacuate immediately, many still went about their usual preparations of taping windows and packing valuables. Those efforts, as it turned out, were akin to using a cardigan for a bulletproof vest. As birds fled the shore for inland safety and the sky turned an ominous purple and then gray and black, some 90 percent of the parish's residents left their homes for safer ground to the north. Peggy Shackelford, six months pregnant, was one of them. She, her husband, her eleven-year-old son, and her infant daughter headed up the coast amid bumper-to-bumper traffic as the wind became a high-pitched wail.

By six o'clock that evening, just ten hours after the first evacuation warning, Betsy, now a full-fledged hurricane, began to move across the state. She would break all records for Louisiana hurricanes, traveling up the river at more than seventeen miles per hour and packing wind gusts up to 160 miles per hour. Century-old oak trees were whipped to the ground and shredded. Homes were tossed into crumpled heaps. As the storm drove the salty seas of the gulf into the muddy Mississippi, walls of water as high as sixteen feet hurdled the levees and swept across the parish. Boats were thrown inland; homes and buildings were washed out to sea. In Boothville, down the road from Triumph, one man clung to a tree throughout the night after his house was splintered. In Pilottown, a community at the river's end reachable only by boat, another man floated for hours, finally washing up a few miles from his yard the next morning.

Despite erroneous early reports that bodies were being removed by the truckload in the parish, only nine of the eighty-one deaths blamed on the hurricane were Plaquemines residents. The reports that everything had been destroyed were closer to the mark. Nearly 95 percent of the parish was flooded. It was no longer easy to distinguish between the gulf, the river, and the land. In Venice, a tugboat rested atop a firehouse. Up

Peggy Shackelford

the road, a brick house blocked the highway. Hundreds of dead cattle were entangled among snapped electrical poles and coffins that had floated out of cemeteries, creating an eerie aftermath. Water moccasins slithered across the parish, and the few cattle that remained alive wandered in a crazed frenzy. The Red Cross estimated that more than 4,600 homes, 700 trailers, 500 boats, 270 business establishments, and 140 farm buildings were either damaged or destroyed. Total damages reached $1.2 billion, making Betsy the first-ever billion-dollar storm.

Peggy returned to find only the shell of her house intact. The Shackelfords lived with four other relatives in a cramped, government-supplied trailer for a few months before their house was remodeled into a bigger, safer, more impressive structure. Their recovery mirrored that of the parish. In a brief editorial only a week after the hurricane, the regional newspaper concluded, "Plaquemines will rise again." And it did. Within three weeks, most of the water was pumped out of the parish, the last spot to dry being Fort Jackson. A few weeks later, schools reopened. By mid-November, 75 percent of the parish's residents had returned.

The inhabitants of the piece of land jutting into the gulf still kept a wary eye on the sea, as evidenced by a poem one of them penned for a book called *Betsy and Camille, Sisters of Destruction*. The poem was titled "That Was No Lady," and its final stanza went,

> It seems like only yesterday, we bid that girl "good-bye"
> As we keep a watchful vigil on that sultry, summer sky.
> And still we pray for tropics quiet, and ask our dear Lord, "Please"
> To tame those tempests to the east, and hope that he agrees.

He agreed for only forty-seven months. In early August 1969, a tropical storm emerged off the coast of Africa and began moving westward into the Caribbean. By August 15, it had been named Camille. Hurricanes are ranked on a scale from I (minimal) to 5 (catastrophic). Betsy had been a Category 3 hurricane; Camille was a Category 5.

When the storm was 140 miles southwest of New Orleans, an air force reconnaissance plane flew into its eye and reported staggering readings—winds of 190 miles per hour, gale-force winds as far as 150 miles from the center, a tidal surge extending out from the eye for 50 miles and reaching heights of 20 feet. The newspapers had called Betsy a once-in-a-century hurricane. This one, four years later, was worse.

On August 17, Camille came up the Mississippi at full force, its top recorded wind velocity exceeding two hundred miles per hour. In the aftermath, strange and unbelievable stories came out of Plaquemines Parish. The tidal surge left a 138-foot barge blocking the main highway for weeks. A trailer was found wrapped around a tree, crushed to a height of one yard by the powerful winds. The steeple of St. Anthony's Church in Boothville was discovered a half-mile away atop the levee, the bell still inside. A pay telephone was found, but not the building it had once been attached to. A woman's purse showed up in a cemetery miles from her home; it was sitting by her nephew's tombstone.

Though only seven Plaquemines residents died, hundreds of people across the South lost their lives to the hurricane, half of them due to flash floods as far north as Virginia. Thousands more were injured. Camille exceeded Betsy in total destruction, the damage to Plaquemines Parish alone estimated at $500 million. Most of what had been rebuilt after the first hurricane was annihilated by its younger sister. "For a short time," noted the 1970 Buras High School yearbook, "it seemed as if our town was gone forever."

While preparing to evacuate for Betsy, Peggy Shackelford had placed her valued photographs and mementos high on a closet shelf. Though her house was severely damaged, the photographs were saved. "So when Camille came, I thought I might be fortunate again," she explained with a sad chuckle. "I had an attic, and I put everything up in it. But when we came back, the whole house was gone."

"If you can meet with Triumph and Disaster and treat those two imposters just the same," Rudyard Kipling wrote, "yours is the Earth and everything in it." Well, Peggy Shackelford had met disaster on the outskirts of Triumph, and there was nothing left.

"I was born and raised here," she said. "And when we came back a few weeks later, I didn't even know where we were. It was like you were out in the desert. I just felt like I wanted to die. Everything you worked so long and so hard for . . . You think you have it all, and then overnight, it's gone."

Once again, however, the people prevailed. Within four months, 85 percent of the parish's residents returned, a total of 1,116 building permits were issued, and 7,500 students were back in school. As for the Shackelfords, they simply started over again. Although they're still forced to evacuate once a year on average, they're not going to let a little thing like a hurricane push them around. "That's right," said Peggy with a defiant shrug. "And I guess if a hurricane takes this house, I'll rebuild again."

Jack Kerouac once compared the Mississippi River to a torrent of broken souls. But I don't think so. Not this part of the river, at least. Bent, perhaps, but not broken.

Age-old questions were rumbling around my brain. Do we each have a destiny, or do we make our own? Do we determine our future or abide by it? In Plaquemines Parish, it might be phrased like this: Can we defy the wind?

I was pondering this because I couldn't quite figure out where the people of Triumph fit in. Some were making the point that no force of nature could force their hand. Others were just as surely subscribing to fate, feeling that no metaphorical retreat to higher ground could stave off the inevitable.

Most people are somewhere in the middle regarding this subject, believing in destiny, but only as a product of choice. I've always been at one of the extremes, feeling strongly that predestination is a crutch for inaction. To me, "It's God's will" has always meant "It's out of my hands." And that means forfeiting a role in sculpting a future.

Then I met Max Latham, a charismatic, enthusiastic ecclesiastic. He was the voice of the other extreme, having placed himself unconditionally in the Lord's hands. He may not have changed my mind, but he did soften my perspective.

I met Max through his sixteen-year-old daughter, who was working at a checkout line at the Triumph Grocery Store. She wore her long, straight black hair pulled back by a red barrette, a red jacket, bright red lipstick, and a large, gold *Sylvia* necklace. Sylvia said her mother was coming by momentarily to take her home. Her father, the pastor of a church down the road in Boothville, would be there, too. She was sure they would love to talk.

Amy and I followed them down the highway and turned right at a gravel road just past a *Jesus Saves* sign. A few hundred feet later, across from an orange grove, was what appeared to be half a house, though it was actually a small structure with the beginning of an addition. A trailer rested in a corner of the front yard, along with an enormous antenna sprouting from the ground and rising so high it seemed to stab the sky. It was as out of place as a high-rise in a wheat field.

Max Latham sat on a swinging bench on the front porch of the house, reading the Old Testament. He was just short of his fiftieth birthday, well tanned, with bright blue eyes behind wire-rim glasses. We settled in some folding chairs on the porch as Max's wife, Rhonda, joined him on the bench. He was thin and angular; she was just the opposite, heavyset with a round face bearing sunglasses and big earrings in the shape of an R. Sylvia brought a pitcher of lemonade out to the porch, and a puppy sniffed around curiously. Lucky, they called him, which spoke volumes.

Max's parents were born at opposite ends of the Mississippi River. His mother was from Minneapolis, his father a native Mississippian. They met while both were in the army. Max spent his early years in Mississippi before his father moved the family down to Plaquemines and took a job driving a truck for a company that rented oil pumps. After his parents divorced when he was thirteen, Max lived with his father and helped raise his three younger siblings. He attended Buras High School and then majored in electrical engineering at Louisiana State University, working his way through school in the oil fields. That was chapter I in the Gumpian saga of Max Latham. The rest was a tale like a feather in the wind.

"I was the first one back in here after Hurricane Betsy," said Max in a voice that was bayou Bill Clinton. "I was at college, and when I heard about the storm, I headed down the road. They told me the place was so totally destroyed that they wouldn't let me through. But I said, 'I'm going in. I want to see what's happened to my house.' So when I got to Belle Chase, they said, 'You can't go any further. They've got National Guards at Port Sulphur. They're gonna stop you.' I said, 'Well, I'm gonna try.' When I got to Port Sulphur, I got pulled over. There was the National Guard. So I pulled out my wallet, and all I had was my LSU student ID card. I don't even know why I did it, but I just flashed that card. They must have thought it looked official or something, because they said, 'Right on through, sir.' "

He laughed at the memory, but it was a bittersweet laugh. "When I got to Empire, they had a drawbridge and the National Guard and rifles to stop looters and all that. Same thing! I flashed that LSU student card

The Lathams

and went right on through. When I pulled up to the Buras school and walked in, Leander Perez and all the government officials were there. They all wanted to know how I got through. I told them I drove in. They said, 'You can't drive in. Did you come across the levee by boat or something?' I said, 'There's my car right there, a '57 Chevy.' They said, 'You can't get in here! It's impossible!' I said, 'Here I am!' "

That moment was Max Latham's life in abbreviated form. Whether it was good fortune or unwavering faith that got him through was a matter of perspective, but Max always seemed to get where he was going.

I asked what it was like when he returned home after the storm. There was a long pause before he answered, and then tears began to form in the corners of his eyes.

"I have never seen such destruction. We never had a bunch of money, and we'd spent years building that house, just a plain, little house. And the thing was just a pile of lumber. You know, I had never seen my dad discouraged before. For the first time in my life, the only time, I saw my father cry."

He let out a deep sigh and reined in his emotions. "Things like that, they're indelibly imprinted in your mind. People still talk about it. Whenever you've got get-togethers, they still talk about the storm. The only thing that's ever come close was a freeze that destroyed all of the orange trees years ago and just ruined that industry. And then the oil bust. But none of those had the same impact."

At the very least, it changed the course of Max's life. Four years later, after the Lathams rebuilt their home, and as he was preparing to accept a commission as a second lieutenant in the army at the height of the Vietnam War, Hurricane Camille hit. Max's father had died of a heart attack a month earlier. Now, nearly everything the family owned was destroyed. Only four credits from graduation, Max dropped out of school to take care of his family. In the eighteen months before he returned to his studies, he found what he thought was his calling. Before he died, Max's father had purchased a thirty-two-foot boat to ferry workers to and from oil platforms. "I felt this was the way to get rich," said Max. "I went back and got my degree and then came right back down here. I didn't even go to the commencement. I was on an oil rig offshore."

Max always thought big. When he started his boat business with the old, rusty tub his father had left him, he didn't settle for naming it Max's Boat Rental. He called it Ocean Transportation Systems. Despite having little or no credit, he began amassing more boats—the *Sea Horse*, the *Sea Raven*, the *Sea Rover*, the *Sea Rider*, and his first hundred-footer, the *Sea Serpent*. He was seeing green.

"He wanted to be a millionaire before he was thirty," said Rhonda, amazement and distaste in her voice.

"That was my goal," he admitted. "That's where I was headed. I mean, I look at it now, and it was just pride and arrogance, you know? I just kept ordering more boats to fulfill my goal."

But then Max Latham found religion, and he found it through Rhonda.

"I married her in 1971."

"Seventy-two," she corrected.

"Okay, '72. She was from the end of the road. She lived in a camp they called the Chevron Camp. They built homes to attract people to work, you know." I pictured an oil-and-water version of copper-and-sage-brush Inspiration, Arizona.

"In 1974, our first child was born with brain damage. So my wife began to attend church a lot. Just looking for healing, for God to do a miracle. In the process of that, she went to this little church where I happen to be pastoring now, the Miracle Assembly of God, and she got saved. Her life changed drastically. I mean, she had been a killer! A real Boothville bomber! She was a wildcat."

"You don't have to tell them all that!" Rhonda boomed.

"Well, in order to know how her life had changed, from a smokin', drinkin', cussin' woman who didn't keep house . . . But her life changed so dramatically that, within a month, I decided to go find out what happened to her. Her mom, who lived down here all her life and was a confirmed Catholic, thought she had gotten into a cult, she had changed so much. So anyway, I got saved." He said this matter-of-factly, but I had no doubt it was the defining moment of his life.

"I simply knelt at the altar one Wednesday night, five people in the church, and I said, 'God, I'm sorry.' And that's when I became changed. I lost the desire to become the biggest crew-boat owner in the gulf. And you know, it's weird the way the Lord does things. When I got saved, my desire then was to preach. But the Lord had different plans. I was not nearly ready. And so I told the Lord that if he wanted me to stay in that business, he'd have to make me excited about it again, which he did. We committed that business to the Lord and began to make it a witness in everything we did."

It was the kind of talk that always makes me uncomfortable. It's one thing to believe in divine intervention. It's another thing to believe in a God with the breadth of vision, the power, and the inclination to set a course for every person on the planet. It's quite another thing still to contend that God, who deals with famines and earthquakes and hurricanes on a daily basis, is concerned with the way a simple man in Louisiana runs his boat business. I was prepared to react with incredulity and cynicism. But the man sitting in front of me with the Old Testament in his hands had an earnestness about him that was hard to dismiss.

"So when I got saved," Max continued, "the Lord tells me he wants me to change the names of my boats. You know what the next three boats were gonna be named? The *Sea Devil*, the *Sea Demon*, and the *Sea Dragon!*"

Rhonda shook her head. "All related to Satan."

"The Lord said to change it, and I said, 'I can't change the names. This is my trademark now.' God says, 'You're a different person now, and I want you to change the names.'"

So Max's boats became the *King of Kings*, the *Redeemer*, the *Resurrection*, the *Rapture*. His last boat was the *Revelation*, which was what he had next.

Having decided to "pioneer a church," as he put it, Max moved the family to the town of Dry Prong in central Louisiana. "Now, here we are in a little church with twenty people, just two men, and only one's got a job," he recalled. "Total income that year was six thousand dollars. My wife and I had just given up a fifty-thousand-dollar-a-year business. I told my brother, 'You're president. I'm leaving.' And I told the Lord, 'If I'm gonna live like this, if I'm a pastor, I'm gonna do it with no help from the outside.' "

"Livin' by faith!" Rhonda announced.

"I didn't have a job, and the Lord provided. Oh boy, you wouldn't believe the miracles—"

"Miracles!" shouted Rhonda.

"—that the Lord provided for us."

"Like what?" I wondered. The question came out sounding like a challenge.

"Well, we get up there, and we make a commitment we're not gonna work. We didn't take any salary from our business, and we had no income from the church. Every week, the kids would run to the basket when everybody left to see if there was any grocery money in there. But soon after we got there, our church decided they were gonna support us with, I forget, two hundred or three hundred dollars a month. Just in answer to prayer, people we didn't even know would bring groceries."

"The light bill would be due," Rhonda explained, "and people would walk up to me and say, 'I felt impressed to bring you this seventy-five dollars.' "

"And then there was the well," said Max. "Rhonda's mom and dad owned some property out on the bayou that had some oil wells on it. The wells would produce a check maybe every quarter. You know, little royalty checks, maybe five or ten dollars. Well, soon as we get up there, her mom and dad write us, 'Man! They worked Grandpa's oil well, and that thing is a gusher right now! So we want to send that to y'all.' That was three or four hundred dollars a month. It was just miracle after miracle.

And four years later, when we were getting ready to leave, we got a call, and they told us the oil well dried up. Well, it lasted through the whole thing."

Apparently, if you look hard enough for miracles, you can find them. If gushers and groceries and a good-hearted congregation will do, then burning bushes need not apply. The miracles continued when the Lathams moved back to Triumph. Max returned to his boat business just in time for the oil industry to go belly up. The miracle, as he saw it through his rose-colored perspective, wasn't that he found his company $2.5 million in debt, it was that his biggest creditors wrote off the judgment for $5,000 in cash.

So Max turned to his next adventure. Like Forrest Gump, he bought a boat and went trolling for shrimp. Unlike Gump, he didn't become a millionaire. "Worst mistake I ever made," he said. "I never did so bad in my life. I'd always had success in everything I tried, and this liked to kill me. It literally liked to kill me." After a couple of years, he gave up on it. No miracles this time.

Then the local pastor resigned, and the congregation in Boothville asked Max to take over. He moved the family out of his brother's double-wide trailer, bought a house for two thousand dollars, moved it to its current location, and began fixing it up.

And then he built a radio station.

"You said you're writing about Triumph? Well, this truly is a triumph of the Lord," he asserted, his preacher's cadence becoming more and more evident. "You know, you don't think things are connected," he continued. "I said, 'Lord, if you was gonna call me to be a preacher, why didn't I go into law? I mean, electrical engineering? I wasted all those years.' But now, I think maybe God did have his hand on me in those prior years."

It was during a mission to Venezuela in 1987 that the concept took root. Shocked at the poverty and impressed by the multitudes in Caracas, he figured he could reach millions of people via the local airwaves. Max seriously considered moving to Venezuela until the Lord instructed him otherwise. "He said, 'You don't have to go to Venezuela. You can reach the world from right where you're at.' And so that's what my wife and I committed to doing—trying to reach the world from right here. From right in Triumph."

A local man had purchased an AM station from the church but still owed money on it. Max convinced him to donate the station back to the congregation. He secured a license for an FM channel, too. He took an unwanted satellite dish from a cable station in New Orleans and reassembled it in his front yard. He and his oldest son spent two years building an antenna for about fifteen hundred dollars; Max estimated it should have cost fifteen thousand. He was able to afford a transmitter when a man walked up to him in the Boothville post office one day and handed him a thousand dollars for it.

Every morning, he stacks his CDs—contemporary Christian music for 91.9 FM, southern gospel for 1510 AM. Every afternoon at twelve-thirty, he offers a sermon. And every day, he gives thanks to the station manager in the sky. "All of this was given to us through prayer," he insisted. "That's the only way."

The deeper I delved into the life of Max Latham, the more I had to question my preconceived notions. I have always felt that triumph means beating the system, choosing a destiny and willing yourself there, even if it means going against the current. Max had simply built a boat, set the sail, and allowed the breeze to take him where it might. His success toppled my precepts.

Certainly, he took fatalism to an extreme. None of his five children, for instance, had ever set foot in a public school. All were taught at home. "We train 'em right here. We use the word of God to train our children," he explained. "And we began to see God really teaching our kids, and he got that rebellious spirit out of them at a young age. I'll tell you, I'd take a dozen more right now, because they are such a blessing. I mean, of all the blessings God's given me, our kids top 'em, by far."

His joy in his offspring led him to write a book, *Abortion in the Church*,

a two-hundred-page, self-published rant against birth control. "The message is this: You need to let God have charge of your family, whether he wants you to have zero children or fifty. Let the Lord do it," said Max. "My wife and I have not taken any prevention methods since right after we got married, and the Lord has only given us five kids. We'd love to have another right now, but the Lord has not given it."

It was for this kind of talk that I had been prepared to be at odds with Max Latham, having long held a bias less against those who use the Lord's name in vain than against those who use it in excess, and who attribute any personal achievement to the machinations of a higher power. And yet he revealed none of the stagnation and acquiescence I expected. He was, in fact, one of the most self-empowered men I had ever met.

Max was an engineer, an oilman, a shrimp-boat captain, a disc jockey, a preacher, a teacher, an author. He was an inventor, having patented a small plastic device used on boats. He was an entrepreneur, having created a business—now run by his son—to market that invention. He was a dreamer, having named his business Latham Industries and his publishing company Light the World Publications. He was a man whose opinions and metaphysical perspective were diametrically opposed to mine. But he was a man I had to respect all the same. No matter whom he gave the credit to, he had triumphed, at least in spirit.

"I tell you," he remarked almost apologetically after revealing his plans to market his invention, "I get off on these tangents."

I told him I thought there weren't enough tangents in life.

Max walked us to our car and placed a hand on Amy's shoulder and one on mine. "Let me tell you something," he said. "You know what happened? Today, you two have received a new set of prayer partners."

"We'll take it," I replied, and I meant it. After all, it couldn't hurt.

He nodded toward the heavens. "'Cause I just don't believe in coincidences. They're all divine appointments."

As we left Triumph and headed back up the west bank of the river, we caught a glimpse of something red and gold soaring high above us against the cloudless sky. It was a kite, dipping and darting haphazardly with each unpredictable gust. Somebody was trying to harness the wind.

GLORY,
GEORGIA

> *'Twas like a battlefield with all the glory missin'.*
> Rudyard Kipling

Over the previous couple of weeks, through Pride and Hope and Triumph, I had sampled a taste of southern attitudes, southern tragedies, southern dreams. Yet I still couldn't seem to grab hold of what it meant to be southern, what made the South a region unlike any other, a geographic state of mind. I was an outsider trying to understand an entire physical and psychological subculture, and I had to admit I was doing so according to criteria that inevitably catered to my biases.

I am your typical northern liberal, a damn Yankee if there ever was one. I was raised amid a northern perspective and view the cataclysmic events of the 1860s and 1960s through a northern lens. When I learned about the Civil War and the civil-rights movement, the North was *us* and the South was *them*. There's an old fable, "The Man and the Lion," in which the lion complains that he will not be so misrepresented "when the lions write history." But I was beginning to understand how difficult it was to swap points of view. And I was beginning to wonder if I was open-minded enough to let the South roar a little.

It took me longer than it should have to realize that the South was no more definable than any other place where the view depended on the angle. Is New York City defined by Broadway, the Village, or Harlem? Is Chicago Al Capone, Richard Daley, or Michael Jordan? Is California a Berkeley protest, a Napa winery, or a power lunch at Paramount? The South that Amy and I had sampled in a fortnight was part of the story. But the whole was greater—and more elusive—than the sum of its parts. I was hoping the journey to Glory might clarify matters, but it's hard to find something if you don't know what you're looking for.

Given my confusion, it seemed appropriate that our route from Triumph to Glory took us through Montgomery, Alabama. Like much of the South, it was an odd juxtaposition of iconic places. Jefferson Davis's home during the first fourteen months of the Civil War sat steps away from the State Capitol, a reminder that Montgomery started the war as the Confederate capital. But just down the block was Martin Luther King's Dexter Avenue Baptist Church, the very genesis of the civil-rights movement. And just steps away from that was the Civil Rights Memorial. We visited Montgomery on a Sunday in late April, when the city was quiet and clean and gentle enough to palliate the physical and spiritual wars it had seen. But if Montgomery taught me anything about the South, it was that here, conceptual crises were met head-on. War and revolution have required this region to confront profound issues without flinching. The result, I think, is a more straightforward society—while much of the rest of the nation still flinches.

From the Confederacy's cradle, Highway 82 would take us straight to Glory. A succession of pastures and pine trees lined the road, which was devoid of any oncoming traffic for long stretches. Counting the distance markers passed for excitement on this leg of the journey, perhaps because it was the first time we saw signs in kilometers as well as miles. It was as if the South had won the war and gone metric. The high drama came when mile marker 192 and kilometer marker 308 stood at the very same spot.

After speeding through historic Union Springs (*A Wonderful Way of Life*), followed (thirty miles later) by the turnoff for Batesville, where a marker commemorated something known as the *Election Riot of 1874*, we finally reached Alabama's end at a quaint, old town with large antebellum homes surrounding a bustling business district. This was Eufala, a name that sounded strikingly familiar to me. I later realized we'd been hearing it constantly since we reached the South—as in, "Just go to the end of the block and take your first right, you follah?" We crossed a bridge over Lake Eufala and into Georgia.

It's popular to say that Georgia was started by convicts, but it isn't necessarily fair. Originally part of the Carolinas, it was chartered in 1733 as the last of the thirteen colonies and named after King George II. Georgia was both a defensive strategy—a buffer zone against Spanish Florida—and a philanthropic experiment. British reformist James Oglethorpe, astounded by the treatment of debtors imprisoned in Britain's jails, conceived a plan to transport them to Georgia, where they could rehabilitate themselves through labor and make some money for the colony's proprietors in the process. So Georgia became a second chance for penniless farmers, sailors, and merchants, as well as persecuted Scots, Protestant minorities, and Jews.

The laws of Georgia, too, were a product of Oglethorpe's reformist ideals. Alcohol and slavery were prohibited, for instance, and trade with the Indians was regulated. But the colonists quickly began to chafe at the restrictions, which fell one by one. By 1742, there was rum. By 1749, there were slaves. As the white population began to grow and its landholdings did the same, Native Americans gave an early name to the region—*E Cunnau Nux Ulgee*, which means, roughly, "People greedily grasping after the red men's land." Eventually, Oglethorpe surrendered power to the British government and returned to his home in Surrey, his utopia a dismal failure.

After crossing the state line, we could have taken the highway straight to Glory, but we opted for a couple of detours that seemed to illustrate the southern dichotomy. First, we headed through unexpected hills to the hamlet of Plains, home of Jimmy Carter. Historians tend to treat the Carter administration harshly; voters in 1980 certainly did. But the man had the youth, the moral backbone, and the trial-by-fire experience to become one of our nation's finest ex-presidents. I looked for a lesson there concerning my regional biases and figured it was no more fair to judge Carter by four years in the White House than to judge the South by four years of war. We bought some boiled peanuts as an homage to the man and a peace offering to the place.

Carter's election, when I was all of eight years old, represented to many the region's reacceptance into mainstream America. He was the New South personified. Our next stop was the other bookend—the tragic end of the Old South, as memorialized at Andersonville National Historic Site.

In November 1863, the Confederacy's War Department ordered the construction of a prison here, amid the sloping meadows of southern Georgia. Slaves and free blacks built a stockade encompassing sixteen and a half acres, but before the prison was ready, the first trainload of Union prisoners arrived. Little shelter was available, and no streets had been laid out. A brook running through the stockade served as a waste system, as well as the site of cooking facilities. The water supply was hopelessly inadequate.

Major Henry Wirz, a Swiss émigré and medical doctor who had been wounded in battle, was placed in charge. Depending on whose history you believe, he was either tremendously incompetent, unfeeling, or overburdened. The prison was built to house ten thousand men. Within six months, there were thirty-three thousand Union soldiers in the Andersonville population—and less than four square yards of space per prisoner. Smallpox, scurvy, dysentery, dehydration, gangrene, typhoid fever, and starvation thinned the ranks of the captives, as did a gang of marauding raiders within the prison walls. By May 1865, when Major Wirz was arrested by Union troops, thirteen thousand prisoners had died.

Not a single Rebel general was tried for treason following the war, but Wirz was sentenced to death and hanged. There's a monument to him in the middle of Andersonville, erected by the United Daughters of the Confederacy "to rescue his name from the stigma attached to it by embittered prejudice." Wirz, the monument's inscription claims, discharged his duty with as much humanity as possible, considering the "harsh circumstances of the times." To me, it seemed a monument to the power of perspective as much as anything.

One hundred thirty years later, a little store, Bill's Good Ole Days Antiques, sat at the site of Wirz's old office. There, we found refrigerator magnets and dolls of large-lipped black figures cooking pancakes and eating watermelon. There were T-shirts and bumper stickers declaring *The South Was Right* and *The South Will Rise Again* and *Old Gray, New Blood*. And there was a constant barrage of Confederate Battle Flags. Indeed, it seemed that everywhere we went in Georgia, we encountered that flag—on biker jackets and teenagers' T-shirts, on decals and bumper stickers, on mud flaps and key chains, on the front porches of houses and the back windows of pickup trucks.

The irony is that the Battle Flag that flies so brazenly as we approach the millennium was never officially adopted by the Confederacy. The first Rebel flag, known as the Stars and Bars, was approved by the Confederate Congress on March 4, 1861, in Montgomery. It featured a broad white stripe between two broad red ones and had seven white stars on a blue background in the top left corner (representing, at that time, the seven seceded states). But it had a fatal flaw. In the heat of battle, it was occasionally mistaken for the Stars and Stripes. Not a good idea.

So the Battle Flag was introduced on the battlefield in October 1861. The Stars and Bars remained the Confederacy's official flag until May 1863, when the Stainless Banner was unveiled. This was a white flag with a smaller version of the battle flag in the top left corner. But this presented problems, too. Hanging limp from a pole, it looked like a flag of truce. Another bad idea. In March 1865, only a few weeks before the South's surrender, a third and final official Confederate flag was unveiled. This one added a red bar across the right end of the Stainless Banner. But it was too late to be of any use. So the Battle Flag continued to be the fighters' favorite throughout the war.

More than a century later, it has emerged as a cultural lightning rod between the compassion of the New South and the recalcitrance of the Old. On one side are those who claim the flag is a tribute to heritage and fundamental southern beliefs like local government and the right to rebel. If you ban the Battle Flag because it is a reminder of slavery, they contend, then you have to ban Old Glory because of Indian genocide. But the other side might point out, for example, that because the Confederate emblem wasn't added to Georgia's state flag until 1956, it was clearly a response to the mandate to integrate. They condemn it as a favorite banner of hate groups, as an opportunity to publicly pledge racism under the guise of regional affiliation, as an example of taunting masquerading as tradition. To them, the flag is as inflammatory as the bumper stickers that serve as its captions, the ones that say things like, *If I had known this, I would have picked my own cotton.*

The debate still rages through Georgia. Governor Zell Miller, the great-grandson of a Confederate soldier, argued that the Battle Flag portion of the state flag should be removed. He urged legislators to have the "sheer guts" to remove an emblem that linked the state to "the dark side of the Confederacy." He eventually dropped the plea when the issue became too divisive—and when he saw that 60 percent of Georgians wanted to keep the present flag. But the battle continues on many fronts. In Dekalb County, Sidney Dorsey, the county's first black sheriff, removed

the state flag from the county jail, saying it represented a time when the country was divided. In Atlanta, black mayor Maynard Jackson signed an ordinance banning the state flag from the city and replacing it with an older, non-Rebel version. In response, several Georgia legislators drafted a bill that proposed to cut off state funds to the city. The sons of sixties-era civil-rights activists rallied; the Sons of Confederate Veterans did the same.

Not only in Georgia but throughout the South, there has been widespread rebellion against the Rebel flag. In Alabama, the Battle Flag was removed from the state capitol. In Mississippi, black citizens sued to remove the Confederate emblem from the state flag, while at Ole Miss, the football coach urged fans to stop waving the Battle Flag at games. Even Hootie and the Blowfish, the integrated rock band from South Carolina, got involved. Darius Rucker, the band's black lead singer, wrote a song called "Drowning" that decried the flying of the Confederate flag above the South Carolina statehouse. The governor proposed moving it to a spot alongside a monument to Confederate soldiers, but three out of four voters said the flag, first raised in 1962, should remain where it was. Rucker received death threats.

The debate has even reached the floor of the United States Senate. Four times this century, the Senate renewed the patent on the insignia of the United Daughters of the Confederacy, a seven-starred Confederate flag. But in May 1993, first-term Illinois senator Carol Moseley-Braun, the first and only black woman in the Senate, argued against it. "This vote is about race. It is about racial symbols, the racial past, and the single most painful episode in American history. It is absolutely unacceptable to me and to millions of Americans, black and white, that we would put the imprimatur of the United States on a symbol of this kind of idea," she stated, her voice shaking. "The issue is whether or not Americans such as myself who believe in the promise of this country . . . will have to suffer the indignity of being reminded time and time again that at one point in the country's history we were human chattel."

In the end, twenty-seven senators reversed their votes, and the patent was not renewed. Among them was Alabama's Howell Heflin, the grandson of a Confederate army surgeon, who said, "We must move forward. We must realize we live in America today."

In Louisiana, Jefferson Davis Elementary School was renamed after the first black mayor of New Orleans. In Mississippi, Ole Miss faculty passed a resolution seeking to end the playing of "Dixie" at university events. In Virginia, the state senate voted to retire the state song, "Carry Me Back to Old Virginia," because of its references to "darkeys" and "old massa." The South is moving forward—as fast as possible, perhaps— on a tightrope between history and humanity.

We hopped on Interstate 75 and took it south for sixty-five miles to the city of Tifton, where we set up camp at Amy's RV Park, which delighted my wife until she learned that Amy was the owners' dog. The following day, we unhitched the Day Tripper and headed east along the same Highway 82 we'd first climbed aboard in Montgomery. Seven miles later, we were in Berrien County, established five years before the Civil War. Nearly half the county consisted of farms that produced corn, peanuts, soybeans, wheat, watermelons, squash, pecans, peas, cotton, and tobacco. Bright lavender wildflowers lined the road, as did a couple of dead skunks.

The first town we passed in Berrien bore the marvelously whimsical name of Enigma, which came about when settlers were unsuccessful in finding an appropriate name for their community and one commented that the place was "just an enigma." So they left it at that. The second

sold
were
rout
had
and
som
rous

wher
Sout

(

some
ries o
tion.
was o
thoug

N
of mo
white
Meth
sermo
his ba
ward h
"Is thi
H
here ar
little tl
"S
"C
the nar
a town

town was Alapaha, a quiet, tree-lined hamlet that the old-timers pronounced "Loppy-haw." The name is believed to have come from the Creek Indian word *apala*, meaning "on the other side."

We stopped at a grocery store to buy soft drinks and were considering asking directions to our destination when a man with wild hair and a salt-and-pepper beard spied Amy's Nikon 6006. "Nice camera," he said. As we walked out of the store, he approached us. "I'm not trying to get all in your business or anything," he said, "but you look like you could use some help."

Did we look that much like tourists? "Well," I explained, "we're looking for Glory."

He ran his hand through his hair. "Glory? Well, about halfway between here and Willacoochie, which is about twelve miles down the road, was a location called Glory. That was the original Glory community. There might have even been a train stop there. I'm not absolutely sure about that."

Mark was his name. He considered himself an amateur historian. He was from the area. He was forty-seven years old. Still, his knowledge of Glory was limited to somewheres and might-have-beens. It wasn't a promising sign.

"Do you know how Glory got its name?" I asked.

"No, I don't. But I never really investigated it, because it was insignificant in certain ways."

I wasn't sure if he meant the origin of the name or the community itself. Regardless, I pressed the issue. I told him of our figurative exploration of the concept of glory, of my suspicion that the South's glory was based more on romantic hindsight than historical fact. He ran his hand through his hair again.

"I don't know. Now, you're talking in abstracts. I'm not a philosopher. I used to think I was. What was the glory of the South?"

"That's what I'm trying to figure out. I'm thinking maybe it's something that continues to be redefined."

"Well, from this area, we had two delegates to the Confederate

Co
cul
for
illu
tho
get
kic
anc
rad
glo

pos
by
It
Ge
tut
tar
rig
Pre
a fe
tur
wal
Sto

mil
but
Gei
cap
his
hur

ing

consider a town. Just that one trading post, and that was it."

"How long ago was that?"

"It must be twelve or fifteen years since it's been gone." The man—his name was Greg—waved at some gnats that were gathering around the conversation. "When I was small, we used to ride our motorcycles over there and get a drink on Sunday afternoons. But that was fifteen or sixteen years ago. It's been awhile."

"So we're in Alapaha now?"

"Well, it really is nothing. But our mail comes to Alapaha. There's probably eight or nine hundred people who live in Alapaha, but Glory's never been maybe two people."

Continuing, we found ourselves behind a pickup truck with a bumper sticker. *Confederate Pride*, it said, next to the Battle Flag. My thoughts turned to those still extolling the glory of the Rebel flag. There are today two national societies of Confederate descendants—the United Daughters of the Confederacy, organized in 1894, and the Sons of Confederate Veterans, formed in 1896. Skepticism was my initial reaction to such organizations. I figured that supporting the Rebel soldier meant supporting the Rebel cause. But the more time I spent in the South, the more I began to understand why Confederate descendants strive to maintain memories that others consider long dead or better forgotten. There are few behaviors more instinctive than protection of a family's honor. There are few nerves more tender than the disparagement of ancestors. Mine were eastern Europeans, and most knowledge of them was lost amid the years and the miles. But southern ties remain fresh and well tended. When you get your hands on an old sepia photograph of your great-great-grandfather in a bushy mustache and a gray uniform, and you see your own eyes staring back at you, it must arouse an instinct to support one who died fighting for a way of life.

And sometimes, the past isn't as far away as we think. This I discovered through a newspaper article I came across about an eighty-nine-year-old Alabaman named Alberta Martin. She was calling for the state to pay her a pension she was entitled to as the widow of a Confederate soldier. That's right, a Civil War soldier. She'd married him in 1927, when she was nineteen or twenty. He must have been in his eighties. Alabama had stopped funding those pensions a decade earlier, believing all war widows had died. But this Confederate wife was still kicking. It was a reminder not to be too hasty in discounting old wounds.

We crept along Highway 82 like a couple of mutts sniffing our way past trees. Each narrow side road meant a short excursion, followed by a dejected return to the four-laner. It was as if the hamlet we were searching for had vanished like a rural Atlantis, swallowed by waves of cotton and pecans. As we stopped by a dumpster at the side of the highway to plan our next move, a woman pulled up in front of us and began disposing several bags of garbage. We gave her a hand, tossing out the trash and talking of Glory.

"Back years ago," she said, "I know there was a store—a big, long, brick store—and three or four houses on each side of it, and then a big two-story building across the railroad. The old original Glory was a railroad stop, but they took the railroad out. I can remember my daddy taking me down there, and a colored man had a little store where you could buy big candy bars for a nickel and penny candy. You could probably get five or six pieces for a penny."

Nell was her name. She was soft-spoken but had a hard face. Nell had lived all of her sixty-six years on this sliver of land between the Alapaha and Willacoochie Rivers. She was born fifteen miles away in a little town that was nothing but a cotton gin and a store. When she was four, her father bought the farm she lived on now, just up the road in a cluster of houses that called itself the Glory community. But it wasn't the original Glory. The name survived when the original place died.

"It never was really a town. Just a stop in the road. I don't know how it got on the map. I really don't." She shrugged her shoulders. "I guess, basically, it's something that used to be, and it's not here anymore."

I wasn't surprised that the name had outlived the town. *Glory* is to the South what *wild* is to the West. But why glory? It seems that myth and rhetoric have bolstered one another for more than 130 years. The rhetoric—or was it the myth?—started with the warriors themselves, who justified their actions by glorifying their side. So it was that Major R. E. Wilson of the First North Carolina Sharpshooters announced, "'Tis the cause, not the fate of the cause, that is glorious." And Corporal Sam Watkins of Tennessee proclaimed, "The South fell battling under the banner of State rights, but yet grand and glorious even in death." The South lost, but far greater would have been the loss of southern pride. So the cause was praised and the soldiers honored. Memories of glory reduced the sting of defeat.

Taking the soldiers' cue, the chroniclers came next. These were the men and women who reshaped the war in its aftermath. Many had lost brothers or uncles or homes. But history is a compendium of reflections, and reflections are the product of biases. So the myth of glory was amplified in verse.

Abram Joseph Ryan, a Catholic priest from Virginia, was the Confederacy's most poetic defender. In "The Confederate Banner" (often called "Requiem of the Lost Cause"), he wrote, "Furl that Banner! True, 'tis gory / Yet, 'tis wreathed around with *glory*." He concluded a poem called "C.S.A.," "The *glory* they won shall not wane for us / In legend and lay / Our heroes in Gray / Shall forever live over again for us." And in "A Land without Ruins," he declared, "Yes, give me the land / Of the wreck and the tomb / There's grandeur in graves / There's *glory* in gloom."

Even as the years went by, as Reconstruction came and went and it became possible for some southerners to distance themselves from the cause, they didn't diminish their praise for the southern soldier. Henry W. Grady, author of the famous "New South" speech in 1886, followed a line about the returning soldiers of the North by saying, "Will you bear with me while I tell you of another army that sought its home at the close of the late war—an army that marched home in defeat and not victory—in pathos and not in splendor, but in glory that equaled yours."

Indeed, the South's inclination to glorify its fight may be much the same as any sovereign body's eagerness to praise its fighters. After all, they risked their lives for the rest of the folks. And *bravery* and *glory* are often mistaken for one another.

Eventually, myth takes on a life of its own. The naysayers and revisionists feel compelled to repeat it even while they discard it. I've known for years, for instance, that Abner Doubleday had nothing to do with baseball. The story of how he invented the game in Cooperstown was a fabrication, an attempt to turn an English derivative into an American creation. Indeed, he probably never saw a baseball game in his life. But more than once, I've used his name in passing, all my knowledge of the facts trumped by the lyrical pleasure of the fiction.

So it might be with the South and glory. A century after the Blue battled the Gray, Albert Gore, Sr., the late Tennessee senator, published his memoirs, in which, among other things, he deconstructed the myths of the Old South and wrote of the tendency of residents to exalt in a past that was gone. When he chose a title for his book, he chose this: *Let the Glory Out.*

Maybe the perpetuation of myths keeps us sane. Maybe we tailor our recollections and histories to our needs and wishes. Or maybe we're just mixing up our legends. After all, thanks to soldiers congregating from the corners of the country, the Civil War greatly influenced the evolution of baseball. And Abner Doubleday? He did distinguish himself after all. As a Union soldier, he fired the first shot at Fort Sumter.

We drove a mile farther along the highway and turned onto a dirt road, followed by a gravel path, which took us past rotting tree stumps and burnt shrubs until we finally came to a clearing that made the hair on the back of my neck stand up. It was a compound of sorts—six or eight tiny trailers, a shack draped in camouflage, some floodlights and rows of plastic chairs set up, as if some sort of gathering were scheduled. It seemed to be abandoned, at least temporarily, but my imagination took charge. It has a tendency to do that in locales best suited to hermits and fugitives. Beset by visions of a Klan revival or a militia hideout, I put the Day Tripper in reverse and backed down the gravel road just a bit quicker than I'd rumbled up it.

It was time, Amy and I decided, to give up the search, and perhaps it was appropriate. The elusiveness of our literal destination seemed to reflect my confusion about its figurative component. But as we made our way back to the dirt road and headed toward the highway, Amy caught something out of the corner of her eye. There, twenty feet from the road, amid the tall grass of the swampy backwoods, was a sign. It was old and gray, rust having eaten away the corners. It had been riddled by bullets over the years, one hole big enough to reveal the thicket of trees behind it. And it said, *GLORY.*

That's all that was left.

LOVE,
VIRGINIA

Love is always a consolatory thing.
Thomas Jefferson

I t was May 14 when we arrived at yet another coincidence of time and place. Three hundred eighty-nine years earlier on May 14, a group of 104 English colonists completed an eighteen-week journey across the ocean by stepping ashore thirty miles inland from what is now known as Chesapeake Bay. They built a precarious fort, the first permanent settlement in North America, and named it James Cittie after the British monarch, King James I. The waterway that led them from the sea to their new home was christened the James River.

One year earlier, a group of investors had been authorized to settle colonists in the New World under the auspices of the Virginia Company of London, named to honor the previous monarch, Elizabeth I, the "Virgin Queen." While the investors remained comfortably ensconced in London, the settlers were destined for tragedy. Due to lack of leadership, lack of food, and lack of protection from malaria-carrying mosquitos, more than half of the original settlers of what came to be known as Jamestown were dead before the summer was over.

Still, English investors, prodded by the Virginia Company's propaganda, continued to finance larger expeditions. Within two years, the town's population grew to nearly five hundred. This led to an even great disaster in the winter of 1609–10, the so-called Starving Time. Ill-prepared for the cold months, the famished settlers were reduced to eating dogs, cats, rats, and snakes. Some even dug up corpses to satisfy a gnawing hunger. Those who didn't starve to death were attacked by disease and by Powhatan Indians. By the time it was May again, only sixty-five settlers remained.

The significance of the ensuing events cannot be overstated. On June 10, 1610, the fort at Jamestown was abandoned. Had it remained so, the Spanish likely would have taken control of the New World. There might have been no colonial discontent, no revolution, no "all Men are created equal," no Manifest Destiny, no democratic superpower. But as the colonists sailed down the James River toward the sea, they were met by a ship bearing a new governor, a load of colonists, and much-needed supplies. Jamestown was saved and reinvigorated. A chance encounter changed the course of history.

The real turning point came two years later, when colonist John Rolfe introduced tobacco cultivation to the New World and shipped the "jovial weed" to England; subsequent tobacco crops would serve as the basis for Virginia's economic viability. Seven years later, the House of Burgesses was established, the first representative assembly in America. That same year, a Dutch captain named Uwe Jope sailed his trading vessel into a port just south of Jamestown and exchanged "twenty and odd Negroes" for fresh water and provisions. These were indentured servants, but the practice Jope began would evolve into outright slavery, which would be legalized in Virginia in 1661. Some 330 years later, Douglas Wilder, the grandson of Virginia slaves, would become the nation's first African American governor.

Driving into Virginia, one can't help but be impressed by the historical eminence of the state. It was here in 1619—not in Plymouth, Massachusetts—that the first Thanksgiving feast was held. It was here that the American family took root a year later, the Virginia Company of London sending a shipment of ninety mail-order brides in return for payment of tobacco. It was Virginia that became an official Royal colony in 1624, the first of the thirteen.

Virginia was where the seeds of rebellion grew, from Nathaniel Bacon in 1676 to Patrick Henry a century later. It was a Virginian, Richard Henry Lee, who introduced the resolution for a declaration of independence, and another, Thomas Jefferson, who wrote it. When the United States Constitution was drafted in 1787, much of it was based on the Virginia Plan, which was largely the work of James Madison. He would go on to draft the Bill of Rights, based on the Virginia Declaration of Rights.

Lewis and Clark were Virginians. John Marshall, chief justice of the Supreme Court from 1801 to 1835 and the man who made an independent federal judiciary the final interpreter of the Constitution, was a Virginian. The first four two-term presidents—Washington, Jefferson, Madison, and Monroe—were Virginians. Four more native sons—William Henry Harrison, John Tyler, Zachary Taylor, and Woodrow Wilson— would later hold the office, earning Virginia the nickname "Mother of Presidents."

Richmond was the capital of the Confederacy, and Virginia was the home state of Generals Robert E. Lee, Stonewall Jackson, Jeb Stuart, and George Pickett. In twenty-six major battles and more than four hundred smaller engagements, more men fought and died in Virginia during the Civil War than in any other state. It was in a Virginia town, Appomattox, that Lee surrendered to Grant—just as, a hundred miles east and nearly a hundred years earlier, British troops had surrendered to George Washington at Yorktown.

Virginia is to America's development what Chuck Berry is to rock-'n'-roll, what Yale is to football, what San Francisco is to the sixties.

Despite this, the state's tourism bureau apparently came to the conclusion that a slogan like *Virginia Is for History Majors* or *Virginia Is for Rebels and Statesmen* was too cumbersome. So the bumper sticker of choice became the incongruous *Virginia Is for Lovers*. We found it to be entirely appropriate.

The plan was this: We would climb aboard the Blue Ridge Parkway at its southern terminus in the Great Smoky Mountains of North Carolina and cover almost all of its 469 miles toward Virginia's Shenandoah National Park. We would ride the ridges of the southern Appalachians past high pastures, deep hollows, and meandering mountain streams. We would pass places with evocative names like Crabtree Meadows, Cumberland Knob, Grandfather Mountain. We would travel through one of the world's great forests—spruces and firs, birches and beeches, maples and oaks, eastern hemlocks and white pines—and past wildflowers in full bloom—dwarf iris, bird's-foot violet, Mayapple. We'd see small farms with picket fences and rows of beans and cabbages and tobacco. We'd smell the faint scent of apple butter and hear the distant sound of fiddles and banjos and dulcimers. Sixteen miles before the road's end, we would turn off at a mountain hamlet on the crest of some of the world's most ancient peaks, ending with a bang at a town called Love.

That was the plan. Reality was nine miles and a whimper.

We overestimated the Rolling Stone's ability to conquer steep hills. We grossly underestimated its size. The manual stated that we were eleven and a half feet tall. As we approached a series of tunnels along the inaugural stretch of the parkway—a stretch we could have jogged faster than we drove—it felt like putting a square peg in a round hole. The sign for the first tunnel claimed it was twelve feet tall. We pushed through. Minutes later, the next tunnel was eleven and a half feet. We held our breath, stuck to the center, and made it. The next one was eleven feet. I eased the RV to the entrance, Amy stepped out to measure peg and hole, and somehow we squeezed our way through. When the color returned to our faces, we made a joint decision: Screw the parkway.

We exited two-lane serenity and set out for a trio of leisure-be-damned interstates. Interstate 40 took us east through the heart of North Carolina. Interstate 77 brought us north into Virginia. Interstate 81 combined both directions and led us to our base camp in the town of Natural Bridge. The following day, we unhooked the Day Tripper and, like Rosie Ruiz rejoining the 1980 Boston Marathon after taking the subway most of the distance, returned to the fabled parkway, having bypassed more than four hundred scenic miles.

The road was worthy of its reputation. From a distance, the Blue Ridge Mountains appeared soft and rounded, like a heap of green cotton balls. But when we drove into them, we saw all the sharp edges and vibrant colors. What appeared to be one deep lime hue was revealed as countless complementary shades of the same, accentuated by the sharp white of blooming dogwoods. The parkway was a tunnel of trees, sunlight filtering through a canopy of leaves, and then, every once in a while, a dramatic emergence to a view of a vast valley below. The Appalachians aren't as tall as younger mountains like the Rockies—not even half the size—but they're quite steep. Many summits tower as much as four thousand feet above the valley floor. It was a lesson in the relativity of grandeur.

The mile markers counted backwards. We were heading toward zero, as if going back in time. At milepost 43, Irish Creek Valley. At milepost 40, Clark's Gap. At milepost 32, Still House Hollow. As we stopped at Big Spy Mountain Overlook, elevation thirty-two hundred feet, a group of exhausted bikers peddled to a stop near us. Today was the end of their nine-day journey. They had started in the Great Smoky Mountains.

"That's where we came from," Amy offered, "only we came on four wheels."

"Oh," responded a breathless biker. "That seems like an easy way. Don't know why I didn't think of it." He rode off, leaving us to ponder the fine line between humor and sarcasm.

Around milepost 17, we spied a group of buildings tucked into a small valley below us. Written large on the side of a barn were the words

Hard Time Hollow. A nearby sign said *No firearms allowed. No exceptions.* It was an eerie spot. We thought this might be Love. We hoped not.

It wasn't. A mile later, we came upon a park ranger placing a toppled street sign in the back of his truck. The sign said *Love Rd.* We turned left, passed a tiny church and cemetery, and then stopped at the Nelson County Visitor Center. As we walked in, a kindly gentleman stepped out from behind a row of brochures. He was Dr. Gervas Taylor, an orthopedic surgeon for forty years and now the county's one-man propagandist. "I'm like the Maytag man," he admitted. "Sometimes, I sit here all day with nothing to do."

He folded his hands on the counter. "So what can I do for you folks?"

"Well, this is going to sound strange, but we're looking for Love," I said.

He gave us a wide smile. "You're in it."

"We're in the town of Love?"

"You're in the community. The post office is gone. They get their mail down in Lyndhurst. But this is still the Love community, and people still address their mail to the people who live here as Love, Virginia."

He handed us a booklet titled *What to Do and See in the Shenandoah Valley.* In particular, he pointed out page 60 and a small boxed advertisement for *Backroads,* which was described as a "homespun newsletter about

A mailbox in Love

backroad ramblin', plain folk and simple living." For more information, readers were advised to call Lynn Coffey. So we did. She and her husband lived just down the road.

After a quarter-mile, a sign informed us we were entering Augusta County. Love straddles the two counties—and thus provides a bit of historical irony. Augusta County was formed in 1738 and named in honor of Augusta of Saxe-Gotha, the mother of King George III. That same year, a man by the name of Thomas Nelson, Jr., was born in Virginia. He was educated in England but returned to the colonies to become an outspoken revolutionary, a signer of the Declaration of Independence, and the third governor of Virginia. Nelson County, formed in 1807, was named after him. So one county was named after King George's mother and the other after King George's enemy. They shared Love. If only it were that simple.

According to the most generous estimates, there are eighty-five people in Love. We passed a handful of houses, cabins, and mobile homes as we drove downhill along Love Road, otherwise known as Route 814. The fifteenth house was the one we were looking for. It had two stories of white pine logs, a stone chimney running up the side, a roof of shiny tin, and a wide front porch complete with hanging ferns, a bench swing, and a view of George Washington National Forest across the road.

A gentle creek ribboned through an immaculate yard. A tractor, a Jeep, a motorcycle, and three pickup trucks, one of them a Truman-era model, were randomly placed along a gravel driveway. A smattering of chickens and turkeys wandered about, along with a pair of yin-and-yang cats, one white with a splotch of black fur above its eyes, the other almost the exact opposite. It was all so beautiful and natural—the endless green of the lawn and the surrounding forest, the cloudless blue of the sky, the natural wood of the cabin, the lazy freedom of the animals. It seemed the way we were all supposed to live.

I took a liking to the Coffeys as soon as I shook their hands. Billy

The Coffeys

wore a baseball cap, a plaid flannel shirt, and jeans. He was soft-spoken and had pensive eyes above a slightly graying beard. Lynn was an attractive woman with curly light brown hair, an ivory complexion, blue eyes, and a button nose. He was fifty-three; she was forty-nine. They both looked ten years younger.

The inside of the house was what it should have been—warm, with only a grudging bow to modern convenience. Surrounding us, as we sat at a long kitchen table handmade by the two of them, were a wood-burning stove, a pie safe, an old Victrola, a stone hearth, and a sturdy trunk. The walls were decorated with antlers, washboards, snowshoes, quilts, and a large crosscut saw. A crescent moon was engraved on the door of the bathroom, which held a claw-foot tub. Old tin store signs— like *White Flyer Laundry Soap—makes dirt fly*—complemented the decor. There was also a plaque on the wall with a heart burned into it and the words, *Love, VA . . . Billy + Lynn . . . November 23, 1992.*

"That's when it started," said Lynn. "We had a neighbor, and a tree fell across her lane, and she couldn't get home. The only man who's home during the day is Billy, because he works the night shift, so I got him to come with a chain saw and cut that tree so she could get in. I rode home with Billy that day. When we were later married, that's what the neighbor gave us, a piece of that tree. So that's where it all began, I guess."

On the outskirts of Love is a place called Chicken Hollow. In Chicken Hollow, there is a sixteen-by-twenty-foot log cabin made of chestnut logs chinked with a mixture of red clay and hogs' hair. In the cabin lived four generations of Coffeys. George Washington Coffey built the place in the mid-1800s. His son, Joseph, raised a family of four boys and three girls there. One of the boys, Saylor Floyd Coffey, inherited the house in the hollow. He had a child and named him Saylor, too. The child's middle name was Junior, but at some point, people began to call him Billy. He lived with his parents and his grandmother in Chicken Hollow for the first ten years of his life.

"When I was raised in the old log cabin, at that time, a lot of the chinks were gone," Billy said, his speech slow and deliberate. "My children don't believe me when I say this, but there were places in the wall where you could put your arm through. It had an old, wood-shingle roof on it, and you could look up and see the stars at night. It didn't leak that bad. The water would shed off somewhat. But if it snowed, and it was a blowin' snow, it was very common you'd wake up in the morning with snow on top of your bed."

"They left the door open summer and winter," Lynn added, "so that they would have light, even if it was snowing."

"There was no electricity?"

Billy shook his head. "No electric. No phones. Plumbing outdoors."

The family lived much as its ancestors had, carving a life out of the Blue Ridge, making clothes, growing corn, raising chickens, doing whatever it took to get by. From the beginning, the land most mountain folks called home tended to be barely sufficient to support them. Houses were as much as a mile apart, separated by ridges and forest. Isolation was the rule, and it bred self-sufficiency. It meant that when 125-pound Saylor Floyd Coffey wasn't trudging a mile and a half to his job maintaining the parkway and a mile and a half back at night, he was cutting wood and milking cows and feeding chickens and fetching spring water and tending crops. It was a work ethic necessary for survival.

"My dad would put a bushel of corn on his shoulder in a sack and carry it across the mountain. I don't know how far it is. It's probably three or four miles at least, right down through the mountains. He'd carry it over to the mill and get it ground into cornmeal and then put it on his shoulder and walk back up the mountain. And they didn't think anything about it." Billy shrugged. "I just come up working. I guess it's something instilled in me. I'm always doing something now." He nodded to his wife and smiled. "I'm never still. She'll tell you that."

In 1953, when Billy was ten, his family moved from the hollow to a house closer to the parkway, not far from where Love's first post office had been established fifty-nine years earlier. The first postmaster was a great-uncle of Billy's, a man by the name of Hugh Coffey, who ran the office in a corner of his general store. As the story goes, the original postmark read *Meadow Mountain*, but the government was pushing for a name with fewer letters. At about that time, Hugh's young daughter, Lovey, died of typhoid fever. As a memorial to her, the tiny community on the county line was renamed Love, sentencing subsequent postmasters to work overtime on Valentine's Day, as letters poured in from all over the coun-

Love's first post office

try requesting a local postmark. As it turned out, the name outlasted the post office, which closed in 1946.

Though the Coffeys moved out of Chicken Hollow, it was still awhile before they enjoyed the luxuries of electricity, phone service, indoor plumbing, and paved roads. The people of the mountains and "hollers" were an insular group naturally sequestered by space and time. There's an old mountain saying, "Never move so far away that you can't see the smoke from your parents' chimney." But the reality of seclusion meant not only that their families were neighbors but also that their neighbors were family, related or not. Their world was as small as a holler, as simple as a butter churn. In many ways, it still is. I was curious about how much traveling Billy had done while growing up. How far did he get?

"How about nowhere?" he replied, a strange mixture of pride and regret in his voice. "I don't know. . . . You just virtually never did see the town. Waynesboro is the closest town. It's probably fifteen miles from here. Dad and Mom would go there maybe twice a year. They'd go once in the summer and then right before Christmas. That was it."

How isolated and independent were they? During high school, Billy didn't ride the school bus to the town of Stuarts Draft; he drove it. But by then, the highlands universe was expanding. There were ways to earn a living outside—even if outside meant a dozen miles away. After graduating, Billy married a girl he'd met in high school and spent ten years painting furniture at a plant in Waynesboro. Following that, he helped a third cousin run a grocery store for eight years, then worked in a textile mill for five before taking his current job as a department manager for Hershey's Chocolate in Stuarts Draft.

But making a vastly different kind of living from his parents and grandparents didn't mean he had to make a different kind of life. He lived with his wife and his four kids right next to his parents and his church, on the mountain, in Love.

Lynn nearly apologized for her childhood. "I wasn't raised in the country at all. We had indoor plumbing, and we always had electric. It was a different world, where I lived."

She grew up in south Florida, near Fort Lauderdale. By the time she was in her twenties, she was married and living in a five-bedroom, three-bath house in the country-club section of Richmond. It was a hundred miles away from Love; it may as well have been a hundred light years. But Lynn and her husband felt an attraction to the margins of society. They wanted to avoid being beaten down by the beaten path, so they acquired a two-acre tract off the Blue Ridge Parkway and, while planning their new house, moved from their swanky Colonial in Virginia's capital to a tiny hunting cabin in Virginia's outback. They lived there for three years and then purchased the house of an elderly neighbor. But their dream house, their living-off-the-land paradise, never materialized.

Still, Lynn found a home. "I remember, as a little child about four years old, having an intense desire to live in the mountains and chop wood and things. So when I moved here, it was like a dream come true. Everybody else thought I was having some sort of horrible hardship, but I was in seventh heaven."

She found a community unlike any other she had seen and discovered a nagging desire to chronicle the culture before it was gone. "I'm not a writer," she insisted. "I mean, I was never trained. I just have a high-school education and three years of typing. But when we moved up here, after about a year, I realized this is a completely different way of life. People don't live like this anymore. I thought it should be captured somehow, so I just started to talk to everybody. And I believe I've talked to everyone in the Love area who's living and who has died over that fifteen-year period."

The first issue of *Backroads* appeared in December 1981. It was a four-page rag dedicated to "the small mountain hamlets that dot the American landscape and to the special people who inhabit them." It was a free publication. Lynn paid for printing costs with income from local advertisers, who received a stack of copies to hand out at their places of business. When locals started asking for extra copies for cousins and friends, the circulation grew, as did the size of the monthly newsletter. When Lynn began to hear that issues were hard to find and began to receive long-distance requests for the newsletter, she started selling subscriptions.

By May 1996, when the 172nd edition of *Backroads* hit the back roads, Lynn could boast a twenty-four-page publication, dozens of advertisers, and nearly a thousand subscribers in twenty-five states. "But they're still free if you want 'em," she pointed out. "People say, 'You can make so much money if you'd just charge a dollar apiece.' But I don't want to charge a dollar apiece. I mean, where can you get free good news?"

Backroads is a treasure trove of mountain lore, mountain humor, mountain history, mountain interests, and mountain concerns. But mostly, it is a loving account of mountain people. Flip through some back issues and you'll find—interspersed with articles about the Appalachian Trail and Virginia's covered bridges—local poetry, samples from family photo albums, and headlines like "Cecil and Eva Boggs Celebrate 50 Years of Marriage" and "Barbara Hunter: Rural Mail Carrier for 29 Years" and "An Interview with Cousin Daisy."

Leafing through Lynn's publication, I sensed a familiarity so often missing from the self-indulgent journalism of the nineties. After I graduated from college, I worked as a reporter for a small local newspaper in upstate New York. Within weeks, I found myself reluctant to admit it. There was a remarkable backlash in the community against the newspaper—much of it, I now realize, because the writers and the readers had two different notions of what local coverage should be. The enterprising reporters, visions of big-city beats dancing in their heads, thrived on hard news—the occasional sports scandal or mayoral election or high-profile court case. Yet most of the residents wanted a form of community service, a shot of civic pride, a sense of recognition. Each side was reluctant to defer to the other.

But I think maybe the readers were right. You want news? Open the

Wall Street Journal. You want insight into a community? Turn to the local newspaper. Better yet, turn to people like Lynn Coffey, who do not substitute irreverence and ambition for respect and passion. I began to suspect that if there were more people like her, people who actually went looking for good news, there would be fewer cynics like me. Then I realized that she and I were essentially on the same mission, only on different scales. We were both trying to distinguish perception from reality, to separate front-page sensationalism from back-roads sincerity.

"I just thought their lives were worth recording. There's a stereotype of the mountain people—like *Deliverance*—and they're not like that at all. I guess there are bad apples in every community or every walk of life, but the mountain people have gotten this hillbilly stereotype," said Lynn. "You know, they had to be terribly resourceful to live here, to earn a living, to eat. They were shrewd. They were smart. They were kind. But they got a bad rap from the outside world. They're very different once you get to know them."

There may be nobody in her part of the Blue Ridge Mountains she doesn't know. Nelson County was where a young country lad named Earl Hamner, Jr., grew up during the Depression. He began writing of his experiences, a project that evolved into a television classic, *The Waltons*. It's that kind of place—big families, small worlds, green valleys, and golden rules. Every article by Lynn or one of her growing stable of contributors is a window to the past.

The regular features in *Backroads* include "Recipes of Love" (Effie's Sweet Bread Cookies), a "Love Notes" section ("Get well wishes to Gene Everitt who was in the hospital last month"), and "Helpful Hints" ("When making blackberry pie, sprinkle the bottom crust with cracker crumbs so the juice won't ooze out"). There's a "What Is It?" section, which presents a photo of an obscure implement (a welder's chipping hammer, a grapefruit corer, an old-fashioned tar bucket), the item's identity being revealed the following month. And there are columns with names like "Down at the Store" and "Old Truck Corner."

One column in particular caught my eye. Called "Letters from Uncle Lem," it is written by an elderly man named Lemuel P. Gooch III, who is apparently a Virginian turned Floridian. "Howdy Bub" is how he begins every column. The rest is a study in dialect and tone worthy of Ring Lardner or Mark Twain: "Went out to the everglades to do some serious bass fishing this past weekend, but when I got there they had these here signs stuck in the ground that said all the fish here is Mercury poisoned and you cain't eat 'em! I'd sure love to find out who the dummy wuz that drove his Mercury into my fishin' hole!!!"

Backroads is a paean to the simple life: "How the Mason Jar Got Its Name," "Making Hand Cranked Ice Cream," "Whatever Happened to String?" When Love finally received private phone lines in 1986, Lynn ran the story under the headline, "Death of the Party Line." When she broke her ankle in 1993, she wrote two thousand words about it. Whenever a family holds a reunion or a pig roast, she's there.

"She can take nothing and make a story out of it. She really can," Billy declared. It seemed to me he said this in an attempt at self-deprecation, believing that a man of the world, a city slicker like myself, would think his wife's newsletter was indeed making something out of nothing. I knew better. *Backroads* preserves a slowly dwindling culture. For the people in the hollows and coves of the Blue Ridge, it isn't nothing; it is a compendium of everything.

One local subject Lynn shies away from is the great flood of 1969, when the aftermath of a hurricane poured an inconceivable thirty inches of rain on the Nelson County–Augusta County area in a six-hour period, destroying more than three hundred buildings and half the county's roads. The flood killed an estimated 134 people. "I've never done an article about it in the paper, because it's still too tender," she explained. "It wiped out entire families."

The hurricane was Camille, the same storm that decimated Triumph, Louisiana. Strange how people's lives can be connected by tragedy.

In 1987, Billy's wife was killed in an automobile accident on the outskirts of town. Billy remained in Love, devastated but bolstered by his family and the only community he'd ever known. Two years later, Lynn and her husband separated after twenty-one years of occasionally rocky matrimony. She moved back down to the hunting camp, living by herself, chopping her own wood, hunting her own food. She was satisfied, if not perfectly content, in her seclusion.

"I really made up my mind to just stay alone. And I did. I was separated for four years and never went out. This is where I wanted to be. And I never considered remarrying, because I wanted somebody who understood the way of life that I had chosen. It's not every person's dream to live like this. The simple life is a lot of hard work!"

There was one person, though, who understood. Lynn and Billy had known each other for nearly a decade. They attended the same church at the top of the mountain. Their children had grown up together. "I always thought maybe I'd be interested if I could ever find somebody who wanted to live this life," Lynn explained. "Well, there he was! He'd always lived this life and would continue to live this life." I detected the hint of a blush. "I don't know what happened. We began to look at each other differently, I guess."

They were married in the spring of 1993. Billy had four twenty-something children; Lynn had a twenty-four-year-old daughter who had known them half her life. Billy and Lynn now share three grandchildren—and tons of cousins. "It's funny," Lynn chuckled. "After all these years writing about Coffeys, I'm one of them."

She and her first husband had constructed only the foundation of their dream house in Love. They never built anything on it. Billy and Lynn took that foundation and turned it into a home. "I had already started to build this when Billy came into the picture, and he said if he would have known the work involved, he would have waited until after it was built and then come courting," she said, and they both laughed. "But he got in right at the start. We hired four young men to build it, but one by one, they started to quit on us. When hunting season came, they all left. They had the shell of the house up, and the roof, and that was all. But we finished the whole thing ourselves in three months. We did all the electric, the plumbing, everything, and we moved in on the second day of December of '93."

Looking around the Coffeys' log cabin, I came to recognize it as a symbol and a sanctuary. Billy and Lynn had created something that represented their love for each other and their shared love for their community, an environment in which neighbors were neighborly, a place where if you left your door unlocked, you'd likely come home to an anonymous gift of hand-carved furniture or fresh venison.

"We have these big snows, and the snowplow can't come to us, so we have networking. I put on my cross-country skis and ski over to the neighbor to see if they need anything. Or we'll make a grocery list, and the people who have four-wheel drive will go down and get food and get the mail. And if two or three people do that, everybody's covered. There's just a respect and love for other people besides your family."

"Could you ever picture yourself living in, say, Manhattan?" Amy wondered.

Lynn almost fell off her chair. "Oh, no! I can't even picture ourselves

Simple Living

living in Waynesboro! People are rude. They don't have time for others. The community here, we depend on each other. The survival of Billy's early life depended on all the people pulling together, and they've never lost that here."

Do unto others. That was the first of Love's Two Commandments. Simplify your life. That was the other.

"The kids kind of make fun of us a little bit. We just have wood heat. We don't have a microwave or an electric can opener. I just don't want those things. We have power outages sometimes in the wintertime that last a day or two, and we just keep on going. I can cook on the wood stove. We can keep warm. We have water just right out the door. There's two streams. We have oil lamps. We can our food, and we butcher it," said Lynn. "We have everything we need right here."

On a universal, give-peace-a-chance level, John Lennon's "All You Need Is Love" is a bunch of bull. Love is personal and intimate, not some general utopian possibility. It is intense, focused, private. Broaden it and you dilute it. In fact, children today are raised amid a constant barrage of lyrics, one-liners, and catch phrases that either trivialize love or ridicule it. Never has such a profound concept been so profoundly misused.

Over the past quarter-century, the number of divorced Americans has nearly quadrupled, the rate of crumbled marriages now reaching upwards of four in ten. There are nearly 1.2 million divorces annually in the United States, half the number of marriages. Of the 2.4 million marriages each year, nearly half are remarriages for at least one of the participants. And the divorce rate for second marriages is 25 percent higher than for first marriages.

We seem a nation of consolation-prize pairings and halfhearted vows. My peers and I have grown to adulthood viewing divorce as part of the natural order of things. That's Generation X, as in ex-husbands and ex-wives. The fallout is that we are exponentially more commitment-wary than our parents were.

It may be a good thing, a generation's hesitation. It may be that, a few decades from now, the divorce rate will dip because we learned how to recognize love by watching it corrupted. Or it may be that we hesitate simply because we don't know how to recognize it at all.

And here I am, one of the lucky ones. Amy and I fell in love at an age when it was an option, not a career move. It was what Sherwood Anderson referred to as that "divine accident of life." But still, I can't really define it.

I know I would dive in front of a speeding train for Amy. I know we ceased to live separate lives long ago, that somewhere along the line, we became a single entity. I know that our dreams and desires and attitudes have merged so that we have become completely enveloped in each other—physically, psychologically, emotionally, professionally. I know that I'm a better person every second I spend with her, and that I can't wait until I'm seventy-seven and she's seventy-six and we're flipping through the photo album of the cross-country journey we took a half-century earlier. I know that I occasionally catch myself staring at her with a stupid grin on my face. I know that when she smiles, I laugh.

I don't know if that counts as a definition of love. All I can really say is this: love is to me what obscenity is to the Supreme Court. I know it when I see it. And sitting around the kitchen table crafted by Billy and Lynn in the house built by Billy and Lynn amid the lifestyle treasured by Billy and Lynn, I no doubt saw it.

"It's nice that you can enjoy the simple life," I told them, "but it must be even nicer that you can share it."

"Yeah," Billy replied, stealing a shy glance at his wife while I stole one at mine. "It makes all the difference in the world."

JUSTICE,
WEST VIRGINIA

> *Injustice is relatively easy to bear; what stings is justice.*
>
> H. L. Mencken

W est Virginia was in a state of emergency. Torrential rains had swollen many of the rivers and creeks that slithered through the state. Eight southern counties had been hit by flash floods and rock slides. Roads and schools were closed. The National Guard was working overtime. One woman had been swept to her death. Two hundred people in the town of Gilbert, three miles from Justice, were stranded because of high water across roads. "We can't get to them," an assistant fire chief told reporters. "Period." Unless the newspapers were overreacting, we were headed to a place where nature was leaving chaos in its wake.

Amy and I were riding Interstate 64 west over the Allegheny Mountains. Mist and fog were our companions as we crossed into West Vir-

ginia, where the climbs began to feel longer and the downy softness of the mountains was replaced by harsh revelations of rock. After the downpour of the previous few days, the mountains seemed to be sweating. Water cascaded down every crevice and gully, as if the Alleghenies were a dam about to burst.

We set a course for the heart of Appalachia. We were looking for a town less than a dozen miles from the point where Virginia, West Virginia, and Kentucky converged. Having been carved out of Virginia in the first place, West Virginia has perhaps the most irregular boundary of any state. It is the shape of a splattered bug. The state is the smallest west of the nation's capital, yet its reach exceeds its size. A resident of the West Virginia town of Chester is at about the same latitude as New York City, but a Bluefield citizen lives well south of the former Confederate capital of Richmond. Huntington is a good sixty miles west of Cleveland; Harpers Ferry is sixty miles east of Buffalo.

Interstate 64 took us to the city of Beckley, a hub around which revolved dozens of small mining and farming communities. It soon became apparent, as we wound along Route 99 southwest of Beckley, that these communities were a remarkable combination of the scenic and the tragic, beauty and poverty coexisting. The drive was a study in juxtapositions—a swaybacked horse standing before a lush hillside, a dilapidated double-wide overlooking a frothy river bend, coal shafts boring into ancient mountainsides, magnificent rock walls layered with punk graffiti. The graffiti was everywhere. On stop signs. On junction signs. On signs with arrows telling us which way to go. Even when we began to see the remains of rock slides, many of the crumbled boulders lining the roadside bore the remnants of spray-painted messages—nature splitting infinitives.

We turned south onto Route 85 and immediately encountered a lengthy 9 percent grade down into the bowels of the hills. Toward the bottom, as we approached the town of Oceana, we came upon a light stream of water flowing across the road, but nothing like what the papers were shouting about. West on Route 10 through the hamlet of Cyclone and the much-publicized poverty of West Virginia began to come into focus—dirty faces staring from the porches of clapboard houses, tattered shirts gripping backyard clotheslines, stripped and rusted pickup trucks decomposing in weedy lawns.

When we reached the Route 80 junction, we drove south, away from a town called Man and toward one called Christian. Now, the Guyandotte River, wide and brown, appeared on our right. A handful of straining bridges took us over the river and back several times, and we saw the water creeping ever so slightly into people's backyards, swallowing the land in sips. Southeast on to Highway 52, past a sign: *Welcome to Gilbert, WV. We are naturally resourceful.* But no sign of stranded residents.

We arrived at Justice a few miles later, having found no evidence of a state of emergency. The town was a thin strip of civilization tucked into the hills along the Guyandotte. It had a business district from the one-of-everything model of community planning. Camped under a green-and-brown monolith of granite as omnipresent as a prison wall were a hardware store, a beauty shop, an ice company, a general store, an accountant's office, a paving company, the United Methodist Church of Justice, Justice Freewill Baptist Church, a Church of God, a discount furniture shop, a bait-and-tackle shop, the Justice post office, the Justonian Restaurant and Motel, and a dance club called Yesterday's.

The businesses lined Highway 52, which paralleled the river, still the most powerful presence in town. Fanning out from the highway and the river were dozens of mobile homes and some permanent ones. About a mile or so through town, we came upon an old school bus parked on the side of the road, produce being sold from under a canopy beside it. We bought a bunch of bananas for a buck. About a half-mile later, we encountered a car sitting perpendicular to the highway, having plowed head-on into a rocky outcropping that was supposed to hold it to the road. Nobody was on the scene, nobody in the car. It was apparently another roadside ornament.

Of all the towns we visited, Justice seemed the most unapproachable, the least inviting. It felt like a community tucked away for a reason, enjoying its solitude as if keeping a sinister secret. And then we noticed a stark white sign on the side of the road, written upon it in blood-red letters the words, *Elect Tennis H. Hatfield, Democrat for Sheriff.* We had avoided the flood; we had discovered the feud.

The feud is a reflection of West Virginia's past, a history rife with dissension and secession from the very beginning. Two New Englanders, Jacob Marlin and Stephen Sewell, moved into what is now Pocahontas County, West Virginia, in 1749 and established what was perhaps the first recorded settlement west of the Alleghenies. Almost immediately, the two had a difference of opinion over religion, and Sewell went to live in a nearby tree. Yes, a tree. The dispute was merely the first of many.

As the country opened up and more settlers streamed over the Alleghenies, western Virginians began to resent their eastern counterparts, complaining of inequality in taxation and representation. In 1810, western Virginia had nearly the same number of inhabitants as eastern Virginia but only one-fifth of the state representatives. By

1816, some newspapers were calling for a division of the state, suggesting it be separated into North Virginia and South Virginia. Thirteen years later, western Virginians called for a state constitutional convention to remedy the situation. Though the convention turned out to be a farce, the western delegates began to sense a unity among themselves, and talk of separation grew louder.

In many ways, the division of Virginia seemed natural, the mountains in the center of the state serving not only as a physical boundary but also as a social and philosophical demarcation. What the movement needed, however, was a significant event to crystalize the situation. That event was the Civil War.

On April 17, 1861, five days after South Carolina fired on Fort Sumter and two days after President Lincoln asked for seventy-five thousand volunteers to put down the rebellion, Virginia seceded from the Union. The western counties, however, voted against it by a margin of twenty-nine to nine. At a convention in June, Union sympathizers nullified the Virginia ordinance of secession, vacated the offices of the state government in Richmond, and formed a "restored" Virginia government.

A popular election in October resulted in a vote of 18,408 to 781 in favor of the creation of a new state, but dissension reigned when the former Virginians met to decide on a new name. Originally, they chose *Kanawha*. But some delegates thought the word too difficult to spell; others feared confusion with a county by the same name; still more were proud of their Virginia heritage and wanted a name to honor it. Despite the exhortation of one delegate who declared, "I for one would want a new name—a fresh name—a name which if it were not symbolical of especially new ideas would at least be somewhat indicative of our deliverance from old ones," the delegates chose the decidedly unimaginative *West Virginia*.

Though the statehood bill passed the United States Senate and House, President Lincoln was troubled by the movement. According to the Constitution, it was necessary for the Virginia legislature to give its consent before West Virginia could break away. In addition, Lincoln recognized the hypocrisy of allowing one part of a state to secede from another but waging a war when states voted to secede from the Union. In the end, he signed the bill after rationalizing that "there is still difference enough between secession against the Constitution, and secession in favor of the Constitution."

On June 20, 1863, in the middle of the Civil War, West Virginia became the thirty-fifth state in the Union. But the fighting was far from over. The state became a microcosm of a torn nation. West Virginia contributed more than thirty-six thousand soldiers to the northern army, but nearly seven thousand West Virginians joined the Confederate side. Families were split; friends became enemies overnight. Most of West Virginia's southern counties and those on the Virginia border sympathized with the South, some so strongly that the "restored" government wasn't restored at all. Counties with divided loyalties fell prey to partisan bands of marauders on both sides, their means of intimidation and revenge ranging from arson to murder.

West Virginia was a state conceived by secession, created by war, raised by irreconcilable differences. When the smoke cleared in 1866, the state constructed its first public institution—a lunatic asylum. And in a not entirely unrelated event, a family named Hatfield cultivated an extreme dislike for a family named McCoy.

The Hatfields and McCoys had always been dim figures on the periphery of my consciousness, cartoon images almost. My imagination conjured toothless, shoeless hillbillies with floppy hats and long, unkempt beards wandering the backwoods with oversize rifles on their shoulders and vengeance on their minds. I wasn't sure where myth ended and reality began with these two mountain families, but the entire affair clearly stood out as an archetypal case of frontier justice.

Justice the township lay on the eastern edge of Mingo County, which was once part of the larger Logan County. After Virginia seceded from the Union and West Virginia seceded from Virginia, Logan County might as well have seceded from West Virginia. It was a place where law and

government were virtually nonexistent, where huge families led by stubborn patriarchs lived in isolated hollows, surviving by fishing, hunting,
logging, and making whiskey.

The Tug River served as the border between West Virginia and Kentucky. In the mid-1800s, the east bank of the river was populated mostly
by the West Virginia Hatfields, while the west bank was home to the
Kentucky McCoys. The leader of the Kentucky clan was a tall, broad-
shouldered fellow named Randall McCoy. "Ol' Ran'l," they called him.
He was a no-nonsense man who fathered nine sons and six daughters.
Patriarch of the West Virginians was William Anderson Hatfield, who
was known to everyone as "Devil Anse." A man fond of tall tales and
pranks, he was as charismatic and clowning as Ol' Ran'l was humorless.
He was only slightly less prolific, having nine sons and four daughters.

Devil Anse was said to have borne a striking resemblance to Stonewall Jackson. He certainly shared the general's sympathies. During the
war, he formed the Logan Wildcats, a feared band of guerrillas who pa-
trolled the Tug's banks in search of anyone with northern leanings. Their
first victim was a McCoy.

Like the Hatfields, the McCoys were Confederate sympathizers. But
Harmon McCoy, a younger brother of Ol' Ran'l, traded family loyalty
for loyalty to the Union, joining the northern forces as a private toward
the end of the war. He was discharged on Christmas Eve 1864 after
suffering a broken leg. Upon returning home, he was greeted by a warning from Jim Vance, a ruthless uncle of Devil Anse, who told him to
expect a visit from the Logan Wildcats. Snubbed by his family and pursued by Devil Anse's gang, Harmon McCoy hid in a cave for several
days. But the Wildcats followed his tracks in the snow, surprised him,
and shot him dead. Suspicion centered on Jim Vance, but nobody was
ever brought to trial for the murder. After all, even the McCoys thought
their wayward relative had sealed his fate by betraying the southern cause.
Still, the first shot had been fired.

For more than a dozen years after the war, there was peace along the border. Past injustices were largely forgotten; Hatfields and McCoys even began to intermarry, there being little else to choose from. Then, one crisp autumn day in 1878, a Hatfield and a McCoy got into it over a pig.

In those days, pigs roamed free until herding time and were marked only by an identifying ear notch. When Ol' Ran'l McCoy popped in to visit his brother-in-law Floyd Hatfield, he spotted a familiar-looking pig. It looked so familiar, in fact, that he claimed it as his own. The case wound up in court in front of a jury of six Hatfields and six McCoys and a roomful of whiskey jugs and rifles. The jury ruled in favor of Floyd Hatfield, thanks primarily to the testimony of Bill Staton, a nephew of Ol' Ran'l McCoy, who nevertheless swore it was Floyd's pig. Within months, Staton was dead. A McCoy was arrested for the murder and later acquitted.

It was at this time of growing animosity that a hillbilly Romeo and a highlander Juliet entered the scene. Romeo was Johnse Hatfield, the eighteen-year-old bootlegging son of Devil Anse. Juliet was Roseanna McCoy, Ol' Ran'l's beautiful daughter. The two met on the west bank of the Tug on Election Day 1880 (though what the West Virginia Hatfields were doing in Kentucky that day is unclear) and decided to elope. Roseanna followed Johnse home to the Hatfield cabin, a development that pleased neither Devil Anse nor Ol' Ran'l.

Roseanna returned to the McCoy side of the river a few months later, after her mother sent her sisters to plead for her return. But she soon fled to an aunt's house, where she could be closer to Johnse. The two lovers were together one night when a group of McCoys captured Johnse and carted him off toward prison. Believing her brothers were going to kill him, Roseanna climbed aboard a neighbor's horse and rode bareback to the Hatfield cabin. Devil Anse quickly assembled a gang, cut off the McCoys, and reclaimed his son.

After this heroic performance, the remainder of Roseanna's life was a steep spiral into tragedy. Her family shunned her, unable to forgive her breach of allegiance. Her lover avoided her, unwilling to risk her company, then adding to the ignominy by marrying her sixteen-year-old cousin. Pregnant and alone, she contracted measles and miscarried her baby. She was dead of a proverbial broken heart before she was thirty.

The feud, however, took on a life of its own. On Hatfield property in 1882, three of Roseanna's brothers finished off an argument with Devil Anse's brother Ellison Hatfield by stabbing him twenty-six times and shooting him in the back. Three days later, the three McCoys were found riddled with bullets. Six years later, the Hatfields raided the McCoy home and killed one of Ol' Ran'l's daughters and one of his sons.

Even Appalachia's chief executives went at it. The governor of Kentucky appointed a special officer to arrest the guilty Hatfields and sent a gang of bounty hunters to their West Virginia hollow. West Virginia's governor responded by suing his neighboring state for unlawful arrest.

By the time the last outburst of violence between the clans occurred—a murder on each side in 1896—the death toll had reached the teens. Jim Vance, the man who started it all, was dead. Johnse Hatfield was in prison for life, his wife having left him for one of the men who put him there. But in an ironic twist of fate, the two patriarchs, Devil Anse and Ol' Ran'l, survived it all, living well into their eighties. Their descendants became entrepreneurs, educators, physicians, even a governor of West Virginia.

Upon our arrival in Mingo County, it had been a hundred years since the last Hatfield murdered a McCoy and the last McCoy gunned down a Hatfield. The feud was ancient history, but the clans were not. Big families only grow bigger. I counted 410 Hatfields and 126 McCoys in the local phone book. We chose three names that seemed a good bet for a story—one a Vance, one a Hatfield, one a Justice.

It made sense to start our exploration of Justice with a descendant of the man who started the whole fracas—the man known in most Hatfield-McCoy histories as "the evil Jim Vance." So, in a room at the

Justonian Motel, we met another Jim Vance, whose grandfather was a cousin of the man who allegedly fired the first shot. The nineteenth-century Jim Vance had arrived in the area after his father, a backwoods preacher, shot a man who refused to marry his pregnant daughter and escaped into the hills. But this Jim wasn't named after that Jim.

"I'll tell ya how I got that name," he said in a drawl as thick as the muddy river a few hundred feet away. "My mama always told me, when I was born, they turned around and said, 'Well, what are we gonna name him?' And the doctor looked up and said, 'I'll tell ya what, ma'am, name him James after me.' So they did. Ya know, that doctor ain't been dead but about seven or eight years. I'm seventy-five, and he was already an ol' man then."

Jim Vance was born in McDowell County, just a few miles from Justice, and moved to town when he was seventeen. He became a coal miner, like his father before him, in 1941, just before Pearl Harbor. He left the mines in 1980.

"When I started workin' in the mines in nineteen and forty-one, the first of November, I got a dollar an hour. Seven hours for seven dollars."

"That was probably a lot of money in those days," I said, knowing it would take a hundred times that to get me into a coal mine.

*J*im Vance

"I reckon it was. I used to go to the store and buy the best pair of wing-tip shoes for two ninety-eight. When I started workin' in the mine, I always had to wear a hard-shell cap. It cost us about two dollars and somethin'. The other day, my wife was with me, and I picked one up and said, 'Do ya see this? Looky here. Here it is for twenty-four dollars!'" He shook his head. "Coal mining's tough."

"Well, you look pretty good for having spent forty years underground," I offered, opening a can of worms.

"Well, for the last year, I been fightin' prostate cancer. I made thirty-eight trips to Charleston. That's 220 miles round-trip. After they give me treatments, they said I have to do some therapy, so I do that in Logan. I been takin' a shot there once a month since back last September, when it started. Man, that shot makes me sick. I also got black lung. Any coal miner that works in the coal mines forty years and runs those machines and eats all that dust and everythin', he's got the black lung. When I went to have an operation on my hands back last July, I was on the operatin' table, nurse come in there and says, 'Mr. Vance, has anybody ever told ya you got the black lung? You got one of the worst cases of it. But as far as the federal government's concerned, you don't have it.' I said, 'I know that. I known since 1972 that I had the black lung.'"

He laughed, paused, and then laughed again. "I can get up and go to the bathroom and a lot of times cough and spit up dust like it was yesterday. Black as coal."

I tried to imagine what it must be like to work in a coal mine. I really did. But I couldn't. Just like I couldn't picture myself ranching in Harmony or mining copper in Inspiration or working a sawmill in Pride or farming in Hope or hunting in Love. I come from a land of gas fireplaces and AAA road service and weekly landscapers and boneless chicken breasts. Show me a flat tire and I'll look for a car phone. Point me to a horse and I'll feed the wrong end. I am a product of my environment, for better or for worse. It's in my blood, like cholesterol.

During our journey, whenever I came upon people whose lifestyle seemed to have nothing in common with mine, I found myself treating the encounter like a session of self-analysis. I'd look at them, then look at myself, wondering if my hands lacked calluses or if my fingernails weren't dirty enough. Then I would wonder if I was being unfair to myself by wondering this. It was an egocentric process, to be sure. But then this trip across America was also an expedition of the mind.

Maybe it's a generational thing or a suburban thing. Maybe it's deeply personal. After all, I can't picture myself on Wall Street either. All I know is that I'm not the kind of person who could scratch out a living exploring a tunnel in a mountainside, risking life and limb, returning home every day covered from head to toe in coal dust. And I'm not sure what that says about me. Still, I respect the people who do it. And Justice was full of them.

"It used to be that we had three, four, five beer joints. Fun every night and Sunday, too!" Jim recalled. "Back around '39 and '40, this used to be the meanest place ya ever seen. Ya couldn't walk from this upper end to the lower end when somebody didn't shoot at ya, crack ya with a rock, or somethin'." He said this with a playful gleam in his eye. I suspected it was an inherited gleam, the kind of look Harmon McCoy probably saw in the old Jim Vance 130 years earlier, just before Vance started shooting.

"A bunch of rowdy coal miners, is that what it was?"

"Exactly right. They'd come from McDowell County, from Logan County, and they'd all come to Justice. They'd say, 'Well, we're gonna take the town Saturday night.' But they never did take the town. We had a bunch of roughnecks here. Man, we've had a lot of murders here in this town. I'd say we had ten or fifteen murders back in them days."

"So where was the justice here?"

"Well, I'm gonna tell ya. It wasn't the people livin' in this town. It was the people that came here from other places. The people that was here at the time, they was excellent people."

"This is no longer a wild town, then?"

"Oh, no . . . Well, I can't tell you that. Yeah, it is, to a certain extent. This club up there . . . As far as this town right now, it's got more dope in it than any town in Mingo County, far as I know."

"The club? Yesterdays, is that it?"

"Yeah. That's it. Of course, they're fixin' to make a raid in there. One of these nights, they'll take every sucker in. They got their names. A lot of dope here. Yeah, if I was the law, I could get out here and catch every one of 'em—on a Saturday night."

"What about the old Jim Vance? What would he do in that case?"

The "young" Jim Vance, two generations removed, began to grin. "Far as I know, he was jus' a mean feller. He mighta been in there with 'em!"

From Jim Vance, it was natural to move on to a Hatfield. For some reason, I was apprehensive about meeting a real live member of the clan, half-expecting some wild-eyed mountain hermit looking to start a new quarrel. Jim Blake Hatfield turned out to be nothing of the sort. A retired strip miner, he was a sweet-faced, grass-stained, laconic lump of a man. We caught him wielding a weed whacker in front of a large white Colonial and spent a few minutes with him while a trio of puppies tumbled over each other in the yard.

"I'm closely related to Devil Anse," he informed us, "on my mother's side and my dad's side. I enjoy history, and I take pride in being related to Devil Anse. He wasn't so bad, you know. Part of it was over the Civil War and part of it over a woman. It was a divided country at that time."

I had to ask the question: "So if you're walking down the street, and you run into a McCoy . . . ?"

"No problem."

"I suppose that ended about a hundred years ago."

"Right. I lived in Washington State for fifteen years. Took more harassment for being a Hatfield over there. They enjoyed it, harassing me. And I worked for a black McCoy."

Jim Hatfield

"A guy named McCoy who happened to be black?"

"Yep."

"I assume he wasn't a descendant."

"No. Heh-heh."

"And I bet you got along fine, didn't you?"

"Got along fine."

"But do you ever stop and marvel that you descend from a famous family—and certainly the most famous feud—in American history?"

"Like I said, when I lived on the West Coast, I took pride in being a Hatfield. See, Oregon had a governor, Mark Hatfield. So I'd go into Oregon and get all kinds of good service."

It was a bit like a descendant of Andrew Jackson getting free tickets to a Michael Jackson concert, but I got the picture. "What about back here in West Virginia?"

"Ah, West Virginia . . ." Jim Blake smirked. "It's a place to love and a place to hate."

"What's to love?"

"I guess the country atmosphere. You know, you can still do your own thing."

"And what's to hate?"

"I'd rather not comment. Heh-heh."

"All right. But it's not the McCoys, right?"

"Right. Well, this town here, it's had a . . . a reputation. One time, we had seven taverns—bootlegged, wasn't legal—and seven churches within a mile-and-a-half radius."

"I hear this was a mean town."

"It still is."

"In what way?"

"No law," he answered quickly, laughing as he did. "Unincorporated, you know. It's a long story. Heh-heh. You get shot when you leave town. Heh-heh."

The conversation ended there, but I was satisfied. Jokingly or not, a Hatfield had warned me I was going to get shot. How many people can say that?

Dotty Joe Justice was different. A Renaissance man, he was an educator, an entrepreneur, a historian, a sociologist of sorts. After majoring in fine arts and social sciences at Marshall University, he earned a master's degree in administration from West Virginia University and technical certification from the Mind, Science and Health Academy in Beckley. Dotty Joe taught school for a decade in Gilbert. He owned land in three states, ran the Justonian Motel in town and a small sawmill up the road, and was in the process of constructing a bed-and-breakfast about an hour north of Justice. "Jack-of-all-trades," he admitted. "Master of none."

My memory of Dotty Joe is of a stocky, fast-talking, coal-country philosopher with a full face, a shock of messy white hair, a rolled up *USA Today* "Money" section in his hand, and a story on his lips.

"Are you from Illinois?" he began. "I see your tags. There's a town called Justice in Illinois, you know. I had a cousin who moved out there. I guess he had to move away from home to find Justice—heh-heh— because there's not any justice in West Virginia."

It was a point he would return to at length, but at the moment, I was more interested in the community than the concept. "I was wondering," I said, "what you could tell me about the history of the town." As it turned out, he could tell me a lot.

"I've traced it back to 1657 in Jamestown. The first Justice came to Jamestown—I believe it was William, there's nothing but Williams and Thomases and Jameses all the way down the tree—and he was in charge of sixty-seven indentured servants who settled in Charles City, Virginia, on his plantation. He had three sons. One went to Pennsylvania. One went to North Carolina. And then one came west and wound up in Floyd County, Kentucky.

"About 1837 or so, my great-great-grandfather, whose name was James Justice, migrated from Floyd County or Pike County. Floyd and Pike have always had a debate as to what their border is, so no one knows. Back in those days, it was still part of Virginia, I guess, and he came into the various valleys that separate Kentucky from West Virginia. Now, James was married to the aunt of Devil Anse Hatfield, whose name was Jenny. I don't know if the feud had actually started at the time, whether or not James was leaving Kentucky in order to get away from it, or if, like most of the people who settled down in that rugged area, he was just looking for a better place. Of course, most of 'em were 'subsistent' farmers. I mean, they farmed on a forty-five-degree angle.

"James eventually made his way down Gilbert Creek to the Guyandotte River, and he actually traveled up the river to a tributary, a place called Little Huff Creek. That's sort of where it started. The then-governor of Virginia gave a grant of land for so many thousand acres to James, who died, evidently, without a will. I don't even know where he's buried. Nobody knows. I don't know how many children Jenny and James had by the

Dotty Joe Justice

time they came here, but the son that remained in the area, who basically inherited the land, was William Epperson Justice, and he was my great-grandfather. He was a gigantic, big ol' guy. Probably weighed 340 pounds."

According to Walt Whitman, "The maker of poems settles justice." According to Dotty Joe, gigantic, big ol' guys do. By the turn of the century, Epp Justice—who was Jim Blake Hatfield's mother's grandfather and Jim

Vance's mother's great-uncle—had acquired thousands of acres and a small fortune, much of it through the timber industry. Around 1907, Epp's land was sold off in lots. The town that sprang up was originally named Alonzo, after Epp's oldest son. About a decade later, it entered the county records as Justice City. Somewhere along the line, it shrank to Justice.

"Epp had a son named Dotty Yaeger Justice," explained Dotty Joe. "That's how I got my name. The name came from Pennsylvania. You see, William Epp was also in the store business, and one of his connections was a company called Dotty and Shiveley out of Lancaster. So he named one of his kids Dotty, and he named one Shiveley. Well, Shiveley didn't make it. He died at childbirth, I think. But anyhow, that's the tradition, and it's been a pain in the neck from day one. The rarity of it! As rare as it is for a male to have that name, there's four of us critters in the area. Four Dotty Justices! I had trouble with it because, basically, it's a female-type name. I was placed in the ladies' dormitory in college, way before coed dorms. Heh-heh. That was back in the sixties.

"Anyhow, my daddy's name was Dallas, son of Dotty Yaeger, and when Dad was discharged from the army, he came back and worked a little in and around the coal mines. Then, in the late forties, the coal industry went bad, so jobs were scarce, and evidently he decided it wasn't for him. Then, in 1952 or thereabouts, he put in a little service station, a small one, rented the place. I remember he had to have $380. I was about eight, and that was a fortune to me. He worked there until 1957 or so, and then he built the service station next to the motel. Then the Corps of Engineers decided to build a dam for flood control and supposed recreational pleasures just outside of town. As a result of that, we decided that they're gonna need a place to stay, the people who worked there. So my daddy bought a forty-by-a-hundred lot and built seven units for a motel. Then the demand was there, and we added a second floor. And then we built another wing and another one and another one, on down the line.

"The motel has gone through some good times. Justice boomed during the seventies, when the oil embargo occurred and coal demand was gigantic. It was just unbelievable how the economy flourished. It's leveled off again, but what happened was that everyone and his uncle became involved in the coal business. Here I was teaching school, but I've always had an interest in everything, so I became involved in coal from 1974 to 1989. Then I sold out, because it started getting tough again. From 1989 to the present, it's been horrible for small investors. What happened to the coal industry happened to the town of Justice. The demand was so great that everybody jumped into the mining business, and they mined out what little was left, so that now there's no future in it. Coal's gone."

Evidently, he envisioned the same future for the town named after his family. There was talk of a new interstate highway being built through southern West Virginia. Most of the land was owned not by descendants of the people who settled it but by big land companies, and it was the people waving the money who were going to decide where the superhighway went.

"So now, the road will totally bypass Justice, but it'll go right through the middle of the land-company land," he said. "Fifty years from now, as the world turns, that will probably be a commercially developed area, and Justice will be one of those little back-road towns with a history, totally insignificant to the rest of the world."

But what about the Hatfields and McCoys? Can a place be rendered insignificant even if its founding families were a mythical part of American frontier culture? Shouldn't Justice have the same resonance as Tombstone or Dodge City or Deadwood? Isn't the feud of all feuds worth something?

Dotty Joe didn't think so. "Oh, I think it's a joke! People here just want to act the fool, being a relative of one clan or the other. But I'm not proud of the fact that I had some ancestors who ran around the woods and fought over a damn hog. In my opinion, that's about as redneck as you can get."

The history lesson over, Dotty Joe, professor of Appalachia, switched gears to social studies. "Ignorance is bliss," he asserted. "And by the way, you're presently in a state of bliss. I call this area down in the hills 'West Vacant.' There's a vacancy of creativity, a vacancy of logical understanding of how things work. And that's why we're where we're at. We stay here because we want to be here in the hills, in the valleys and nooks and crannies that flatlanders like y'all can't stand to drive to. It's always gonna be that way, and that was the call of it to start with."

He then embarked on a story that shed some light on the kind of people attracted to Justice and the surrounding nooks and crannies. "I know this guy by the name of John Thomas that lived in Justice once upon a time. He lived in a place called Groundhog Creek. Growing up, I'd see him every so often on the back of a mule. He had two white sacks tied together, hanging over each side of the mule, and he had something in them, but I couldn't tell what it was. And behind him on a mule would be his wife, and she would have two white sacks tied together, hanging over the sides. Couldn't tell what that was either. Behind them on a mule were his two children, Grover and Woody. Grover had rickets, was all drawn over. Still lives in Gilbert, by the way. But anyhow, John Thomas, you never talked to him. The only time you saw him was when he rode through town, and what they were deliverin' was quart jars of moonshine. Nobody knows where it came from. But lo and behold, one day, a state trooper pulled into the Justice Exxon station, wanted to know if anyone knew a John Robert Thomas. And somebody said, 'Yeah, he lives over in Groundhog.'

"So, next thing you know, John Thomas has been picked up for committing murder in Virginia—for shooting a federal agent. He escaped to this part of West Virginia because it's vacant. It's vacant of law. It's vacant of authority. It's vacant of roads. It's isolated. And that's the draw of it all. He lived in that hollow all those years, and they finally caught him. See, in the hills, as rugged as they are, you just don't call the police. I mean, if you call 'em in Justice today, they won't come. Justice has had nine murders in my lifetime—in a little town with a population of 250!"

The purpose of my journey through the lower forty-eight was not only to probe the American psyche but also to examine biases and preconceptions, including my own. I hoped that maybe I could even debunk a few of these, replace my simplistic prejudices with the complexities of actual experience. But here I was in the heart of Appalachia listening to stories about moonshine and murders and shotgun feuds. It was too . . . expected.

"It's hard to avoid stereotyping a state even if you're trying not to," I admitted, "but West Virginia . . ."

"The southern counties in West Virginia and eastern Kentucky have been stereotyped by people who don't really understand what it's all about," he replied. "Now, I'm sort of being critical of West Vacant and all that, but it depends what you're looking for. I mean, West Virginia produced Cyrus Vance. George Washington was from what was then western Virginia. Chuck Yeager was a West Virginian. I can name fifty people from here who have influenced the world in one fashion or another."

"But the southern counties . . ."

"Those are in trouble. The draw that the Tug Valley and the Guyandotte Valley had for the early settlers who came here was independence. But it's not important anymore, because it's an impossibility. You can't be independent anymore with a population of 260 million. You can't be a loner." Dotty Joe was now leaning forward on the edge of his seat.

"My point being that it's another way of life, and it was a selected way of life—until 1960, until John Kennedy and Lyndon Johnson came through and told these people, 'Hey, you're poor! You live in this little ol' tarpaper house, even though you got a color TV and a refrigerator and a freezer on the back porch and a cellar full of canned goods. You got the finest coon dogs ever to chase coons in this world sittin' on that doghouse there, right beside your home. And you got the best crop of fightin' chickens ever to mess in the yard. But you don't realize this—you're poor. Listen to me, I can help you. You don't have to live like this no more. You just come down and sign up for this adult education class. We got a fine teacher here. He's gonna teach you to read and write. And as soon as you learn to read and write, we're gonna put you on a program where you start drawing checks from the government. And then you don't have to worry about planting your garden, 'cause now all you have to do is wait for the fifteenth of the month.' "

His was the confident tone of someone who had thought long and hard about the problem. Mine was the wide-eyed expression of someone who hadn't.

"Now, you think I'm punnin', but in a sense, I'm not," he continued. "Do you know the strongest industry in the state of West Virginia? What would you say?"

"I would think that coal would be."

"That's what most people think. It's not. It's banking. Banking! The strongest industry in the state! And West Virginia has the third-strongest banking industry in the U.S. Now, how can that be, when you drive through and see all of this visual poverty? Well, some of those folks are getting thirty-eight hundred dollars a month, because they're drawing social security, because they have SSI—supplemental social security—for those people who are indigent, physically impaired, or in any way needing help.

"Lyndon Johnson, with his Great Society, convinced these people that they were poor. Now, they're uneducated and they're ignorant, but they're not stupid. They were told that they don't have to work in the mines anymore, that they don't have to work anymore period. You can just go down and sign up at the social security office. Tell them that you didn't graduate high school, that you're an ol' hick who just went to grade school. That qualifies you so that you don't have the intellectual level to be a productive citizen. Then you tell them you don't have any skills." Here, he adopted a high-pitched, hillbilly twang. "'Alls I know is coal minin', and coal minin' done left.'

"So he then qualifies for a monthly stipend from SSI. Now, all he has to do is not get caught when he wants to work. We have a black-market industry in southern West Virginia that is unbelievable. I employ people. I pay them five dollars an hour. If I want to write them a check for five dollars, they won't take it. Now, that tells you they're not dumb, because they know that anything in writing will get traced, and they'll get caught for working when they're supposed to be unable to work, because Lyndon Johnson told them they were too poor and too physically and mentally impaired to work. Or I write 'em a check to their son's name or their uncle's name. I've got people making thirty-eight thousand dollars a year and more, counting what they get from the government. It's unbelievable.

"You read all the statistics. West Virginia has the highest unemployment rate in the nation and all these people on welfare. But here they are, they're getting $446 a month if they're married or they have a woman at home. They get $126 a month in food stamps. They get free clothes for the children when they start school, and if they plan right, they can get enough clothes to last them all year. They get 100 percent hospitalization. So I figured it out. It comes to about $800 a month, which is no fabulous fortune. But they're living in an area where they can raise a little garden, raise all the critters they want, work when they want to, eat chicken when they want to—the old way of life. They got enough money to leave if they want to, but they ain't about to leave, 'cause they got it too good. 'Cause they're poverty-ridden."

I hadn't expected a lecture on the evils of public assistance—or "draw," as they call it in West Virginia. But then I hadn't expected a need for it. At least not here. Like much of the nation, I had been brainwashed into envisioning the face of welfare as a black one, even though a greater percentage of those receiving government handouts is white. I'm cynical enough to think that both sides of the issue see an advantage in portraying welfare as largely an African American and inner-city phenomenon. The program's supporters provide dramatic examples of families subjugated by a racist society. Its opponents appeal to that very racism, allowing an eager working class to label black Americans as lazy.

But here I was, in one of the poorest counties of perhaps our poorest state, and the only black faces I saw were those covered with coal dust. And I was being told—by an educated man with intimate knowledge of the subject and an obvious, if paternal, love for the people of his state—that Appalachian poverty was a practiced science and that a program based on giving was being taken for all it was worth. I had long scorned those who proposed to eliminate the welfare system as compassionless and removed, but I was beginning to think that my perspective was just as distant. I could feel my bleeding heart clotting just a little.

"You know that saying that beauty is in the eye of the beholder?" asked Dotty Joe. "Well, I think culture is in the eye of the beholder. When people go looking at another culture without understanding the background and the whole scenario, then they're gonna have this misconception. These people here have become wards and slaves of the system. They depend upon that check totally now."

"So are you saying that ignorance is bliss, in the sense that a little awareness for them is dangerous?"

"I don't know if you'd call it dangerous. They're doing pretty good. The reason West Virginia has such a strong banking industry is that these people get this monthly check, and they save a portion of it."

If the welfare system has indeed run amuck, the problem, as I see it, is placing blame. Do we blame the government for its good-hearted intentions or the residents of the Appalachian hollows for taking advantage of a system that had long taken advantage of them? We are a nation of educated, wealthy, comfortable people who have few qualms about diving through tax loopholes, forcing frivolous lawsuits, and filing padded insurance claims. When those who have everything are willing to cheat the system, can we blame those who have nothing for doing the same? Isn't the pot calling the kettle black?

I found myself looking for a third option on which to pin blame and wondering if I would have the moral fortitude to wave off some distant, faceless entity willing to pay me for not working.

"You know that you would rather earn your bread than have it given to you," Dotty Joe insisted. "You're an intelligent, educated fellow. You've never been in the pits that I'm talking about, and neither have I. I've grown up around it, but I've never been in it. If you're a farmer, you understand this. If you're a chicken farmer, you understand it well. If you got a handful of corn and you got your chickens running free and you start spreading it out on the ground, do you know which chicken gets the most corn? The one that's there first. The one that's at the front of the line. Did somebody teach them that way? No. It's just their nature. If you can get something free, you take it. Now, it just so happens that it used to be you were rewarded for being independent. If you lived in the hills of southern West Virginia or eastern Kentucky, you could stay there, and nobody bothered you. But now, the chicken farmers in Washington have come in and started spreading out the corn. As a result, two generations have been lost."

The amazing thing to me, as I listened to Dotty Joe's diatribe, was that a region of the country so associated with a lack of government interference, settled by people who hid in the hollows to avoid laws and lawmakers, was now so thoroughly immersed in public aid. Would Appalachia have been better left to itself in the first place? Or was the problem in today's Appalachia one of systematization without supervision?

Dotty Joe seemed to think the government had introduced a diseased perspective into the hills of southern West Virginia and then left the region to fester. "The only place I've seen so many roadside flea markets was in the Pueblo Indian reservation in Arizona. You come to West Virginia, and they sell every damn thing in the world by the side of the road—and about two-thirds of it is stolen," he lamented. "Because there's no regulation. There's no police. There's no need for it, because everybody takes care of their own situation. So as a result, the drug culture, which has been brought in from big cities, has now begun to destroy what little was left of the ancient culture that James Justice came here to find—that independence, that self-sufficiency.

"It used to be that people where I came from would raise corn on a forty-five-degree angle," he said. "Now, they raise children."

As Amy and I pulled out of town, we had no way of knowing that only a few weeks later, President Clinton would sign a sweeping welfare reform bill. Some said it was just the thing to get America working again. Others feared it would cut a lifeline for people in places where health care and child care were expensive and jobs were scarce—that it might turn coal-country communities, in particular, into ghost towns.

I'll have to reserve judgment—until I return to the Guyandotte Valley someday to see if Appalachia survived, to see if Justice was served.

BLISS,
NEW YORK

> *Where ignorance is bliss, 'Tis folly to be wise.*
> Thomas Gray

"Each of us is all the sums he has not counted: subtract us into nakedness and night again, and you shall see begin in Crete four thousand years ago the love that ended yesterday in Texas."

In the first paragraphs of *Look Homeward, Angel*, Thomas Wolfe articulated the notion that every epic saga was the product of smaller events of unheralded consequence. "A stone that starts an avalanche . . . a pebble whose concentric circles widen across the sea."

Bliss was the product of such occurrences, those tangents that became foundations. Because an Englishman heard the call of the wild 350 years ago, because an American pioneer lost his mind in 1832, and because a turn-of-the-century German suffered an accident with an ax, Amy and I found ourselves sitting across a table from Frank Noble, the town historian of a tiny hamlet in western New York.

We had set off from Gettysburg, a town itself immortalized by happenstance—a chance meeting of opposing armies. From the place made famous by Pickett's charge and Lincoln's words, Route 15 took us straight through the heart of Pennsylvania, past Harrisburg and Lewisburg and into the Allegheny hills. The Susquehanna River, the largest nonnavigable river in North America, accompanied us most of the way, rushing in the other direction.

I was struck by what an integral part rivers played in many of the communities we had visited—the Guadalupe in Comfort, the Tennessee in Pride, the Mississippi in Triumph, the Guyandotte in Justice. Sometimes, it was the rush of water as historical narrative that transfixed me. Or the river as giver, as a region's vital artery. Here in Pennsylvania, I found myself considering rivers' unpredictability, the fact that, though constancy defines them, they are actually subject to radical fluctuation. At its peak, the Susquehanna fed 650 billion tons of water to Chesapeake Bay per day. Yet it could move as little as 2 billion during a drought. If the river was a storyteller, it was a temperamental one.

Today, the final day in May, the Susquehanna was serene and reflective after a morning rain, twisting and turning with the highway until it left us at Williamsport and headed west. We continued north through the Tioga River Valley and into New York, where we were met by a picture postcard of rolling hills, strolling herds, and primary colors—deep blue sky, lush green meadows, brown fields, yellow dandelions, white houses, red barns. After a succession of zigzags and one long detour around Letchworth State Park, a seventeen-mile gorge known as the "Grand Canyon of the East," we stopped at the intersection of Routes 39 and 362. Just then, a motorcycle with a sidecar zoomed past us. Peering out from the sidecar was a fluffy white poodle. This surreal crossroads was Bliss.

Bliss wasn't a one stoplight town. It was a one stop sign town. Bliss was Main Street and its periphery tucked into a bend in some lonely railroad tracks. It was a little town of 250 people decorated with a little of everything. The former Bliss High School was now a tiny recreation center. Bliss Library was 150 square feet of books. Bliss International Speedway was a go-cart track on the outskirts of town, bails of hay surrounding a blacktop oval. There were a couple of churches, a town hall, an American Legion post, a hardware store, a grocery store, a garage.

At first glance, it seemed an idyllic rural outpost—men riding lawn mowers, laundry hanging from clotheslines, dogs running in backyards, windmills spinning, flags waving. But a closer look revealed a hamlet, like many we visited, that was past its prime. A school bus with shattered windows lay dead in a lot, a few boarded buildings inhabited Main Street, too much litter marred an otherwise pristine landscape. Bliss was a Norman Rockwell painting left to fade and wither in a damp attic.

Frank Noble lived in a small two-story house—pink on the bottom, white on top, brown shutters. It looked like an enormous slab of Neapolitan ice cream. Sitting at one end of his kitchen table, his dog, Angel, at his feet, he was a stout, cherubic fellow with a gentle, scratchy voice somewhere between Cronkite and Kuralt. He pulled out a file

Downtown Bliss

and carefully showed us a document he'd inherited from the previous town historian, who had received it from his grandfather. It was the only copy of the 164-year-old deed marking the exact origin of Bliss. Of course, origins were a matter of perspective. Thomas Wolfe: "Each moment is the fruit of forty thousand years." For Bliss, it was at least 400.

The genealogy of a hamlet: Thomas Bliss was born in 1588 in Daventry, England. He married Dorothy Wheatlie at the age of twenty-six, and they had seven children, three of whom died young. When Thomas turned fifty in 1638, he and his family climbed aboard a vessel headed for New England. Their reasons were lost to time. A blacksmith by trade, Thomas was not a poor man, though he spent most of his money transporting his family overseas. They landed in Boston, moved just south to Braintree, Massachusetts, and then joined fifty-seven other settlers in obtaining a grant of land on both sides of the Palmer River. They called their new town Rehoboth. Thomas received an eight-acre plot of land. At the time of his death in 1647, he owned forty-five acres.

His youngest son, Jonathan, also a farmer and blacksmith, rose to prominence in the community. Over the years, he augmented the family's holdings and was appointed to various positions of respect in the town, including surveyor, grand juryman, and constable. His first daughter was named Experience; she lived to be seventy-two. His second, Rachel, was brutally murdered during an Indian war in 1676. His seventh child was Jonathan II.

Jonathan Bliss II became one of Rehoboth's leading citizens. He had eight children with his first wife, four more with his second. His oldest was Jonathan III, who begat Abraham, who begat Eleazar Elias, who made the first significant move in the Bliss family since it came over the pond. In 1785, at the age of forty, Eleazar moved to Berkshire, Massachusetts, where he worked as a miller. From there, he headed west into New York, eventually building a home in Hartwick, a sparsely occupied tract where the paths from one settlement to another were marked by blazed trees. He stayed there until his death at age eighty-eight.

His son, Eleazar Elias Bliss, Jr., born in Massachusetts in the months between the Boston Tea Party and Paul Revere's ride, raised eight children in New York, many of whom came to personify American expansion. One daughter married a man from Michigan; another moved to Wisconsin; a grandson wound up a cotton broker in Mississippi. Eleazar's third child was Sylvester. "A stone that starts an avalanche . . ."

In this case, the stone was a man a couple hundred miles west in Allegany County who went certifiably nuts. The deed Frank Noble held in his hands affirmed the sale of 182 acres in Allegany County to Sylvester Bliss. The land had belonged to a fellow named Justin Loomis, but Justin Loomis was judged insane. His lawyer sold the 182 acres for $575. It was July 12, 1832.

Frank pointed to his favorite phrase in the deed—"in the matter of Justin Loomis, a lunatic"—and noted, "I guess they didn't mince words, did they?" He laughed a rumbling Santa Claus laugh.

Sylvester Bliss cleared his newly purchased land of timber and established a profitable farm. He shipped butter and cheese to New York City and sent wool to New England mills. In 1865, he sold the farm to his youngest son, Stephen, the pilgrim's great-great-great-great-great-great grandson. Stephen erected the family homestead that still stands today. In 1870, the house was made a post office along a regional mail route, and Stephen was named postmaster. In 1878, he oversaw the completion of the Rochester & State Line Railroad through the area and the launch of the hamlet's first general store. Finally, on February 7, 1881, the settlement was named Bliss in recognition of its founding family.

Within a decade, the town could boast two general stores, a clothing store, a furniture store, a meat market, a livery stable, two wagon shops, two blacksmiths, a hotel, and a newspaper. Over the years, several businesses came and went—a cheese factory, a salt factory, a pump manufacturer, a sawmill. There was a Bliss brass band and a Bliss orchestra. Still, the railroad was the community's lifeblood. The train's whistle, according to one local account, "was sure to draw a crowd of young folk . . . and was equal to a fire or a dog fight in appeal." It proved an unfortunate choice of words.

Frank pulled out another faded piece of paper, this one a copy of the front page of the *Rochester Herald* dated August 12, 1919. The boldest headline: "BLISS PLANS REBUILDING ERE SMOKE OF DESOLATING FIRE CLEARS FROM RUINS." Two days earlier, at about five in the afternoon, some children playing in the hotel barn with cattails dipped in oil had caught the structure on fire. Pushed by a northwest wind, the fire began to spread. The town's water system failed, and calls for help were sent out to neighboring communities before the phone lines burned. By the time help arrived, an entire block of Main Street was in flames. In all, the three-hour blaze consumed sixty-five buildings—including the Bliss & Sons general store and Bliss National Bank—and caused an estimated two hundred thousand dollars in damage. Thirty-five people lost their homes.

"Little except heaps of smoldering ashes and stone foundation walls remains of the business section of Bliss," announced the *Herald*. "A chimney still standing, a charred tree, a toppling pole and debris of all kinds scattered around with curls of smoke rising from the ruins made a dis-

*F*rank Noble

mal scene not unlike views of France where the Huns had passed." Within a few years, several brick business blocks arose from the ashes of the old, but the fire marked the end of an era. Industry drifted away; the town began to fade into the present state of Bliss.

It's remarkable how the forces of nature can conspire against a small town's survival. Hundreds of years of concentric circles lead to the formation of a community. A pebble here, a pebble there. And then it can be gone in a heartbeat, a quantifiable day of reckoning. A fire in Bliss, August 10, 1919. A hurricane in Triumph, August 17, 1969. A flood in Love the next day. Sometimes, too, the end is gradual, though perhaps more permanent. Corporate encroachment put an end to Inspiration. Economic stagnation was killing Justice. Old age apparently took old Glory.

"Each moment is the fruit of forty thousand years." Small towns, like one's state of mind, take years to ripen but just days to rot.

"My mother was born in Germany. She was only three or four weeks old when she came over here in 1883. I asked my older brother last year why they came over when she was so small. He told me our grandfather had to leave. He was cutting wood from the kaiser's forest, and he slipped and cut his leg. And they didn't dare go to the doctor, because the doctor would have turned him in." Frank let out a faint laugh. "So here we are because our grandfather was a crook!"

Frank was born in Centerville, New York, in January 1918. His family moved down the road to Bliss just weeks before the fire. That same year, Frank suffered a permanent scar of his own. "My folks had bought a brand-new horse-drawn mowing machine. My brother was putting grease in there, and this big wheel was going around and around, and I stuck my finger in it. Cut if off," he said, holding up a stump that should have been his left index finger. "I never missed it. I mean, I was a year and a half old. I just grew up without it."

He became a carpenter, absent finger be damned. Most of his work was commercial—schools, colleges, hospitals. Every town needs its Sylvester Bliss, someone to claim the ground in the first place. But just as important are people like Frank Noble, those who construct the town from the ground up. Now, having retired to a $150-a-year role as Bliss's historian, he no longer built things but rather preserved them.

Frank showed me how he held his hammer wedged between his would-be pointer and his middle finger. "It's never bothered me," he said. "You know, you can overcome a lot of things. I talk to blind people. It amazes you what they can do. My wife had a relative who was blind, and he was tuning pianos. He'd stay with us overnight sometimes when he was in the area, and he'd say, 'I've got to go to so-and-so's place.' My wife would say, 'I don't know where that is.' He'd say, 'Well, you go down this road and down that road.' He'd tell us where it was, and he'd been blind since he was six years old."

I wondered if Frank had been living with blinders on, too. With the exception of a twelve-year span in early adulthood, he had spent all his life in Bliss. Had it colored his perceptions? Had it simplified them? Did Bliss foster a sort of unsophisticated contentedness, and, conversely, was there truth in Thomas Gray's oft-repeated line, quoted by Dotty Joe Justice only a few days earlier?

Is ignorance bliss? Frank became my case study.

"I grew up during the Depression," he explained. "I didn't know I was poor. You don't realize it, because everyone else is. You're all in the same boat. I was born on a farm, raised on a farm. I went to school in a one-room schoolhouse. Our desks were quite wide. They were big enough for two people. The teacher would call a grade for, say, history, and you'd sit on a bench in front of her desk. So anybody who was in the first, second, and third grade, they heard the lessons for the eighth-graders and the seventh-graders, and they learned a lot of stuff that they normally wouldn't. I wouldn't say I got a great education, because I went to high school in the sixth grade and graduated when I was sixteen." He smiled. "I think they needed the seats.

"When I was a teenager, I don't remember anything about world news. The big stock market crash in 1929? That didn't mean a thing to me. I didn't know what they were talking about. The only scandal we ever had here is somebody was caught out with another man's wife, and that was about it." Frank laughed. "Course, everybody in town knew it. That was way back in the thirties. The telephone was quite a source of gossip. Everyone on the street was on one line, so when the telephone rang, it rang in every house. But each house had a different ring—two longs or two longs and a short or three shorts."

"So everybody knew everybody's business," Amy said.

"Except the neighbors down the street," Frank said. "They came from Wales and talked Welsh, and no one could interpret that."

Amy and I smiled at each other. One of the reasons we had been eager to take this trip was to get a breath of fresh air, to escape big-city worries and obligations. For us, small towns represented a gentler state of mind. But the pundits of the metropolis tend to ascribe ignorance to anyone without a subway token and a health club membership, anyone so far from the city skyline that it fails to block their view.

And what is ignorance anyway? From the Latin *ignorare*, meaning "not to know," it is the condition of being without education or knowledge, of being uninformed. But was it ignorance that characterized Frank's experience of Bliss, or merely isolation? And doesn't isolation breed imagination?

"You don't have all the things to do," he explained. "Whatever recreation we had, we had to make ourselves. Like in the winter, sliding down the hills and playing different games in the snow. When I was real small, we used to have a game called Wood Tag, where as long as you could touch a piece of wood, you were safe. And Run, Sheep, Run. That was played in the dark. And Fox and Geese, where you formed a circle. Simple, simple games."

Perhaps childhood is an appropriate analogy. Children are uninformed. Their lives are simple, unencumbered by the complexities that arrive with adulthood. And yes, they're supposed to be happy. But is it due to the boundaries of ignorance or their boundless imagination? That is the heart of the issue.

"Where ignorance is bliss, 'Tis folly to be wise." Thomas Gray's line has been quoted out of context for decades. It hints at the foolishness of underestimating wisdom. It also suggests the absurdity of inferring cause from correlation—that if ignorance leads to bliss, then only the empty-headed can find spiritual joy. It's like saying, "If fat people are jolly, then who wants to be thin?" I hear sarcasm in the line, not sagacity.

Yet there have always been proponents of the know-nothing philosophy. They bring up Van Gogh or Poe or Oppenheimer to show that genius is somehow equivalent to discontentment, and they blame the cynicism permeating the country on the demise of naivete. They dredge up historical figures who somewhat disingenuously lamented the bane of their intellect—Sherwood Anderson speaking of the "sadness of sophistication," Mark Twain claiming that success could be attained simply by combining ignorance and confidence, Frederick Douglass suggesting that learning to read in captivity had been a curse rather than a blessing ("In moments of agony, I envied my fellow slaves for their stupidity").

Film, television, and literature abound with similar examples, from Forrest Gump to Mr. Magoo. The last lines of Jerzy Kosinski's *Being There*, a tale about a mentally challenged man named Chance whom the social and political elite misinterpret as suave and farsighted, are these: "Not a thought lifted itself from Chance's brain. Peace filled his chest." In the end, the reader is left wondering if Chance is about to be nominated for the vice presidency of the United States. But who are the ignorant ones in that story? The intellectual elite who talk about the happy, uninformed masses are also the ones whose lives are filled with complications.

Growing up in a place like Bliss, you can't see as much, but my guess is you can see more clearly. There's one hardware store, one grocery store, one coffee shop. Life isn't cluttered with choices.

"Course, it doesn't really prepare you for the real world," Frank admitted. "You know, growing up in this farm community, I never heard a woman swear until I went up to Buffalo. I couldn't get over that. It boggled my mind."

"I'm curious," I said. "Why didn't you become a farmer?"

"I left the farm as soon as I could. I hated it. I didn't like cows. I didn't like horses. I didn't like the hard work involved. I didn't like seven days a week. I didn't like daylight to dark. Today, it's different. It's no longer manual, it's mechanical. But I never milked the cows because of that hand," he said, lifting his left hand again. "I couldn't squeeze."

"On a dairy, that gets you out of a lot of work," I admitted. "But this is farm country."

Frank shook his head. "You can hardly find boys today who want to stay on the farm."

The statement took me back to Comfort, Texas, where Gregory Krauter had offered economic reasons to explain a generation's reluctance to take over the family farm. Frank's reasons were more internal: "Too much work, too little pay, and no time for recreation. The only recreation we had on the farm was the county fair in August and a once-a-month social at someone's house. People would bring dishes to pass around. My father would bring a radio. That thing squeaked and squawked and faded out and had static." And then he added the kicker: "Oh, we thought it was wonderful!"

That's simple contentment, but is it bliss? Only if we sell the concept short. What you don't know won't hurt you, and it may lead to some level of satisfaction, but extreme happiness? To go there, it's necessary to have a healthy supply of insight to power the emotion. You can't be extraordinarily joyful, not truly blissful, unless you discover profound understanding. It takes big thoughts to reach a superlative state of mind.

In *The Demon-Haunted World*, Carl Sagan put it in metaphysical and astrophysical terms: "To discover that the Universe is some 8 to 15 billion and not 6 to 12 thousand years old improves our appreciation of its sweep and grandeur; to entertain the notion that we are a particularly complex arrangement of atoms, and not some breath of divinity, at the very least enhances our respect for atoms; to discover, as now seems probable, that our planet is one of billions of other worlds in the Milky Way Galaxy and that our galaxy is one of billions more, majestically expands the arena of what is possible. . . . When we recognize our place in an immensity of light-years and in the passage of ages, when we grasp the intricacy, beauty, and subtlety of life, then that soaring feeling, that sense of elation and humility combined, is surely spiritual."

Frank Noble, it turned out, thought on that kind of scale. He'd spent the bulk of his life in small-town isolation, but he'd let his mind wander. He was an explorer of sorts, and that meant more than just his winters in Florida. "When I first started school, my father got a little magazine of western stories, and I used to read them. I always read a lot from then on. I've studied a lot of religions, and boy, there were some honeys, too. . . . I love history, and I love to watch the Learning Channel."

Frank paused for a moment. "To tell you the truth," he said, "I question a lot of things now."

"Like what?" I asked, opening the floodgates.

In the next half-hour, Frank touched on a wide array of subjects. He mused over the hypocrisy of religion, evident in a rift that had appeared recently in his local Baptist church. ("Now, I'm pretty cynical about religion, but if you profess to be Christian, wouldn't you work it out? This is what happened years ago. That's why you have thousands of different religions, every name under the sun.") He scoffed at the shortsightedness of fundamentalism. ("You can't read a passage and say, 'Well, that's it.' You've got to know the whole thing. No one will ever convince me that Adam and Eve ate an apple because a serpent in a tree told them to. It was a story to tell the people at that time, so they would understand.") He pondered the egocentricity of man. ("Why did the dinosaurs live for 200 million years before man? And they died out 60 million years ago. Why were they first?") And he laughed at the selectivity of memory. ("I go up to the coffee shop about once a week and talk to a couple people my age. We reminisce about the old days, but the old days weren't so good. You forget the bad times and remember the good ones.")

It wasn't so much what he said that warmed my heart, but the fact that he said it at all. He was a man who valued simplicity but also acted on his curiosity. Though he'd gained wisdom, he remained the same person who had stuck his finger in that mowing machine as a one-year-old. Ignorance is satisfied stagnation; insight—though it can take you to both extremes—is bliss. Frank had spent his life in Bliss, but in my book, he was still searching for it.

"Every year down in Florida, the first Sunday in March, we have a get-together of all the people from the county who go down there. I met our old minister there, who was our minister for twenty-five years. He was a character in his own right. But anyway, this is how he introduced me to his wife's cousin. He said, 'I want you to meet Frank Noble. He's different.' "

As he said it, Frank smiled knowingly.

UNITY,
NEW HAMPSHIRE

> *The unity of government which constitutes you one people . . . is a main pillar in the edifice of your real independence.*
>
> George Washington

New Hampshire is hardly a microcosm of the nation. Eighty-five percent of it is covered by forest. Just 93 miles wide at its widest and 180 miles long at its longest, it is smaller than all but six states. It has not a single city of over a hundred thousand people; only nine states are less populous. It is mostly white, generally conservative, and predominantly middle class. In 1996, the state's unemployment rate was 3.2 percent, the lowest in the United States. Only 4 percent of its residents are foreign born, and half of those are Canadians. And only 2.7 percent of its people are classified as minorities.

The state cannot even find a representative of itself within itself. None of its ten counties is typical of New Hampshire as a whole. The northern counties are snowy, sparsely populated mountain hamlets. The southeastern counties are virtual suburbs of Boston. The state's center and its shoreline are increasingly dominated by tourists and summer homes. And while New Hampshire has given us Daniel Webster and Franklin Pierce, it is otherwise so politically bland that it has had no fewer than eleven different governors named John, with the odd Ichabod and Huntley thrown in.

But every four years, New Hampshire becomes the epicenter of American politics as the site of the nation's first presidential primary, which provides the state with political clout well beyond its size. Indeed, it is more important in determining who wins a presidential nomination than even California, which, if it were an independent country, would have the sixth-largest gross national product in the world. Jerry Brown or Ted Kennedy can win the West Coast, but it's too little, too late unless he enjoyed a head start in New Hampshire. For better or for worse, for richer or for poorer, right or wrong, the Granite State has come to be a bellwether of the American political process.

It began, for all intents and purposes, on February 10, 1952, when Democratic senator Estes Kefauver of Tennessee made a speech at the Elm Street Junior High School auditorium in Nashua, New Hampshire, becoming the first candidate to campaign in the state's presidential primary. Though President Harry Truman had not said he would seek reelection, he was the Establishment choice, and Kefauver was the darkest of dark horses. But when the votes were tabulated, Kefauver won by 10 percentage points. Truman tabled a reelection bid, and Dwight Eisenhower—the surprise Republican winner—was on his way to the White House.

Since then, only one person has won the presidency without first winning New Hampshire. That was Bill Clinton, who finished second to virtual native Paul Tsongas of Massachusetts in 1992. Yet even that was a strong second place, considering Clinton overcame attacks ranging from draft dodging to infidelity. Christened the "Comeback Kid," he, too, was on his way.

New Hampshire's memorable political scenes have far outweighed the state's percentage of the United States population, whether it was Ed Muskie crying in the snow or pro–Eugene McCarthy students getting themselves "clean for Gene" or Clinton's "I've caused pain in my marriage" admission or Gary Hart's triumph over Walter Mondale. Though New Hampshire's unpredictability shouldn't come as a surprise anymore, the state still manages to deliver a quadrennial shock or two. Truman lost in 1952. Ronald Reagan lost in 1976. Ted Kennedy lost in 1980. For many candidates, this tiny New England state at the beginning of the presidential primary season is the beginning of the end.

Even New Hampshire's winners don't always leave victorious. In 1968, President Lyndon Johnson received forty-two hundred more votes than McCarthy, but experts thought that an incumbent president should have trounced an obscure senator. The moral loss led to LBJ's decision not to toss his Stetson into the ring. Four years later, Muskie beat George McGovern by about nine thousand votes. But New Hampshire is as much about meeting expectations as about meeting voters. Muskie didn't meet the former and eventually didn't get nominated.

In the end, it's all about momentum. A solid performance in the Granite State translates to more media attention, more money, more volunteers, more endorsements. Is it fair? Critics have called it New Hampshire's private practical joke on the rest of us, "the tattle of jesters which we have come to believe is the pronouncement of kings." But is it fun? Definitely.

The press may love it most. If the nation's first primary were held, say, in Nevada—sprawling, featureless, isolated Nevada—it would hardly merit such a print and electronic invasion. But New Hampshire is close to major media centers. And in New Hampshire itself, everything is close to everything. Reporters can canvass the state with little difficulty and catch up with old cronies at the same time. And what editor or producer doesn't foam at the mouth thinking of Yankee citizens standing on snow-covered streets and shaking hands with the future president, then making a grand pronouncement about personal choice. There's a joke about the self-important New Hampshire voter who, when asked what he thought about a particular presidential candidate, answered, "Don't know. I only met him twice."

Indeed, that joke indicates why New Hampshire maintains its position as the ultimate winnowing machine. The media may be obsequious there, but it is also irrelevant. New Hampshire is retail campaigning, face-to-face politics, comparison shopping without the media's distorted filter. The playing field is leveled. Long shots can emerge as contenders, incumbents can become lame ducks, front runners can recede into also-rans. But as Amy and I drifted through Texas in February and watched the 1996 primary unfold on our television in the steel confines of the Rolling Stone, the theoretical appeal of the process faded into distaste for politics in practice.

The four main contenders for the Republican nomination were the prototypical choices—the Establishment (Bob Dole), the Extremist (Pat Buchanan), the Outsider (Steve Forbes), and the Alternative (Lamar Alexander). As the primary unfolded, the candidates' missteps multiplied. Alexander visited a local grocer and then couldn't come up with the price of milk and eggs. Buchanan's camp created a television ad that included video of the *Challenger* explosion, forgetting that Christa McAuliffe, the teacher killed on the flight, was from New Hampshire. Dole made an offhand remark comparing Forbes's whining about negative ads to the guy who shot his parents and then asked for mercy because he was an orphan—but he did it on the day New Hampshire awoke to shocking reports of two teens arrested for shooting their parents. The seventy-two-year-old also made an appearance at a product unveiling at a brewing company, only to discover too late that the product was Old Man Ale. Finally, he waxed eloquent with this bit of profundity: "You know, we've never had a president named Bob. Think about it."

The campaign deteriorated into mudslinging and finger pointing. Alexander fielded attacks about insider deals during his term as Tennessee governor by which he made a $620,000 profit from a $1 investment. Buchanan was informed that one of his campaign cochairmen had appeared at a gathering of militant hate groups. Other reports detailed how Buchanan had plotted dirty tricks during Richard Nixon's 1972 reelection campaign. Buchanan said Dole's campaign was "hollow at the core." Alexander said Dole had "absolutely nothing to say." Everyone said Forbes was trying to buy the nomination.

As the candidates charged each other with making negative phone calls to voters, as discussion of ideas was replaced by talk of advertising, as a debate became so testy that front runner Dole quipped he was putting in for another Purple Heart, and as the candidates were dismissed in sound bites (Dole was said to be too old, Forbes too rich, Alexander too slick, Buchanan too scary), a reporter covering the campaign summed up the citizens' sickened feelings. "This is revolting to exasperated voters here, who have been reduced to choosing a candidate the way one shops for shampoo," she wrote. "At this point, they just want the one that leaves the least dirt and greasy residue."

Polls showed a neck-and-neck race between the man with the résumé (Dole, who had the support of every prominent Republican in the state) and the renegade (Buchanan, who was their worst nightmare), with 17 percent still undecided. The media prepared the nation for what was to come. Conservative columnist Robert Novak predicted, "The Republican and independent voters of this tiny upper New England state hold in their hands the fate of Sen. Bob Dole's long march to the Republican presidential nomination." Should Dole win, Novak said, he would confirm his front-runner status. Should he lose, he'd be in serious trouble.

Well, he lost. The final tally gave Buchanan 28 percent of the vote, Dole 26 percent, Alexander 23 percent, and Forbes 12 percent. Exit polls asked voters whether they would have chosen Colin Powell instead. Thirty-seven percent said gladly.

Although just 16 convention delegates were at stake out of the 996 needed to win the Republican nomination, and although there were a whopping twenty-seven primaries scheduled during the next thirty days, the headlines read like apocalyptic screams: "DOLE WOUNDED IN CLIFFHANGER," "RIGHT-WING REBEL SPOILS THE PARTY," "TRAUMA FOR REPUBLICANS." Dole, who had seen his presidential hopes shattered in 1980 when only 597 New Hampshirites voted for him and in 1988 when George Bush beat him, responded, "I know why they call this the Granite State. Because it's so hard to crack."

All this because of New Hampshire? A look inside the numbers made the state's status even more perplexing. Of nearly 1.3 million residents, about three-fourths were of voting age. Of those, about three-fourths were registered to vote, of whom two-thirds were registered as Republicans or independents. And of those, about half voted in the primary. In the end, that meant that the number of people voting for Buchanan was about equal to a ward in Chicago or a county in Oregon. But in New Hampshire, it was enough to make a presidential front runner. The difference between the gloating winner and the mortified loser was a few thousand votes. Yet the spin created by those few thousand votes made its way to all corners of the political landscape.

Instead of alleviating the confusion, the New Hampshire primary seemed only to illuminate the shortcomings of those governing at the national level and to reveal an increasing sense of dissatisfaction among an ever-decreasing number of participating voters.

When I was in college, all eager and idealistic, I'd jumped at the chance to play a part in the first presidential election for which I was of legal voting age. I was the editor of the *Students for Dukakis* newsletter, which someday may have the value of a New Coke marketing brochure. But the shallowness and shortsightedness of that campaign soured my taste for the political challenge and eroded my respect for the political animal. I began to lose my faith in the very workings of government.

Four months after New Hampshire's latest horse race, as I headed for Unity, I was looking for something to hold on to.

The journey there took us across the Empire State to Albany, which still felt very much like upstate New York, and then to its sister city of

Troy, which began to feel like New England. Of course, being that the area won the honor of having the least courteous drivers we encountered in the entire trip, we also knew we weren't too far from Manhattan. Clearly, though, we were getting close to Vermont. We could sense it in businesses' decreasing blandness, the nondescript gas pumps and motels giving way to commercial establishments with names like Candy Kettle, Trading Post Dairy Bar, and Man of Kent Tavern.

Every other store along the drive across the bottom of Vermont seemed to offer antiques, handmade crafts, maple syrup, or aged cheese—or often an odd combination of two or three. Highway 9, cutting its way from Bennington to Brattleboro through Green Mountain National Forest, was quite literally a gentle slice of New England—farmhouses, country stores, cider mills, and stark white churches. But it was also steep and winding and occasionally dense with fog. It took us an hour and a half to travel forty-four miles. After reaching Brattleboro and turning north, it took us exactly half that time to move forty-four miles along Interstate 91. But while the expansive Connecticut River tagged along with us the whole way as we zoomed up Vermont's eastern edge, we caught a glimpse of it for exactly thirty seconds. Therein lay the pros and cons of the interstate system.

We exited at the Vermont town of Ascutney and crossed the river into the New Hampshire city of Claremont, where there was a red-brick house with a Playboy banner hanging off its side and an exhortation on its front: *Call me, ladies.* Though it was June, we shuddered at the thought of the long winters that must have created such desperation.

We found Unity eight miles away in Sullivan County. Actually, there were three communities—East Unity, Unity Center, and West Unity. A divided Unity was ironic but not surprising, considering that in Sullivan County alone, you had Newport and North Newport; Lempster and East Lempster; Acworth and South Acworth; Grantham and North Grantham; Croydon and Croydon Flat; Washington and East Washington; Plainfield and East Plainfield; Springfield and West Springfield;

Charlestown, South Charlestown, and North Charlestown; and Cornish City, South Cornish, Cornish Center, Cornish Mills, and Cornish Flat. In New England, names were less fun than functional.

Cutting through Unity from northwest to southeast was a road with the lofty name of Second New Hampshire Turnpike. It was surrounded by landmarks that evoked colonial images—Potato Hill, Butcher Knife Corner, Quaker Meeting House. And no wonder. Unity was the only hamlet on our itinerary that was named before the nation.

Indeed, New Hampshire has a history as starred-and-striped as they come. It was settled in 1623, just three years after the Pilgrims landed in Massachusetts. A century and a half later, New Castle, New Hampshire, was the site of one of the first conflicts of the American Revolution, when colonists routed the British garrison at Fort William and Mary and seized arms and powder later used at the Battle of Bunker Hill. Five months later, New Hampshire became the first of the thirteen colonies to declare its independence from England and then the first to adopt its own constitution. New Hampshire was subsequently the ninth state to ratify the United States Constitution, officially putting the document into effect.

All this history was crystallized when we came upon a well-manicured park in the center of Unity Center. It was surrounded on one side by the Unity Volunteer Fire Department and on the other by an imposing white Colonial that served as the town hall. Rising from the grass of the park was a pole bearing an American flag and a New Hampshire flag, and next to it was a sign. *Town of Unity*, it announced, *Incorporated 1764*.

The town's origins actually dated back eleven years earlier. In 1753, King George II awarded sixty-nine grantees six square miles of land in the province of New Hampshire. The area was to be called Buckingham. Whether any of the grantees actually settled there is unknown. They probably didn't, because in 1764, several New Hampshire families, having lost their holdings in their old communities, petitioned the governor

Unity Center town hall

for land of their own; King George III granted them those same six square miles, but this time, the town was incorporated under the name Unity, the thinking being that the new tract would unify these people who had no land of their own elsewhere.

The list of original grantees included New England-to-the-bone names like Ebenezer Copp, Enoch Sawyer, Archaleus Stevens, and Bartholomew Heath. In March 1776, four months before the Declaration of Independence, they and the other settlers of Unity sent out a resolution that read in part, "We the subscribers do hereby solemnly engage and promise that we will, to the utmost of our power at the Risque of our Lives and Fortune, with ARMS, oppose the Hostile Proceedings of the British Fleets and Armies against the United American Colonies." Twenty-five Unity men signed the declaration; four refused. "Live Free or Die" became New Hampshire's motto. At least eighteen Revolutionary War soldiers were buried in East Unity Cemetery.

Over the years, the town continued its patriotic, arms-bearing course. Muster Field, a level stretch of land in Unity, was where one of the town fathers, Colonel Nathan Huntoon, trained his men for service in the War of 1812. Two dozen years later, the short-lived Unity Scientific and Military Academy went into operation, offering classes ranging from topographical drawing to fencing. In 1862, when the nation found itself in civil war, sixty men from Unity answered the Union's call.

As the list of American wars grew, the list of Unity veterans did likewise. In the park, Amy and I spied a plaque next to the flagpole. It read, *Erected by the town of Unity in memory of men who served in the World War.* Under the thirteen names included on the plaque came the announcement, *These men pledged their lives to the call of their country.* Nearby, a veterans' honor roll listed two hundred; it was surrounded by American flags. Across the street from the park sat three solid-color farmhouses—one red, one white, one blue.

Not far from the town hall was a dirt road that may have qualified as the strangest of our journey, if only for its mysterious and haphazard nature. Maybe it was the clubhouse on the side of the road that sparked our imagination, the one with the big black flag with the big white *F* by the yellow sign that said, *Unauthorized Travel Prohibited.* Or maybe it was the dilapidated wooden shack nearby, the one with the *For Sale* sign. Or it could have been Rainbow Acres Farm just down the road, with the big picture of a rainbow and a dove flying through it, and below it the words of Psalm 133: "Behold, how good and how pleasant it is for brethren to dwell together in unity!" Finally, it might have been the beer cans lining the road until we reached a moth-infested graveyard set back in the forest, surrounded by stone walls. About twenty granite tombstones sat there at odd angles, like something from a Disney haunted mansion. The inscriptions revealed that there were ancient Unity bones underneath, all the graveyard's inhabitants having died between 1832 and 1872, some before adulthood. Seventeen-year-old Olive Marshall, died 1846. Ten-year-old Daniel Welch, died 1845. Three-year-old Charles Henry Walker, died that same year. It was isolated and empty and eerie, and we didn't stay long.

We breathed easily only back at the road's beginning, where it met up with Second New Hampshire Turnpike. On the corner stood a general store called Will's Place. That's where we met Will. He told us how he used to live just outside Boston, how the constant crime wore him down, how he used to keep spare tires at work because his were always being slashed. The final straw, he said, was when his wife had her wedding dress all boxed and cleaned and packaged for preservation, and it got stolen out of their pickup truck. They moved to Unity immediately after that.

Will also told us that if we really wanted to get a taste of the town, there was a board of selectmen's meeting that evening at seven. I'd already decided I couldn't stomach New Hampshire's role in determining government from the top down. I figured maybe it worked from the bottom up. Maybe government was better in small doses.

New Hampshire's form of local government has been called one of the purest forms of democracy in the world. Each of the state's 221 towns is a little republic. Every year on the second Tuesday in March, the townspeople assemble for a meeting in the town hall, where they approve budgets and elect officials. Any registered voter may stand up and speak his mind on any issue put forward. The vote is direct; the government is of the people, by the people, and for the people.

Unity changed the rules only slightly, in an effort to make an already supremely democratic process even more equitable. The town's practice was to elect its officers on the second Tuesday in March and then postpone the remainder of the meeting until the following Saturday, so that average working stiffs could participate. Usually, about a hundred citizens showed up. The meetings often lasted eight hours.

There were 305 votes cast at Unity's town meeting in 1995. Among those elected were the community's chief administrative officials, the ones who carried out the mandates of their friends and neighbors. They formed the three-member board of selectmen, and on a quiet Tuesday in June, they sat before us in Unity's town office, a crowded, little room in back of the local elementary school.

Mary Gere, a no-nonsense, ash-blond thirty-something, was a pressman by trade; she worked at an area newspaper to support her husband and two children and make payments on their mobile home on the out-

A meeting of Unity's board of selectmen

skirts of town. Scott Levanovich, a long-haired, sleepy-eyed chain-smoker, owned a rental store in Claremont. Ed Gregory, the chairman of the board, was a friendly, bearded fellow who worked as a custodian for the Claremont schools. This was the town's triumvirate. This was the beauty of democracy.

On a bulletin board in the room was an offer for a tax booklet and an accompanying poem:

> Tho "Live Free or Die"
> Be Our State Motto
> The State doth tax
> Because it Gotto.
> Of death and taxes, please to note,
> On only One do You get to vote.
> So inform Yourself and be not lax—
> Who levies?
> Who gathers?
> Who gets your tax?

Ed Gregory commenced the proceedings: "I want to suggest that the first thing we do is handle the Freelancers' permit. That's going to take just about a minute, instead of having them sit here all night long. You're only fourth on the list, but that's probably about three hours from now."

He directed his comments to a pair of men sitting next to us. Tom and Bob were their names. They wore combat boots, gray-green vests covered with patches, and what appeared to be multihued sleeves—until a closer look revealed them to be arms thick with tattoos. Each wore a large patch on his back that said, *Freelancers—New Hampshire.* Suddenly, the mystery was removed from that black flag with the white *F* flying over the clubhouse along the dirt road. The Freelancers were a biker club. They were here to obtain a permit to stage their annual August blowout, attended by some thousand folks at ten bucks a head.

Priscilla, the town secretary, who emerged as possibly the hardest-working person in the room, asked the date of the party: "August the tenth to . . . ?"

"Whenever," said Bob, a smile creasing the unshaven face beneath his shaved head.

Ed's "All in favor?" was followed by a couple of quick "Ayes," and the permit was signed, no red tape in sight.

"Well," said Ed, "I hope you have good weather."

As the bikers roared away on their Harleys, an engineer overseeing a repaving project took center stage and commenced a lengthy discussion about bids, budgets, banks, and schedules.

After various bids were considered, a full-bodied man named Mo

*T*om and Bob from the Freelancers

took his turn. His property was along a road that wasn't maintained by the town, so he was maintaining it himself. He asked for overdue repairs.

"I just want to be able to get up there without bottoming out," he said, his voice thick like gravel. When after a brief discussion his wish was granted, he lifted himself out of his chair, and with a thank-you wave, he joked, "I hope I never see you again."

An application for a storage building for the local landfill was next on the agenda, and while I couldn't understand much of the discussion, I could see quite clearly the look of frustration on Selectman Scott's face. "We have to be addressing what's happening to the whole lot," he insisted, "not just that little chunk of land in the middle of it." And with that, he hurried outside for a cigarette break.

"Are you paid for this?" I asked the selectmen when the opportunity presented itself.

"Certainly," said Ed.

"Not really," said Scott.

"Sorta," said Mary. "We get a flat rate per year—$750. The chairman gets an additional $250."

The numbers explained Ed's and Mary's disparate answers. Scott's frustration accounted for his. "But," I started, "when you add up your hours versus your salary . . ."

"This is community service," Mary finished.

In my eyes, Mary, Scott, and Ed represented government without the muddle of politics, but they didn't see themselves as governors at all.

"I think we're business managers. That's more like it. Really, we have a very distinct set of rules to follow," said Scott, whose voice was as deep as the town's roots. "If you think about it, it's very much like stockholders and executives. The townspeople are the stockholders, and we're the executive officers of the corporation."

"But you choose who gets what bids," I countered. "You make decisions."

"That's part of the administration," Mary replied. "You always have to be accountable. Politicians say one thing and do another. We have a direct line. The townspeople say, 'We elected you, we hired you to act on our behalf, and this is what we've given you to work with.' "

Accountability. For some reason, it brought to mind the presidential primary. I wondered if any candidates had come through town.

"No, Claremont is about as close as they get. They try to stay in the cities," Mary said. "This year in particular was real strange. There weren't as many coming to this area as there had been in the past. They went up north to Coos County and down to Merrimack County, even to the sea-coast. There was a lot of campaigning out there. But not here."

I tried to think like a campaign manager. "I would think if I was a candidate, if I was Pat Buchanan and everyone was talking about how I was so divisive, I would come up here and schedule a photo shoot next to the Unity sign."

Scott shook his head and allowed a grudging smile. "We don't even have a parking lot big enough for them to come here."

The meeting continued with the next order of business—fixing Unity's police cruiser. The town's lone law enforcement vehicle had lost all its oil, probably the result of a blown head gasket. Ed asked Priscilla how much money was left in the till. Priscilla told him nine thousand dollars. Unless the Pentagon was buying, there was plenty of money.

Next issue: a mobile home without the proper permit. "The way I look at things," said Ed, "he's in violation right now."

I later discovered that a related issue was an area of disagreement between him and Mary. Ed believes in zoning, to an extent. He believes that sanitary conditions should be met and that taxes, the lifeblood of the town, should be equitable. Why should a family send six kids to the local school but pay nothing in taxes because that's what their property is worth? Mary, who calls herself a libertarian, disagrees.

"He and I are very different on that. I feel everybody has a right to live to their means. If all somebody can do is live in a twenty-by-forty shack or a mobile home, then who is somebody else to say, 'I don't want you in my town.' I know what Ed's saying, as far as taxes being inequitable. But generally speaking, people aspire to have more. They try. They work to have a little more, whether it's a car or a boat or a big garden or a horse or flowers or a barn. People aspire to the things they want in life. When some people aren't fortunate enough to have good things, I don't think they should be forced into a subsidized housing apartment in Claremont, which is basically their only other option."

Mary spread her arms and smiled. "To me, I always loved that about New Hampshire. I always thought 'Live Free or Die' meant something. Here is your piece of land. Do what you can."

The minutes turned into hours as the meeting dragged on. Much of it was consumed by the selectmen passing vouchers to one another, discussing bills, and signing off on them. Two new tires for a backhoe for the landfill. Lumber for street signs. Will from Will's Place, who was one of the few townspeople to watch the entire proceedings, joked, "I don't know if they should call them vouchers or vultures."

It wasn't the most exciting evening I've ever spent. But the experience was enhanced when a sense of history was brought to bear on it. I held in my hands a booklet called *Highlights in History of Unity, N.H.*, compiled by the Unity Historical Society. So while Mary, Scott, and Ed managed the business of Unity in 1996, I discovered that three fellows named Abner, Amos, and Elijah had done much the same in 1774 as the town's first selectmen.

As the modern triumvirate dealt with road repair, I noted that most of the time during the first-ever town meeting was spent finding people to create such roads. And I witnessed the evolution of a community by perusing the votes of its citizens through the years. They voted $600 toward education in 1779. Six years later, they voted to give $5 to any resident who killed a grown wolf within the town limits. In 1793, they voted to have a minister come to town to preach a few Sabbaths. They discussed a town seal in 1805 and decided that each local soldier should have a pint of good West Indies rum on Muster Day in 1811. In 1877 came the following announcement: "A new era has dawned. . . . FREE- DOM FROM DEBT!" Six years later, the town purchased its first hearse, for $242.65.

The historical perspective helped me reinterpret the mundane issues confronting Mary, Scott, and Ed. The party permits and lumber pur- chases and vehicle repairs were merely the continuation of a 232-year- old effort to maintain and define a community.

Ed called Unity's two policeman to the selectmen's table. The younger of the two, a patrolman named Chris, was dressed in his uniform. The older, an ample-bellied sergeant named Barry, wore a T-shirt touting *Cops: The Good Guys*. Good guys or not, they were here to hear complaints from the townspeople they protected, the biggest being that the cruiser was out of town too often. Just last week, there had been a burglary in town, and a state trooper had been forced to respond. Sergeant Good Guy pointed out that two cops couldn't possibly be expected to be at the town's beck and call twenty-four hours a day. Ed wondered if it was time to add a part-time officer.

The complaints about police response had been voiced not to the cops but to the board. Fielding gripes is a part of any public office. But was it worth it? Did they get grief, for the most part, or gratitude?

"Actually," said Ed, "you get both. It depends on what's happening in people's lives at the time. If, like tonight, they get broken into, and the police officer wasn't there in five minutes, then you get the grief."

What was it, then, that led them to run for office? There were no perks. There was little appreciation. The pay seemed several notches be- low minimum wage. Could it be that *public service* wasn't an antiquated term after all?

"I came from Long Island. Down there, you were so far removed. You had no voice, no opportunity to speak, no opportunity to know what was even going on. The tax bill just came, and that was it," Mary explained. "When I came here, I found myself so overwhelmed by the process of going in and listening. Neighbors would say, 'I'm not going to pay such and such for that.' And it meant something. And everybody listened. And it went back and forth. To me, it was so awesome. Anybody can get up in front of a group and say, 'Wait a minute. Have you thought about this?' And people listen, even if they don't agree."

Eventually, she saw a need to make the system, so wonderful in theory, live up to its potential in practice. "I always went to town meetings, always participated in what was happening, watching, trying to understand the process," she said. "A lot of it really didn't make sense. One year, you'd go to town meeting, and everything would seem very established and understood. The next year, you'd come back, and they didn't do anything that they were supposed to do. You think, 'Was I at the same meeting?'

"Mostly, what drew me into it was the idea that if you're not part of the solution, if you're not trying to help, if you're not working at it, then you're part of the problem. And you really shouldn't be complaining. Get into it, find out, and then you have a new perspective and respect for what the job is."

Mary moved to Unity in 1982. She lived here more than a decade before deciding to run for office. But that still may have constituted a meteoric ascent to local acceptance.

"The kind of neat thing about local government is, you can come into this town with a million dollars, and people won't vote for you," Ed declared. "You don't buy your way into this town. You don't come here without being a native and say, 'I'm going to run for selectman.' Unless nobody else is running."

"And then you still might not get any votes!" added Mary.

"I've been in town since '59," he continued. "The thing I found, running for office, is you basically don't have to do any campaigning. In New Hampshire, they don't like people coming in and just running over the town. They like people who have been there for a while."

Mary nodded. "The people who have been here all their lives, they're the salt of the earth. They're independent—stubbornly so—and they're hardworking. And they're always going to look a little bit askance. 'You're new in town? Who are you? What are you trying to do?' They're always a little bit suspicious. So, generally, if you can win over this group, if you can show you're hardworking, you're honest, and you've got integrity, you're generally okay."

In a few breaths, she had encapsulated why the New Hampshire primary is such a litmus test. I wondered if any of them had larger political aspirations.

"Not me," said Ed.

"Nope," said Mary.

"Uh-uh," said Scott.

In fact, none of them was even sure about running for selectman again. For all the talk about little republics and serving the public and earning respect from a populace that offered it grudgingly, the most salient rewards at the end of the day were headaches and whispers.

"I won't do it again," said Mary. "My feelings are hurt too easily. You have to have a hard, tough skin to be in that office. And I don't have it. When people don't agree with you, sometimes it turns personal and malicious. I won't be a quitter. I won't give anybody the satisfaction. I'll stick it out my last year and a half. But I think it's weaned me off of wanting to do public service."

Amy and I hadn't gotten that impression at all. If anything, we were moved by how hard she worked and how much she seemed to care. But Unity, apparently, didn't always live up to its name.

"People can come and tell me I'm stupid or I'm wrong or I didn't understand it. If they say it to my face, that's fine," she insisted. "But you can't fight innuendo and rumor, because you don't know what it is, and you don't always know where it's coming from."

The meeting was crawling toward conclusion. Sergeant Good Guy informed the board that seventeen fire alarms had been pulled at the elementary school in the past six months, to which Ed responded, "What it basically comes down to is a ninety-two-dollar solution—a new door latch." Unfortunately, the selectmen didn't have jurisdiction over the school; the school board did.

Will turned to Amy and me, whispering, "And you thought everything was so simple in a small town. It's the little things that are big."

Next on the meeting's agenda, it was revealed that Priscilla had called the *Boston Globe* and the *Hartford Courant* about advertising some property in town. It was a reminder that Unity, like Harmony and Inspiration and Glory and Bliss, was no longer quite what it once was. In 1790, the first United States census listed 538 Unity residents. Within thirty years, the number rose to 1,277. But that was its peak. By 1860, there were 887 people in Unity. By 1960, there were 675. Today, the population has crept back over 1,000, thanks in part to the construction of a nursing home in town.

Unity didn't used to have to advertise. Indeed, a couple of the town's tall tales concerned immigrants and their land.

The first told the origin of a certain willow tree. In the early nineteenth century, a man and his wife traveled overland from Connecticut by way of the Connecticut River Valley. They each rode a horse, and their belongings were piled atop a third. When they finally arrived in Unity, they dismounted, stuck their riding whips into the soil, and apparently left them there. The woman's whip, which was actually a willow branch, took root and eventually grew into a tree that still stands, without another willow in sight.

Another story concerned the little-known New Hampshire gold rush of 1908. In the 1830s, an old gold digger claimed to have found the mother lode in rock-strewn Unity. When heavy snow halted his operations, he said he would be back in the spring to collect his strike. He died that winter, and nobody returned to his claim—until 1908, when some old Pacific coast miners dug up the legend and then dug up the site. Blasting away granite, they found several pieces of quartz and what the newspapers suggested was "a nugget of no small value."

The story struck me as strangely incongruous in New England, like a three-cornered hat in Dodge City. Then again, before this journey, I would have said the same thing about a radio tower in the bayou, a Union monument in Texas, and a game show in the New Mexico desert.

The second-to-last topic of discussion at the meeting concerned a bell tower to be placed atop the town hall. It reminded me of Comfort, Texas, and its attempts to restore the crumbled spire of the Treue der Union monument. One was an unincorporated community founded by freethinkers; the other was an incorporated town home to the Freelancers. Each had a different perspective of self-government, but neither wanted to forsake its most profound symbol.

Finally, garbage was dessert that evening—the last item on Ed Gregory's list. The local landfill was open on Saturdays, but a resident busy that day was asking for a key to the dump for another day.

"It's a bad precedent," said Mary. "I'm not comfortable with it."

The issue brought into focus the challenge of one neighbor making decisions concerning another.

"I happen to know the woman fairly well. I happen to work with her. She's as honest as the day is long," Mary later explained. "But sorry, no. I'd trust her with the key, but I can't say, 'Sure, go ahead.' Because tomorrow, somebody else might want a key who maybe I don't know or maybe I don't trust."

"Basically," said Ed, "the rules and regulations are made up at the town meeting, and we have to follow the rules. Whether it's my neighbor, my friend, or my enemy, everybody has to be treated the same. It's not political."

"That's why there's three of us," Scott added.

It was decided to keep the landfill open on Saturdays only. But Mary offered an addendum, muttering mostly to herself, "Maybe I'll give her a ring—not as a selectman thing, but as a neighborly thing."

Finally, three and a half hours after it had begun, Scott made a motion to adjourn the meeting. Ed seconded it. Their work, for now, was done.

FRIENDSHIP,
MAINE

*Laughter is not a bad beginning for a friendship,
and it is the best ending for one.*

Oscar Wilde

The ninety-four-year-old Friendship sloop moved effortlessly through the blue-gray waters as we inched slowly past the islands of Muscongus Bay. The silence of the sea was broken occasionally by a sea gull's squawk, a flapping sail, the distant hum of a motorboat. But for a moment, when the wind slowed, the only sounds we heard on this picture-perfect afternoon on the cusp of summer were the dull creak of the boat and the smooth voice of Andy Zuber, first mate and storyteller.

"I come home from fishing the other day theah," he began, affecting a New England accent as thick as fog, "and I tell ya I hear this awful screamin' in the upstairs windah. I didn't know what the hell was goin' on, so I run into the house figuring I had to dial 911—we don't have

*F*riendship Harbor

9II here, but you get the idea. I come to find out what was in the upstairs windah, and it was my wife in the upstairs bathroom. So I banged
on the door, and I says, 'Deah? What's the mattah?' And she says, 'I can't
get out.' I says, 'You can't get out?' And theah and then, I remembered I
had enameled that toilet seat earlier that mahnin'. Then I went fishing.
And she must have set on it just at the peak of dryin'.

"Course, she's a bit vain and all, and she had the door locked, and I
couldn't get in theah. I had to go back down to the shack and get my
house ladder, a screwdriver, a putty knife, some tuhpentine, and a monkey wrench. So I climbed the house with the house ladder, and I opened
that windah with the screwdriver, and I climbed on in theah. I surveyed
the situation, and I says, 'Deah, you push and I'll pull.' Well, she pushed
and I pulled, and she didn't budge none. I says, 'Deah, this may smaht a
bit,' and I took some of that tuhpentine and that putty knife and went
round the edges the best I could, trying to ease her off, you know. I says,
'You push and I'll pull.' Well, she pushed and I pulled, and still she didn't
budge none.

"Course, by then, I was so damn mad that I took that monkey wrench
and unbolted the whole damn thing, seat and all. I slung her up over my
shouldah and took her straight down to the back of my pickup truck. I
set her up on all fours in the back, and we drove straight to the doctor's

office. Well, you can imagine we drew quite a bit of attention goin' through town, and they didn't have her settin' in that waiting room long, I tell ya. Finally, we got in, and I put her up on the table theah, and old Doc Walker comes in and looks her over. I says, 'Doc, have you ever seen anything like this?'

"Well, he looks at her again, and he turns to me and says, 'Well, of course I have, but I've never seen one framed.' "

How we came to be sampling the local humor aboard a spectacular antique sloop in the Gulf of Maine is easy enough to explain. The 225-mile journey from Unity to Friendship took us across New Hampshire west to east, from Newport to Concord to Portsmouth. We then climbed aboard Interstate 95, crossed the Piscataqua River into Maine, and headed north up the coast, past Kittery and Kennebunk, Biddleford and Brunswick, York and Yarmouth. Just past Portland, we turned on to Route 1, once the main north-south artery down the coast but now just a shadowy adumbration of the interstate. There, the Maine coast loosened into a succession of peninsulas and inlets and bays, as if someone had ripped his way up the rest of the seashore instead of using neat scissors.

After watching the road dwindle from three lanes to two to one, we came upon a roadblock. Without explanation, the state police herded us on to a side road, where we followed a long line of cars around a six-mile, thirty-five-minute labyrinth that would have taken about thirty-five seconds had we not been misdirected. It was the third detour en route to our past three states-of-mind destinations.

It was another two dozen miles or so before we turned south onto Highway 220 and into the heart of a peninsula shaped like a gnarled claw jutting into the sea. Driving through Waldoboro and South Waldoboro and Lawry, the disappointing McLobster feel of our Maine experience up to then gave way to the Maine of expectations, the one we'd seen in photographs.

Friendship rested at the point of the peninsula. At the crest of a hill was the intersection where 220 dead-ended into Highway 97. At the intersection sat the Friendship Library, housed in a modest Colonial the color of a blank page. The town fanned out to either side in a semicircle around Friendship Harbor. It was the image of an idyllic, unspoiled coastal village. In much of the landlocked rural America we'd traveled, the lawn ornament of choice was a trailer lying forgotten among the weeds. Here, there were precious, half-refinished boats on blocks, lobster traps stacked in front yards, glorious fields of lupine dipped in florescent shades of lavender and purple, well-tended houses as white as a Maine winter set against a deep green countryside, and above all, the smell and serenity of the sea.

Friendship traced its origins to Plymouth Rock and the Boston Tea Party. Located between the Muscongus and Penobscot Rivers, it began as part of a territory granted to a Londoner and a Bostonian in 1629. More than a century later, it came into the possession of Samuel Waldo, who colonized the town that came to be known as Waldoboro and then, in 1743, turned his attention to another community on the peninsula, originally called Meduncook Plantation. *Meduncook*, they say, is an Indian word for "place by tide where sun shines over islands and warriors make beautiful canoes."

By 1754, there were twenty-two families in the area, several of them descended from the Pilgrims. When the rebellion in Boston Harbor came two decades later, Meduncook's residents hastened to the side of the patriots, realizing in the process that official town organization was the best way to protect their liberties. It wasn't until 1805, however, that twenty people sent a petition to the general court of Massachusetts (Maine was still fifteen years from statehood) asking that Meduncook be incorporated as the town of Friendship. Soon, another faction sent a counter-petition asking that the first one be disregarded and stating that the land was "destitute of natural advantages" and could "never be expected much to increase in population or wealth." It proposed instead that the community be annexed by Waldoboro, which Waldoboro promptly voted down. On February 25, 1807, amid conflict and rejection, Friendship was incorporated.

The source of the town's name is unclear. One story suggests that the townsfolk simply named it after the community's most valued commodity, although Lobster might have been a better choice. Another story says that a boat with the name *Friendship* stenciled across her stern arrived in the harbor and sparked the locals' imagination. My favorite explanation, however, is that when the Abenaki Indians and white settlers finally decided to end years of hostility with a hatchet-burying ceremony in a place still known as Hatchet Cove, the town that grew around it was named Friendship.

Strolling through the half-mile business district of the 250-year-old community, we passed a boatyard, the town hall, a couple of churches, a hardware store, a bed-and-breakfast (the Outsiders Inn), the Friendship Market, the Friendship Highway Department, and the Friendship Fire Department. Parked alongside the latter building was an antique, open-air fire truck, circa 1941, a siren rising up from the center, a horn protruding from above its bright red bumper. It must have caused a stir in its day.

"Yup, she's quite a piece of machinery," a fire department volunteer volunteered as we inspected the truck like a couple of kids at an antique auto show. "She's gone from New Yahk to Bahston to Camden to Waldoboro, and then we bought her off Waldoboro. She's still in good wahking condition. You could see yourself in the paint up until last year. But we got a brand-spanking-new pumpah, and we had to make room fah it, so we're gettin' rid of this."

"It must get pretty chilly riding this thing in the winter," I said, startling myself a bit with my laziness in pronouncing the last *r*.

"That's why all we use it fah is to clean out chimneys," he explained. "We don't really have any use fah it, 'cause we have a mutual aid system. You know, Waldoboro's got a ladder truck, Thomaston's got a snorkel, Camden, Rockland, they've all got ladder trucks. If we ever needed one in a fire, they'd all come anyway. So this one's for sale."

A block away, the Friendship Market was selling T-shirts that read, *Friendship, pop. 1099, deer 710, elvers 43, sloops 260, lobsters 4,831,262.* There was a bulletin board covered by local notices and advertisements. It was in the faded words of one of those notices, nearly hidden by a plea for a lost cat, that we discovered our destiny in Friendship: "1902 Original Friendship Sloop *Gladiator*—See the Beautiful Untouched Islands of Muscongus Bay—Sailing Daily from Friendship Harbor Town Landing—Reservations Recommended." There was a phone number attached.

"Well," said the voice on the other end, "this is the first day we're taking her out this summer. We were planning on taking just the family, but come on along. We'd love to have ya."

Captain Bill Zuber gave us a hearty welcome and introduced us to our shipmates for the afternoon. There was his red-headed wife, Caroline; their twenty-something son, Andy; their nephew, Rob; Caroline's brother, George, who had outdueled Down syndrome to middle age; Rob's girl-friend, Lauren; and Andy's girlfriend, a brunette named Nirvana. To Tao-ists, *nirvana* means, literally, "a state of no wind." That's irony.

The town landing in Friendship Harbor was a jungle of kelp-stained lobster traps, warped crates, and well-worn fishing vessels of all shapes and sizes. There was a colorlessness to the scene—the aura of a working harbor—except for the shiny sloop tied to the pier in the middle of it all. *Gladiator* was magnificent, all polish and class, like an ageless Audrey Hepburn. Sailing Muscongus Bay aboard this turn-of-the-century charmer was going to be like cruising the Blue Ridge Parkway in a Model-T Ford.

The Friendship sloop was once defined as "a sloop built in Friend-ship by Wilbur Morse." Of course, that was Wilbur Morse's definition. Though its origins have been obscured by the vagaries of time, what is known is this: when offshore fishing became popular off the Maine coast in the late 1800s, fishermen in the Muscongus Bay region saw a need for a boat large enough to provide stability, strong enough to withstand rough offshore weather, and fast enough to outrun a gale.

Morse found a suitable design known as the Gloucester sloop and simply cut down the dimensions to make it more affordable. In 1874, at the age of twenty-one, he built his first sloop just off the coast on Bremen Long Island. Eight years later, he moved to the mainland and Friendship, where he set up shop in the upper level of a barn, employed as many as a dozen men working sixty-hour weeks, and began building sloops in a manner approaching mass production. He built all kinds of boats—five hundred in all—before launching his last one fifty years after the first. But because of the sheer number of the modified Gloucester type produced in town by Morse and others, it came to be known as the Friendship sloop.

Built for function, she has been described as the pioneer equivalent of a Ford pickup. Her broad waist translated to a comfortable working platform. Her low sides made it easy to lift fish and lobster traps aboard. Her bow, high and sharp, cut the sea and kept her crew relatively dry. The early sloops were built from wood—oak for the keel and stem, pine for the planking and decking, spruce for the mast and boom.

It was function with an eye for form. Combing through the Friendship Library, I came across a testimonial written by a man named James Rockefeller, who wondered what it was about his Friendship sloop that warmed his heart. "No one thing, perhaps, rather a blending of the whole," he concluded. "There is an aura of honesty; no gimmicks and the proportions are right."

Indeed, the Friendship sloop's form has outlived its function. By 1915, gasoline engines were here to stay, and boatyards turned from crafting sloops to churning out powerboats. Though occasional Friendships were constructed over the years, the once-proud vessel was relegated to the scrap heap, its memory kept alive by a few stubborn lobstermen and nostalgic yachtsmen. It was one of the latter, a sailor named Bernard MacKenzie, who sparked the rebirth of Wilbur Morse's creation.

After his Morse-built sloop crossed the finish line first in a race off the Massachusetts coast in 1960, MacKenzie came up with the idea of planning a race reserved for Friendships only, an event to be held, naturally, off the coast of Friendship. On July 22, 1961—Friendship Day, as proclaimed by Maine governor John Reed—fourteen boats competed in the first-ever Friendship Sloop Regatta. Within two decades, five times as many boats were competing. There is still a Friendship Day the last Saturday in August, a small-town celebration complete with a parade of kids on bicycles trailing paper streamers. But the regatta has moved up the coast to the town of Rockland in an effort to handle the hordes.

More important than the race was its offshoot—the formation of the Friendship Sloop Society, a gathering of sailor-sentimentalists dedicated to reviving the spirit of the old sloops. It worked. Today, there are more than 250 registered Friendships, including century-old originals, teenage replicas, and two dozen sloops no longer in existence (listed under the heading "Gone but Not Forgotten"). For the owners of these vessels, the society is the validation of a deep-seated belief in the sailboat as symbol.

"Friendships are more than just a pleasure to the eye. They take our minds and spin them down a hundred different paths," James Rockefeller explained. "They stand for good fellowship in the rounded cockpit amidst clean air and water. They stand for a job well done, a day well lived, and Maine. . . . The stuff of dreams, this is what boats are all about. A bit of magic is a basic need in life, get it where you will."

I have always felt enlightened by the sea. To me, standing on a lonely, rocky shore peering out into the rippling vastness is the antithesis of, say, standing on the corner of State Street and Madison Avenue at rush hour, smothered by skyscrapers and distractions. The ocean is like a Copernican revelation that we are in the grip of something bigger, something so profound it tests our understanding. More so than even the most imposing mountains, which can be conquered, or the endless prairie, which lacks mystery, the ocean is perspective and, consequently, humility. It inspires a subdued sense that we haven't begun to decipher millions of life's secrets.

But landlubber that I am—Dramamine cruising through my system even as we drifted on Muscongus Bay—I had always been a humble observer, not a participant. Actually being out there, being carried along by waves that had rolled past more answers in a day than I could find in a lifetime, I felt more lucid, yet more insignificant, than ever.

"There were more people living on the islands in the state of Maine before 1900 than there were on the mainland," Bill Zuber told us, pointing to a spruce-clad slab of land to the east as green as *Gladiator's* painted hull. "The town of Friendship really began here, on Friendship Long Island, which is about two miles long. Each little town along here had an island that they referred to as 'Long Island,' because it was the longest island in the area. But there are sixty-three islands in this bay right here."

An occasional house peeked out from behind the trees on the island. They were obviously summer residences, the last year-round islanders having moved to the mainland in the late eighties. "That's a typical, old island house," said Caroline, pointing to a canary-colored one. "That's

Bill Zuber

where the original settlers were. We had a lady on the boat who was in her eighties, and she was born in that house in 1908."

"She told us a story," Bill recalled, "about how lightning hit the house and went down the wall. The wallpaper fell down, and the cow didn't give milk for a week. She also told us they used to run a store in the back, her mother did. Her mother and father met in the store. He was a stonecutter back in the

1800s. There was a big granite quarry on the island."

"The quarry went out of business," added Caroline, "when they blasted a hole and the ocean came in."

I would later learn that some of that granite—indeed, the last order before the quarry closed—found its way to New York and Ulysses S. Grant's grave site. So the next time somebody asks what you can find in Grant's Tomb, tell them a little bit of Friendship.

"Let's see if we can get upwind," said Bill, half to himself. "Let's see if we can't get around this island."

Caroline leaned forward and pointed to what appeared to be a gate across a pond on the island. "See over there on the right? That's called a lobster pound, and they actually store lobsters in that, usually in the fall. The tourists leave, and the price goes down, so they put them in this big corral. The pound keeper lives in that house there and feeds them, sometimes into January or February. Mostly, though, they sell them off around the holidays."

I listened intently and saw that Amy did the same. I had a feeling we were both thinking the same thing—that this was something we should know. It was the same feeling we had while driving past, say, the artichoke farms of Salinas and the cattle ranches of Missoula, embarrassed at our ignorance about the core of people's lives.

The Zubers helped as best they could. We learned that lobstering is as seasonal as farming, that the locals might rig their boats for shrimp in the winter and scallops in the spring, and that Muscongus Bay is good lobstering territory because it is rather shallow. We learned that cold water means sweet fish, that each lobster trap has its own buoy and its own color marked with the owner's number, that at the peak of summer, there is a rainbow of buoys across the bay. We learned, too, that the lobsterman is part businessman, part scientist, and part psychic.

"The reason that Friendship, despite its name, has remained so insular is that all of these lobstermen are self-employed. Their success is directly proportional to the effort they put into running their business.

And each wharf along the shore of the harbor is sort of like the ranch out west. You fish, and you deal with a certain lobster dealer who has a wharf, and he furnishes you with your bait, your salt, your fuel for your boat. You sell to him, only to him, and he takes care of the wholesale end of it," Caroline explained, as *Gladiator* cut a swath through a clump of spruce pollen.

"So each wharf has its own stable of lobster boats. You have to have someone who will buy your product, and you have to know where you can set your traps. And they're moving the traps all the time. You never commute to the same place if you're a lobsterman, because they sort of sense when the lobsters are on the move all the time, depending on the weather, the wind, whatever. The lobster decides this is the time to go someplace else, and they all move."

It was an amusing image, those little lobsters with their little lobster brains dictating the movement of a fleet of fishing boats. There was a message in there somewhere.

Bill yelled hello to a neighbor as we passed his boat, and we watched the lobsterman pull a trap aboard. "There you go," Bill said. "Is there a lobster in it? Yeah . . . Well, a little one. He'll probably throw it overboard. You see, there's only a given amount of lobsters that are keepers. You can't keep the big ones, and you can't keep the little ones."

"You can't keep the big ones?" Amy asked, not letting on that she's allergic to lobsters of any size.

"No, and Maine is the only state that has an upper size limit. So you're catching a class of lobsters."

"The middle class," I offered.

Our captain nodded and shrugged. "The middle class always gets it in the end."

Bill Zuber grew up on a farm in New Jersey. More accurately, his father was a farmer-fisherman with a degree in horticulture and a fleet of boats. Bill began sailing at the age of four, but he thought he wanted to be a doctor. "I went to Rutgers for about a year and blew that after getting out of military school. That was a little too much freedom," he explained. "I went on to Glassboro State Teachers' College and graduated from there. I was an educator. After that, I decided that there were too many politicians in the schools, so I went to work taking people fishing."

Eventually, he started his own boatyard on the New Jersey coast. He ran it for a decade. Then, one rainy day in April 1967, the Zubers and an older couple they were friendly with spent an afternoon in a boatyard along New Jersey's Barnegat Bay. They were in the process of completing the hull of what was to be a replica Friendship sloop, and they were searching for a used mast. There, in the headwaters of the bay, they spied two white Friendships, both for sale, both named *Downeaster*. One had the builder's name and the year 1963 carved under the bowsprit. The other, obviously older and leaking slightly, bore only the serial number 86611. The two families huddled for a few minutes, made an offer on the older boat, and found themselves co-owners of a thirty-three-foot Friendship sloop.

"We both borrowed twenty-five hundred dollars," said Caroline, meaning the Zubers and their friends Stu and Dot Hancock. "We went to the bank, and they asked, 'What do you want it for?' And we said, 'To buy a boat with a friend.' And they said, 'Well, that's a good way to lose a friend, and the money.'"

That summer, they sailed the sloop to Friendship for the annual regatta and spent their free time in a dusty attic poring over old records in an attempt to find her origin. They discovered that they had purchased an original, built in 1902 and christened *Gladiator*. "This boat was built by Alexander 'Bug' McLain over on Bremen Long Island, which is right around the corner about two miles from here," said the proud captain, as a pair of cormorants glided by, skimming the water. "There was a family of McLains that built Friendship sloops, and they built 'em like the proverbial brick house, more so than some of the others. Wilbur

Morse is probably the most famous builder of Friendships, but he built the Fords. The McLains built the Pierce Arrows."

In 1970, after adding a new topmast and upper sails, the owners sailed the sloop to Friendship again, won first place in the regatta's "Original" class, and then sailed home to New Jersey. The following year, the Zubers bought some property in Friendship, property they decided to call home once Bill found a job working on the boats of the Hurricane Island Outward Bound Program, headquartered in Rockland. "The boat brought us here," said Bill. "If you've got a Friendship sloop, what the hell, you might as well live in Friendship. So here we are."

For nearly a decade, *Gladiator* was moored at Hurricane Island, the Hancocks still sharing the expenses and visiting Maine for two weeks each summer. But in 1982, Bill decided it was time to fix her up a bit. He took her out of the water, built a plastic shed around her, and spent the next five years rebuilding her. When she was launched again in June 1987, she had a modern engine and interior, new decking, and new sails. Her cracked ribs had been replaced and her planks refastened. She was eighty-five years old and good as new.

"Roger Duncan, who owns a Friendship sloop and sails out of Boothbay, has written books about Friendship, excellent maritime histories of the coast of Maine," said Caroline. "He came and looked at it, and he said, 'This boat will never come apart.' "

"Short of a major nautical disaster," Bill pointed out.

"Like getting run over," said Caroline.

"By a cruise ship!" shouted Andy.

By 1989, Dot Hancock had passed away, and her husband had sold his share of the sloop to the Zubers, becoming "owner emeritus." Bill had left Outward Bound and turned instead to a seasonal job with the Sea Education Association, taking college students out for six weeks each winter through the western Atlantic and the Caribbean aboard a two-hundred-ton schooner. "I usually go as the engineer, because if I were to go as captain, I wouldn't be able to spend enough time teaching the kids," he explained. "So I go on deck and teach about celestial navigation. That's good. I like doing that."

The rest of the year, Bill does some carpentry work, while Caroline works for the Maine Department of Human Resources. Meanwhile, for the first time since World War II, *Gladiator* earns her keep by taking paying passengers for day trips and charters, hosting everything from weddings to funerals to whatever rite of passage Amy and I were experiencing. *Gladiator* cost $450 when she was built in 1902. The Zubers and Hancocks paid ten times that for her sixty-five years later. Three decades after that, she is insured for ten times more. To the captain and his wife, however, their Friendship sloop is nothing short of priceless.

"A couple of things these boats are famous for," Bill said. "One is their ability to take care of themselves. You just set the sails and let her go, and she'll hold the course within about five degrees as long as the wind doesn't change. The other thing is they're comfortable. You get a feeling that this boat is something maybe you want to be on, that it'll all be okay."

His eyes took on a faraway look as a porpoise performed a water ballet a few hundred feet away. "When you're on this boat, you get the feeling that you're not going to die today," he said. "Maybe tomorrow, but not today."

The ship's bell rang six times, meaning it was three o'clock. We had circumnavigated Friendship Long Island and were heading north again, through Otter Passage. The plan was to continue our course, squeezing between Morse Island and Gay Island before sneaking back into Friendship Harbor through the back door. To our left, we spotted a seal sunning himself on a rock, the top of which just barely broke the surface of the water. But the sun was beginning to fade as low clouds came into view.

"C'mon, sun. Then we'll get some wind." Caroline shaded her eyes. "See, the breeze is changing from an easterly to a westerly."

"Yup," said Bill. "It's trying to make up its mind."

Thunder in the distance sounded like muffled cannonballs. Nearly two centuries earlier, the cannonballs had been real. During the War of 1812, when the British occupied all of eastern Maine as far as the Penobscot River, there was a brief naval battle between the American frigate *Enterprise* and the British frigate *Boxer*, a battle fought within sight of Friendship. The vessels, each carrying eighteen guns and just over a hundred men, poured broadsides into one another for forty minutes. When the cannons' thunder subsided, one boat surrendered to the other, but nobody in Friendship knew which one. The townsfolk waited impatiently to see whether the vessels would turn north toward Halifax, meaning a British victory, or south toward Portland, meaning an American triumph. A cheer rose as the boats headed south.

Maine had been saved for America, but to this day, there is still something removed about it, something different from the other lower forty-seven. Maybe it's because Maine is the only contiguous state bordered by only one other. Maybe it's the location; Maine looks like a northeastern addendum, as if the United States took one last bite out of Canada. Perhaps it's the fact that civilization is an afterthought here. Four-fifths of the state, some 17 million acres, is covered by forest. There are twenty-five hundred lakes and ponds, thirty-two thousand miles of rivers and streams, and thirty-five hundred miles of coastline, when all of the two thousand coastal islands are accounted for. Maine is the largest state in New England but the most sparsely populated east of the Mississippi River. It is an isolated place that breeds a unique character.

"The down-easter is a funny kind of person," Bill explained. "They're very nice people, easy to get along with. But they won't say much to you, and they're not outgoing. I mean, if you move in, they don't have a big party to welcome you to the neighborhood and all that sort of thing. But if you ask for help, by God, they're there."

"They're there," echoed Caroline.

The Zubers had lived in Friendship for nearly a quarter-century, yet the state-of-Mainers were still "them." Tourism notwithstanding, Maine is as insular as it is isolated. Just one-tenth of one percent of its population consists of people who arrived from another country between 1980 and 1990, fewer than any other state. More than 70 percent of its residents are home-born. "From away" is what they say of anyone without a Maine pedigree, particularly in Friendship, which is a secluded citadel all its own.

"You know, Friendship's a strange little enclave," Bill declared, "because it's surrounded by places like Boothbay—lots of people, lots of tourists, all kinds of things going on. Rockland is getting the same way, and Thomaston is a fairly touristy place, where people go to see the big, old homes and that sort of thing. But Friendship? There's nothing. There's no restaurant. There's isn't even a public telephone."

He glanced up at the mainsail and then back down to the water ahead. "I think there are a few reasons why Friendship has remained that way," he continued. "One is that the families of the people who started coming here years ago still come here. Another is that it's a dry town. You can't buy booze or wine or beer. Also, the lobstermen have kept it lobsterin'. We're the only other commercial operation in the harbor. That's why these islands are as unpopulated as they are. It's sort of a place nobody goes."

His analysis complete, Bill perked up, almost like a dog hearing a distant whistle. "The wind's shifting. We're gonna get a nice breeze from the west here all of a sudden. Feel that nice, warm breeze? That's a front coming through." He tried to maneuver to avoid the coming rain, but it was unavoidable.

"Look at it!" said Andy. "Here it comes."

It turned out to be only a light drizzle. While the raindrops fell, I noticed the smiles on the faces of our captain and crew, smiles that suggested more than momentary pleasure. These people were unabashedly content out here on the Atlantic, and I wanted to know why. What was it about the sea that led them to build their lives near it?

"Well, there's no telephone, there's no television, and there's not much politics out here," said Bill. *Politics* was a term he used often, his favorite and least-favorite word. It was apparently a sort of catchall for all the mainland, fast-track, stress-inducing nonsense he couldn't stomach. "You can go anywhere you want to go, and when you're at sea, you're constantly looking at things, because you always have to observe things in order to get along. You gotta know what's happening."

He thought for a moment and then continued with a renewed passion in his voice. "It's just getting to be part of that whole cosmos that surrounds the sea. It's so interesting, and it's calming, and it's nice. You feel like you're secure in yourself, because you know what you need to do and when you need to do it in order to get where you want to go."

"And it's self-reliance," added Caroline. "You're in control, and there are very few times in your life when you feel you can control what you're doing."

It was then that I realized what I admired so much about Bill and Caroline Zuber. They were in control of their lives. They had taken it upon themselves to define the moment. It was a concept that became the credo of our cross-country tour and, indeed, a blueprint for our future, so much so that Amy and I turned the journey into a search for a home, setting lofty criteria for the life we wanted to live and looking for an environment that would meet them. We even began a list of fifty things we wanted to do before we died—attend a rocket launch, raft the Colorado River, catch Springsteen at a small venue—to make sure our epiphany wouldn't be lost over the years amid the haze of compromise.

Too many people I know—and these are young people, people with options—seem to settle for entrenched mediocrity, merely tolerating their day-to-day existence. A few even seem to revel in their misery, the late hours or cold winters or tyrannical bosses or shunted dreams. They trudge through fifty weeks of tedium to enjoy two weeks of reprieve—maybe three weeks, if they're lucky enough to get a promotion.

The Zubers decided to make life a vacation. They had been mindful enough to recognize when they were being handed bull and courageous enough to grab it by the horns. When they found themselves involved in something they didn't care for, they escaped it. When they saw something they loved, they pursued it. These people were smiling because they were where they wanted to be. They understood that life is too short for what-ifs and complications. Life, they found, can be as simple as reading the wind.

Hemingway wrote, "They say the seeds of what we will do are in all of us, but it always seemed to me that in those who make jokes in life the seeds are covered with better soil and a higher grade of manure."

The rain had lasted only a few minutes, the mid-June sun was back, and the captain and his first mate were warming to their role as entertainers.

Maine humor, Andy explained—or, as he called it, "Maine humah"—is a breed of comedic folk story. The fun is as much in the telling as in the tale. "It's sort of long-winded," he admitted, "but you have to be careful listening to it, because later, when you're driving in your car, you may break out into a fit of giggles and drive off the road."

Bill cleared his throat, and the son gave way to the father. "There's one that I remember about Mr. Perkins's privy," he said, slipping into his Maine storytelling voice. "You see, Mr. Pahkins needed to have himself a new privy, because he was afraid Grandpop might fall through and have himself a heaht attack. So he called over old Elmer Tasker to come over theah and figure him a new privy.

"Elmer come over, and he says, 'Well, Mr. Pahkins, where would you like to have this privy?' And Mr. Pahkins says, 'Well, I believe I'd like to have it right over theah by them chestnut trees.' Well, Elmer looked at 'em, and he says, 'Well, all right, Mr. Pahkins, it's your privy,' and he commenced digging. Well, he got the hole dug, and Mr. Pahkins come out, and he says, 'You know, Elmer, I been thinking some more about that privy of mine, and being out theah by them chestnut trees in the wintertime might be quite a long walk. I believe that perhaps we should have that privy right theah by them lilac bushes.' Well, Elmer looked at him and says, 'All right, Mr. Pahkins, it's your privy.' Then he covered up that hole and commenced to diggin' again.

"Well, he just got the framing up, and Mr. Pahkins come out again and says, 'You know, Elmer, I been ponderin' all night long about this here privy, and I noticed that being over heah by them lilac bushes, with the wind in the summertime being from the sou'west, it's gonna be a little uncomfortable for them lady folks. I think we've got to have that privy about halfway between them lilac bushes and them chestnut trees.' And Elmer says, 'All right, Mr. Pahkins, it's your privy.'

"He covered up that hole, and he commenced to diggin', and he had just gotten the interior decorating all fixed up theah with a nice new holly seat and a brand-new Sears and Roebuck catalog in theah when Mr. Pahkins come out that morning with a head o' steam and says, 'Damn it, Elmer. When we contracted for this privy, I told you I wanted a two-holer, and you've got it fixed up as a one!'" Here, Caroline's brother, George, began a fit of giggles before the punch line. "Elmer looks at 'im and says, 'Mr. Pahkins, I don't mean to be dictatin' to you or nothing like that. But if you come out heah some morning pressed for time, by the time you figured out which one of them holes to set on, it will be too late, that's all.' "

We all laughed, not a slap-your-knees, grab-your-gut kind of laugh, but an appreciative laugh at a story well told. To add a note of absurdity to the festivities, it was at that moment that I caught out of the corner of my eye what appeared to be a piece of driftwood draped in seaweed floating by. As we drew closer, it became clear that it wasn't driftwood at all. It was a baseball bat. As my mind generated wild theories of how it wound up so far north on the Atlantic (probably took ten years to drift up from Boston after the 1986 World Series, I concluded), our captain threw the gauntlet back to his son. "I like the one about the bugle," he offered with a nod of his head.

Andy, now steering the boat, kept one hand on the wheel and used the other to tilt his cap back on his head. "Well," he began, turning from sailor to actor, "this being an election yeah and all, this is a good election-yeah joke. . . .

"Now, see, Hubert was runnin' for town office, and he is kind of numb, you know. Of course, Hubert runs that swing bridge down at the hahbor, you know. And if the boats want to get in the hahbor, they toot the horn, and he opens the bridge, you see. Well, Bubba come up to my fahm one day—of course, Bubba is Hubert's cousin trying to solicit my vote—so Bubba comes up to my fahm, and he says, 'Are you gonna vote for Hubert?' And I says no. And he says, 'Why not?' And I says, 'He killed my cow.'

"He says, 'He killed your cow?' I says, 'Yes! Last spring, my cow had a case of the collywobbles theah, and I took it down to the vet'rinarian to see what I should do. And the vet'rinarian said I should give my cow an enema. I says, 'Are you sure?' And he says, 'Yeah. That'll fix her up straight.' So I went back to my fahm, and I fixed her up a good bucket full of warm, sudsy water theah, and I went out to my barn and had a talk with my cow. And I says, 'Deah, you're not gonna like this much, but you just hang with me, and we'll get through it together.'

" 'I didn't have a funnel or nothing. All I had was this old bugle I had from my army days. So I took that, and I lubed her up a bit, and I eased her in, and, well, the cow didn't like that too much. But I put that hot, sudsy water to her, you know, and I got her just about topped off when that cow o' mine decided she'd had just about enough. She broke free and started running down the road towards that bridge. Well, about halfway theah, things started to break loose on her, you see, and that bugle started to go. Just like 'The Star-Spangled Banner.' And of course, Hubert runnin' that swing bridge thought it was a boat in distress, and he opened that bridge right wide, and that cow ran right off the end of the dock into the middle of the hahbor and drowned.

" 'And I tell you, I will never vote for a man who doesn't know the difference between a foghorn and a bugle stuck up a cow's ass.' "

When the laughter subsided, there were still smiles all around, as the sun warmed our faces on the day before Father's Day and we drifted back home into Friendship Harbor.

Gladiator *at home*

HONOR,
MICHIGAN

Mine honor is my life; both grow in one;
Take honor from me, and my life is done.

William Shakespeare

As June melted into July, we embarked on a tour of extended family. A visit with my cousin and her family outside Boston, a reunion with Amy's grandparents, parents, and sister at her cousin's wedding in Philadelphia, a few days roaming my mother's hometown of Butler, Pennsylvania, where long-lost relatives descended on us. Finally, a headlong rush to Chicago, where my brother's five-day-old son, the first of a new generation, squinted and yawned to welcome us home. It was four weeks in which two weary travelers grew to appreciate the ties that bind. Then we set out for Honor, where such ties were paramount.

Bordering four of the five Great Lakes, Michigan has more coastline than any state but Alaska. We seemed to traverse most of it as we followed the shore of Lake Michigan up the western edge of the state. Henry David Thoreau believed lakes to be land's most beautiful and expressive feature—"earth's eyes," he called them. But I don't think he meant lakes this size, too immense for romance, too sprawling to seem a window into nature's soul. When a person in Gary, Indiana, can look upon the same waters as another in Michigan's Upper Peninsula, hundreds of miles and a separate time zone away, those waters lose something. Expanse dilutes a sense of figurative depth.

Halfway up the coast, we stopped for the night in Muskegon, where my uncle and two cousins from Grand Rapids were spending the night in their cottage near the lake. One cousin had just graduated from West Point. Top 10 percent of his class. He was preparing to head out to Fort Lewis in Washington, where he'd be a second lieutenant in an armored division, piloting a tank.

We're first cousins, Todd Vydareny and I. I admit I'd never envisioned myself driving a Winnebago, but a tank remained completely out of the question. I am a knee-jerk pacifist, repelled by regimentation, questioning authority on an hourly basis. I sleep late; I'd never held a gun; I don't even jog. I wouldn't survive an hour of basic training. Indeed, I'm not alone among a generation that has never had to consider a military stint and has never felt the profound tug between preserving a way of life and preserving life itself. I'm lucky, lazy, and selfish. Todd, on the other hand, is a soldier. "Duty, Honor, Country." That's the West Point motto. We talked about honor.

"What they always told us is, it means doing the right thing when no one's around," he explained. "The full Honor Code at West Point is, 'A cadet will not lie, cheat or steal, and will not tolerate those who do.' That was the minimum standard. I'm not going to say I've never done any of those things. It's a personal line. For me, if a little voice makes me feel bad about doing something, that's where the line is."

Perhaps honor is malleable, and inseparable from personality. At the United States Military Academy, cadets take classes on the subject of honor, in which they discuss and debate scenarios, the aim being not to find a correct answer but to learn something by searching for it. Still, there are times when orders and honor don't jibe, and it's not always a My Lai kind of drama. Often, it's mundane. Todd offered an example: "The army spare-parts system doesn't work. If I'm driving my tank and a piece of it breaks, it could take me two weeks to get a new piece. And while I'm waiting for it to come in through the proper channels, I can't train. But let's say I've got a sergeant in my unit who will go and either take it from another unit or trade for it, and he'll get my tank back up and running. Now, is that right? That's against army regulations, but they always say, 'Whatever you have to do, get this done.'" The mission comes first, he implied. Duty.

"It seems to me," I said, well aware that we came at the subject from entirely different angles, "that out of duty, honor, and country, honor's the most noble."

Todd nodded. "Of all three of those things, at least for me, honor is always pure."

But when one of them has to go, it tends to be the pure one, the internal one. Did our nation's Japanese internment episode or our Vietnam policies place country above honor? Did Oliver North sacrifice honor for duty? Honor, coming from within, should trump the others. Yet my cousin pointed out that in his case, the honor is in the duty, and the duty is for the country. "The way I see it, I don't choose where I'm going to fight. I've chosen to go wherever the country says, whatever the national leadership says, whether or not I agree with it. You can voice your opposition, but when they give that order . . ."

Maybe that's why the military seems so foreign to me. The military is about unquestioned obedience, about America first, about right and wrong as black and white. But the lessons of my lifetime have been about abuse of power, about a global village, about shades of gray. I'm too cynical to be devoted to someone else's ideals, yet too broadly idealistic to be wholeheartedly patriotic.

I don't know. Maybe I'm the kind of person who claims selflessness without having a willingness to sacrifice, who has conviction without commitment, honor without courage. Regardless, I knew I wasn't what the army wanted. But why had my cousin decided to make a career of it?

"It's a purpose, just like some people find purpose in religion," he told me. "It's a way of waking up and feeling like you're doing something important every morning. I feel like I'm doing something good, that I'm making a difference."

Then he hit me with both barrels—logic and emotion. "I think the easiest way to put it—why I'm in the army—is I've always been very protective of my family and the people I love, and it gives me purpose in my life to know that what I'm doing is indirectly protecting my family."

So there it was. He wasn't doing it for politics or patriotism or testosterone release or discipline or pension or glory. He was doing it for Mom and Dad and Little Brother and Big Sis. Honor and family were cousins after all.

W e continued up Highway 31, heading due north along the western edge of the state. If Michigan is a great big oven mitt, then we entered the pinkie at about the town of Ludington, where the highway shrank from four lanes to two. In theory, we were hugging the coast, but we couldn't catch sight of the big lake. There were only pint-size versions along the way: Manistee Lake, Portage Lake, Bear Lake. Michigan was dotted with earth's eyes.

At Crystal Lake, the highway took an eastward and more dramatic turn. The forests became deeper, the water bluer, the hills hillier. We passed the Cherry Bowl Drive-In, a throwback theater that opened just after the Korean War. *Courage Under Fire* was playing, I noted, appreciating the irony as we crossed the Platte River and rolled into Honor.

Honor was a village of three hundred inhabitants in the winter, a number that swelled considerably when the sportsmen arrived with the sun. U.S. 31 masqueraded as Main Street for a mile and two-thirds, Main

Street seeming like an almost perfect but incomplete row of teeth. Interspersed among the polished ivory businesses (the Honor Motel, Honor State Bank, Honor Insurance Agency, Honor Building Supply, and a strip mall known as Honor Plaza) were a handful of vacant storefronts. Honor was either eroding or rebuilding.

Or maybe it was hung over. Nailed to one house was a plaque that read, *Happy Birthday, Honor,* and attached to electrical poles along Main Street were dozens of banners celebrating, *Honor 1895–1995.* Over each banner hung an American flag. We'd missed the centennial bash—three full days of parades and raffles, beard judging and basket weaving, horseshoe tournaments and organ recitals—by a scant twelve months. Timing is everything.

We spent an hour exploring Honor's outskirts along the tangents that led from U.S. 31. Platte Street was a little loop from the highway. Scenic Drive was just that, rising to a dead end and a breathtaking view of the valley. Covey Road was a dusty trail toward wheat fields and farmhouses. Soon after exploring the latter, we discovered there was a resident in town named Norm Covey. With nothing to go on but the name, we chose him as our person of Honor.

After lunch at the Sleepy Bear Lounge—which, according to its owner, doubled as a brothel during Prohibition—Amy and I strolled toward Covey's house on one end of Main Street. It was a beautiful ninety-degree afternoon in July, and the lazy air hung around us like a shawl. There was serenity here, the kind you find off the beaten path, even though Honor was very much on it. Cars hummed past us. To them, Honor was just a stretch of highway where the speed limit changed. Then we heard a chugging and rattling that relegated the hum to the background. Gobbling up the highway at about twenty miles per hour was a 1921 Ford Model-T roadster with a convertible top, running boards, a spare tire on the back, wooden wheels, a tilting windshield, kerosene parking lights, and a driver who looked as though he should have been aboard a John Deere.

Don Andrews was smiling the smile of a man on display. We stopped him across the street from Covey's house and inquired about his means of travel, which was as antique and impractical as our beloved Rolling Stone was comfortable and cutting edge.

"I did it from pieces," he told us. "I knew what I wanted. Being that my profession was also my hobby, I decided to build one. So I started gathering parts from all over. The top comes from a car show in Zephyr Hills, Florida. The body comes from down by Grand Rapids. The motor is from up the road in Empire. The wheels are the original wood. They're seventy-five years old."

Don, whose wife was named Donita, had run an auto-body shop outside town before retiring. The car was a seven-year project, a collection of parts from around the country that formed a whole representing life as it was three-quarters of a century earlier. It later struck me that Don's search for the right parts was analogous to the journey that brought me to him.

"This car's ten years older than me," he announced, petting the dashboard as if it would purr.

"For me, that would mean a '57 Chevy."

He waved his hand. "Fifty-seven Chevys are a dime a dozen. They don't

Don Andrews and his 1921 Ford Model-T roadster

mean nothing to me, because they're too new for me to really enjoy."

I thought about that one later, too. It was a comparison that neatly summarized the generation gap. Different views of what America once was could lead to different views of what it is. Generations are molded, not born. For better or for worse, we are the products of our parents' prime. His *Hindenburg* is my *Challenger*. His polio is my AIDS. His Roosevelt is my Reagan.

Of course, this is all subtext added in hindsight. Mostly, it was just a conversation about cars. When we finished talking, Amy asked if he had a business card he could give us, something to remember him by. Don said no, he didn't. But he took out a card belonging to a fellow antique car collector, wrote his own name and number on the back, and handed it to us.

There's a passage in William Goldman's book about screen writing, *Adventures in the Screen Trade*, in which he discusses the notion of a "movie moment." "The reality of a movie," he explains, "has almost nothing to do with the reality of the world we, as humans, inhabit." His point is that some moments in the real world are simply too unbelievable for the movie screen. Like when you wonder what the weather's going to be to-morrow and then turn on the radio just in time to hear, "Tomorrow's forecast calls for . . ."

That business card Don Andrews handed us provided us with a movie moment. At the bottom was the summer address of his friend in nearby Empire. At the top was the friend's winter address—in Comfort, Texas.

What were the chances that we would be strolling down Main Street in Honor just as Don Andrews chugged by in his Ford? That he would be carrying his friend's card in his wallet? That he would hand it to us? What were the odds of choosing eighteen tiny hamlets in the middle of nowhere and finding a link between two of them located a thousand miles apart? It was like writing your name on a dollar bill, spending it in Miami, and getting it back five months later in Milwaukee.

We would soon discover a tie between the two communities that went beyond that coincidence. Comfort was a study of roots. Honor became a lesson in family.

Norm Covey's turn-of-the-century white Victorian was a museum—a gallery of photographs, a collection of artifacts. On the walls of his den were more than a hundred snapshots—grainy photographs of upstanding subjects, most of them with the unsmiling visages that passed for nineteenth-century posing, men with handlebar mustaches and women with parasols. They were family photos. The room—indeed, the entire house—was an homage to ancestry.

Norm pointed to a photograph dated February 7, 1909, that included his grandfather. "Fat Men of Honor," said the inscription below the photo of fourteen 250-pounders. "It used to be a sign of being a bourgeois," he explained. Then he turned the picture into a story. "My grandfather was a Civil War lieutenant. The Coveys had come out of New York and up through southern Michigan, but at some point, my grandfather had joined the Seventh Illinois Infantry and became a medical officer. His name was Israel. Israel Palmer Covey."

It had dawned on me, particularly in Georgia, that there were people whose grandfathers had fought for the Blue or the Gray. But I figured those people were by now elderly anomalies, feeble and confused. Norm was young enough to remind me of a man who had spent his boyhood summers in northern Michigan. He resembled an Idaho-era Ernest Hemingway, with his salty eyes and tight white beard. He was only sixty-three, but generations are malleable, too.

"My grandfather married," Norm continued, "and they moved up through Muskegon, where he was a town marshal. On the way up, he began practicing medicine, using his army training. They came into Honor just one hundred years ago last year."

That was when Honor began, when the maple forests were so bountiful that they drew an English industrialist to the Platte River Valley. William Gifford represented the Guelph Patent Cask Company, manufacturers of wooden containers. On the shores of the Platte, he saw a generation's supply of hardwood, a convenient river, and the potential for rail service—a perfect site for his company's newest lumbermill. In August 1895, Gifford purchased a tract of land in the area and brought his wife, son, and daughter to their new home in the valley. The daughter was fifteen months old. Her name was Honor.

Almost immediately, two railroad lines built tracks into the new community. The Pere Marquette was strictly a freight line—no passengers, save the occasional adventurer riding the caboose. The Manistee and Northeastern soon followed with its own spur, a lonely stretch of railroad dubbed the M & NE (as in "Mine and Nobody Else's"). The M & NE offered passenger service, and by the turn of the century, Honor had grown into a legitimate logging center. Meanwhile, Israel Covey's son, Ezra, had become a medical student.

"This was in the basement for seventy years," said Norm, pointing to a chair on his front porch covered with the dust of decades. "It's a real medical chair, given by my grandfather to my father when he graduated medical school. That was June 18, 1900."

That was the heyday of Honor, when the forests seemed endless, the trains came and went, the mill yard bustled with activity, and the town's population exceeded five hundred. In 1908, Honor even began an eight-year stint as the seat of Benzie County, the smallest county in Michigan. One of the more memorable occasions during those years was an all-out Fourth of July celebration complete with a balloon ascension, no minor treat. "So great was this event," say the histories, "that for some time thereafter, impressionable children reckoned time from the day that 'the balloon went up' in Honor."

But what goes up . . .

The Giffords left town in 1912, deciding they wanted to spend their summers in England. Honor Gifford was eighteen years old, and she never returned, dying before her thirtieth birthday. By then, the glorious stand of maples that had drawn the Giffords to the Platte River Valley was depleted. Honor was a lumbermill town surrounded by stumps. With the forests gone, the mill went next. With the mill went the railroads and the prestige. The Pere Marquette suspended service in 1915. The county seat was snatched away by a neighboring town a year later. The M & NE struggled on for another seven years, finally rattling to a halt in 1923.

But towns, while made by industry, are made up of families.

Norm glided over to the wall of photographs. "Here's the house and my dad, about 1905. Here he is with his dog. Here he is with the first car in town. . . . Of course, he started out practicing in a horse and buggy."

In the days when small-town America was a study in self-sufficiency, Ezra Lincoln Covey was that most honorable and antique of professionals—the country doctor.

"He would make house calls and OB calls, and my mother would go along and stay overnight in people's houses," said Norm. "Or he would be out practicing, maybe, making a call late at night. And somebody, maybe next door or down the way, would hear him rumbling around in their kitchen late at night. You know what he'd be doing? Getting coffee. He felt that free about it. In the middle of the night, he'd come in and pour himself some coffee."

Norm looked out into the street with an expression somewhere between wistful and whimsical. "It's nice to bump into people who remember. He's been gone such a long time that there aren't a lot of people, except real old-timers, who remember him." He reached into a closet and blew the dust off a tuxedo as old as the town. "These are Dad's tails he was married in back in 1900."

Ezra Covey's first wife had lived across the street. She was the daughter of a Civil War veteran herself. Her father had been a fourteen-year-old Union drummer boy. She and Ezra were married for twenty-nine years, until she died after suffering a stroke and spending several years as an invalid. Later, Ezra met Evelyn Dana at the hospital up north in Traverse City, where she was a nurse. They married in 1931. She was twenty-five. He was fifty-seven.

Norm led us into a sitting room across the hall. "I was born in this room in 1933. It was quite a thing for a sixty-year-old man to have a child in those days. I think it turned out to be a bit of a plus growing up, certainly with Dad and his wisdom. I remember I would lie there on the couch, and he would read poetry to me. He taught me to fly-fish, too. You don't really look for someone to play catch with. I suppose you've got your boys for that. What you want is somebody to set the pace for you, to set an example for you."

Norm paused before reflecting on what the walls of that sitting room had seen. "My father died in this room. He passed away the first of February 1948. It was a Sunday morning in February, very snowy that winter. He had been down in the basement checking the furnace, and he came up and didn't like the feeling in his chest. He lay down, and Mom and I sat with him. He lay in that couch that was in that corner." He pointed as he spoke, his finger shaking slightly. "He was a little concerned that there might have been a pain down his arm, and he knew what that was. At 3:35 P.M., my mother was washing dishes. He asked for a little drink of whiskey, and my mother gave it to me to take in to him. I handed it to him, and he had a coronary right there."

Having a father sixty years older than he, Norm had tried to prepare himself for the moment. His father was vigorous, but his age was a constant consideration for a son who feared most a loss that was more probable with each passing year. Norm would listen to his father breathing at night, just to make sure. He told himself he was ready if the moment came, but of course, he wasn't. Nearly half a century later, his recall seemed recent and vivid, still tender to the touch, like a deep bruise on his memory.

He shuffled to a collection of photographs. "Here's my dad making a house call in about 1915. . . . Here he is when he was in the band. He played the snare drum and cornet in different bands. . . . Here he is balancing a girl sitting on a chair on his chin. . . . Here he is balancing a canoe paddle. . . . Here's a ladder. . . ."

And then the son, describing his long-dead father, lapsed into present tense: "He's a Renaissance man. . . . Here he is as a football player. He was very athletic. I keep hearing that he would run and vault over fences with his medical bag."

And with that, Norm brought out the medical bag itself—wrinkled, black, still containing half-full vials of medicine. He dug out his father's medical books, too. And he proudly produced the shingle—*Dr. E. L. Covey*—that had hung in front of his father's office. There seemed to be no end to the ancestral antiques.

Norm graduated from high school a few years after his father died. He enrolled at the University of Michigan, where he bused tables with James Earl Jones and joined Delta Kappa Epsilon. The more time he spent in the Deke house, the less time he spent on his studies, until finally, his grades plummeting and his money dwindling, he dropped out. He returned to Honor, took a job in construction, and thought about returning to school for his medical degree, just like his father. Instead, he was drafted into the army in 1954. He joined the medical corps, just like his grandfather, and went from Fort Leonard Wood to Fort Sam Houston to Fort Bliss and finally to France.

College had opened up cultural doors for the boy from Honor. He'd roomed with a black student in the days before integration was mandated. He'd made friends from New York and Chicago, from Shaker Heights and Grosse Point. Europe opened the doors further. Norm visited London and Paris, Copenhagen and Edinburgh, Venice and Rome. "It was the nicest way and nicest time to see Europe," he explained. "I was a medical technician. There wasn't much soldiering to do."

Norm Covey and his father's medical bag

Norm returned home and then

to Ann Arbor for a brief spell before dropping out of college again. Medicine wasn't in the cards. Soon, he found himself at the other end of the lower forty-eight, in Miami, where he spent a couple of years as an orderly in a local hospital. He saw JFK down there late in 1963 and was surprised by how little protection the president seemed to have. "I thought at the time, 'My gosh, with the Cubans down here, he could be shot right here in front of me,'" Norm recalled. "That was Monday. On Friday, he was assassinated."

Miami was too far from Michigan, too far from his mother, who had gone back to work as a registered nurse when his father died. She had earned eight dollars a day, scrimping and saving to send her only son to college.

Norm made it as far north as Flint, where he became part of the Michigan mainstream, manufacturing cars for the masses. He stayed there for twenty-four years, but he constantly visited Honor, often driving the three hours there just to get a glimpse of home and Mom and the old Victorian with the medical bag and the grainy photos—the shingle, the tux, the memories.

He even managed to save enough money to pay his mother back. He grabbed the dog he had found years earlier shivering in a snowbank and put him in the back seat. He grabbed Mom and put her in the passenger seat. He climbed behind the wheel and drove off to see America—three different times, three trips to reduce the continent to one big thank-you postcard.

"First, we went to the Northwest, a very nice trip through Washington and to the coast," said Norm. "It was her first look at the Pacific Ocean, and she really related to that, because our lake here lies to the west. The next year, we ended up in Nova Scotia. The third one, we were heading to Lake Louise but only got as far as Idaho. She was getting a little tired."

Evelyn Covey died on May 14, 1984. She went to a nearby town to do some shopping, called on a cousin, told her she didn't feel well. She was taken back home to Honor, where she lay on the same couch where her husband had taken his last breath thirty-six years earlier. Norm was there, of course.

"I helped her to the bathroom and then set her back on the couch again. Then she said something like, 'Oh, there's something wrong here. I want to get out of here.' It was as if she wanted to escape her body or something," Norm recalled.

He took her to the emergency room, where it was discovered she'd had a minor stroke. Norm sat with her day and night, but then, when he happened to be out of the room, she choked on a piece of food. She had another stroke and passed away the next day. Norm was by her side. "It was eleven-fifteen in the morning," he recalled. "May 14. The day after Mother's Day."

The black-and-white photos were hung in the Covey house in honor of the Honor centennial. That was a year ago, but Norm hadn't bothered to take them down. After all, at the end of the day, what do we have but family and flashbacks? As Norm put it, "There are some things that you don't sand out when you refinish." Memories should be preserved, not polished away. There was nothing remarkable about the village of Honor, but it served as a reminder of the first rule of gratitude and respect: Honor thy father and thy mother.

That being the case, Norm worried about his own demise and what he would do with the beloved house he'd called home for sixty-three years, a Covey landmark since 1902. He considered leaving it to the town, but then he thought better of it. "I figured the way town politics change, I'd almost rather deed it to a committee of my friends. I don't have any heirs, so I thought, 'Well, I'll pick five of my closest friends.' Some of them don't have a place to land in Honor, so they could look after the house and would always have a place to go," he explained.

"I didn't think I'd end up single, not by choice, but now I appreciate it. I'm not lonely. I love living alone. I just wish I had a son or a daughter. I'm sorry because Mom would have made a wonderful grand-mother. That's kind of my immortality anyway. I don't worry too much about me, but Dad and Mom, they were really special. I even thought up till I was sixty, which was only three years ago, that there was time, but . . ."

I looked hard at him as his voice trailed off, and once again, I thought of Hemingway, of a passage in *Death in the Afternoon*: "There are some things which cannot be learned quickly, and time, which is all we have, must be paid heavily for their acquiring. They are the very simplest things, and because it takes a man's life to know them, the little new that each man gets from life is very costly and the only heritage he has to leave."

Amy and I left Norm Covey to his memories. Then we found a pay phone and called our parents.

FAITH,
SOUTH DAKOTA

> *To revive faith is more difficult than to create it.*
>
> Benjamin Disraeli

Travel chroniclers have often tried to identify where the cluttered East becomes the open West, the physical and spiritual point where the American map should fold. The evidence is in the terrain. The prairies begin to expand and toughen. Cornfields become cattle ranches. The scarcity of trees and hills and vertical obstructions allows the sky to match the land's vastness. They've tried to pinpoint where the dust devils start dancing along the horizon like spinning tops, where towns no longer bump up against one another, where the road ahead appears longer and city streets grow wider. It is an impossible determination, like blasting into the atmosphere and attempting to mark the place where sky turns to space. But wanderers have chosen their spots regardless.

Jack Kerouac selected Des Moines, Iowa, where he procured a gloomy hotel room and awoke with a strange sense of not knowing who he was. "I was half-way across America," he wrote, "at the dividing line between the East of my youth and the West of my future." William Least Heat Moon chose the western state lines of Minnesota, Iowa, Missouri, Arkansas, and Louisiana. Kansas City, Missouri, was the last of the East, he explained. Kansas City, Kansas, was the first of the West. Traveling westward as well, John Steinbeck waited a bit longer, but he was sure he'd found the place: Bismarck, North Dakota, located where the Missouri River took a sharp turn south. The green, wooded, well-watered landscape on the eastern side stood in stark contrast to the brown, treeless, semiarid flatlands to the west. "The two sides of the river," he mused, "might well be a thousand miles apart."

I have no idea who's right. But I do know this: Faith is at the center of all things.

When Alaska and Hawaii became states, the geographic center of the nation shifted from Kansas to an uninhabited area in the west-central portion of South Dakota. The city of Faith is exactly seventy miles east of that point—and seventy miles west of the Missouri River, which makes as if to cut the country in two. Or if you prefer to think of the United States as being sliced into three sections by the Mississippi River and the Continental Divide, Faith is almost exactly equidistant from the two.

Our excursion toward the middle started at a famous beginning—at Minnesota's Lake Itasca, the Mississippi River's headwaters. From there, we traveled south to Park Rapids and then east to the North Dakota border. It was along this stretch that the landscape began to change. Enormous forests became scattered woods. Rippling lakes became rolling fields. Narrow roads became broad highways. After climbing aboard Interstate 94 at Fargo, North Dakota, we began to pass the famous amber waves of grain—and we agreed that the sight was worth singing about. Fields of wheat and corn surrounded us, extending as far as the eye could see. When the fields finally ended, green waves of grass took their place.

Soon, trees disappeared entirely, and we experienced the sensation of being surrounded by grass and sky on all sides. Slicing through the solid colors was a road so straight that I was tempted to put the Rolling Stone on cruise control, go back to the kitchen, grab a soft drink, gulp it down, and return to the wheel. Even then, our left tires still would have been hugging the centerline.

We spent the night in Jamestown, North Dakota, which was home to the National Buffalo Museum, as well as a small herd of the animals beside it. Towering over all was the largest buffalo in the world, a sixty-ton statue twenty-six feet high and forty-six feet long. As late as the mid-1800s, there were an estimated 30 to 40 million buffalo in the West. By 1894, there were eighty-five left. They were killed for meat, for hides, for furniture, for trophies, for the hell of it. And while they're no longer near extinction, Jamestown's homage to them felt like kitschy compensation.

Back on the straight and wide again the following day, we turned south an hour west of Jamestown on to U.S. 83. Upon entering Emmons County, we were informed that we were traveling the Lawrence Welk Highway. His hometown of Strasburg was just down the road. I half-expected the discussion of soybean, wheat, and cattle prices emanating from the Bismarck radio station to be backed by an accordion polka.

Minutes later, we were in South Dakota, which looked like a faded green tabletop stretching into infinity. Technically, South Dakota is not the nation's flattest state. Neither is North Dakota, Kansas, Nebraska, or Iowa. The honor goes to Florida, which has only a 345-foot difference between its highest point and its lowest. Delaware (442 feet) is next, followed by Louisiana (543 feet). But the lack of trees in most of South Dakota, the lack of anything to take the eye's attention away from the sprawl, makes the country seem empty and endless. It is the land of the lonesome stretch.

For people who are uncomfortable turning inward, it can be an interminable drive. But Amy and I loved it. There was something profound

The land of the lonesome stretch

and revealing about South Dakota, something humbling. It was haying season, and as we rumbled along the highway, we were slack-jawed at the quantity of collected hay dotting the landscape. Bales of hay, rolls of hay, stacks of hay. Hay in cut rows. Hay piled in pyramids. With regard to sheer volume, this must have been what the buffalo herds used to look like.

The sight helped clarify the scale of the scenery. What a journey from east to west does, more than anything else, is offer perspective. Without skyscrapers and neon and shopping malls, one gains an appreciation for nature's enormity and power. We sensed it along the way—in the bubbling brook that matured into the mighty Mississippi, in the memories of massive bison herds, in the fields covered for miles in nature's bounty. We didn't feel tiny as much as our surroundings felt huge. In an urban setting, a thirty-four-foot Winnebago felt like a bull in a china shop. On the Great Plains, it felt like a buffalo bull on an endless graze.

The 1990 census put South Dakota's population just short of seven hundred thousand, about the same as San Francisco's. The state can be a harsh place to live—thanks to its temperature range of about 140 degrees, its frequent tornados, its relentless winds—but it is populated by survivors who have learned to adapt to the elements.

The problem is that they are increasingly messing with the elements, too. There are 250 natural lakes in the state, but nearly five times as many artificial lakes. The Missouri River, once revered for its power and feared for its unpredictability, has been harnessed and tamed. Gold mines have hollowed out the hills. The land has been portioned into lots. When your perspective has been sharpened and your respect for nature enhanced by the West, you begin to feel that attempts to alter it are affronts to whatever higher power may oversee it.

That consideration, coupled with the knowledge that we were heading toward Faith, put me in mind to reexamine my own faith. I've long struggled with the concept, either thinking too deeply about it or, some would say, not thinking deeply enough. I am what I consider a cultural Jew, but a spiritual agnostic with an eye toward atheism. My faith is as empty as the South Dakota landscape, prone to as many misgivings about organized religion as there are bales of hay in July. I resolved to confront those doubts at our next stop.

After 183 miles on U.S. 83, we turned west again on U.S. 212. Ten miles later, we came upon the Missouri River, dammed to form massive Lake Oahe. A bridge took us into Mountain Standard Time and the Cheyenne River Indian Reservation. The road through it would take us right into Faith.

Almost immediately, we were met by a sign warning, *Rough Road Next 19 Miles,* and we found ourselves slowing down to twenty-five miles per hour over loose gravel. Cars speeding in front of us were reduced to swirls of dust. Soon, clouds crept in on all sides, as the sky became a kaleidoscope of dark and light. Some of the darker clouds seemed to be clawing at the ground. When we began seeing lightning in the distance, we suspected it represented rain at best, the makings of a tornado at worst.

Soon, the clouds massed like an army moving into formation. Only in wide-open spaces can you actually see the weather coming in its entirety. There were showers straight ahead, still more to our left, and two additional swaths of precipitation to our right. We were moving slowly on a ribbon of road surrounded by nothing but rain.

For a while, as we passed through the towns of La Plant and Ridgeview, we thought we might avoid it. Through Parade and Eagle Butte, we felt a few light raindrops. Through Lantry and Dupree, the sky grew increasingly threatening. Finally, about the time we hit Red Elm, just thirteen miles from our destination, we drove straight into the weather.

It wasn't rain at all. It was a hailstorm, chunks of ice as big as marbles crashing against the metal roof of the Rolling Stone like BBs on a tin can. The sky grew so dark and the hail so thick that our way became more a guess than a road. It must have lasted a good ten minutes, and then, just like that, it was over. We came out of the storm into blinding sunshine and a completely dry stretch of highway. If I were a religious man, I would have suspected that some higher power had aimed the storm directly at us.

I shot a glance into the rearview mirror in time to see a giant rainbow arching across the prairie. Then we continued toward Faith.

The calm after the storm

Faith was as western as places come. Main Street was fifty feet wide, dusty, and dramatic. If I squinted, I could see an outlaw at each end, hands twitching in anticipation of a draw, while the citizens peered from behind curtains in store windows. Even the businesses along Main Street, with their yellow-and-brown signage and Old West lettering, evoked a sense of place—Frontier Family Clothing, Prairie Oasis Mall, the Steakhouse Lounge, the Wrangler Café. This was a town of big belt buckles and bolo ties.

And grasshoppers. Thousands of them, an infestation of near-plague proportions.

They've always been my least favorite insects, if only because they fly like drunken kamikazes and crunch when you step on them. Almost everywhere we walked in town, we scared up a dozen with each step. As the insects jumped in and out of our way, it was as if the ground itself moved. Doors and windows had to be opened and closed quickly, for fear of inviting a swarm in. Cars and pickup trucks were covered in green grasshopper grime.

In the story of the Exodus, locusts followed hail. I found our succession of plagues that day ironic, it being a journey to Faith and all, and ominous, my faith being in question. Keeping a lookout for boils and frogs, I collected my doubts and looked for the proper outlet for vocalizing and examining them. There were only 540 people in Faith, but there were a half-dozen places of worship—a Catholic church, a Methodist church, a Presbyterian church, two Lutheran churches, and a Church of Christ. On a slow Saturday amid a dry July in the plains, two men of the cloth—Wayne Hjermstad, a Norwegian Lutheran pastor, and Dennis Riss, a Catholic priest—had the pleasure of defending God to a visitor playing devil's advocate, so to speak.

I later admitted to myself that perhaps I was testing them. Maybe I wanted to see if they could answer the tough questions, juggle the generalities, reconcile the contradictions. Here, in the middle of nowhere, I found them to be articulate in their defense, unwavering in their convictions, and eager to preach to a skeptic, as opposed to the choir.

The two clergymen had come to Faith via different paths.

Father Dennis was born a hundred miles southeast in Rapid City but had taken a circuitous route back home. He wandered through schools

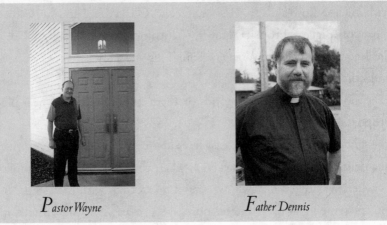

Pastor Wayne   *Father Dennis*

and seminaries in Missouri, Minnesota, Iowa, and Colorado and accepted his first assignment in a rinky-dink town near the Nebraska border before finally finding his way back to western South Dakota. He had decided on a career in the clergy as a child, then realized later that he yearned to be unique. And what better fit that word than the priesthood and the celibacy that accompanied it?

"But I think the ultimate reason is mystery," he concluded. "The whole concept of the mystery of God is very compelling to me—and overwhelming. That's probably the key to my priesthood."

Pastor Wayne grew up in Minnesota. At age nineteen, in 1966, he joined the air force and was shipped to Guam, where he worked with the Strategic Air Command, sending bombers to Vietnam. He returned home expecting to forge a career in business. But someone else had other plans. "I had a will for myself," he explained, "but I guess I kind of knew in the bottom of my heart that God had a will that was in conflict with my own."

I could hear the snowy forests of Scandinavia in his speech, in his "yah know" and "yah, yah, okay, yah." His great-grandfather had immigrated to Minnesota from Norway in 1857, and it was on a visit to his century-old homestead that Wayne had done his business with God.

Having been led to the pulpit, he spent thirteen years ministering in the suburbs of Minneapolis and St. Paul, all the while yearning for the rural environment in which he and his wife had been raised. Then the phone rang. Faith was on the other end.

"It was quite remote, but it fit the bill for us. We had our kids enrolled in a private school in St. Paul called Faith Baptist School. So it was just a matter of moving the kids from there to Faith Public School." He smiled. "Out here, we realized there wouldn't be any aspect of our life that wouldn't be public. But we realized that if we wanted to live a life that would glorify God, there wasn't any better place to do it."

Both men qualified as spiritual versions of the country doctor, traveling great distances and spreading their medicine. Along with his Faith congregation, Father Dennis had churches thirty miles south in Plainview and fifty-five miles west in Red Owl. Pastor Wayne ministered in Faith and in Eagle Butte, forty miles east. Their travels covered an area about the size of Connecticut. But an hour's drive in this part of South Dakota was equivalent to a trip to the corner store in Hartford.

It was a drought year, 1990, when both moved to Faith. There was tension in the air that summer, and much of it was directed at the clergy. They represented God, and God had stopped the rain. In fact, the weather being so entwined with the daily existence of the residents of "Faith Country" (defined as the area seventy-five miles in all directions), religion took on a particular flavor here. There was a sort of intimacy with God on a grand scale.

"It's a very cowboy environment. In fact, cowboy almost becomes the religion. There's a whole ritual, a costume, a culture to being a cowboy," said Father Dennis. I could see his point. Religion appeals through its repetition and familiarity; ranching offers a familiar pattern with the changing seasons. March means calving time. May signals branding time. July is haying season. August brings the rodeo to town.

"If you stop and think about it, each rancher is the king of his or her kingdom, just like the religious kingdom. He has control over life

and death, for animals at least. He participates very much in the beginning of life, as well as the end of life," Father Dennis continued. "You
know, there are ranchers out here who would call ten thousand acres a
medium-sized ranch. That's a lot of kingdom. So there's a natural tendency toward religion when there's that intimate contact with creation."

What I was interested in—the first issue I broached with the priest
and the pastor—was the distinction between religion and faith. I've always felt that one can have the latter without believing in the former,
and a recent poll on the subject seemed to back me up. Ninety-five percent of Americans claimed to believe in God, but only about a third of
them classified themselves as religious. To me, it indicated that faith, being an internal phenomenon, has no need of an outward manifestation.
But Father Dennis suggested that kind of faith may be no faith at all.

"Faith needs religion," he insisted. "If it's true faith, it needs expression. And the best form of expression of that internal faith is to share it
with others. Our faith should lead us naturally to the church. Some may
think churches are formed to form faith. Hopefully, faith forms churches."

I've long considered faith in God easier to come by than faith in
religion. The trappings of religious observance have always troubled me,
and they are much the same in any religion. There are prayers to recite,
rituals to perform, books to study, laws to obey, holy days to honor,
places to frequent, other places to avoid. I perceive it as more style than
substance, the behaviors repeated so many times for so many years that
we don't ask why anymore; we just ask what to do. So I understood why
so many Americans claimed a belief in God without adhering to a rigid
means of expressing it. Religion is hard, I figured; faith is easier.

Pastor Wayne took the exact opposite view. Complementing Father
Dennis's contention that you can't have true faith without a need for
religion, he claimed there was much religion out there with no foundation in faith.

"You can lead a very religious life, in our opinion, and still go to
hell," he said. "In the Old Testament, there were times when the Israelites
were very strong in their faith, and there were times over hundreds of

years when their faith wasn't as strong. When they were just bringing their sacrifices to the temple and just going through the motions while living whatever way they wanted to without regard for God's laws, God said, 'Don't bother to bring your sacrifices and offerings. It's an offense to me.' And I'm afraid a lot of Christianity is that way today—form without any substance to it. Faith needs to be kept real and alive and vital. We want people doing what they do for the right reasons, not just for any reason. That's what I'm striving for as pastor."

But even Martin Luther himself stated that to have a god is to "have something in which the heart trusts completely." That could mean a supreme being, or it could mean something as worldly as pleasure or power. Religion is the means to such ends. It is neat and orderly, and it tells you what to do to get there. Metaphorically, I could see it in the streets of Faith—eight avenues going north-south, five streets going east-west, all carefully numbered and perpendicular. Everything is laid out for you. Just follow the right path and you'll get there.

The concept of faith, on the other hand, is like the city's surroundings. Meade County is the largest in the state, 2.2 million sparsely inhabited acres that consist mostly of nothing at all. The concept is as broad as the landscape. And for some of us, that makes it difficult to find our way.

Faith was created by an all-powerful entity—the railroad. When the Milwaukee Railroad started to construct a branch line into western South Dakota in 1910, speculation as to how far it would go led to settlements springing up overnight. Merchants anticipated where the track would be laid and came any way they could—by rail, by horse, by foot—to set up businesses on what they figured was prime real estate. Rumors sent them into action. It was not unlike the boom-or-bust mentality in the Arizona desert, or the whims of lobsters determining the movement of fishing fleets in Friendship, Maine.

Finally, the railroad announced its destination by securing title to land in Section 10, Township 12, Range 17—just beyond the western edge of the Cheyenne reservation. Dozens of settlers with pioneering in their hearts and dollar signs in their eyes made a headlong rush toward the spot. The president of the Milwaukee Land Company named the inevitable hamlet for his daughter, Faith.

In the beginning, the area was void of development, but within just one day, three buildings were raised. The next day, there were five. The day after that, there were seven. On May 23, 1910, the first edition of the *Faith Gazette* was published, and reporter F. G. King gushed about the little houses on the prairie. "Presto change, in just two weeks time the amazed traveler sojourning across the prairie is astonished to come upon a town of 25 well-built substantial buildings comprising banks, hotels, lodging houses, stores, printing offices—in fact, every line of business usually found in a town 10 or 15 years old," he wrote. "Everybody is as buoyant, hopeful and enthusiastic as at a country fair or the rush to a new gold digging. They welcome the new arrival, dozens of whom are coming every day, with the glad hand. And his first wonder is if all the town are politicians, and the next is the fear that they have all gone crazy."

Then the Milwaukee Land Company came to inspect the chosen site, and the company saw the community, and it wasn't good. Faith had been constructed on the north side of the tracks; the company announced plans to plot it south of the tracks. All of it had to be moved. At a one-day public auction, the land company sold fifty thousand dollars' worth of lots. By January 6, 1911, there were already three hundred people in town. Days later, the first freight train arrived, bearing the train depot itself.

Most settlements evolve over time into communities. But not this settlement. In the Faith Public Library, I came across a photo of the area taken on April 19, 1910. It showed a shed and a man on a horse. That was all. But a photo of the same location taken exactly one year later showed scattered railroad cars alongside some four dozen buildings. There were a couple of banks, a handful of saloons, a newspaper, a post office, a barbershop, a doctor's office, a hotel, a blacksmith, a livery, a department store, a hardware and furniture business, and a pool hall.

Faith no more evolved than did the Garden of Eden. The account of the city's creation—in about six days, no less—would be hard to believe if there weren't photos to back it up. But there are. In the Book of Genesis, of course, there aren't. That's the essence of faith and the question I posed for Pastor Wayne: What happens when faith conflicts with reason?

"If you base religion on reason," he answered, "then it becomes an intellectual exercise."

"As opposed to what?" I wondered.

"Faith," he said, leaning back in his chair. "God is reasonable, whether I can appreciate God's reasonableness or not."

Yet I always find myself wanting more. Clearly, a little bit of doubt is a prerequisite of faith. But I have more than a little bit. Are less obscure prophecies and more salient signs too much to ask? If there is a God, and he's all-powerful, why didn't he print the Ten Commandments on Mount Everest? Why not talk through a redwood instead of a bush? Why limit the miracles to ancient word of mouth and mysterious sleight of hand?

Why is faith such a challenge? Or am I just trying too hard?

"If I'm too simplistic in my faith, I believe God won't hold that against me," said the pastor. "But if I try to be too reasonable in my faith, it may take me in a direction that will take me away from God. I find that it's safer for me to accept what the Bible says literally, unless there's a reason from Scripture to see that God meant it as an allegory."

Is it blasphemy, then, to look for proof? Certainly, over the years, thousands have done so. In some instances, science has confirmed the Bible, or at least lent credence to it. Archaeologists have found a twenty-six-hundred-year-old text of the Old Testament, suggesting that at least some of its books described events in recent hindsight. They've also unearthed a nearly three-thousand-year-old inscription carved into rock referring to the "House of David" and the "King of Israel," evidence that the monarch was more than just a biblical legend. But science can neither confirm nor deny some of the Bible's most seminal events—slavery in Egypt, the conquest of Jericho, the very existence of Jesus Christ.

Israeli archaeologists in the Sinai conducted an exhaustive search of the area from 1967 to 1982, and though they found Stone Age artifacts, they discovered nothing to suggest the Israelites' forty-year march through the desert or the destruction of an Egyptian army.

There are two ways to deal with such dilemmas—unbridled skepticism and unwavering belief. I took the perspective of H. L. Mencken, who described faith as "an illogical belief in the occurrence of the improbable." Pastor Wayne responded with the words of Saint Augustine, that understanding is the reward of faith. But perhaps I am an agnostic because I lack the courage of my convictions at either extreme. After all, even atheists believe in something.

There was a time when religion bound itself to reason. Philosopher-theologian Thomas Aquinas attempted to reconcile the two, formulating five proofs of God's existence. The medieval church tried to incorporate ancient scientific assertions about the earth and the heavens into its system of belief. But then, out of fear that belief would crumble if its scientific base were removed, the church resisted new discoveries that contradicted the old.

Today, the faithful tend to discard much of science as an all-too-human pursuit. "When man is in conflict with the Bible, when human reason is in conflict with God's reason, who's going to win?" the pastor wondered. "Assuming there is a God, assuming the Bible is the word of God, who's going to win?"

But there are many who have devoted their lives to reason and are not quick to jettison faith. There is, for instance, a group called the Society of Ordained Scientists, who believe that faith and science share a common ground of intellectual inquiry. There is a course at MIT called "God and Computers: Minds, Machines, and Metaphysics." And after decades of trying to shed its mystical elements, medicine seems to be embracing them again. Several medical schools now offer programs in spirituality and healing. Harvard Medical School stages an annual conference on the subject.

We live in a century in which scientific advancement has dwarfed that in all the centuries before it, making it easier for doubters to cite fact in rejecting faith. Indeed, compared to the percentage in the population at large, about half as many scientists believe in God. But there's an interesting footnote: in the past eight decades, their attitudes haven't changed. In 1916, a psychologist asked a thousand randomly chosen scientists if they believed in a personal God to whom they could pray and who would answer. Forty percent said yes, 40 percent said no, and the rest didn't know. Eighty years later, the same study was undertaken, and the numbers were the same.

"Albert Einstein, if I understand correctly, wanted desperately to believe that God did not exist—until he reasoned in his mind, by what he saw in the heavens, that there had to be a beginning and there had to be a God that set it in motion," said Pastor Wayne. "What would you say? That man has to be like Einstein to reasonably conclude that there was a God who started it? If that's the case, how many of us have a prayer of a chance?"

Indeed, Einstein did say, "Science without religion is lame." But he also said, "Religion without science is blind." Somehow, I had a feeling Pastor Wayne's faith in God was stronger than mine in science. I may have been confident that man evolved from apes, but he was positive that man was made by God.

"I have a feeling the smarter the scientific community becomes, the more they'll have to agree with God," the pastor said. "So let's cut to the chase. If God is going to be right in the end, then I'll just agree with him now and not go through all this other monkey business."

He shrugged and smiled. "That may seem like ignorance to you, but what's ignorance to one is faith to another."

The *Faith Independent*, a newspaper published in town since 1927, was as local as local rags come. It was full of birthday notices, anniversary reminders, rodeo results, church schedules—all the minutiae of small-town living and none of the hard news of life beyond the grasslands. In that week's paper, I learned that ranchers Jack and Ann Freeman had received a state Excellence in Grazing Management award. I was informed that eight Faith swimmers had raised $204 for the American Heart Association. And I discovered that local rider Ryan Miller had placed fifth in bareback at the National High School Rodeo. In my favorite section, called "Faith Locals," it was revealed that Robert Fisher and Danny DeKnikker had gone spearfishing over the weekend, Lucille Fairbanks had been visited by her late husband's cousin, the Vig family had taken in an Australian boarder, and Walt and Virginia Gerbracht had traveled to Rapid City to see the movie *Independence Day*. When Pastor Wayne suggested that every part of your life became public in Faith, I didn't realize he meant it would be publicized in the paper of record.

But the international headlines on the day we arrived told a different story. They told of a flood rampaging through thousands of Chinese villages, a military coup in Burundi, a war-crimes tribunal in Bosnia, a hunger strike in Turkish prisons that had already left three dead, and the aftermath of a TWA flight that had fallen from the sky. Faith the community didn't ignore hardship in its newspaper. It just didn't deal with it directly. I've often felt that faith with a small *f* does just the same.

How did the clergymen square all the misery in the world with their faith in God? I was thinking of the Holocaust and Elie Wiesel referring to the "flames which consumed my faith forever." Of Indian genocide and Chief Seattle contending that "the white man's God cannot love our people or He would protect them." Of slavery and Harriet Beecher Stowe wondering how it was possible "for the untaught heart to keep its faith, unswerving, in the face of dire misrule." Of abject poverty and Maya Angelou reflecting that "God didn't seem to be around the neighborhoods I frequented."

Pastor Wayne put forward the original tale of bad things happening to good people—the story of Job. He was perfect in God's eyes, yet God allowed him to lose his possessions, his family, his health. All along, Job remained strong in his faith—faith in a God using misery as a lesson plan. I must have looked unconvinced. Perhaps I lacked enough faith to accept God's word in defense of God's world.

So Pastor Wayne provided a less ethereal example: "I had a friend of mine who's a pastor, and his wife was carrying a baby that died in the womb. She was forced to carry it to term. Now, I don't know another situation that would be as heartrending as that. And I will never, never be the same as a result of seeing the grace of God sustaining them through that situation—how they were thankful to God for allowing that to happen for reasons that they had no conceivable idea about. It was beyond conception, beyond philosophy. There's only one thing that it boils down to, and that's a true and living faith. That's it."

God was preparing us for eternity, the pastor explained. But I must have looked unconvinced again. Perhaps this time, I had too much faith in the significance of my own life to consider it an insignificant precursor to something more profound. He read it in my eyes.

"You've got to be awfully careful when you're talking to somebody about this—that they're going through this misery because God thinks it's better for them. It isn't the kind of thing people like to hear. There are a few things that are beyond us, where you just have to trust God to work through it in some way without asking too many questions. You know what? You can't figure God out using philosophy. You can't."

Besides, he said, a lot of people bring it upon themselves. "They get disgusted with God for allowing it to happen, when they were just doing their own thing and didn't give a rip about God or the consequences. Then all this misery comes, and they say, 'Well, why did God allow this in my life?' And that's not a bit fair. Most people give God a bum rap."

The lesson, if I understood correctly, was that we're asked not to fault God for allowing misery, because it's all part of a grand plan. Instead, we're asked to praise him for sustaining us through it. Faith in this sense is just one huge, metaphysical benefit of the doubt.

Pastor Wayne's contention that some people bring misfortune upon themselves led me down another avenue of apparent contradiction—faith versus tolerance. Why is it that a claim to faith brings with it a right to moral judgment?

"I don't know if this answers the question," said Father Dennis, "but we need some kind of focal point of our human potential, a kind of perfect humanity or perfect divinity. Of course, God is the best definition of that. And we have to set out a guideline or guidepost of what is the best for humanity, and in particular for the human. There has to be that set of perfect ideals. I think it's our job, in a sense, to look at our own imperfections. The first call is to look within ourselves, and if we've made that journey, then we can begin to look at the imperfections of others or other institutions. Now, that can easily be interpreted as self-righteousness or intolerance. Yet if I look at my Christian religion, Jesus himself was very tolerant."

"If I don't feel there's a line that you've got to draw, then there isn't much point in my being here—if it's just making people feel comfortable wherever they are in life, whatever they believe, and whatever they do," added Pastor Wayne. "God has a will, and I want them to come closer to it. Because as they do, I know they'll be happier, and our community will be better off."

I had difficulty with that notion, that people can claim a relationship with God based simply on a moral code of conduct, and that somehow they know what's best for those who've strayed from their interpretation of God's will.

"What if a member of the community is gay?" I asked the pastor.

He seemed to expect the question. "I might love him dearly. I might. I couldn't encourage this, personally. And I couldn't preach tolerance of that lifestyle from my pulpit, because that's where I cross the line, see? Tolerance of him or her? Absolutely. But I don't have to approve of what they do."

Funny thing, that was where my line was crossed as well, only going the other way. Disapproval on the part of a massive institution and in the name of God opens the door for persecution. "But isn't there a point," I asked him, "where not approving of what they do is interpreted by the people following your lead as not approving of them?"

"Oh, absolutely. Isn't that what's happening everywhere? But then what happens is I'm the one that's railed against for having the convictions I do. I'm the homophobe now. I'm the one that's persecuted, simply for not tolerating a lifestyle that, according to my beliefs, isn't justifiable or approved in the eyes of God." He paused, then executed one of those quick turns preachers can handle so smoothly. "But if that person needed a helping hand, I would like to think of myself as being the first one there."

I believed him. I really did. He was a good soul, doing his best within the framework of unyielding faith. But the Bible, unlike the Constitution, isn't open to amendment.

"Are we to say now that God has changed his mind about this, when it clearly speaks in his words what he thinks about it?" he asked. "If this is what I'm basing everything I hold sacred on, this word of God that I have, am I safe to tamper with it?"

The pastor leaned forward and invoked the name of one of my own heroes. "You know, Thomas Jefferson had a Bible, and he cut out everything he didn't agree with. What do you have left? You have holes in your faith."

The endurance of the new settlement called Faith was tested by a severe drought that first summer long ago. May came and went without rain, and June and July did the same. Thunderheads could be seen scuttling across the horizon, but nothing fell in Faith. The water holes dried up, the buffalo grass died, the gardens remained lifeless, and the wind blew across the prairie like a sneering catcall. It wasn't until late August that the first raindrops fell, but by then, dozens of homesteaders, discouraged by the elements and racked with doubt, had given up their claims and returned to the more predictable Midwest. The brave ones who remained learned that this was a climate more suitable for ranches than farms. When a brutal winter followed, stopping train service for a month and sending the thermometer to forty-one below, Faith's numbers thinned even more.

In *Miles from Nowhere: In Search of the American Frontier*, author Dayton Duncan called the process "Municipal Darwinism"—survival of the fittest along community lines. "Founding a town on the western frontier was both an act of faith and an exercise in false advertising," he explained. "The winnowing process of natural selection started immediately. The odds of success were long."

But plenty of Faith's settlers stuck it out. The fiftieth-anniversary edition of the book *Faith Country History* recalled that the "hardy soul who came early and stayed had the courage and perseverance of a champion, the nerve and audacity of a deep sea diver, and the imaginative boldness of an astronaut." That perseverance paid off. On February 13, 1912, the city of Faith was incorporated. By that autumn, eight grades were being taught by four teachers in the local school. The city had its first theater by 1913, its first telephone switchboard by 1917, a high school and water and sewer lines by 1923, a public library by 1924. Faith became the largest initial shipping point for livestock on the entire Milwaukee Railroad system, drawing cowboys and herds from all over the county and sending several trainloads of stock out daily, heading toward eastern markets.

The settlers' endurance might be interpreted as an example of faith, but I saw it as a story of self-reliance, which was my next question for my clergy friends. When does absolute faith in God take away from a faith in humanity? Walt Whitman claimed to be troubled by "large masses of men following the lead of those who do not believe in men." Sigmund Freud rejected religion as "infantile helplessness." Is there a point when devout faith in a higher power erodes our faith in ourselves?

"That's a balance to maintain, for sure, and I suppose I struggle with it personally," said Pastor Wayne. "I found my self-worth in knowing my position with God, more so than the best I would be able to do as a human being. I want to have that self-worth, and yet I think if I find my value in God, I'm better off than if I had too much self-worth. Go back to the Old Testament heroes. The ones who got into the most trouble were the ones who had too much faith in themselves, not the ones that didn't have enough."

I often wonder if people confuse faith and fate, if saying "It's God's will" becomes an excuse for inaction. If we are all destined to a predetermined fate, where does self-reliance enter the picture? When I think of this, I think of Amy's ancestors. At the turn of the century, her great-great-uncle had tickets to come to America from central Europe. But his wife felt like she couldn't leave her mother. They had a choice, and they chose to stay. They gave the tickets to his sister, who chose to emigrate to the United States. The brother who stayed perished during the Holocaust, as did most of the family. The sister who left had a son, who had a son, who had a daughter—my wife.

As with the account of Faith's survival, some might conclude it's a story of fate, that two siblings were destined to have two ends. But once again, I think it's a tale of decisions, a lesson that we're empowered to choose our own destiny and are not part of some cosmic puppet show. It's all a matter of interpretation, which is a product of bias, which is a barometer of faith.

Father Dennis tried to clear up the confusion by insisting that decisions aren't made by man or God, but by a cosmic combination of the two. "The faithful person makes decisions with a sense of the greater good and avoidance of evil. And God is the divine interpreter of good and evil," he explained. "It's a tremendous cooperative effort between our humanness and our divine selves. Religion should teach us how to be fully human. And if we're fully human, we're divine."

Pastor Wayne continued the thought. "I make my choices. I don't necessarily feel that the tie that I pick in the morning is because God predestined it to be. But you know, a ship at sea is only turned by the rudder when it's moving. God wants us to be active and alive and moving in life, and he will be our rudder if we allow him to be."

Prophets and signs are God's modi operandi, usually in the form of misunderstood men in desperate circumstances—men like Loren Slocum, one of Faith's own. Slocum arrived in the area at age thirty-nine in 1909, a year before the town was formed, and proceeded to carve out a home, quite literally. For many years, he lived in a hole in the ground, a five-by-eight-foot section of hollowed-out prairie two and a half miles west and one mile north of Faith. His bed was a ledge formed from the earth, his mattress a bunch of clothes piled in heaps. He did it, he said, because he was "too poor to survive above ground," even though he owned a hundred acres of land.

Slocum was hardly a hermit. He would walk into town dragging a crippled leg and sell vegetables from a baby buggy or peddle printed material—diet information, gardening advice, prayers. He experimented with bizarre diets, eating onions for a week at a time. He would offer to read your palm or the bumps on your head for a price. Once, he even ran for political office, carrying around a sign saying, *Slocum for Governor: Kiss Babies over 18*. He lived to the age of eighty, and by the end, he was convinced he had been sent to the prairie as a beacon of light—albeit underground. "I have spent most of my life here in Faith," he wrote, "for the good of all nations and peoples and languages."

Would Loren Slocum have been revered as a prophet in ancient days? Are the characters in the Bible who converse with God as they roam the desert equivalent to modern-day schizophrenics conversing with themselves as they shuffle along Broadway? Is it conceivable that a religion called Slocumism might emerge two thousand years from now, one in which his hole in the ground—by then a prairie Mecca—is interpreted as a rejection of worldly possessions, his crippled leg is a sign of man's imperfection, his palm readings are prophetic warnings, and his onions—the earth's bitter offerings—are so sacred they're saved only for the Sabbath?

Cynical? Certainly. Blasphemous? Perhaps. It all depends on what one considers the origins of belief in a higher power. Either belief is rooted in the words and deeds of that supreme being or it is rooted in human ignorance. If belief arose when we couldn't explain fire or thunder or the stars, and now we can, where does that leave faith?

Again, the city of Faith provided an analogy. The railroad breathed life into the formless prairie, but only for a time. Eventually, local livestock commission companies emerged, and there was no longer a need to ship animals to distant stockyards in Omaha and Chicago. At about the same time, highways replaced railroads as America's main arteries of commerce, and automobiles made train passenger service obsolete. Soon, the train was coming to town only once a week. Finally, in 1978, it no longer came at all. Two years later, the tracks were gone.

Faith no longer needed the railroad, the powerful force that had created it. Whether that was a good thing or a bad thing is a matter of perspective.

FREEDOM,
WYOMING

> *Freedom in general may be defined as the absence*
> *of obstacles to the realization of desires.*
>
> Bertrand Russell

F ive routes to Freedom:

I. If Manifest Destiny had a Mother Road, it was the Oregon Trail. For nearly three decades in the middle of the nineteenth century, it served as a 2,170-mile track into a nation's future, guiding four hundred thousand emigrants from the banks of the Missouri River to the salty shores of the Pacific.

A confluence of events and attitudes led to Oregon fever. Farmers and merchants were frustrated by economic depressions. Easterners wanted to escape increasingly crowded and polluted cities. Concerns were growing about British inroads into the Pacific Northwest. And churches saw an opportunity to civilize and convert the Indians of Oregon Country.

When a couple of tribes sent word of their interest in the "White Man's Book of Heaven," it was construed as an invitation.

In 1836, Marcus and Narcissa Whitman headed for Oregon as Protestant missionaries. With them was another couple, Henry and Eliza Spalding. On the Fourth of July, at South Pass in Wyoming, the two women became the first white females to cross the Continental Divide. Eight months later, Alice Whitman was the first white child born west of the divide. The Whitmans founded a mission among the Cayuse Indians not far from present-day Walla Walla, Washington, and sent back enthusiastic reports about a region teeming with opportunity. Their letters spurred the Great Migration.

In 1843, the largest wagon train ever assembled set out from Independence, Missouri. Led by Marcus Whitman and guided by mountain man Bill Sublette, the Applegate Wagon Train included a thousand people, 120 wagons, and five thousand head of livestock. Within six months, these pioneers made it all the way to the Columbia and Willamette Rivers in present-day Oregon. At the time, it was British territory, but almost immediately, there were calls for the United States to annex the entire region up to fifty-four degrees, forty minutes north latitude. "Occupy Oregon!" was the refrain during the election of 1844, and "Fifty-four forty or fight." Two years later, a treaty with Great Britain established the forty-ninth parallel as the boundary between the United States and Canada.

In 1850, just over twelve thousand people lived in Oregon. By 1860, there were four times as many, and Oregon became the nation's thirty-third state. By 1870, completion of a transcontinental railroad meant a cross-country journey counted in days instead of months, reducing the Oregon Trail to a seldom-used anachronism. But the short-lived road paved the way for a coast-to-coast nation. "When God made man," explained the diary of one pioneer poet, "He seemed to think it best / To make him in the East / And let him travel West."

Whitman's wagon train proved the feasibility of an overland trail.

Within a decade, astounding numbers of Americans repeated his example, representing the greatest peacetime migration in history. Pioneers rolled into Indian lands, accompanied by a measles epidemic. The population of Whitman's own Cayuse Indians was decimated, and soon the Whitmans themselves were dead at the hands of the vengeful tribe. By then, however, the Oregon Trail was on its way to killing off the last of the American frontier.

Almost as soon as the trail emerged, crafty entrepreneurs began to sell guidebooks describing its route, sights, and terrain. Some were reliable sources; others were quite the opposite. Often, the distinction meant success or fatal failure. An estimated one-tenth of emigrants never made it to their destination, accidents, disease, and early-winter storms leaving thousands of unmarked graves along the trail. It was a lesson in traveling light, traveling fast, and traveling well.

Although emigrants also traveled by stagecoach, on horseback, and on foot, the wagon train came to symbolize American expansion and adventure along the Oregon Trail. Your basic covered wagon was forty-eight square feet brimming with supplies and heirlooms, the latter often discarded along the way. Shelter was a secondary consideration; occupying every square inch with tools and food came first. Each group of wagons was a community, dependent on one another for survival.

The pioneers, following on the heels of the fur trappers who first braved the frontier, quickly learned the dos and don'ts of overland travel. They generally left in the spring, hoping to avoid the snow and cold as much as possible. They traveled six days a week, knowing that the mountains came toward the end, and that winter wasn't the time to cross them. If they left early enough, they could reduce the risk of overgrazed campsites and fouled water holes. Indeed, cholera, caused by contaminated water, proved to be the Oregon Trail's number-one killer. The pioneers learned to spread out in columns in an effort to raise less dust, to rotate positions in the train, and to constantly monitor the condition of their wagons. They made sure their animals were well fed, knowing that their own health depended on that of their livestock. Often, as pioneer myths relate, the emigrants circled their wagons. But it wasn't for the romanticized purpose of warding off Indian attacks; it was to corral their livestock.

In fact, many pioneers never even encountered Indians. When they did, they found most of them to be of great assistance. The Indians often provided food, medicine, and wagon teams, guided the settlers along unclear trails, and piloted them through dangerous crossings. It wasn't until later, when the emigrants began to multiply beyond all expectations, when the wild game so important to the Indians grew scarcer, and when unfamiliar diseases came calling, that relations took on a less cordial tone. If anything fanned the flames of hostility between the Native Americans and the emigrant Americans, it was the sheer numbers heading west.

The Oregon Trail began in Independence, Missouri, on the banks of the Big Muddy. From there, wagon trains rumbled through the northeast corner of what is now Kansas and the southeast corner of what is now Nebraska to the Platte River. There, at mile 319, Fort Kearny was constructed in 1848. It was the "Gateway to the Great Plains."

As the travelers rumbled across the gentle landscape of the Platte River Valley, there were tolls to be paid at bridges and ferries and supplies to be purchased at trading posts or from fellow pioneers. By the time they reached Chimney Rock, a landmark located at mile 561, most emigrants had an idea whether or not their money would last until Oregon. Scotts Bluff, thirty-five miles west of Chimney Rock, signaled that almost a third of the journey was over.

Fifty-four miles—and usually about one week—later, the emigrants arrived at Fort Laramie in what is now Wyoming, the trail's primary resupply point. Food and whiskey could be purchased, worn-out stock could be traded for fresh animals, wagon wheels could be repaired. All were vital precautions, because from that point, as the emigrants followed the Sweetwater River and the road rose in elevation, the trail grew more difficult and dangerous. The supply of water and grass dwindled, and the buffalo herds—which supplied fresh meat—thinned considerably.

Two hundred sixty-four miles west of Fort Laramie, the emigrants reached South Pass and the Continental Divide and passed into the Pacific watershed. The pass was so level and broad that many didn't even realize they had reached what was then the beginning of Oregon Country. From there, as winter closed in and speed became paramount, they followed the Snake River Valley through what is now Idaho, crossed the Blue Mountains, and either floated down the Columbia River or climbed over the Cascades, finally descending into the Willamette Valley and Oregon City.

But it was here, just west of South Pass at a place known as Parting of the Ways, that our trail diverged. Two shortcuts pursued a northern route. One, the Sublette Cutoff, crossed a fifty-mile stretch of barren country with no water and little grass. If the emigrants survived, they saved eighty-five miles and a week of travel. Farther north, the Lander Cutoff brought the emigrants into what later became known as Star Valley. That route came within a few miles of what is now Freedom, Wyoming, before veering west to meet up again with the main trail. But it was a southern detour at Parting of the Ways that in fact spawned Freedom, a detour into Utah along the Mormon Trail.

II. The history of a Wyoming hamlet began in Vermont with the birth of Joseph Smith on December 28, 1805. Fourteen years later, while working on his father's farm in Palmyra, New York, Smith began to experience a series of spiritual visions. Prepare for an important assignment, the spirits told him, and God will reveal to you the true nature of Christianity. Later, when Smith was twenty-one, he claimed to have been visited by an angel named Moroni, who pointed him to a hill in western New York, where a book written upon gold plates was buried. It was written in a kind of hieroglyphics, and Smith was able to read it "by the gift and power of God." It took him three years to decipher it.

The gold plates told the story of a group of Hebrews who left Jerusalem for North America about 600 B.C. They eventually split into two factions. One faction, the Nephites, received an earthly visit by Jesus Christ, whose teachings were recorded on gold plates by a prophet named Mormon. His son, Moroni, then buried them. The other faction, the Lamanites, forgot their ancient religion and became the ancestors of the American Indians. Around 400 A.D., they destroyed the Nephites. The gold plates were forgotten, said Smith, until he was chosen to retrieve them.

After translating the plates into the six-hundred-page *Book of Mormon*, Smith gave them back to Moroni, and they were never seen again. But Smith knew that Christ had vowed to return to the continent once a new, "true" church was established. On April 6, 1830, Smith, the chosen prophet, founded the Church of Jesus Christ of Latter-day Saints, more commonly known as the Mormon Church.

Within a year, he attracted several hundred followers and hundreds more detractors. Smith prophesied that the Mormons would be a wandering people until they found their new Promised Land. To avoid nonbelievers, he led his Latter-day Saints first to Ohio, then to Missouri, and finally, in the winter of 1838, to the tiny Mississippi River hamlet of Commerce, Illinois. Within five years, the community, which Smith renamed Nauvoo, was the second-largest in the state, boasting twenty thousand inhabitants. It had its own hilltop Mormon temple, its own militia, even permission to operate as its own nearly autonomous principality.

But there was trouble brewing at Nauvoo, from both within and without. Smith claimed that, as early as 1831, he had received a divine command sanctioning plural marriage. By 1844, it was discovered that he had taken forty-nine wives, some of them already married. A rift arose within the church, and many Mormons opposed to the practice printed newspaper accounts detailing his polygamous behavior. At about the same time, Smith decided to announce his candidacy for the presidency of the United States. This further fueled anti-Mormon sentiment. Smith was attacked as a fraud, his teachings as blasphemous, and his church as an attempt to create a nation within a nation, to preach radical economics, and to sanction polygamy—some or all of which were true. "The Mormons are the common enemies of mankind," said one Presbyterian minister, "and ought to be destroyed."

On June 24, 1844, Illinois governor Thomas Ford persuaded Smith to give himself up in the town of Carthage. "We shall be butchered," Smith predicted. Three days later, he was, shot along with his brother and two comrades by a lynch mob that attacked his jail cell.

The assassinations shook the foundation of the fourteen-year-old church. Several splinter groups arose, the most lasting of them the Reorganized Church of Jesus Christ of Latter-day Saints, founded by Smith's first wife and son. But most Mormons followed the lead of another Vermont farm boy, who became the prophet's successor. Forty-three-year-old Brigham Young believed their new Zion lay somewhere west, where they could construct a kingdom far from troublesome nonbelievers, or "gentiles."

In September 1845, anti-Mormon vigilantes burned two hundred homes and farmhouses outside Nauvoo, and the Illinois legislature revoked the city charter in an attempt to force the Latter-day Saints to leave. But by then, Young had already begun to put his plan in motion, setting a course for the unsettled and unforgiving territory around the Great Salt Lake. They would travel much the same path as those searching for land in Oregon or early gold in California, but these pioneers were hoping to find freedom.

In the late winter of 1846, two thousand emigrants in five hundred wagons headed west. They were, in the words of Wallace Stegner, "the most systematic, organized, disciplined and successful pioneers in our history." Young developed a regimen for his people that included bugle calls in the morning, well-ordered companies of emigrants supervised by captains and lieutenants, and departures at regular intervals. Small teams preceded the large companies, sowing seeds and creating rest stations for those to follow. Bridges were built and fields replanted by each succeeding company. Businesses such as ferries were established along the way to help finance the movement.

Young essentially followed the Oregon Trail, though he stayed to the north bank of the Platte River, leaving the south bank to the gentiles. At Parting of the Ways in what is now southwest Wyoming, Oregon-bound emigrants veered northwest toward the Snake River, but the Mormons headed for the Wasatch Mountains, following the faint trace pioneered a year earlier by the ill-fated, California-bound Donner party. Finally, on July 24, 1847, Young and his followers reached the valley of the Great Salt Lake and the end of the trail. According to legend, upon arriving at that location, eight hundred miles from the nearest settlement, Young declared simply, "This is the right place."

Despite their preparations, seven hundred Mormons died during that first migration, victims of high winds and torrential rains, prairie fires and oxen attacks, rattlesnakes and spiders, measles and cholera. As many as six thousand emigrants were buried along the Mormon Trail over the next two decades, but seventy thousand successfully made the migration, many of them walking the thirteen hundred miles with handcarts.

"We do not intend to have any trade or commerce with the gentile world," said Young the day after his arrival. "I am determined to cut every threat of this kind and live free and independent untrammeled by any of their detestable customs and practices." He organized a state covering much of the Southwest, called it Deseret, and asked to be admitted to the union. But Congress, put off by the Mormons' continued refusal to outlaw polygamy (Young himself had at least twenty-seven wives and fifty-six children) and the close link between the church and the proposed state, created a smaller territory instead and named it after the Ute Indians. Young was named territorial governor.

He also remained president of the church until his death in 1877, directing the establishment of Mormon settlements in Utah, California, Nevada, Arizona, Idaho, and Wyoming. It was during that effort that one of his delegates, the apostle Moses Thatcher, arrived on the banks of the Salt River, just east of what is now the Idaho-Wyoming border, and declared the region "the star of all valleys." In 1879, a Latter-day Saint named Arthur Clarke emigrated to Star Valley in an effort to avoid persecution in Idaho for plural marriages. He named the valley's first permanent settlement Freedom, in honor of his right to practice his religion and his freedom to have multiple wives. Just over a decade later, word came from Salt Lake City that polygamy was no longer a tenet of the Mormon Church. By then, Freedom, Wyoming, had grown into an insular and isolated refuge, just like Brigham Young wanted.

III. Freedom is at the core of the American ideal, but we seem to have a variety of definitions. Scrolling through United States history as we rolled across the United States, I decided to examine the rhetoric of freedom over the years, the defining words of the people who shaped the country. It started at the beginning, nearly a third of the 102 passengers aboard the *Mayflower* being members of a separatist congregation in search of religious freedom. The word to them meant immunity. But there are as many freedoms as voices.

Four decades before the American Revolution, an attorney named Andrew Hamilton defended a New York newspaper publisher who was jailed for criticizing the policies of the colonial governor. He concluded his successful defense by telling the jurors, "Every man who prefers freedom to a life of slavery will bless and honor you as men who have baffled the attempt of tyranny."

Freedom, then, is truth.

A quarter-century later, another colonial lawyer, James Otis of Massachusetts, argued against the British government's writs of assistance, which empowered customs officials to search any house for smuggled goods. In this early argument in favor of limiting search and seizure,

Otis claimed that "one of the most essential branches of English liberty is the freedom of one's house."

So freedom is privacy.

In January 1776, English-born Thomas Paine published *Common Sense*, a fifty-page pamphlet calling for independence that may have been read by as much as a fifth of the colonial population. "Freedom," he wrote, "hath been hunted round the globe. Asia and Africa have long expelled her. Europe regards her like a stranger, and England hath given her warning to depart. O receive the fugitive, and prepare in time an asylum for mankind."

Freedom is escape.

Liberty was the buzzword of the Revolution, from Patrick Henry's "Give me liberty or give me death!" to Thomas Jefferson's unalienable rights of "Life, Liberty, and the Pursuit of Happiness." Indeed, the word *freedom* is nowhere to be found in the Declaration of Independence. Once the nation was formed, however, the word became the foundation of the Bill of Rights, the First Amendment establishing the right to freedom of religion, speech, assembly, and petition.

But increasingly, as the institution of slavery collided with the moral foundation of the young government, freedom was the focus of antislavery oratory. It started even before the Revolution, when a group of slaves in Massachusetts presented an appeal to the Royal governor of the colony. It read, in part, "We have in common with all other men a naturel right to our freedoms without Being deprev'd of them by our fellow men."

In 1843, at the National Negro Convention in Buffalo, New York, escaped slave Henry Highland Garnet gave what became known as the "Call to Rebellion." He declared, "The gross inconsistency of a people holding slaves, who had themselves 'ferried o'er the wave' for freedom's sake, was too apparent to be entirely overlooked. . . . Inform them that all you desire is freedom, and that nothing else will suffice."

And in 1852, Harriet Beecher Stowe wrote in *Uncle Tom's Cabin*, "What is freedom to a nation, but freedom to the individuals in it? . . . To your fathers, freedom was the right of a nation to be a nation. To [the slave], it is the right of man to be a man."

Freedom is emancipation.

During the Civil War, the best-loved Union song began, "Yes, we'll rally round the flag, boys, we'll rally once again, shouting the battle cry of freedom." At Gettysburg, Abraham Lincoln concluded his best-remembered speech by saying, "We here highly resolve that these dead shall not have died in vain—that this nation, under God, shall have a new birth of freedom—and that government of the people, by the people, for the people, shall not perish from the earth."

Freedom is preservation.

The first black newspaper in the country was called *Freedom's Journal*. Indeed, freedom became the conceptual centerpiece of the civil-rights movement, whether the early rhetoric cautioned patience and moderation (as in Booker T. Washington's concern that "in the great leap from slavery to freedom, we may overlook the fact that the masses of us are to live by the productions of our hands") or cautioned against patience and moderation (as in future Morehouse College president John Hope's words, "God forbid that we should get the implements with which to fashion our freedom, and then be too lazy or pusillanimous to fashion it").

Freedom is opportunity.

When the United States Supreme Court decided, in its 1896 *Plessy v. Ferguson* ruling, that separate but equal facilities were constitutional, lone dissenter John Marshall Harlan wrote, "The arbitrary separation of citizens, on the basis of race, while they are on a public highway, is a badge of servitude wholly inconsistent with the civil freedom and the equality before the law established by the Constitution."

Freedom is access.

Woodrow Wilson promised a "new freedom" when he campaigned for the presidency in 1912. But after his victory, his administration quickly introduced racial segregation in several government departments. Black newspaper editor William Monroe Trotter protested, telling Wilson, "As

equal citizens and by virtue of your public promises, we are entitled at
your hands to freedom from discrimination, restriction, imputation and
insult in government employ. Have you a 'new freedom' for white Americans and a new slavery for your Afro-American fellow citizens?"

Freedom is equality.

Half a century later, in his "Letter from Birmingham Jail," Martin
Luther King, Jr., wrote, "We know through painful experience that freedom is never voluntarily given by the oppressor; it must be demanded by
the oppressed. . . . Oppressed people cannot remain oppressed forever.
The urge for freedom will eventually come. This is what has happened to
the American Negro. Something within has reminded him of his birth-
right of freedom; something without has reminded that he can gain it."
Later that same year, in his "I Have a Dream" speech, King used the
word *freedom* eighteen times.

Freedom is deliverance.

The women's movement, too, unfurled the banner of freedom for its
cause. When Elizabeth Cady Stanton addressed the legislature of New
York on women's rights in 1854, she lamented the tragedy of woman as
wife, claiming such a person "has no civil existence, no social freedom."
When Susan B. Anthony spoke two decades later about the tragedy of
woman as citizen, she wondered, "Is there a man who will not agree with
me that to talk of freedom without the ballot is mockery to the women
of this republic?" Finally, in 1898, Charlotte Perkins Gilman discussed
woman as intellectual. "What we do modifies who we are," she explained.
"The freedom of expression has been more restricted in women than the
freedom of impression, if that be possible."

Freedom is independence, input, impulse.

"The basic freedom of the world is woman's freedom," birth-control
crusader Margaret Sanger wrote in 1920. "A free race cannot be born of
slave mothers. A woman enchained cannot choose but give a measure of
that bondage to her sons and daughters. No woman can call herself free
who does not own and control her body."

Freedom is choice.

Freedom has also been a mainstay of presidential rhetoric in the twentieth century.

Woodrow Wilson. After asking Congress to declare war on Germany in April 1917, he explained, "Neutrality is no longer feasible or desirable where the peace of the world is involved and the freedom of its peoples."

Herbert Hoover. In a speech during his successful 1928 presidential campaign (and before the stock market crash), he declared, "Economic freedom cannot be sacrificed if political freedom is to be preserved."

Franklin Roosevelt. In his State of the Union address in 1941, he explained the nation's position regarding the spreading world war by listing four principles he considered essential for world peace—freedom of speech, freedom of religion, freedom from want, and freedom from fear. "Freedom," he concluded, "means the supremacy of human rights everywhere."

Two decades later, John F. Kennedy began his inaugural address by saying, "We observe today not a victory of party, but a celebration of freedom." And later: "In the long history of the world, only a few generations have been granted the role of defending freedom in its hour of maximum danger. I do not shrink from the responsibility—I welcome it." And still again: "My fellow citizens of the world, ask not what America will do for you, but together what we can do for the freedom of man."

In four years, JFK was dead and Lyndon Johnson was left to define the concept at a Howard University commencement address: "Freedom is the right to share, share fully and equally, in American society—to vote, to hold a job, to enter a public place, to go to school. It is the right to be treated in every part of our national life as a person equal in dignity and promise to all others."

Finally, in 1988, Ronald Reagan addressed the students of Moscow University. "We Americans make no secret of our belief in freedom. In fact, it's something of a national pastime," he began. "Freedom is the right to question and change the established way of doing things. It is the continuing revolution of the marketplace. It is the understanding that allows us to recognize shortcomings and seek solutions. It is the right to put forth an idea, scoffed at by the experts, and watch it catch fire among the people. It is the right to follow your dream, to stick to your conscience, even if you're the only one in a sea of doubters. Freedom is recognition that no single person, no single authority or government, has a monopoly on the truth, but that every individual life is infinitely precious, that every one of us put on this earth has been put here for a reason and has something to offer."

The United States has celebrated the word in song, carried it into space, hammered it into brass medallions. The second verse of "America the Beautiful" avows, "O beautiful for pilgrim feet / Whose stern, impassioned stress / A thoroughfare for freedom beat / Across the wilderness." In 1961, civil-rights activists sang of traveling "down Freedom's main line" and called themselves "Freedom Riders." Alan Shepard made America's inaugural flight into space aboard *Freedom* 7. The United States Marines' hymn claims leathernecks are "first to fight for right and freedom." The nation's highest civilian honor is the Presidential Medal of Freedom.

It is ubiquitous, this word of a thousand meanings. It has been the subject of a poem by Langston Hughes, an essay by E. B. White, diatribes by immigrant activists at the turn of the century, labor organizers during World War I, judges during World War II, and senators in response to McCarthyism. It has been synonymous, in various contexts and eras, with franchisement, representation, latitude, exemption, and autonomy.

But as I set out for Freedom, Wyoming, the ever-evolving concept still seemed indefinable. Two centuries and two decades after the Declaration of Independence, as the twenty-first century loomed into view, what did *freedom* mean now?

IV. What better starting point toward Freedom than Mount Rushmore? As Washington, Jefferson, Lincoln, and Theodore Roosevelt nodded good-bye, we headed for the northern edge of the Black Hills and Deadwood, South Dakota. We stopped there briefly not for the historical resonance or the postcards but to see if we could spot Big Dave Murra, the "Terror of the Rockies." When he wasn't posing for pictures along Arizona's Apache Trail in the winter, he was supposed to be performing in Deadwood, but a cursory glance in town revealed no eighty-six-inch gunfighters. We thought it safe to assume he wasn't there, else we would have seen him sticking out like a mountain among foothills.

North of Deadwood on the interstate, we promised the Rolling Stone that we'd provide her the best roads we could if she would just make it over the mountains. Interstate 90 is the main route across the northern United States, stretching 3,016 miles from Boston to Seattle. We covered the middle 165 miles, or thereabouts, through places with delightfully western names like Spearfish and Sundance, before coming to a halt in Buffalo, Wyoming.

Although Buffalo's Main Street ran along an old bison trail, and although the name fit like a worn saddle, the town was actually named after Buffalo, New York. The settlers picked it out of a hat, according to the histories—but I'm guessing it was a Stetson. The region was the site of an iconic western event (the Johnson County War, a shoot-'em-up cattle-rustling standoff in 1892) and a home to mythical western characters (Butch Cassidy's famous Hole-in-the-Wall hideout was southwest of town; his partner, the Sundance Kid, earned his nickname while spending time in the Sundance Jail just up the road). The ranch war was the basis for *Heaven's Gate*; the outlaws' movie fared better.

The following day, we headed east on U.S. 16, and the Rolling Stone wheezed over Powder River Pass (elevation 9,666 feet) in the Bighorn Mountains. Eighty years ago, this road was the main link among Chicago, the Black Hills, and Yellowstone. The "Black and Yellow Trail," it was called, after the poles with alternating black and yellow bands that marked the highway. But there was little traffic during our passage, just sixty-five miles of pine-covered Alps. The final miles took us into Ten

Sleep Canyon, with rust-colored cliffs on all sides and enough switchbacks to catch sight of every one of them. The mountain pass and the steep canyon were our first realization, later confirmed, that Wyoming may trump all other states in sheer magnificence. Colorado, California, Arizona, Utah—they're all spectacular. But Wyoming is an explosion of the senses.

The twenty-seven miles between the towns of Ten Sleep and Worland were twenty-seven miles of absolutely nothing but the sharp colors of the high desert and the sluggish movements of an occasional oil rig. Other than the rigs' periodic dips into the soil, there wasn't a sign of civilization. Indeed, though it is the ninth-largest state, Wyoming is the least populated, and only Alaska boasts fewer than its five people per square mile (if in fact it boasts about it). Even South Dakota is nearly twice as densely populated. In comparison, New Jersey, the most densely populated state, has over a thousand people per square mile. Wyoming is also last in projected population growth, with only a one percent increase expected by the year 2020. Bottom line: America's most unmatched scenery is somehow uninviting at the same time.

At Worland—a relative metropolis of fifty-seven hundred residents— we merged onto U.S. 20, which took us south through the Wind River Canyon and more breathtaking tableaus. We clung to the east bank of

The Rolling Stone at rest in Wyoming

the river, while the tracks of the Burlington Northern Railroad paralleled the west bank. Canyon walls rising as high as twenty-five hundred feet hemmed us in. When we reached the hamlet of Shoshoni, we veered southwest into Riverton, a city surrounded by the 2-million-acre Wind River Indian Reservation, which in turn was surrounded by Fremont County, the largest in the country.

This was the closest we'd come to the main route of the Oregon Trail. Not forty miles south was South Pass, the pioneers' route over the Continental Divide. "Today we entered Oregon," wrote one emigrant at the spot, undoubtedly huddling under a blanket to ward off the chill air. "We nooned beyond at a small spring and drank the waters of the Pacific!" A century and a half later, Amy and I spent the night in Riverton drinking chilled spring water in bottles, the wind glancing harmlessly off our twentieth-century covered wagon.

We headed northwest along U.S. 26 the next day, through Kinnear (population forty-four) and Morton (population five). As we followed the loops and bends of the Wind River, crossing it several times, the mountains of the Wind River Range offered a collage of color combinations—gray-green, orange-pink, maroon-black—arranged in layers and stripes and swirls. After coasting past the town of Dubois (which, in true western fashion, the locals pronounced *DEW-boys*), we made our own crossing of the Continental Divide—a breezy drive over Togwotee Pass (elevation 9,858), through lodgepole pine forests, past sweeping meadows, and into the Pacific watershed. Soon after, we were greeted by one of the most majestic sights the continent offers—Grand Teton, rising like a 13,770-foot fist thrust into the air.

We would be coming back to spend a few days in Grand Teton National Park, so we didn't dawdle, save for a jaw-dropping pullout at the base of the snow-covered range. We headed south through Jackson Hole, where we encountered more traffic in a half-hour than we'd seen in the past three days combined, then followed the canyon of the Snake River to the town of Alpine. From there, U.S. 89 took us into Star Valley. The turnoff for Freedom came fourteen miles later.

What was it the Beatles claimed? Happiness is a warm gun? Well, Freedom, at first glance, was a gun factory. Three hundred yards after turning onto Highway 239, we came upon a long, green building on which was printed, *Freedom Arms—The World's Finest Handguns.* The building's lobby was a museum of cause and effect—display cases bearing the models manufactured there (50 Action Express, .357 Magnum, .44 Remington Magnum) and walls covered with animal heads that had once stared into the wrong end of such instruments (antelope, elk, mule deer).

"The factory's been here fifteen years," said employee Vicki Price. "We sell all over the world, mostly for competition shooting and big-game hunting." She then pulled out the flagship firearm of Freedom Arms—the 454 Casull. "It's the world's most powerful manufactured handgun, twice as powerful as the .44," Vicki explained. "The 454 has taken elephants, rhinos, buffaloes, grizzly bears. There's nothing it can't take."

While examining the 454 Casull (suggested retail price $1,677), I was stunned by the realization that it was the first time I had ever held a real gun of any kind. It was smooth and shiny and immensely powerful, but it was also heavy and unfamiliar and sort of creepy. The experience of holding one in my hands did nothing to reduce my general distaste for weapons. For that matter, neither did the glassy stare of the four-horned ram on the wall.

Vicki wore a black T-shirt bearing a drawing of a handgun, a grave-stone, and the words, *Better to be judged by 12 than to be carried by six.* It was her way of stating that she'd rather own a handgun and risk the wrath of the courts than not own one and risk the wrath of an attacker. After all our efforts to reach Freedom, however, I found unsatisfying the notion that freedom here concerned the right to bear arms, a right about which Charlton Heston and I didn't necessarily see eye to eye.

But if I can't shoot straight, I can certainly rationalize with the best in the West. I decided that, since we weren't technically in the town of

Vicki Price

Freedom yet, Freedom Arms didn't really count. Of course, tell that to the mule deer.

We continued west. Less than a mile later, we came upon a sign reading, *Freedom: Pop. 100, Elev. 5900.* Moments later, the highway stopped at State Line Road. When they said Arthur Clarke founded his town just over the border, they weren't kidding. The Idaho-Wyoming border ran right through town. Half was in one state, half in the other.

State Line Road was Freedom's version of Main Street, but it was sort of a postapocalyptic version. Aside from the Freedom General Store and the sturdy, brick Church of Jesus Christ of Latter-day Saints, it was a road lined with had-beens. On one corner was what used to be a service station, but the two ancient-looking gas pumps in front of it looked as if they hadn't seen any action since the Edsel. Across the street were two buildings, one announcing *BILLIARDS* in big block letters, the other saying *GARAGE*. Neither was either. The post office, still in use, occupied a stark white building without a single sign to identify it, as if it were embarrassed at being the edifice that qualified Freedom as a town.

It was Sunday afternoon, and this devout Mormon community seemed deserted save for a white-haired boy in green camouflage sweatpants riding his tricycle on the front porch of the store and making racecar noises. He seemed to have the run of the place. Nearby, at the intersection that constituted the hub of the hamlet, what once had been a stop sign was now warped and cracked and lying in the street. It occurred to me that it was a metaphor for both freedom, the state of mind, and Freedom, the town in a state of disrepair.

Star Valley offered beautiful scenery—Wyoming's Salt River Range to the east and Idaho's Caribou National Forest to the west. The mountains, matted by pines, seemed smaller than they really were, an optical illusion that succeeded only until you saw a house imbedded like a tiny pebble in a mountainside or a tractor-trailer cruising past its base like a Matchbox car past an armoire. When you saw Freedom from a distance, from U.S. 89, it looked like a quaint settlement tucked among the mountains. But upon closer inspection, my impression was that it was less a town than a repository. It was tin roofs, tottering shacks, ragged mobile homes, leaning fences, rusted cars, forgotten pieces of pipe, abandoned spools of cable, broken barbed wire, cows with their heads down, swaybacked horses watching traffic, hay bales, wagon wheels, satellite dishes, clotheslines, sagebrush, gravel, and dust. Sure, the church sparkled, as did a handful of well-kept houses. The cemetery was well tended, and a baseball diamond shone from amid the rough. But for all intents and purposes, it appeared Freedom had gone the way of nearly every other town on our itinerary. This hamlet surrounded by mountains was well past its peak.

A Freedom farm

V. As we stood on the corner in front of the church, a middle-aged fellow rode up on a motorcycle. He was Kendall Jenkins, and he ran four farms in the area. "That's just the way it is," he told us. "Most of the people who are still doing it are running three or four." The American small farm was like many American small towns—either disappearing due to lack of self-sufficiency or being consolidated as part of a larger whole. Still, Kendall told us not to believe the sign at Freedom's town limits. The elevation was on the mark, but the population was off. With a Mormon church in every town throughout the valley, and five hundred members in the Freedom church alone, the numbers supported his contention.

Like the majority of Freedom's residents, Kendall descended from polygamists. "My grandfather worked in the Caribou Gold Mine. Had two wives." He grinned. "The story goes that he came home one night, got all shaved up, and splashed on the aftershave, and she said, 'Where are you going?' And he said, 'Down to see the other one.'" He shook his head and laughed. "I don't know. If you're living with two women, seems like you'd at least want them in two different cities."

If we really wanted to learn some of Freedom's history, Kendall decided, we should visit Lorna Haderlie. He pointed us down the road to a light blue aluminum building that looked like a tiny warehouse. In fact, it was attached to one. But it was surprisingly homey inside, even if it was not meant for those who scraped low ceilings or feared enclosed places. Lorna was neither. She was short and shy and had spent all of her seventy-one years in Freedom.

"At one time, our town was one of the biggest in the valley," she said. "The bank started here, the one that ended up in the upper valley. We had a garage, three stores. And we had some of the biggest celebrations in the valley on the twenty-fourth of July."

"The twenty-fourth of July?" I asked, then realized that was the day Brigham Young had reached his destination.

"We always celebrate the twenty-fourth of July. It's the main day of celebration for the Mormons. We had big rodeos, dances, parades. You would never know it now. It's like a ghost town now, compared to what it used to be. One by one, our businesses left, until we ended up with nothing but a church and a post office."

Lorna's great-grandfather, William Henry Harrison Heap, was among the first settlers in the lower Star Valley, arriving from Utah in 1880 with his young family and twenty-seven other emigrants. "He brought the first cattle and sheep into Freedom," Lorna explained, a hint of pride in her voice. "When they got here, it was utterly beautiful, because no man had messed it up. The grass was tall, the streams were full of fish, there was wild game everywhere. It was a perfect summer." She lowered her voice for dramatic effect. "Then it snowed—six feet that winter— and they lost almost all of their animals. They had it mighty hard, but the next year, they were ready."

Although Heap was named after the man whose claims to fame as United States president were the shortest time in office (one month) and the longest inauguration speech (given amid the pouring rain, which led to his death from pneumonia), his Wyoming community proved long-lasting. Those were the last days of Mormon polygamy. Heap brought only one wife to Freedom, but she was his third. His son, Joseph, took Kendall Jenkins's advice, keeping one family in the Freedom area and another across the border in Idaho.

The practice having long been abandoned, Lorna was able to reflect on its legacy. "It was a hard thing. Some of the families got along good, but many didn't," she said. "I think it's the only blemish we have in the church. But it served its purpose, which was to increase membership."

It certainly worked in Lorna's family. Her late husband, Earl, was the grandson of a polygamist who married two sisters. Each wife bore thirteen children, meaning Earl grew up with at least two dozen aunts and uncles. Earl and Lorna had seven children. The two girls were Erlean and Chandra. The five boys were Darren, Darrell, Dallie, Dannie, and Dennis. ("When we were first married, I said I'd name the girls and he'd name the boys," Lorna shrugged.) At age seventy-one, Lorna counted thirty-one grandchildren and thirteen great-grandchildren. Those kinds of numbers—as well as the Mormon practice of sending nearly every nineteen-year-old man and twenty-one-year-old woman on an eighteen- to twenty-four-month mission—are why the church has grown to more than 10 million members in less than two centuries of existence.

Today, Freedom's children attend elementary school in Etna and high school twenty miles south in Afton, but Lorna informed us that there were once three schools in Freedom alone. That was because Freedom owns a distinction that may be unique among American hamlets. Not only is it located in two states, it is claimed by three counties—Wyoming's Lincoln County and Idaho's Bonneville and Caribou Counties. For a time, that meant three different elementary schools, and it translated to a post office in one county, a general store in another, and a cemetery in the third. It also meant that someone like Lorna Haderlie had no voting rights over what happened across the street from her house. Come to think of it, Lorna seemed to suggest that a politically divided Freedom was a metaphor for the social evolution of the community.

"We don't work together like we used to," she explained. "I often heard my grandparents say how everybody used to help everybody. When it was time to thresh the grain, all the men worked en masse and helped each other, just moving from farm to farm until all the work was done. They did the same when they built a house. They could put up a home in no time flat, you know? Now, we're more independent of each other, and they just won't take time to be together like we used to. You can do your own thing, so you do your own thing."

Lorna might have looked wistfully out a window had there been one available. "I'd sure like to go back to the good old days," she said, her voice trailing off, "but it's the way of the world."

A mile south of Lorna's humble home, State Line Road ran almost directly into the driveway of a house belonging to one of her old class-mates. Resting atop a knoll, nestled against a grove of trees, and sur-rounded by two and a half acres of immaculate green grass and undulat-ing white fences, the house was a sunflower among dandelions. We paid a visit to Merrill Weber, also seventy-one, and his wife, Jo, in this, their summer home.

Jo was a southern Californian by birth, but Merrill was a Freedom native. Samuel Weber, his grandfather, had emigrated from Switzerland in 1887, heading first for Utah and then, four years later, for Star Valley. Samuel's son, Fred, was the first white child born in Freedom, at least according to *his* son, Merrill. The Webers were dairy farmers. They owned quite a bit of land. Later, they gave some of it to Freedom for its cemetery and its baseball diamond.

Merrill's father was an outstanding baseball player—so good, in fact, that the St. Louis Cardinals once came calling. But for his religion, he might have been on his way to the major leagues, and Freedom might have been a memory. "They had a contract all drawn up, and my grandmother was all ready to sign it. Then one of the recruiters happened to mention that their big game was on Sunday," said Merrill, chuckling at the thought. "That was the end of his professional career." Fred Weber remained a fine pitcher until he was well into his fifties. As a youngster, Merrill even watched him pitch two no-hitters in one day. But that was in the Star Valley leagues, not the major leagues, all because he was closer in spirit to Brigham Young than Cy Young.

Freedom in the early twentieth century was what Arthur Clarke wanted it to be—secluded and self-sustaining. The residents didn't seek to escape the town in search of entertainment. It was all there—the rodeo in the summer, dances every Saturday night, baseball and basketball games. The townspeople were essentially forced to provide for themselves and entertain themselves, and a thriving town sprouted around the necessity.

The Webers

"It's rather remarkable to me that the composition of the town, in terms of the number of people, hasn't changed since I was a boy. There are about the same number of families," said Merrill. "But when I was a young man living here in Freedom, we had two grocery stores, a bank, a hardware store, a blacksmith shop, a barbershop, a pool hall, a service station, rodeo grounds with grandstands. . . ."

Lorna had recited the same litany of losses. Maybe Janis Joplin sang the truth. Maybe freedom *is* just another word for nothing left to lose.

"Why is it all gone?" I asked. "What happened?"

"Modern transportation made it so the people could roam far and wide for their entertainment. The businesses couldn't compete, because bigger stores in larger communities were able to offer more."

Funny thing was, Merrill was living proof of the transformation. The child from the provincial town in the protected valley in the sparsely inhabited state spent much of adulthood roaming far and wide. In 1944, he went right from high school to the navy, which sent him to San Diego to train. When he returned home in 1946, he went straight to Brigham Young University—"also known," quipped Merrill, "as the 'Marriage Factory.'" That's where he met Jo.

Merrill then attended graduate school at Northwestern University and became an accountant in Pocatello, Idaho. He was given C.P.A. certificate number thirteen, meaning that just twelve people in the state had earned it before him. During the next thirty years, the Webers moved from Pocatello to Salt Lake City to San Diego, visiting Merrill's hometown every three or four years. It was on one of those visits a quarter-century ago that they decided to purchase some property in Freedom. Like the Lawrences in Harmony, they didn't expect much to come of it, but it soon became their summer home, a complement to their winters in San Diego.

Among the many changes in town during Merrill's long absence were the names. Sure, just about everybody was a second cousin of everybody else. But the Weber family didn't marry within the town nearly as much as, say, the Jenkins family. "It used to be, at one time, there were about the same number of Jenkinses as Webers within the community of Freedom," Merrill explained. "Now, since we've moved back here, there are four Weber families and there must be twenty Jenkins families in town."

Just as he said it, as if on cue, the doorbell rang, and a couple of Jenkinses walked in. Chad and Pam Jenkins were dropping off some pineapple cake. They looked little older than Amy and I, but they had eight children. The oldest was roaming Australia for two years on a Mormon mission, just like the Webers' granddaughter was serving in Germany and their grandson in Mexico. Indeed, twenty-one young adults from Freedom were among the nearly fifty-six thousand Mormons spreading the word in 161 countries. It was a missionary, Marcus Whitman, who had blazed the trail that led to Freedom in the first place; now, the missionaries left *from* Freedom.

Merrill and Jo Weber had fashioned missions of their own, only they spread the gospel of arts and crafts on cruise ships for a month or two every year, teaching needlepoint classes and sailing the seas on discounted fares. Good work, if you can get it. When they weren't wintering alongside the Pacific or coasting atop it, their Freedom seemed like a slice of heaven in the Rockies.

The Webers can sit on their deck overlooking the Salt River Range and watch the deer and elk cautiously approaching the salt block in their yard. They can enjoy the hummingbirds flitting around their bird feeders. They can grow raspberries in their garden and watch the blue spruces they planted twenty years ago sprout into a shady grove. When their grandchildren visit, they can build a bonfire in the open pit in their yard, help them roast marshmallows, then send them off to sleep in their massive basement bedroom.

The overwhelming feeling Amy and I took from our visit with them was that theirs was a life well lived. But when I asked Merrill if he would redesign his retirement differently if he could, I was surprised by the answer.

"You mean if I could design the ideal retirement?" he asked, then paused for several moments. "Yeah. I would travel for about four months every year."

Jo nodded and added, "I'd love to do what you're doing."

Once again, I was reminded of Harmony and Jim and Kay Lawrence, who decided that life was too short and the world too large not to spend time exploring it. I thought about it later and found it ironic. Freedom—the town—went from hub to has-been because the once-restricted world of its residents grew larger and more accessible. Self-sufficiency was no longer necessary; isolation was no longer feasible. But it may be that as the twenty-first century approaches, freedom—the state of mind—is synonymous with that flexibility. In a world of endless possibilities, perhaps it means the opportunity to act on your desires. That can mean spending a lifetime in a place full of family and memories, like Lorna Haderlie. Or it can mean fashioning a comfortable existence out of a combination of favorite experiences, like the Webers. Or it can mean setting a course for discovery and letting freedom take the wheel.

WISDOM,
MONTANA

> *A man never reaches that dizzy height of wisdom*
> *when he can no longer be led by the nose.*
>
> Mark Twain

I t was the greatest real-estate deal in history. In 1803, Napoleon Bonaparte, needing money for his war against England, offered to sell the twenty-eight hundred square miles around New Orleans to the United States for $2 million. But President Thomas Jefferson's negotiators, Robert Livingston and future president James Monroe, convinced him instead to sell the nearly 600 million acres of the Louisiana Territory—everything from the Mississippi River to the Rockies except Texas—for only $15 million. Ironically, the deal was underwritten by the Baring Brothers banking house in London, meaning Napoleon indirectly received money to fight the British from the British themselves.

The deal had its detractors, who believed that the new territory was useless, that it cost too much, that it was too far-flung, and that the whole thing was unconstitutional. But for two and a half cents per acre, the Louisiana Purchase doubled the size of the country and placed the United States en route to becoming a world power. "The consequences of the cession," Jefferson said at the time, "will extend to the most distant posterity."

In the early nineteenth century, the region west of the Mississippi was shrouded in myth and rumor—fantastic legends about prehistoric beasts roaming the wilderness and a race of red-headed Indians stalking them. At a time when the American flag held just seventeen stars, most of the Louisiana Territory was a cartographic void, a blank space on a new map. Explorers were familiar with the mouth of the Missouri River, fifteen miles north of St. Louis, but knew only that the mighty watercourse rolled and tumbled from uncharted points west. And they were aware of the mouth of the Columbia River, discovered from the Pacific in 1792. Everything in between was the Great Unknown.

But Jefferson had a plan. He would send a band of men into the wilderness—the "Corps of Discovery," he called it—to chart a path to the sea for American commerce. It was believed that there was a Northwest Passage to the Pacific, a route that would take the explorers up the Missouri River to the Continental Divide and then down the Columbia River on the other side. That was the mission's primary objective, but it was to be far more than exploration for financial gain. It would be a venture in natural history, ethnography, geography, geology, and diplomacy. The Corps of Discovery would be both a company of backcountry scientists and a band of messengers charged with informing any natives they encountered about the "White Father" in the East and the American traders who would soon arrive.

It was an expedition in keeping with Jefferson's diverse interests. Politician, philosopher, scientist, inventor, educator, ambassador, architect, author—he was a universal genius. Needing a worthy representative to carry his banner, he chose his private secretary, Captain Meriwether Lewis, to head the party. Lewis in turn asked Lieutenant William Clark, his friend, to be co-commander. So began the journey of Lewis and Clark.

The journey of Brad and Amy began with decidedly less fanfare, but our mission shared some of the same lofty intentions. We would push into territory we had never explored. We would catch sight of scenery more spectacular and animals more exotic than any we'd ever witnessed. We would follow the waterways, trek the plains, cross the Continental Divide (several times), head for the ocean. And we would study the natives with care. It took the Corps of Discovery 447 days to reach Wisdom; it took the Winnebago Adventurer half as long.

The last leg, from our camp in western Wyoming, took only a week. We started by pointing ourselves north and speeding through Jackson Hole into Grand Teton National Park, where we expected to hike the trails at the base of the glacier-carved mountains, working up a sweat befitting the memory of Jefferson's explorers. But somewhere between Faith and Freedom, we had both acquired head colds. So we opted instead for a placid afternoon float down the Snake River and a motorized sunset cruise across Jackson Lake.

Lewis and Clark had neither luxury on May 14, 1804, when they and forty-three others pushed off in a fifty-five-foot keelboat and two pirogues. For them, it was upstream all the way. Today, the Missouri River is used for commercial navigation, for irrigation, for hydropower, for fishing and sailing and water-skiing. But back then, it was a wild and unpredictable river. A mile wide, they said, and a foot deep. If the explorers covered fifteen miles against the current, that was a day well spent. But Lewis and Clark slowly made their way into the Great Unknown, their determination inherent in the words that appear in their journals more than any other—"We proceeded on."

Over more than twenty-eight months and eight thousand miles, the explorers experienced their share of near-misses. They suffered frostbite in the winter, relentless heat in the summer, hunger at mountain passes, river rapids so dangerous even the local Indians avoided them, and flash floods that nearly swept them away. There were close escapes from grizzly bears, rattlesnakes, and buffalo trampling their campsite. One soldier survived being lost from his hunting party for sixteen days. Four others survived a battle with eight Blackfoot Indians, who tried to steal their horses and guns. Lewis even survived being shot in the rear by his one-eyed French hunting partner, who mistook him for an elk. But on August 20, 1804, with the expedition barely two months old, the Corps of Discovery suffered its only fatality of the entire journey when Sergeant Charles Floyd had a ruptured appendix. He uttered his final words to Clark—"I am going away. I want you to write me a letter"—and became the first United States soldier to die west of the Mississippi River. Floyd Monument, overlooking the Missouri, was our first National Historic Landmark.

The expedition proceeded on. By the time Lewis and Clark reached the villages of the Mandan and Hitatsu Indians, near the mouth of the Knife River in what is now North Dakota, it was already October, and the Missouri was about to freeze. So they constructed Fort Mandan and settled in for a long winter.

When spring finally arrived, the keelboat was sent back to St. Louis, along with fourteen men, dispatches for Jefferson, and dozens of animal and plant specimens. The Corps of Discovery now numbered thirty-three, including York, Clark's slave, who became both the first black man to see the western half of the continent and the first black man its natives had ever seen. The total also included three newcomers to the expedition— French interpreter Toussaint Charbonneau, his Shoshone Indian wife, Sacagawea, and her four-month-old son, whom she would carry on her back for the remainder of the journey. The Shoshones lived in the Rockies at the headwaters of the Missouri. Sacagawea had been abducted five years earlier and sold to Charbonneau. Now, she was headed back to her people.

Setting out in two pirogues and six cottonwood dugout canoes constructed at Fort Mandan, the expedition headed west. When in late April it reached the mouth of the Yellowstone River, where North Dakota and

Montana meet today, it entered territory no American had yet explored.

When Amy and I reached Yellowstone National Park, we saw more people than wildlife. While the explorers were paddling up the Missouri, huge buffalo herds fording the river occasionally forced them to halt their travels. Here, in the crown jewel of America's national parks, buffalo crossings still stopped traffic, only it was along Highway 89, where cars, campers, and RVs were backed up a few hundred yards.

Yellowstone offered a little bit of everything—high desert stretches and lodgepole pine forests, serene mountain lakes and spectacular river canyons, waterfalls of rushing water and frozen black lava, ten thousand geysers, fumaroles, hot springs, and mud pots, and the greatest concentration of mammal species in the lower forty-eight. The handful of animals we glimpsed—some elk, a black bear, a whole bunch of bison—were of interest because it was the first time we'd seen many of them. Lewis and Clark's catalog of encounters was of interest because it was the first time many of the animals had been seen at all. Mule deer, pronghorn antelopes, coyotes, jackrabbits, prairie dogs, gray wolves—all were new to the Corps of Discovery and to science itself.

Though most people associate Yellowstone with Wyoming, three of the park's five entrances are actually in Montana. We exited through West Yellowstone and took U.S. 287 into Big Sky Country. In the four months it took Lewis and Clark to traverse Montana, they didn't encounter any human life. Within four minutes of our entrance, the quiet of beautiful Hebgen Lake was shredded by motorboats and wave runners. Alongside Hebgen, which was created by damming the Madison River, was Quake Lake, which was a reminder that Mother Nature still prevails. On August 17, 1959, an earthquake measuring 7.1 on the Richter scale shook the Madison River Canyon, collapsing a seventy-six-hundred-foot mountain into the river and creating a tidal wave. As we sped past the lake, rubble still covered the hillsides, and barren trees rose from the water like periscopes.

Montana is still sparsely populated, though not by Lewis and Clark's standards. A fourth of its fifty-six counties have fewer than three thousand residents. In fact, there are a dozen cows for every human in the state. The average ranch or farm consists of more than twenty-five hundred acres, further evidence that Montana is Texas with bigger hills and longer winters. U.S. 287 was a succession of massive ranches with names like Circle W, Longhorn, High Valley, and Lonesome Dove. The road followed the Madison, moving in the same direction. When we finally came upon a town forty miles later, the sign said, *Welcome to Ennis: Population 660 people, 11,000,000 trout.* Another forty miles brought us to Interstate 90 and the exit at Three Forks, a spot that the Corps of Discovery recognized 191 years earlier as "an essential point in the geography of this western part of the Continent."

Throughout their journey along the Missouri, Lewis and Clark encountered forks in their river road. At such times, they explored the mouth of each branch to determine which was the main one, then named each fork. Rivers were named after members of the expedition, significant events that happened there, the appearance of the waters, even random people in their lives. Near what is now Nashua, Montana, a river described by the explorers as "about the colour of a cup of tea with the admixture of a tablespoonful of milk" was accordingly named the Milk River. At what is now Loma, Montana, Clark named a northern tributary after his cousin Maria Wood. It is now known as the Marias River. And the Judith River, winding through the center of the state, was named in honor of Miss Judy Hancock of Virginia, who later became Mrs. William Clark.

But when Lewis and Clark reached the Three Forks area in late July 1805, they faced a dilemma. None of the three streams there was sufficiently large to warrant calling it the Missouri and calling the other two feeders. They solved the problem, here at the Missouri's headwaters, by naming the "three noble streams" after the secretary of the treasury (Albert Gallatin), the secretary of state (James Madison), and the president (Jefferson). "You went fairly far west," Jefferson later teased, "before you found one to name for me."

Finally determining the main branch, the Corps of Discovery turned west along the Jefferson River, which soon ended in another triple fork. Lewis and Clark named these three branches for attributes of Jefferson himself—the placid stream to the southeast was Philanthropy, the main, middle fork was Philosophy, the bold, rapid, clear stream was Wisdom. Trappers and prospectors later renamed the three rivers less abstractly, calling them the Ruby, the Beaverhead, and the Big Hole, respectively. But two towns along the latter river still bear the marks of Jefferson's genius. One is Wise River; the other is Wisdom.

Once again, the expedition chose the correct stream, this time following the middle fork, but the captains were beginning to worry. They had hoped to reach the Pacific and return all the way to the Mandan villages before winter. By now, however, they weren't even sure they would be able to cross the Rockies in time. And in order to do so, they needed to find the Shoshone Indians, who might provide them with horses for the mountain portage. But there was no sign of them.

Within a few days, Sacagawea gave her companions some welcome news. She recognized the scenery, in particular a prominent bluff known to her people as Beaver's Head. Today, Beaverhead County is Montana's southernmost and largest, encompassing 5,619 square miles and four mountain ranges. Here, the people are few (just 1.4 per square mile) and the ranches large (6,800 acres, on average). And here is where Wisdom lies.

Heading west along Interstate 90, we came upon the fourth coincidence of date and locale in our excursion. In Triumph, we had reached Fort Jackson 132 years to the day after its great battle. In Comfort, we had explored the heart of Texas 150 years to the day after the state's independence. And we had arrived in Love exactly 389 years after the first settlers arrived in Jamestown. Now, on August 12, the interstate took us over the Continental Divide—6,393 feet at Homestake Pass. Twelve miles later, we turned south on Interstate 15, and due to the whimsical route of the divide, we crossed it again.

It was on August 12, 1805, that the Corps of Discovery reached the Great Divide. After becoming the first white man to cross it, Lewis wrote in his journal, "I had accomplished one of those great objects on which my mind has been unalterably fixed for many years." Climbing to the top of the ridge, he hoped to see the watershed of the Columbia River, the light at the end of the tunnel. Instead, he saw only more mountains.

The expedition soon came upon the Shoshones, who were of great assistance, thanks to a bit of remarkable happenstance in which the tribal chief happened to be Sacagawea's long-lost brother. But it was also soon after reaching the Great Divide that Lewis and Clark realized their hopes were dashed. The Rockies were not within a week's paddle of the coast. The Columbia's watershed did not cozy up to the Missouri's headwaters. There was no Northwest Passage, and thus the expedition had failed in its prime objective.

It was at about this time, on his thirtieth birthday, that Lewis wrote in his journal some thoughts that hinted at future emotional trouble— yet presaged many of my own ideas regarding a youth left in the wake. Surmising that he had probably lived half his life, he reflected that he "had as yet done but little, very little, indeed, to further the happiness of the human race or to advance the information of the succeeding genera- tion." He greatly underestimated his historical influence, and he overesti- mated his life span just as badly. But I could only think, "If Meriwether Lewis was unsatisfied with his accomplishments, what hope is there for the rest of us?"

Amy and I proceeded on anyway, exiting the interstate over a cattle grate at the town of Divide and heading west along Highway 43. We followed the Big Hole River, formerly the Wisdom, into the Big Hole Valley, a horseshoe-shaped basin also known as the "Big Hole Prairie" (because it is one of Montana's highest and flattest stretches), the "Land of Big Snows" (because there was so much snow that it kept settlers out for many years and moved them on quickly when they came), and the "Valley of 10,000 Haystacks" (for the local ranchers' preference for stacks of unbaled hay).

Rimmed by the Bitterroot, Pioneer, and Anaconda ranges and sur- rounded by Beaverhead National Forest, it was supposed to provide breath-

taking scenery—row upon row of pines and row upon row of mountains. But Big Sky Country on this day in mid-August was one big, smoke-
filled haze, the result of three massive forest fires in southwestern Montana. This lent a mysterious air to our drive through the Big Hole, because we knew there were dramatic vistas behind the gray curtains but
could only imagine them. The closer we got to Wisdom, the more few
were enveloped in the haze. We could barely make out the snow-topped
peaks of the Bitterroot Mountains across the valley.

The Bitterroots were Lewis and Clark's most harrowing ordeal, an
eleven-day crossing in which the explorers were forced to eat horses and
candles to survive. But survive they did, and by early November, they
paddled down the Clearwater, Snake, and Columbia Rivers to the sea.
They hadn't found the Northwest Passage, but they had discovered the
most practicable route to the ocean. "O! the joy!" wrote Clark, who estimated that the expedition had traveled 4,162 miles from the mouth of
the Missouri to the Pacific.

The group spent a rainy winter on what is now the Oregon side of
the Columbia River before heading east again in March. It divided into
several parties upon reaching Montana—Clark even spending a couple
of days in the Big Hole Valley—before regrouping at the mouth of the
Yellowstone River. At the Mandan villages, Lewis and Clark took leave
of Sacagawea and her family, paying Charbonneau five hundred dollars
for his services. Finally, on September 23, 1806—two years, four months,
and nine days after their departure—the thirty remaining members of
the Corps of Discovery reached the mouth of the Missouri. A populace
that had long thought them scalped or drowned or ripped in two by
prehistoric beasts rejoiced in their arrival, greeting the great explorers as
heroes back from the dead and the unknown.

As Amy and I pulled into Wisdom, we were greeted by only a cloud
of dust blowing across the highway.

Like Faith, Wisdom had a highway running through it and a few dozen residences sitting to the south of the main road. Like Freedom, much of the place had the feel of haphazard western residue—a flimsy shack here, a broken-down car there, trailers, satellite dishes, piles of firewood, stacks of hay. Like Pride, a turn from the highway into the heart of the hamlet meant going from pavement to gravel and dust. Like Harmony, the half-block business district revolved around food, spirits, knickknacks, and artwork.

I decided to try something different in Wisdom, replacing depth of discovery with breadth of exploration—not unlike Lewis and Clark. I would stop a handful of the town's inhabitants, extract some background about their own journeys to Wisdom, then try to pry from them some words of wisdom. Maybe then some of the haze would clear.

We started with lunch at what appeared to be the social hub of this valley crossroads, a sixty-four-year-old institution known as Fetty's Beer Garden and Burger Barn. The marquee outside promised, *Homemade service and homemade smiles.* I wasn't quite sure how either could be anything else, but I got the point. It was a bustling establishment, so much so that it startled us when we came in from outside, where a tumbleweed would have turned heads. The decor was tavern catchall—animal heads on the walls, an aquarium behind the bar, old baseball pennants, beer signs, pool tables, keno machines. Also scattered around the restaurant were black-and-white photographs of Wisdom's past. A panoramic view of the town over the caption, "Wisdom, the commercial center of the Big Hole basin." A photo of a band playing on a motel balcony over a banner shouting, *Celebrate the lighting of Wisdom—dance tonight.* A snapshot of horses and Model-T Fords crowding Main Street.

The front of Fetty's menu included a drawing of a cowboy riding a fish, an appropriate depiction for a ranching community beside a trout-filled river. Inside, it offered "world-famous burgers" with names like the Cowpoke, the Pioneer, the Bitterroot, and the Big Hole. These were burgers from a burger hatchery, truly homemade. Naturally, I ordered a chicken sandwich and felt as blasphemous as I had in Faith.

Most of the waitresses in Fetty's were women in their teens or early twenties. I sidled over to a man sitting contentedly in a corner chair, soaking in the scene. His name was Leon Cheever, and he was wearing a checked shirt, red suspenders, and the lines of eighty-three years on his face.

Leon was originally from Macon, Missouri, not fifty miles north of the Missouri River and the early stretch of Lewis and Clark's trail. He pronounced it "Mizzura," which was one way of validating that he was, indeed, a Show Me State native—just like you can be sure of other natives when you hear "Lewuhville" or "Bahston" or "Nawlins" or "Joejuh."

"When I was a kid back there in Mizzura, my grandmother used to come out and stay with us for about a month at a time. She told me a lot of Indian stories," he recalled. "Her mother played with the Indians, ran footraces with 'em, the friendly Indians around there, see? She taught me how to count to ten in Indian." After releasing about eighteen syllables that sounded—to my untrained ear—like gibberish with a speech impediment, he announced, "That's counting to ten, see? I never forgot it all these years."

A mechanic and machinist by trade, Leon had moved from Missouri to Colorado, staying there thirty years until his first wife died. "When my wife passed away, I married a neighbor lady, a preacher's wife, a year later," he explained. "The minister passed away, and I married her, and we come up here to Montana."

His second wife had been dead about five years, and Leon's family had urged him to spend his twilight years with them in Wisdom. Apparently, he spent most of that twilight in Fetty's, which happened to be owned by his granddaughter.

"Do you usually spend your days sitting here?" I asked.

"Oh, yeah. Watching the people go by," he answered, and then his mind ran to another, more recent memory. "Last summer, a man saw me on the street from a magazine. Asked to take my picture. He was taking pictures of a western town."

I smiled at the non sequitur, after which my own thoughts turned to Holden Caulfield and his assessment of his teacher in *The Catcher in the Rye*: "You never knew if he was nodding a lot because he was thinking . . . or just because he was a nice old guy who didn't know his ass from his elbow." I wasn't sure about old Leon.

"So what's the most important thing you've learned in your eighty-three years? What words of wisdom can you give me?"

"Oh . . . Heh-heh . . . I don't know. It's just a quiet place to retire in, you know?"

I told him I didn't mean the town. I meant wisdom. Words of wisdom.

"Oh," he said again, followed by a long pause. "The thing here is the cattle business. And hunting. I used to hunt."

I tried a different tack. "Is there anything you learned when you were younger that proved to be an important lesson?"

"Oh," he reiterated, then stopped.

I gave him a for-instance. "Never shoot a deer that's wearing a hunting cap?"

He laughed, or maybe it was more of a courtesy giggle. "I don't know. I got a whole bunch of guns. Kind of my hobby. The gun show just left here, you know."

Indeed, we had just missed the biggest weekend of the year in Wisdom, including a street dance attended by about twice the hamlet's population. The photograph on Fetty's wall depicted a dance in celebration of electricity; now, they dance over gunpowder.

"Is there anything you've learned watching all the people come through here?" I asked.

"Yeah, you see everything. All kinds of styles, the clothes they wear."

"So what's the important thing you've learned, then?"

I was about to give up when he replied with a lesson profound in its simplicity: "Oh, it pays to listen more than anything else."

"To listen?"

"You stay outta trouble that way."

As Leon settled back into his chair, I wandered over to a Montana Draw video poker machine in the corner of the bar. A huge moose head peered at me from behind the machine. It seemed to be telling me I'd have to be an idiot to put a quarter in. I did anyway and was handed four diamonds and a heart. I went for the flush and got a six of clubs. I should have listened.

Leon's granddaughter had a delightfully appropriate name. Here, in a town indirectly named by a group of explorers who wintered along North Dakota's Knife River, in an eatery along a watercourse that led to one of the famed Three Forks of the Missouri, the proprietor was an attractive twenty-nine-year-old named Julie Spoon.

Julie spent much of her childhood on the move. Her mother was married a couple of times and took her to Colorado, to Wyoming, to Alaska. By the time she was in high school, she was in Dillon, Montana, a city of four thousand residents about sixty miles southeast of Wisdom that served as the cultural hub of Beaverhead County. There, she met her future husband, Randy, who soon graduated from high school and joined the marines, presenting Julie with her own fork in the river.

"I was going to go to college the next year, and he was getting ready to go to Okinawa," she explained. "I thought about it and decided I better go and follow him and see if this is the real thing."

They moved to southern California, to Camp Pendleton, and Julie Owens became Julie Spoon, with a little Spoon soon to follow. When Randy's military stint ended, there was another fork. They'd had enough of California, and Randy remembered Wisdom as a fine place to live

*L*eon Cheever and Julie Spoon

and raise a family. So he asked his wife if she wanted to go home.

"It's really funny," Julie recalled, "because when I was in high school, even before I dated Randy, I was friends with his cousins in Wisdom. They would invite me to spend the night, and for me, it was a lot of fun. There was always something going on here. After the first time I came to Wisdom, I went home and told my mom I wanted to live there."

Upon discovering that Fetty's was for sale, the Spoons jumped at the chance to become the fourth owners of an establishment so constant that when it burned down in the early 1960s, food was served out of a bus for three months while the restaurant was rebuilt. Just about everybody comes to Fetty's when they come to Wisdom, even the handful of celebrities who make their way to southwestern Montana. Country music singer Terry Clark had stopped by a couple weeks earlier while filming a music video. Actor Michael Keaton had come through a few weeks before that, doing some fishing in the Big Hole. Hank Williams, Jr., even owns a place on the outskirts of town, though he's rumored to be less personable than most folks in the valley.

Seven years after taking over Fetty's, as Julie took stock of the lessons she'd learned, her words of wisdom were not unexpected. "I think it's better to live in a small town than a big town," she avowed. "When you're in a big town, everybody's kind of plastic and fake. But when you live in a small town, everybody is so close."

Ask Julie and she'll second Norman Maclean's notion, as expressed in *A River Runs Through It*, that the number of bastards increases rapidly the farther one gets from Missoula, Montana—just a hundred miles from Wisdom. "Here, everybody's just different. I thought it was strange that I made the decision to come here when I was twenty-two. Usually, when you're twenty-two, life is just beginning, and you want to go places that are a lot of fun." Julie shrugged. "But this *is* a lot of fun. You can horseback ride, you can snowmobile, you can ski, you can go fishing, you can go for a walk. You can talk to everybody. You don't have to be afraid. It's a paradise, as far as I'm concerned."

Of course, if you don't like winters that last from October through May, or if you're put off by the invasion of mosquitos in June and July, or if you're allergic to dust or hay or hamburgers, then it may not be *your* paradise. But Eden is in the eye of the beholder.

"I love it," said Julie, smiling amid the lunch-hour chaos in her simple town. "If you stay a little bit longer, you'll find out why."

After lunch, while stopping at Wisdom's post office to drop off a few postcards left over from Yellowstone and Grand Teton, we ran into a lively woman named Nina Johnston. She called herself "Nine-uh," saying in a southern twang, "Mine is the old-fashioned pronunciation." Her husband was Don Johnston—"like *Miami Vice*," she said, ignoring the *t* in the middle, "but he's not *the* Don Johnston."

"And you're happy about that?"

"Oh, yes! I'll take my Don Johnston."

Old-fashioned Nina and Not That Don were a couple of retired schoolteachers from southwestern Missouri. She taught biology for three decades; her husband was the principal at the same school. They still live in Missouri, but they've spent most of the past ten summers in the Big Hole, which, like Lewis and Clark, they discovered in transit.

*N*ina Johnston

"I have a daughter who lives in Washington State, and we would travel through Montana to see her," said Nina. "When we would get through putting up hay on our farm, we'd put a camper on the pickup and take our children camping out west. When we would drive through Montana and Wyoming, we'd think, 'Wouldn't it be nice to stay long enough to get to know people?'"

When they retired, they decided

to take on summer work as park rangers, choosing a couple of sites in southwestern Montana. One was Grant-Kohrs Ranch National Historic Site, a depiction of western cattle ranching, located seventy-five miles northeast of Wisdom. The other, just ten miles due west of town, was Big Hole National Battlefield.

"We consider this our second home," said Nina. "It's sort of like it was twenty-five or thirty years ago around here. People still have kind of a pioneer spirit, and they're not afraid to help out strangers. People accept you for what you are. There's something about it that grabs you. There really is."

Funny, though. The Battle of Big Hole was everything unlike Wisdom. In fact, it was a piece of historical and geographic irony that this town, so connected to a couple of heroic American explorers, was the closest community to a battlefield that symbolized the cultural devastation wrought by that very exploration. Wisdom was thus more than just a crossroads for cattlemen and tourists; it was a crossroads between the wonder and sorrow of Manifest Destiny.

The traditional home of the Nez Perce Indians was where present-day Idaho, Oregon, and Washington meet. But when trappers, miners, and cattlemen began encroaching on Nez Perce lands following the Corps of Discovery's discoveries, the Indians opted in 1855 for a treaty confining them to a reservation that included much of their ancestral lands. The treaty also required their consent for any non-Indian settlement within those boundaries. As so often happened, however, gold was soon discovered on those lands, and the Nez Perce were forced into another treaty. This one reduced their reservation to just a portion of its original size. About a third of the tribe refused to capitulate. Those five bands, known as the "nontreaty Nez Perce," remained in their homeland for more than a decade—until 1877, when the United States Indian Bureau ordered them to move to the reservation within thirty days. The army was sent in to oversee the process.

The nontreaty bands—about eight hundred men, women, and children—quickly gathered as much of their scattered livestock as they could and made their way across the dangerously high Snake and Salmon Rivers to a camp near the reservation. But three young warriors then attacked and killed four white settlers they believed had murdered some tribal elders. Within two days, other warriors joined the attack, and seventeen settlers were dead. Fearing retaliation, most of the nontreaty Nez Perce fled eastward, pursued by the army. After a series of skirmishes in the Idaho Territory, the five bands decided their only hope for survival was to leave their homeland and join up with their Crow allies in Montana. By early August, they reached the Big Hole Valley, where, believing they were well ahead of the army detachment, they stopped to rest for a few days. They were unaware that Colonel John Gibbon and 162 members of the Seventh Infantry, along with 34 civilian volunteers, had been sent to ambush them.

Before dawn on August 9, 1877, with the soldiers arranged not two hundred yards from the Nez Perce tepees, a lone Indian stumbled on to the concealed infantry. He was shot and killed, the gunfire waking the rest of the nontreaty warriors and inaugurating a full attack on the Nez Perce as they emerged from their tepees. Braves, elders, women, and children were killed indiscriminately as the soldiers took control of the south end of camp. Several warriors finally took up sniper positions and forced the infantry back. For the next twenty-four hours, the snipers kept the soldiers at bay while their tribesmen headed south. By early on August 10, the last shots had been fired and the last warriors had retreated. As many as ninety Nez Perce may have died, along with twenty-nine of Gibbon's men.

The Nez Perce continued their flight, but the battle had taken a toll. After several more encounters with pursuing troopers, they reached Crow country, only to find that their old allies would be of no help to them. They realized their only hope was to flee to Canada. Six weeks after the Battle of Big Hole and just forty miles south of the Canadian border, the nontreaty Indians were surprised by army troops under the command of Colonel Nelson A. Miles. After six days of sporadic fighting and negotiating, the renowned Chief Joseph surrendered to Miles. By then, barely half of the original eight hundred nontreaty Nez Perce remained. Some had made it to Canada, some were hiding in the hills, and the rest were dead. "I am tired; my heart is sick and sad," Chief Joseph told Miles. "From where the sun now stands, I will fight no more forever."

Gibbon, the man who led the Big Hole attack, later characterized the tribe's stand as a "gallant struggle." Miles, the man who accepted the surrender, claimed the Nez Perce were "a very bright and energetic body of Indians; indeed, the most intelligent I had ever seen." The famous William T. Sherman, still a general of the army, declared that the Nez Perce had "displayed a courage and skill that elicited universal praise." But the Congressional Medal of Honor was still awarded to seven of the soldiers who ambushed them in the Big Hole Valley.

Nina Johnston, a native Arkansan who moved to Missouri and spent her summers in Montana, found her words of wisdom in the lessons she'd learned at Wisdom's nearby battlefield. "Appreciate other cultures," she said, then pointed out a couple of aspects of Nez Perce culture she found fascinating. "One is the place that they accord their older people. Their grandmothers are the ones who teach the children the tradition, and grandparents have a very high place in their society. I think sometimes we've sort of forgotten that," she explained. "And also, there's their attitude toward material things. They have what they call a giveaway. When someone dies, a year after they're dead, they have a gathering, and they give that person's possessions away to honor that person. I think sometimes we could learn from that."

As if to underscore her interest in cultural exchange—though culture of an entirely different sort—Nina then handed me a copy of a book written by her husband and brother-in-law. It was called *Sassy Sayin's and Mountain Badmouth*, and it was described as "a treasury of country sayings, adages, quips and putdowns." The authors, as sarcastic as they were sassy, promised that after one reading, "you will find your formerly bland, uninteresting conversation has taken on a new life, and you are starting to turn people's heads."

Leafing through the pages, I found amusing Ozarks insults like "He's been pissin' on my head and tryin' to convince me that it's raining" and "He's built backwards. His nose runs and his feet smell." I learned that people can be as crooked as a barrel of snakes, as broke as the Ten Commandments, as worthless as air brakes on a snail, as jumpy as a long-tailed cat in a roomful of rocking chairs, as ugly as the north end of a southbound mule, and as quiet as a bastard at a family reunion.

I even found some words of wisdom, like "You can't get blood out of a turnip" and "Almost shot rabbit don't make stew." And one that seemed appropriate, given the event that had occurred 119 years earlier just ten miles west of Wisdom: "Sorry don't feed the bulldog."

Two doors down from Fetty's was a building from the anything-goes school of design. Its facade was a mint green wall of sheet metal rising three stories, accentuated by assorted lanterns, handcuffs, Stetsons, and rifles. Above the name—*Conover's Trading Post*—was an oversized rendering of a sexy, lounging Native American woman. It looked like Sacagawea posing for *Playboy*.

You could buy anything but groceries at Conover's—hunting supplies, postcards, binoculars, boots, lollipops, suspenders, canteens, saws, toasters, plastic fruit, portable cots, an antique film projector, a Snoopy fishing kit, even a cattle skull for $395. It was one of those general

Conover's Trading Post

stores—like the one run by Gregory Krauter in Comfort—found only in isolated communities with one foot in the past. Even the selection of books read like a time-capsule canon—a twenty-four-year-old set of the *New Age Encyclopedia*, a copy of the 1964 *Writer's Market, a Better Homes and Gardens Decorating Book* from 1956. As in Fetty's, there were old photos of Wisdom on the walls, including one of the building we were in, which had been, at one time or another, a harness shop, a hardware store, a post office, and the offices of a telephone company.

"You can see that it's definitely changed," said Judy Mohr, a thirty-four-year resident of Wisdom who started the store in 1976. "The town's gotten smaller through the years. It takes fewer men to run a ranch, and the local people don't trade as much in town as they did when the roads were tougher to get over."

Wisdom's current population was estimated at 150. Judy's words to the wise were offered with an eye toward the other 149. "Don't say anything flip," she cautioned, adding with a chuckle, "because it changes as it goes down the street."

"Especially in a small town?" I asked.

"Well, it comes back to you quicker." She winked. "Gets you in more trouble."

Staying out of trouble seemed to be a Wisdom pastime. I figured the Antler Saloon across the street might be where trouble brewed. Decorated in antlers, heads, and hides, it was one of those dark taverns where the patrons used one hand to hold their drink and the other to shield their eyes from the sun streaming through an opened door. Sitting in the dim light, in what seemed to be the town uniform of checked shirt and suspenders, was Bruce Helming.

Bruce's roots were so deep in the Big Hole that he could actually say, "The thing that's different about me from most folks is I remember when we didn't have electricity. We didn't have roads. This is a tremendous thing. People don't realize how they rely on electricity. In those days, your status in society was determined by what kind of lights you had, because lights were so important at night."

Sixty-seven-year-old Bruce had spent sixty-seven years in Wisdom, a town with roots way back east in Maine. Following an 1862 gold strike in Bannack, which is now a ghost town in the center of Beaverhead County, a New Englander named George Noyes arrived in the Big Hole area. Two decades later, George's son, Al, and his seventeen-year-old bride, Haddie, eloped and settled in a log cabin with a dirt floor at what is now the town site. At the time, the community was called Crossings, said Bruce, "because that's where they crossed the river with their wagons." Al and Haddie started a ranch and named it Ajax. When a post office was placed in the area, the town was nearly called Noyes. But Haddie chose Wisdom, in honor of the river of that name. The river's name changed a few years later; the town's didn't.

By 1917, the ranch failed, the Noyes family moved to Dillon, and Al was killed by one of his bulls. But by then, Harry Helming, Bruce's father, had arrived in Wisdom. He and his brother opened the first auto garage in the valley in a building that used to house the Ajax Saloon. Bruce pointed to a framed newspaper article on the wall of the modern-day saloon and explained, "There was a murder in there. They closed the saloon down."

"MURDER AS RESULT OF AJAX SALOON BRAWL," shouted the headline from July 29, 1909. It was a prototypical western tale involving a poker game, a bar fight, a murder, and a posse.

After two days of rain in the Big Hole, a couple of hay diggers who had recently moved from Kentucky, brothers named Louis and Schuyler Cundiff, were unable to work in the drenched fields. So they spent the whole day drinking in town and playing poker at the Ajax Saloon. During the game, Schuyler, the older brother, got into an argument with a local named Frank McLain. They scuffled, McLain connected with a punch, and Louis pulled a knife but could not make good on his attempt to skin his brother's foe like a buffalo.

The Cundiff brothers left the bar, but Louis, whose friends called him "Rivets," returned a short time later. According to the article, he entered and, "with a smile upon his face, walked leisurely up to McLain, who was making his way towards the bar for a drink, and pulling a revolver when not more than two feet away, shot his victim in the left ear, the bullet entering the base of the brain." After pointing the gun at the bartender, who dove behind the bar, Louis Cundiff ran out, made his way up the river, and planned to catch a train to take him out of the area. But a posse caught up with him and took him into custody following a brief standoff.

Clearly, Wisdom wasn't always a gentle western hamlet geared toward tourists and nomadic celebrities. But in today's interconnected culture, perhaps no community can remain what it once was without becoming a caricature of itself.

Bruce bought the garage—and thus the murder scene—from his father in 1952. He ran it for forty-three years, selling it only six months before our arrival. He had just returned from Cambridge, England, where one of his sons was an officer in the United States Air Force. His other son was a consultant in Helena.

His words of wisdom bespoke pride in his offspring. "The one thing that I found out," he said, "was that growing up in a small town like this wasn't a disadvantage. It was an advantage. Everybody from here, not just myself but everybody, their kids all went out of here and became successes. It's because they knew how to work."

Next door to the saloon was an establishment that never would have existed in the Wisdom of Bruce Helming's youth—an actual art gallery. It was an indication that a sort of urban sophistication was creeping into the cowboy culture. The Wisdom River Gallery was a collection of creations with western and wildlife themes by local and national artists—lodgepole pine chairs, wagon wheels, elk prints, tree-root lamps, a juniper table. There was also a T-shirt for sale that seemed to encapsulate the town's new status as a cultural crossroads. Under drawings of a cowboy boot and hat, it said, *Shop 'til you drop—Wisdom, Montana.* We were somewhere between Butch & Sundance and Lord & Taylor.

Having the Wisdom River Gallery next to the Antler Saloon was like putting a manicurist next to a blacksmith. But Kay Jacobson's establishment had been there twelve years. A Seattle native but a forty-year Montana resident, Kay moved to the Big Hole Valley when she married her first husband, a rancher. The gallery started as a small gift shop formed by Kay and five other ranch women. When her partners ducked out of the business, she kept it going. "There's never been anything like this here, so we just had to learn by hit and miss," she admitted. "Some things sold, and some things didn't."

Somewhere along the line, Kay discovered a formula that worked, catering both to tourists who wanted to take home a taste of the valley and to locals who lived it daily. "We don't do the traffic they do at West Yellowstone," she said, "but . . ."

Her voice trailed off, but I assumed she was going to suggest that was the price of living in one of the slower sections of one of the most sparsely populated counties in a state where if the cows banded together, they could engineer a bloodless coup. "Did you ever think of leaving the valley?" I asked.

"No. Well, yes. I did move out of the valley several years ago for one year. But I couldn't wait to get back."

"Where did you move?"

"Over by Twin Bridges," she said. Twin Bridges was where the Jefferson River was formed by the streams once called Philosophy, Philanthropy, and Wisdom, not fifty miles east. "This isn't for everybody," Kay cautioned. "I've seen a lot of gals who just hate it here, because we're so far from everything. But I enjoy it."

I don't imagine it's easy being an entrepreneur in a community dozens of miles from anywhere, but Kay's words of wisdom were a call to self-empowerment. "If you really want to do it, you've got to get it done yourself," she declared. "No one else will."

By now, the sun was beginning to set, its light refracted by the haze so that it looked like a big red balloon. The rest of the sky was breaking apart into wisps of lavender and pink and gray. The mountains surrounding the

Big Hole were shadowy hulks. We started back east, but as we reached the outskirts of town, we made one last stop at an establishment with an incongruous name—but no more so than hundreds of others around the country. In Helena, Montana, near where the Corps of Discovery ran out of whiskey, you can visit the Lewis and Clark Distillery. In Hannibal, Missouri, you can stop at the Huck Finn Shopping Center, named after Mark Twain's penniless protagonist. And in Wisdom, not far from where Chief Joseph and his tribe came to the horrible realization that it wasn't safe to spend the night, there is the Nez Perce Motel.

As her springer spaniel dozed next to a wood-burning stove, Barbara Challoner, the motel's thirty-something owner, told us the story of how she made her way from Wisconsin to Wisdom—by way of Alaska. Like Amy and me, she and her husband, Wayne, were both from the Midwest, had grown up in the same community, and had started dating when she was sixteen and he just a bit older. They were married and remained in that small Wisconsin town for several years, Barbara earning money baby-sitting while Wayne worked the swing shift at the local paper mill. Then one day, they decided to pack up and head for the forty-ninth state.

I asked why.

She shrugged. "The adventure, I guess."

Wayne found a job as a packer for a back-country guide. Barbara managed a bed-and-breakfast. They stayed there for about a year, much of it spent alone in the wilderness, just the two of them. "They flew us in by airplane," she said. "We were the only ones there for a month and a half until they picked us up again."

It was interesting, or maybe sad, that the most frequently asked ques-

Barbara Challoner

tion of Amy and me, following our eleven-month trek through the lower forty-eight, was not "Where was your favorite place?" or "What was your most memorable experience?" but rather "How did your marriage survive?" I usually answered the query with another: "How does any marriage survive without it?" Barbara and Wayne came to much the same realization in the Alaskan outback.

"Oh, you become closer," she insisted. "You do a lot more things together. We always wanted to be together. A lot of people can't say they've been married fourteen years and are still happy."

Alas, Alaska proved financially unforgiving, so the Challoners packed up just before winter and headed home to Wisconsin for Christmas. Their route brought them through Montana, and they took a liking to Wisdom. They spent the winter in a campground along the Big Hole River, actually living out of their pickup truck. When the Nez Perce Motel was put up for sale, they bought it. They'd already bought into the ways of Wisdom. "Here, we're about twenty years behind anybody else. It's back to the old way of life, more or less," she said, echoing a familiar refrain of Wisdom's wise. "We would have liked to stay in Alaska, but we just couldn't afford it. So we found the next best place."

Since taking over the motel, they'd met many travelers—like the group that decided to hike the Continental Divide from Canada to Mexico, and the Ukrainian couple who decided to take a year off and bicycle around the United States—who shared a similar yen for adventure and a willingness to define the moment. Indeed, that was the crux of her words of wisdom, which she offered without hesitation. "Don't do something just because," she said. "Go with your heart. Follow your dream."

As we departed Wisdom, I tried to make sense of the wisdom we'd elicited. These people weren't philosophers, and they'd been put on the spot without fair warning, asked to serve up sage advice along with a chicken sandwich, a beer, or a fifty-cent postcard. But collectively, there was a profundity to their responses.

Appreciate cultural diversity. Savor small-town values. Simplify your life. Pursue your dreams. Listen and learn. They were more than just the lessons of a trip to the Big Hole; they were the accrued epiphanies of an eleven-month journey.

Driving along the Big Hole River, trying to keep up with the current, I thought of the aftermath of the Corps of Discovery's far more arduous voyage. After each of the men was given double pay and at least 320 acres for his part in the expedition, the explorers met various fates. Two were killed by Blackfoot Indians while trapping at the Three Forks. A handful fought in the War of 1812. One lost a leg during a battle with Sioux Indians, then married an Osage woman and became a United States attorney in Missouri. Another lived to the age of ninety-nine, long enough to see the nation he explored ripped asunder. York, the slave, was given his freedom, though what he did with it is unknown. Sacagawea is believed to have died in 1812, followed by her husband, Charbonneau, a quarter-century later.

Clark became an Indian agent for the Louisiana Territory and then the first appointed governor of the Missouri Territory. He named his eldest son Meriwether Lewis Clark. And Meriwether Lewis himself became governor of the Louisiana Territory—but he also became an alcoholic, debt-ridden manic-depressive. In 1809, just three years after the expedition, he checked into a small inn on the Natchez Trace in Tennessee and died under mysterious circumstances, perhaps by his own hand.

I found lessons in that, too—that discovery is only as powerful as its application, and the journey's end is only the beginning.

JOY,
ILLINOIS

> *You are seeking joy and peace in far-off places.*
> *But the spring of joy is in your heart. The haven*
> *of peace is in yourself.*
>
> Sathya Sai Baba

lthough reflection is often considered the postscript to experience, it's actually part of it. When we approach the completion of anything—rebuilding a car, reading a book, sharing a meal, celebrating a New Year's Eve—we begin to reflect even before the engine purrs, the last page turns, the dessert arrives, or the ball drops. Looking back is part of moving forward.

With our adventure nearing an end, I peeked into the rearview mirror in an attempt to determine the single most salient moment of the sojourn—the person, place, event, or experience that made the greatest impact on my psyche. I recalled Spanish moss in Savannah, grasshoppers in South Dakota, drunken hordes on Bourbon Street, a sunset in Montana, sand dunes in Michigan, covered bridges in Woodstock, the green mounds of the Blue Ridge, the granite majesty of Grand Teton. I considered the education that became such an integral part of the excursion and the historical figures who became our temporary companions—Devil Anse Hatfield, J. Robert Oppenheimer, Brigham Young, Lewis and Clark, Schwerner, Chaney, and Goodman, Honor Gifford, Sylvester Bliss, James Justice.

I rummaged through the artifacts of the journey—a bottle of Harmony Cellars wine from Chuck the Winemaker, a photo of the Friendship sloop *Gladiator* on the back of a business card, a King James Bible from Wayne Hjermstad in Faith, a *Book of Mormon* from Freedom, a refrigerator magnet from the Apache Trail, postcards from Comfort and Wisdom and Love. I thought of the casual defiance of Jim Lawrence, the lined visage of August Faltin IV, the simple spark between Billy and Lynn Coffey, a bear hug from Chicken Owen Foster, a prayer from Max Latham, a tall tale from Andy Zuber, a whispered name from Ollie Mae Welch.

But if I had to pick one moment when it all crystallized, the most significant epiphany among hundreds, I'd choose a fleeting inquiry in the southwestern desert during a brief pit stop en route from one stay to another. As the numbers on the fuel pump in Socorro, New Mexico, slowly clicked forward, the gas station attendant squinted through the dust and sun. He glanced at us, then at the Rolling Stone, then back at us. Tilting his cap back on his head, he turned to me and asked, "Did you guys win the lottery or something?"

I still smile at the slap of perspective, at his hypothesis that if someone could do just about anything he wanted, maybe he'd be sitting in my driver's seat. Here we were, two twenty-somethings driving a brand-new vehicle as big as many houses in the area. It was the middle of the day in the middle of the week in the middle of the winter, and we were fueling up for a leisurely exploration along the open road. We had hit a spiritual jackpot, and the realization felt like a million bucks.

Amy and I embarked on this journey because we believed that by discovering the real America, maybe we would discover a little more about ourselves. Certainly, that was the case, although it was a mixed bag of discoveries. We saw that every town told a fascinating story and every resident could recount his own remarkable journey there. However, what appeared to be widespread contentment was occasionally accompanied by a prevailing sense of resignation. And most were resigned to the knowledge that their communities, once regional hubs, were now local afterthoughts.

We were bowled over by the hospitality and generosity of the folks we encountered, by how a knock on the door would evolve into a dinner invitation or a quick phone call would translate to an afternoon sail. There's nothing like sincere kindness to soften a cynic. But we also knew that if we weren't a couple of clean-cut Caucasians, we would not have been as eagerly accepted.

We marveled at the sheer diversity and spectacle of the American landscape, cultivating a love of the outdoors that had been lacking when our outdoors consisted of skyscrapers and bus stops. But we also noticed that about half of the voices we heard in America's national parks were speaking foreign languages. Like the Manhattan resident who has never visited the Statue of Liberty, many Americans have yet to explore their nation's jewels. It's as if they're too close to appreciate them.

As a journey of self-discovery, it wasn't as much an amalgamation of insight as it was a means of peeling away the layers that concealed self-awareness. In fact, it could be that the most significant moment of all came when we decided to embark on the search in the first place. It meant that we had the harmony of joint aspirations, the love and friendship to share them, the inspiration to pursue them, the freedom to make it so. It could be that the hope was in the adventure, the honor in the pursuit, the pride in the doing.

Unequivocally, it was a life-changing experience. Now, we intended to apply the lessons by formulating criteria for our own utopia and defining our future accordingly. Having traversed the country from Albuquerque to Atlanta and Boston to Baton Rouge, it came time to make a decision: Where did we want to be? All we were sure of was that we didn't want the adventure to ever end.

As if being led by the hand, we drifted through Idaho, Washington, and Oregon, down to California and the central coast. We stopped three hours north of Harmony at a point where the waves sprayed the rocky shore, the hiking trails passed through a canopy of cypress trees, the small Victorian homes still bore the names of the original occupants— *Alvina Hoffman, 1888*—and their myriad stories, and the residents traded smiles. Choosing a community that billed itself as "America's Last Home Town," we landed in the land of Steinbeck, who had discovered that "after years of struggle . . . we do not take a trip; a trip takes us."

But while the search was over, the journey was not. We had to come full circle, to finish our sojourn where we had started it. So we made a sharp left turn toward Middle America.

The next few weeks were a blur of scenes and stopovers, a last-gasp attempt to canvass the rugged West. The Mojave Desert, yellow and diminished like a faded newspaper. Las Vegas, where neon-lit wise guys have been overtaken by pyramids and pirate ships and castles and clowns like a surreal storybook. The Grand Canyon and a hike past green-and-gold aspens to a sunset-tinted window into the earth. The national parks of Utah—lush Zion, otherworldly Bryce, stark Canyonlands, mysterious Arches.

By then, we had hit the wall. There comes a point in every journey, no matter how magical, when you realize it's time for it to end. You find yourself squinting more often toward the end of the road than at the roadside civilization. Impatience becomes the dominant sensation. So while the first 307 days of our adventure were a stroll around the states, the last week became a dead run for home.

From Arches, we took Interstate 70 through Colorado canyons and—after a brief detour through a corner of Nebraska—into Kansas monotony. At Kansas City, we made a northeast turn into Iowa, the forty-eighth state on our to-do list. From there, we set an eastern course along U.S. 34, which took us toward the Illinois border.

Maybe the anticipation of arrival numbed my vigilance, but I don't remember much of the last part of the drive, save for a series of gentle hills, endless cornfields, and passing attractions. I recall a water slide in Ottumwa, a sign for Deb's Home Cookin' Café in the town of Agency, the House of Chrome in Batavia, and a billboard for the city of Fairfield touting, *10,000 Partners in Progress*. I remember passing the tiny hamlet of Rome (probably built in a day) and hundreds of bright orange school buses in an enormous depot in Mount Pleasant, where U.S. 218 led us to Highway 92.

More images: a sign promoting *Sywassink for Sheriff* in Swedesburg, a life-size lawn ornament of an ape in Olds, The Countree Store in Crawfordsville, a white-steepled church in Columbus Junction, a lonely, graffiti-smothered shack in Fredonia, a collapsed barn next to a topless silo in Grandview, and a pumpkin patch in Muscatine. The road crept along the western shore of the Mississippi River, which we would cross for the fourth and final time. We saw the wooded shore of Illinois on the other side, a long fly ball away.

Gassed by the adrenaline rush of homecoming, I pushed the Rolling Stone across a bridge spanning the great river, causing a great rattling of plates, pots, and pans in the RV's pantry. But I could hear the words of Jack Kerouac above the din: "The bus roared on. I was going home in October. Everybody goes home in October."

After entering Illinois, it was twenty-four miles before we came upon the first hamlet in our last state. Autumn was evident in all its glory here—in the flaming oranges and vivid reds of the maple trees, in the massive sycamore leaves carpeting the lawns, in the imminent harvest of acres of corn, in the leftover banners from the previous weekend's homecoming football game, in the pumpkins and cobwebs and witches in the windows.

This was Joy, and for some reason, this village in the heartland reminded me of the coastal town of Friendship, a quiet community surrounded by a harvested sea. Joy was a dozen or so blocks surrounded by an ocean of crops, shoulder-high as they awaited the combine, cozying up to the street corners like kelp forests to a wharf.

Nestled between a cornfield and a soybean field, an immaculate white ranch house sat on the edge of town like a lighthouse above a rocky bay. It was All Hallowed out with ghosts and skeletons and skulls in the windows, a half-dozen black cats in the yard, and bright orange pumpkins resting under a maple tree. Here lived the mayor of Joy. His name, so very appropriately, was Richard Treat.

He wore a flattop haircut, a striped dress shirt, and large, square glasses. He had lived in Joy since 1961, and he *looked* like 1961. The mayor of Joy was also a faculty member at the local high school, where he taught a class in agriculture. Indeed, to Dick Treat, an education in farming was no less important than reading, 'riting, and 'rithmetic.

"It's still the foundation of our country," he said, casting a glance toward his backyard crops. "It's fun for me to visit with elementary-school kids, whether it be in our own community or the Quad Cities or wherever. I ask them, 'How does agriculture affect you?' And most of them don't know anything about it. But when I ask them if they eat, of course they eat. 'Well, where does your food come from?' They say, 'We get it at the grocery store.' 'Well, where does that supplier get that food?'

*M*ayor Richard Treat

They say, 'Well, it comes in a big truck.'" He chuckled and shook his head. "They haven't the slightest idea."

The mayor was a farmer once upon a time, one of the first in the area to plant soybeans. He owned more than 120 acres just outside town. But like so many other farmers in the mid-1980s, he fell victim to a nationwide agricultural depression. "We lost the farm in the spring of '86," said the mayor. "The bank didn't go under, but it was about to, and they started cleaning out farmers to save themselves. We thought we were in the clear, but we were one of the last three farmers that they cleaned out in order to get their debt service down enough to be able to sell the bank." He paused. "We didn't owe the bank a nickel when they took us out." He shrugged. "So there you go."

Joy, too, was a victim of that depression. Located in Mercer County, it was laid out just after the Civil War by two fellows named Thompson and Ungles. Named after J. F. Joy, president of the Chicago, Burlington and Quincy Railroad, the village was one of the largest hog-shipping terminals in the Midwest. But while its 450 residents are as many as it has ever had, its regional significance has dwindled. The train stopped coming through town, reducing it to a historical footnote by the same means that changed the face of Faith. Most of the residents work outside the village, many of them commuting to the nearby Quad Cities of Rock Island and Moline in Illinois and Davenport and Bettendorf in Iowa. Few in Joy still farm. We didn't see a single hog.

Once an integral part of the farm culture in western Illinois, Joy was now a bedroom community known primarily as the site of the local high school, which drew students from four area communities. Almost the entire northern side of Main Street, which runs through town parallel to Highway 17, was boarded up. When local farms went belly up, local businesses followed.

Main Street

"When I came to town in 1961, it was a booming community. Lots of things going on. There was a Joy barbecue here that went on for two or three days, and a number of other activities," the mayor recalled. "It just seemed as those folks got older, I don't know whether they were not allowing the young people to do their thing, but it all began to kind of fizzle out. The town began to go downhill. Not just Main Street, but homes began to get run-down. But now it's changing, because we're getting a lot of young people to move in and buy homes here. And they want some activity. So I guess you can say we've been to the top of the hill and to the valley, and I hope we're headed back up again."

Over the previous three hundred days, we had never known if we would arrive at a community that was on its way up or down. Sometimes, it was hard to tell. Often, the gradual erosion was noticeable to residents only in the bright light of direct comparison between then and now. But nearly always, I viewed the evolution of those towns in terms of outside forces—a hurricane, a fire, an encroaching commuter society, the demise of a railroad. The mayor of Joy saw an opportunity for his village to pick itself up by its bootstraps. All it needed was new blood.

"Although I think all people see the value in youth, I think sometimes they're a little hesitant about turning things over to them and letting them do what they need to do," he explained. "But that's where our leadership comes from, and if we don't allow them to express themselves, they'll either sit back and do nothing or they'll leave."

Under the warm blanket of Indian summer, we took our leave of the mayor and wandered around Joy. There was little happening—a couple of people smoking on a front porch, a waitress closing up a diner, a carpenter hammering on a rooftop. It was a still, unremarkable atmosphere, and I found myself discouraged by it.

For the past several weeks, we had wondered how our journey would end. How should it end? I half-hoped we'd struggle to make it, limping home on three shredded tires and a wheel rim, arriving like long-forgotten explorers given up for dead. Perhaps we'd run into a fisherman-seer on the banks of the Mississippi, casting his line into the Father of Waters and philosophizing a dozen and a half states of mind into one neat summary. "Hope? Inspiration? Wisdom? Pull up a bedroll and let me tell you a little story about that." Or maybe we'd conclude our search by finding a personage who encapsulated all our encounters—a copper-mining, cattle-raising, Bible-toting polygamist named Chicken Dotty Mae Covey IV, who owned a town, a newspaper, a sailboat, and a one-eyed dog named Meriwether.

Instead, as we strolled to Joy Park in the center of town, we found only bare branches and fallen leaves. But then a hand waved at us from a pile beneath a shedding sycamore. There, sitting alone amid autumn's calling cards, and not far from Mark Twain's mighty Mississippi, was a blond-haired boy straight out of *Tom Sawyer*. His name was Kyle Tompkins, and he lived just down the street. A Big Wheel sat nearby, clearly his means of transportation.

"How old are you?" I began, after we introduced ourselves and sat across from him at a picnic table.

"Six," he answered, then thought better of it. "Seven, I mean."

"When's your birthday?"

He looked up. "Right now."

Amy and I glanced at each other and then asked in unison, "Today?"

Kyle nodded and began wiping his hands all over the table, then wiping them on his face.

"Well, happy birthday!" I offered. "Did you do anything special?"

"At seven o'clock, I'm going to open my presents."

"Presents from whom?"

"My mom, Jimbo, Grandpa, Logan, Jessica, Samantha."

"Who are they?"

"My family."

"Who's Jimbo?"

"My dad. My stepdad."

Joy Park

"Who's Logan?"

"My brother. He's five. I'm the biggest kid in the family."

"Who's Jessica?"

"My sister. She's one. And Samantha's still zero. She hasn't had a birthday yet."

"When was she born?"

"In . . . July. July 8."

"So what were you doing out here? Just sitting and thinking?"

"Yeah."

"What were you thinking about?"

"My . . . nothing. I was getting ready to play."

"You come here a lot?"

"Yep." Now, he was sliding all over the bench.

"Are there usually other kids here?" Amy asked. "Or is it usually pretty empty?"

"Usually full and empty," he said, as he continued sliding.

"What do you mean by that?" I asked.

"I mean, some kids play when I come here, and when it's empty, I just play by myself. When it's full, I still play. And when it's dark, I go home."

It sounded like an excellent philosophy of life. "There are lots of leaves around here to play with."

"I know," he said, picking a few up and throwing them into the wind. "They fall from trees. It's fall now."

"Do you know that today's a holiday, as well as your birthday?"

"Yep."

"Do you know what holiday it is today?"

"Uh-uh."

"It's Columbus Day," I informed him. And indeed it was, ironically, as we concluded our rediscovery of America.

"What," he asked in a voice dripping with incredulity, "is that?"

"Did you ever learn who discovered America?" He shook his head. "His name was Christopher Columbus."

Kyle sat up on the bench and threw me a look of disbelief. "Who's that?"

"He's a guy who came from Spain. Do you know what Spain is?"

"No!" he nearly shouted, then added, "I usually don't know anything."

"Well, ever hear of Europe?"

"Nope."

"How about the Atlantic Ocean?" I sensed a glimmer of recognition. "Spain is on the other side of the Atlantic Ocean."

"I know," he said, as if he had all along. "They say there's usually gold stuff over there."

"Gold stuff? Really?"

"Usually. I've never been in the ocean. I don't like the ocean, 'cause they have sharks."

"I agree with you there." Just try seeing *Jaws* as a child like I did, I felt like telling him—then you'll really develop a phobia.

"When they hit the boat, you fall in the water," he said. "I don't like that. I'm never going to go over there."

"Well, Spain is where Christopher Columbus came from. It was more than five hundred years ago. He came over and found this place. They called it the New World, but there were already people living here. You know who was living here already?"

"Hmm . . . Yeah." He pondered this for a moment. "Uh . . . Lindsey?"

"Who's Lindsey?"

"She's ten."

"Oh, so you think she was probably living here when Columbus came over?"

"Maybe. We don't know. I wasn't even born yet."

"It was a long, long time ago."

"She was born a long, long time ago," he insisted.

"Because she's ten?"

"Right."

"Who else might have been living here?"

"Chris," he replied, pointing. "He lives in that pink house."

"Anyone else?"

"Bryan. Over there with the red truck. And Bryant. It has a *t* at the end. It's like Bryan, but it doesn't have a *n*. He lives in the same house. They're twins."

"Bryan and Bryant?"

"Yeah, one's seven and one's eight."

"I thought they were twins."

"I know, but they're not the same age," Kyle explained. "When you look at them, they have the same face and the same shirts and the same pants and the same shoes and the same hair."

"But they're not the same age?"

"Nope."

I took his word for it. "Well, a long, long time ago, even before Bryan and Bryant were born, when Christopher Columbus came over and discovered America, the people already living here were called Indians."

"You know what Indians are, right?" Amy asked.

"Yeah, they speak Spanish."

"You think that's what they speak?"

"I think . . ." He backed off. "Was Chris Columbus an Indian?"

"Actually, he was Italian," I said.

"What," he asked, "is that?"

"He was from Italy."

"Italy?"

"It's a country near Spain shaped like a boot."

"None of us was born when he was there." Kyle suddenly understood. "No one was."

"Right. Now you get it."

"There wasn't no houses around here."

"Exactly."

"There wasn't no trees," he continued.

"No, I think there were trees. But maybe they were a lot smaller."

And then Kyle turned his attention to some construction across the street, offering one of those magnificent non sequiturs only a child can provide. "There are ten guys building that house right there," he announced.

"That's neat," I said.

"I know that."

Thirty years earlier, as he wandered through Utah's Canyonlands preparing to compile his thoughts in *Desert Solitaire*, naturalist-philosopher Edward Abbey wondered if joy had any evolutionary value. "I suspect that it does," he wrote. "I suspect that the morose and fearful are doomed to quick extinction. Where there is no joy there can be no courage; and without courage all other virtues are useless."

In many respects, Amy and I had combined a search for American virtues and an excursion into history. How were regions settled or towns formed or homes made? The vast majority of the people we encountered were older than we were, usually twice our age, mostly because small-town America was getting older, too. But for the most part, we found solace in their stories. We found substance and staying power in America's nooks and crannies.

However, Kyle Tompkins was a reminder that it wasn't confusion about our nation's past that had set us on our way, or even concern over the present state of the union, as much as it was apprehension about what the future held. It took a child's perspective, the joy of youth, to reveal the immensity and wonder of a world yet to be discovered.

"Do you know who the first president of the United States was?" I asked Kyle.

"Uh-uh."

"Ever hear of George Washington?"

"Oh, yeah! He was. He was. He was. He was on the dollar and a penny and a nickel."

"Really?"

"I think."

"You know what? He's on the quarter."

"I know that, too," he said, now standing on the picnic-table bench. Then he furrowed his brow and sat down. "Huh? George Washington is on a quarter?"

"Does that surprise you?"

"I never knew that."

A small, green insect began crawling across the table, and Kyle pushed it along with his finger. "When you turn the dollar backwards, you know that thing kind of like a house, and it has stripes?" he asked. "There's a chair in there, and George Washington is sitting on it."

"Between the pillars?"

"Yep. It's hard to see."

"Must be because it's pretty small. So George Washington must be just that big," I said, leaving a centimeter between my thumb and forefinger.

"Naw," Kyle replied, turning the centimeter into an inch. "He's about that big."

"Ever hear a story about Washington chopping down a cherry tree?"

Kyle giggled. "Yeah. But I can't remember. It was a long, long time ago. I've seen it."

"Really? What did you see?"

"Not in real life, but in a book."

"What did the book say?"

"It said . . . I don't know. I can't read," he explained. "Well, now I can read."

"Did you learn your letters?"

"Yep."

"What letters?"

"Mmm . . . One, two, three . . ."

"Those are numbers."

"Oh, letters? A, B, C, D . . . I can go all the way to Z." And so he did, singing it the way we all learned. I thought of Leon Cheever in Wisdom and his boast about counting to ten "in Indian," further proof that life is a circle from childhood to adulthood and back again.

"Wanna watch me play?" Kyle asked, clearly tiring of the inquiry.

"No, I want to ask you more questions," I persisted. "Do you know who the president of the United States is right now?"

"Who?"

"The president."

"Nope."

"You know what the president does? He's the leader of the United States."

"He's the leader of the United States," Kyle repeated. "Does it start with an *L*?"

"It has an *l* in it."

"George Washington?"

"No, he was the first one, and it doesn't have an *l* in it. Have you ever heard of Bill Clinton?"

"Bill Quinton?"

"Clinton."

"Clinton?"

"President Clinton. He's the president of the United States."

"Right now?"

Kyle and Logan Tompkins

"Yep."

"Well," he said, "that doesn't start with an *L*."

"Right," I conceded, as a cool October breeze started the leaves quaking. "You know, there's a vote coming up where people get to choose the president of the United States."

"Cool!"

"But you don't get to vote."

"I know that."

"You know why?"

"I'm not big enough."

"How old do you think you have to be to vote?"

"Mmm . . . Nineteen."

"Close. It's eighteen."

"Oh. I'm only seven. I have to have . . ." He counted on his fingers, losing his way en route. "Eighteen more years."

"Eleven more for you."

"Eleven more! Whoa!"

"You think you'd like to vote?"

"Uh-uh. No, no."

"Why not?"

"I wouldn't be eighteen when they were done."

"But you get to vote every four years."

"Cool! Why? So everyone can get a chance?"

"Well, the way our country works is we get to choose our leaders. It's called a democracy."

"Cool."

"You know what else you can do someday? When you're thirty-five, you could be president of the United States."

"C-o-o-l!" Now, he was truly impressed.

"What do you think you'd like to do if you were president?"

"Mmm . . . I would . . . Um . . ."

"What rules would you want to make?"

"Uh . . . In school, we could get a magic scope and see what's in the leaf."

"A microscope?"

"Yep."

"You know, I think you can already do that in school, when you get a little older."

"Cool!" He picked up a sycamore leaf as large as his head. "I could look at this."

"Let's think of some other rules. How about on your birthday—"

"No school!"

"How about no school on anyone's birthday?"

"Okay!"

"Why do you think it's important for people to vote?"

"To give different people a turn to be the leader of the United States."

It was as good a reason as any. "Who do you think would make a good president?"

"Me."

"You? How come?"

"Because I'm good."

"You go to bed on time?"

"Yep."

"You eat all your vegetables?"

"Yep."

"You don't pick on your sisters?"

"Nope. Sometimes. I pick on my brother." Kyle was pushing the green insect again—until a faint crunch indicated he'd pushed a little too hard. "Whoops."

"You're picking on the bug now, aren't you?" I teased. I found myself caught up in this child's imagination. "You think you'd like to make a rule if you were president that everyone can fly?"

"Yeah, that's cool!" said Kyle, laughing. "You could fly high as you can and see God."

"See God? That's pretty high up," I allowed. "Have you ever flown in an airplane?"

"Yeah. We were really high up!"

"Where'd you fly, just around here?"

"To Venus."

Now, it was my turn: "Cool!"

"We flew pretty fast. My hair was standing up. It about fell off."

"My hair just about fell off, too," I admitted, removing my baseball cap. "See?"

"I know," he said. "When? How?"

"That's what I keep asking myself."

Just then, Kyle's five-year-old brother, Logan, rode up on his bike, threw it down, and dove into a pile of leaves. After some brief introductions, he watched as his increasingly antsy older brother continued to handle queries from a pair of strangers straight out of the thin autumn air. I turned the conversation to geography.

"Do you know what town we're in right now, Kyle?"

"Joy," he answered. "Joy Park."

"Do you know what state we're in?"

"Mmm . . . What's a state?"

"A state is a section of America," I offered, struggling to come up with a suitable definition. "Can you name one?"

"Um . . ." For some reason, he began counting on his fingers. "Uh . . . Our world?"

"That's bigger than a state," I said. "Ever hear of Illinois?"

"Yep. That's a state?"

"Uh-huh. Can you think of any others? Ever hear of Iowa?"

"That's a state," Kyle said confidently.

"Yep. It's right next door," I said, pointing west. "Ever hear of the Mississippi River?"

"Yep."

"Where is it?" I asked.

"That's in . . . uh . . . Iowa."

"Well, it's between Iowa and Illinois. It's a river that goes thousands of miles, all the way to the ocean."

"Whoa!" This time, he nearly fell off the bench.

"Isn't that neat?" I said.

"Yep."

"People travel down the river on boats."

"Why?" he wondered, his eyes narrowing. "There's a twister in the middle of there."

"In the middle of the river?"

"Yep."

"Oh, you mean a whirlpool."

"It sucks you in," he explained. "I don't like to go in there."

"But there's no sharks in the river."

"I know that."

"You know, before there were roads, before there were cars, people used to travel on the river."

Kyle sat up and looked me straight in the eye. "How do you know all this stuff?"

"Because I'm older, I guess."

"Have you seen it?"

It sounded like a challenge, but I was up to it. And I was proud of that—even in the face of a first-grader. "Yep. I've seen it," I answered. "We've traveled all around the country the past year. Forty-eight states. I learned a lot."

And that's when seven-year-old Kyle Tompkins summarized the

journey for me. No big words. No fancy generalizations. Just a gut reaction coated with youthful exuberance.

"C-o-o-l!" he exclaimed, and it covered it all.

Moments later, we all left the park—Kyle on his Big Wheel, Logan on his bike, Amy and I in the Rolling Stone. It was time to make a wish and blow out the candles.

ACKNOWLEDGMENTS

States of Mind was a three-part journey—Before, During, and After.

Before we headed for the highways, we needed two things in particular—support and some wheels. I thank Bud and Hazel Herzog and Richard and Carol Hillsberg for providing the former, as always. By barely blinking when told of our grandiose plan and by seeing us off with sincere enthusiasm, they left no room for second thoughts. For that, I am eternally grateful. How do you thank parents for being parents? As for the wheels, Tom "Detes" Deters at Motorhomes Unlimited also sent us off with a smile. He's probably still smiling.

During the road voyage, we were met with constant kindness, including an unexpected openness on the part of the people whose lives became fodder for our examination of the American experience. To all the people who offered us their time along the way, I offer in return my gratitude and respect. I especially would like to thank those who gave us more than a little time—Kay Lawrence and her late husband, Jim; Dave and Irene Johnson; Bob Tooley; Ann Wellborn; Jay Rubin; Gregory Krauter; August Faltin IV; Chicken Owen Foster; Ollie Mae Welch; Max and

Rhonda Latham; Billy and Lynn Coffey; Dotty Joe Justice; Jim Vance; Frank Noble; Bill and Caroline Zuber; Norm Covey; Father Dennis Riss; Pastor Wayne Hjermstad; Lorna Haderlie; Merrill and Jo Weber; Kyle Tompkins; Unity's triumvirate; and Wisdom's wise. Meeting them made the journey; their lives made the book. I am grateful, as well, to the family and friends who provided hospitality and companionship in various parts of the country, making the road seem like home.

In the "After" department, while our cross-country excursion may have renewed my faith in the state of the union, the folks at John F. Blair renewed my faith in the publishing industry. I thank Steve Kirk for his meticulous and understanding editing, Debbie Hampton for her design, Anne Waters for her expertise, and Carolyn Sakowski for having the courage to try something a little different with this book—all of which made the journey complete. Much of the writing of *States of Mind* was accomplished in a perfect creative environment amid the snow-capped mountains of Ridgway, Colorado. I thank Chuck and Ruth Adler for that wonderful opportunity. Finally, I couldn't ask for better karma than that provided by Robert Preskill. Rob was my friend long before he was my agent, which proves to me that sometimes good things happen to good people.

SELECT BIBLIOGRAPHY

Although I used a number of excellent sources, particularly in compiling the histories of various towns and states, the following books were invaluable.

Anderson, William L., ed. *Cherokee Removal: Before and After*. Athens: University of Georgia Press, 1991.

Cagin, Seth, and Philip Dray. *We Are Not Afraid: The Story of Goodman, Schwerner and Chaney and the Civil Rights Campaign for Mississippi*. New York: Macmillan, 1988.

Duncan, Dayton. *Out West: American Journey along the Lewis and Clark Trail*. New York: Viking Penguin, 1987.

Ehle, John. *Trail of Tears: The Rise and Fall of the Cherokee Nation*. New York: Doubleday, 1988.

Goodchild, Peter. *J. Robert Oppenheimer: Shatterer of Worlds*. New York: Fromm International, 1985.

Hall, B. C., and C. T. Wood. *The South: A Two-Step Odyssey on the Backroads of the Enchanted Land*. New York: Simon and Schuster, 1995.

Jewell, Judy, and W. C. McRae. *Montana Handbook*. Chico, CA: Moon Publications, 1994.

Pitcher, Don. *Wyoming Handbook*. Chico, CA: Moon Publications, 1993.

Ravitch, Diane, ed. *The American Reader: The Words That Moved a Nation*. New York: HarperPerennial, 1991.

Ruppersburg, Hugh, ed. *Georgia Voices*. Athens: University of Georgia Press, 1993.

Walton, Anthony. *Mississippi: An American Journey*. New York: Alfred A. Knopf, 1996.

INDEX